T0388208

VOLUME SIXTY FIVE

Advances in Experimental
Social Psychology

VOLUME SIXTY FIVE

Advances in Experimental
SOCIAL PSYCHOLOGY

Edited by

BERTRAM GAWRONSKI

Department of Psychology
University of Texas at Austin
Austin, TX, United States

ACADEMIC PRESS

An imprint of Elsevier

ELSEVIER

Academic Press is an imprint of Elsevier
50 Hampshire Street, 5th Floor, Cambridge, MA 02139, United States
525 B Street, Suite 1650, San Diego, CA 92101, United States
The Boulevard, Langford Lane, Kidlington, Oxford OX5 1GB, United Kingdom
125 London Wall, London, EC2Y 5AS, United Kingdom

First edition 2022

Notices
Knowledge and best practice in this field are constantly changing. As new research and experience
broaden our understanding, changes in research methods, professional practices, or medical
treatment may become necessary.

Practitioners and researchers must always rely on their own experience and knowledge in evaluating
and using any information, methods, compounds, or experiments described herein. In using such
information or methods they should be mindful of their own safety and the safety of others, including
parties for whom they have a professional responsibility.

To the fullest extent of the law, neither the Publisher nor the authors, contributors, or editors, assume
any liability for any injury and/or damage to persons or property as a matter of products liability,
negligence or otherwise, or from any use or operation of any methods, products, instructions, or ideas
contained in the material herein.

ISBN: 978-0-323-99078-3
ISSN: 0065-2601

For information on all Academic Press publications
visit our website at https://www.elsevier.com/books-and-journals

Publisher: Zoe Kruze
Acquisitions Editor: Sam Mahfoudh
Developmental Editor: Jhon Michael Peñano
Production Project Manager: Abdulla Sait
Cover Designer: Christian Bilbow

Typeset by STRAIVE, India

Working together
to grow libraries in
developing countries

www.elsevier.com • www.bookaid.org

Contents

Contributors

Chad M. Danyluck
Carleton University, Ottawa, ON, Canada

Robin S. Edelstein
University of Michigan, Ann Arbor, MI, United States

Naomi Ellemers
University of Utrecht, Utrecht, The Netherlands

Kelci Harris
University of Victoria, Victoria, BC, Canada

Yoel Inbar
Department of Psychology, University of Toronto, Toronto, ON, Canada

Cara C. MacInnis
University of Calgary, Calgary, AB, Canada

Ian D. Miller
University of Toronto, Toronto, ON, Canada

Elizabeth Page-Gould
University of Toronto, Toronto, ON, Canada

David A. Pizarro
Cornell University, Ithaca, NY, United States

Kai Sassenberg
Leibniz-Institut für Wissensmedien; University of Tübingen, Tübingen, Germany

Daan Scheepers
Leiden University, Leiden, The Netherlands

Annika Scholl
Leibniz-Institut für Wissensmedien, Tübingen, Germany

Chadly Stern
University of Illinois, Urbana-Champaign, Champaign, IL, United States

CHAPTER ONE

The intergroup perspective on cross-group friendship

Elizabeth Page-Gould[a],*, Kelci Harris[b], Cara C. MacInnis[c], Chad M. Danyluck[d], and Ian D. Miller[a]
[a]University of Toronto, Toronto, ON, Canada
[b]University of Victoria, Victoria, BC, Canada
[c]University of Calgary, Calgary, AB, Canada
[d]Carleton University, Ottawa, ON, Canada
*Corresponding author: e-mail address: elizabeth.page.gould@utoronto.ca

Contents

Abstract

Cross-group friendship has long been considered a powerful component of positive intergroup relations, largely because cross-group friendship was assumed to be an "optimal" type of intergroup contact (Allport, 1954). While we recognize that cross-group friendship cannot exist in the absence of intergroup contact, we argue that cross-group friendship is something greater than extremely good contact. Cross-group friendship is the manifestation of intergroup cooperation at the individual level of scale. Describing our asymptotic model of intergroup contact (MacInnis & Page-Gould, 2015), we discuss how intergroup contact can improve or worsen prejudice. When contact involves repeated intergroup interactions with the same outgroup member, then a cross-group friendship has the potential to emerge. Drawing on complexity theory, we suggest that cross-group friendships are complex adaptive systems that emerge from repeated intergroup inter-actions with the same outgroup member. Cross-group friendships exhibit many features of complex adaptive systems, such as being chaotic, dynamic, and self-organizing. We organize our research on cross-group friendship into early, intermediate, and established stages of cross-group friendship development to explore this idea. We conclude that cross-group friendships are complex manifestations of intergroup relations at the individual level.

Cross-group friendship is a special type of relationship. It is defined by platonic, interpersonal closeness between people with different social identities (e.g., cross-ethnic friendship). Friendship, more generally, is functional. Friends provide us support when we need it (DeScioli & Kurzban, 2009) and satisfy our basic need to belong (Demir & Özdemir, 2010; Harris & Vazire, 2016). Friendship norms further encourage helping and cooperation among friends (Nagamuthu & Page-Gould, 2017). In this chapter, we use complexity theory to explore cross-group friendships as complex adaptive systems that emerge from repeated intergroup interactions with the same person. While others have considered friendship as a complex adaptive system (DeScioli & Kurzban, 2009), we discuss how the emergence of cross-group friendship suggests that intergroup cooperation is fundamental to individual and human survival.

As a title, the word "friend" is not mutually exclusive of other relationships. We call people "friends" who are also our romantic partners, family members, or coworkers (Fig. 1; Harris & Page-Gould, 2021). This suggests that characterizing someone as a friend provides added meaning that the other relationship label does not completely capture. Drawing from many scholarly perspectives, we view the term "friend" to imply support, cooperation, and coalition (DeScioli & Kurzban, 2009; Harris & Vazire, 2016; Nagamuthu & Page-Gould, 2017). Modern views of intergroup relations argue that perceptions of social groups, as categories, are the end result of a more basic cognitive process that detects the potential for coalition in the social environment (Cikara, 2021). When friendship emerges between people from different social groups, the cross-group friendship is an existence proof that coalitions are possible between these groups.

Intergroup researchers studying cross-group friendship have generally shown interest in these relationships as interventions or tools of prejudice reduction. A large part of the focus on cross-group friendship was because it was assumed to contain the "optimal conditions" under which intergroup contact was most likely to reduce prejudice (Allport, 1954; Pettigrew, 1998). These optimal conditions of contact were that (a) interaction partners have

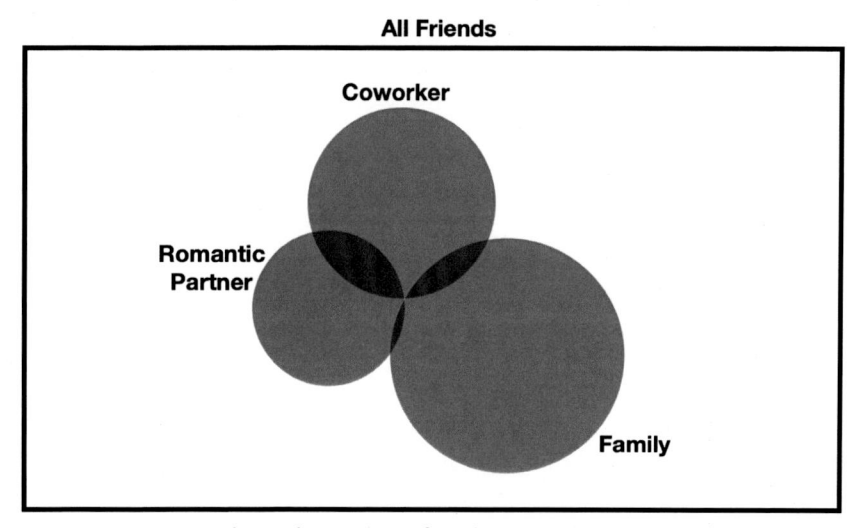

All Friends

Coworker

Romantic Partner

Family

Fig. 1 Co-occurring relationships among friends. Note: The total space represents all people whom an online sample nominated as friends. The white space outside the circles is proportional to the proportion of reported friends with whom respondents had no other relationships. The circles represents all friends who were also identified as coworkers, family members, or romantic partners. Further overlap between those mutual relationships are represented by overlap of these circles, proportional to their co-occurrence in the data.

equal status during the intergroup interaction, (b) there not be competition in the intergroup interaction, (c) the intergroup interaction needed to be sanctioned by authorities, and (d) interaction partners had shared goals. Wright, Brody, and Aron (2005) went further to propose that these optimal conditions *only* promoted positive contact outcomes when the interaction held the potential for cross-group friendship. Supporting the hypothesis that cross-group friendship is a special form of contact, cross-group friendship predicts more positive attitudes in contexts where contact does not (Levin, Van Laar, & Sidanius, 2003; Paolini, Hewstone, Cairns, & Voci, 2004; Van Laar, Levin, Sinclair, & Sidanius, 2005).

The idea that cross-group friendship inherently contains the optimal conditions of contact has advanced research on cross-group friendship considerably. As such, this idea was beneficial, but we think it may not be accurate. Evidence from both within and beyond the intergroup contact literature suggests that cross-group friendship does not inherently involve the first three optimal conditions (Nagamuthu & Page-Gould, 2017). The idea that friendship would equalize societal differences in status was based on the idea that friendship has strong equality norms (e.g., Hatfield, Utne, & Traupmann, 1979). Friendship does have strong equality norms, but status differences nonetheless exist between friends and affect the friendship (e.g., Veniegas & Peplau, 1997). Further supporting the idea that status hierarchies are incorporated into friendships—in contrast to being erased by them—we interrupted pre-existing status relationships between friends and found that this interfered with friends' performance (Nagamuthu & Page-Gould, 2017). At a more basic level, we know that friendships can exist across status hierarchies (e.g., friends between employees and bosses). Friendships across status hierarchies are also observed among non-human primates (Palombit, Seyfarth, & Cheney, 1997). Similarly, while competition among friends is generally perceived negatively (Schneider, Woodburn, del Toro, & Udvari, 2005), competition occurs between friends and is not related to friendship quality in a simple way (e.g., friends whose primary shared activity is a competitive sport). Finally, specific to cross-group friendships, cross-group friendships are less socially sanctioned and less supported than same-group friendships (e.g., Fletcher, Rollins, & Nickerson, 2004). We do believe that friendships fundamentally involve shared goals. Self-expansion theory suggests that we show motivational biases in favor of close others (Aron, Aron, Tudor, & Nelson, 1991), and it has been widely applied to explain prejudice-reduction processes of cross-group friendship (Davies, Tropp, Aron, Pettigrew, & Wright, 2011; Page-Gould, Mendoza-Denton, Alegre, & Siy, 2010). Altogether, the optimal conditions of contact appear useful for prejudice reduction when applied as a set (Pettigrew & Tropp, 2006), but they are likely not the reason that cross-group friendship is beneficial for intergroup relations (Nagamuthu & Page-Gould, 2017).

Instead, we think the very existence of cross-group friendship reflects the necessity of intergroup cooperation for individual and human-level survival. Drawing on complexity theory (see Mitchell, 2009), we argue that cross-group friendships are not so much tools as they are emergent phenomenon of complex adaptive systems. Complex systems can be recognized as having lots of pieces that somehow produce an unexpected outcome when examined as a whole. Complex *adaptive* systems additionally are responsive to the environment and promote survival within it. Complexity research is concerned with the description of such systems. Fig. 2 provides a simplified overview of complexity theory. Complexity theory has wide relevance across areas of science, with complexity research being conducted in various fields like psychology (e.g., Van Rooij & Wareham, 2008), geography (e.g., Manson, 2001), ecology (e.g., Norton & Ulanowicz, 1994), and computer science (e.g., Chaitin, 1992).

Features of Complex Adaptive Systems

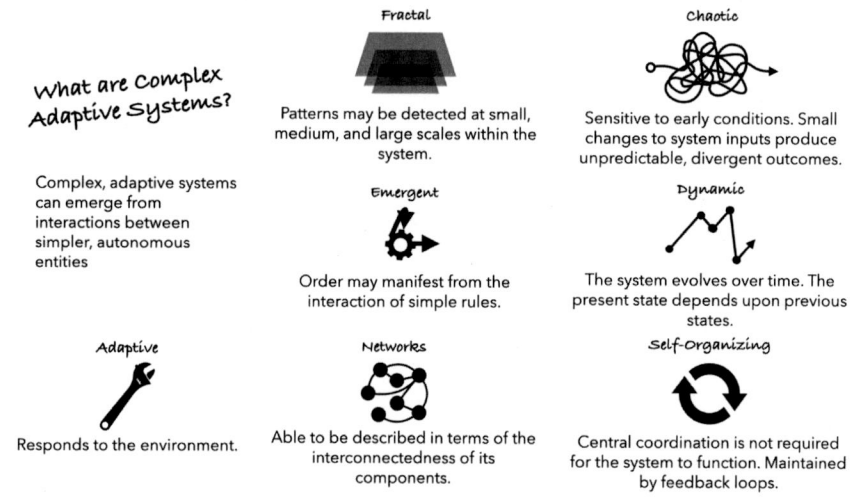

Fig. 2 Features of complex adaptive systems.

Complex systems are sensitive to starting conditions, which means small changes to the system produce unpredictable, chaotic outcomes. Complex processes unfold dynamically over time such that the current state of a system depends upon the accumulated history of previous effects within the system. Emergence occurs when the repeated interaction of simple rules across time permits complex systems to manifest novel outcomes. One common emergent property observed in many complex systems is that of self-organization, in which there is no central coordination required for the system to function. Whether examining the system as a whole or zooming in to the individual level, many complex systems exhibit fractal patterns that are observable at multiple scales. Finally, complex systems are often described as networks due to the interconnectedness of the individual components that the system may consist of.

Arguing from complexity theory, emergent phenomena arise in complex adaptive systems because they are adaptive for the system. We assert cross-group friendships are a core component of human survival that promote intergroup cooperation and thus both reflect and contribute to the complexity of global intergroup relations. It is important to note that cross-group friendships are not the only components of the human-level system of intergroup relations, but we believe these processes to be entangled across levels of scale.

We are not the first psychologists to apply complexity theory to friendships, as DeScioli and Kurzban (2011) laid out a set of arguments showing that friendships are adaptive for the survival of both the individual human and collective society by promoting cooperation. Indeed, like complex adaptive systems, friendships are fundamentally dynamic. As long as both humans are alive, there is the potential for a future social interaction to change the relationship. If social interactions are indeed the components of relationships, as we propose here, then every new interaction with a friend increases the complexity of our mental representation of the relationship. While we expect all friendships to promote cooperation at the human level (e.g., DeScioli & Kurzban, 2011), we see cross-group friendship, however, as a specific type of friendship that has unique functional qualities for the complex systems that characterize intergroup relations at the human level.

A major goal of this chapter is to disentangle the constructs of cross-group friendship, intergroup interaction, and intergroup contact. These constructs are intertwined in the intergroup relations literature for epistemological and structural reasons. We start by discussing the basic premise: That intergroup contact and cross-group friendship are fundamentally comprised of intergroup interactions. We dive into the implications of this assertion for intergroup contact through the lens of our "asymptotic model" of intergroup contact (MacInnis & Page-Gould, 2015). We use these ideas to argue that cross-group friendship is, in some ways, a special case of intergroup contact and, in other ways, something much more than intergroup contact. We discuss the idea that cross-group friendship is an adaptive phenomenon that emerges from the interplay of repeated intergroup interactions with the same person. Supporting this view, our research has identified two feedback loops that occur at different points across the lifespan of cross-group friendships that promote and maintain these friendships (e.g., Danyluck & Page-Gould, 2018, 2019; Page-Gould, 2012; Page-Gould, Mendes, & Major, 2010). Table 1 provides a glossary of key terms used in this chapter.

Viewing cross-group friendships as complex adaptive systems has broader implications for intergroup relations. If cross-group friendships are complex adaptive systems, then they are functional at other levels of scale, beyond the individual and interpersonal levels. It implies that cross-group friendships serve an adaptive function at the scale of the human community in a way that reflects individual-level friendship, and we propose the higher-level system is intergroup cooperation. Taken together, cross-group friendships are positioned as dynamic components of intergroup cooperation. Intergroup cooperation (e.g., coalitions among people with different sociocultural and ethnic identities) is inseparable from cross-group friendship.

Table 1 Glossary of key terms.

Term	Definition
Agent based model (ABM)	A form of simulation where autonomous Agents exist, act, and potentially interact in a simulated universe. Agent behavior can be programmed based on a theoretical model, allowing researchers to explore their theories by observing emergent behavior and manipulating features of the agents and the environment.
Agents	Simulated people in an agent based model.
Asymptotic model of contact	The model of intergroup contact that views each person as having their own trajectory for the impact of their intergroup interactions on their prejudice, changing more during early intergroup interactions and stabilizing in later intergroup interactions (MacInnis & Page-Gould, 2015). Compare with *Linear Model of Contact*.
Complex adaptive systems	Complex systems that are responsive to the environment and promote survival in it. See Fig. 2. Compare with *Complex Systems*.
Complex systems	Systems with many simple components that interact with each other in ways that produce novel outcomes when examined as a whole. Complex systems exhibit certain characteristics, such as being chaotic, fractal, emergent, dynamic, self-organizing, and representable as a network.
Contact effect	The relationship between prejudice and social interactions, traditionally treated as a linear relationship. In the asymptotic model, the direction and magnitude of the contact effect differs between individuals. See *Asymptotic Model of Contact* and *Linear Model of Contact*.
Contact threshold	In the asymptotic model, the point at which the impact of intergroup interactions on prejudice levels off. Subsequent interactions have less effect on prejudice after this point.
Cross-group friendship	Platonic, interpersonal closeness between people with different social identities.
Default prejudice	In the asymptotic model, the amount of prejudice a person has toward a group prior to ever interacting with a person from that group.
Intergroup contact	Amount of intergroup interaction. In the asymptotic model, intergroup contact is the limiting function of intergroup interactions on prejudice as intergroup interactions increase toward infinity.

Continued

Table 1 Glossary of key terms.—cont'd

Term	Definition
Intergroup interaction	A social interaction involving people with different social identities.
Linear model of contact	The model of intergroup contact that views intergroup interactions as having a stable and consistent relationship with prejudice across the lifetime. Compare with *Asymptotic Model of Contact*.
Physiological reactivity	Changes in physiological activity in response to a stimulus or event.
Physiological synchrony	Covariation of physiological activity during social interactions.
Prejudice	A negative attitude about a social group. Prejudice is the affective component of intergroup bias.
Rate Parameter	In the asymptotic model, the speed and amount of change in prejudice as a function of intergroup interactions. Most factors that modulate a person's personal trajectory of intergroup contact affect the system by changing the rate.
Social interaction	A back-and-forth exchange between two or more people.

1. Intergroup interactions as the substance of cross-group friendship and intergroup contact

Although intergroup interaction and intergroup contact are somewhat conflated in the literature, we propose that they are quite distinct. Intergroup interactions are discrete events. Intergroup contact is a term that typically refers to a person's history of intergroup interactions. We previously argued that intergroup interactions were the units of intergroup contact (MacInnis & Page-Gould, 2015). We extend that argument here to further clarify the relationship between social interactions, intergroup interactions, and intergroup contact (Fig. 3).

Intergroup interactions are social interactions between people with different social identities, such as interracial interactions between people categorized in different racial groups (Trawalter, Richeson, & Shelton, 2009). The defining feature of social interaction is that there must be an opportunity for a back-and-forth, interactive exchange between two or more people (American Psychological Association, n.d.). All people involved must have a chance to communicate with or influence each other in real-time for an event

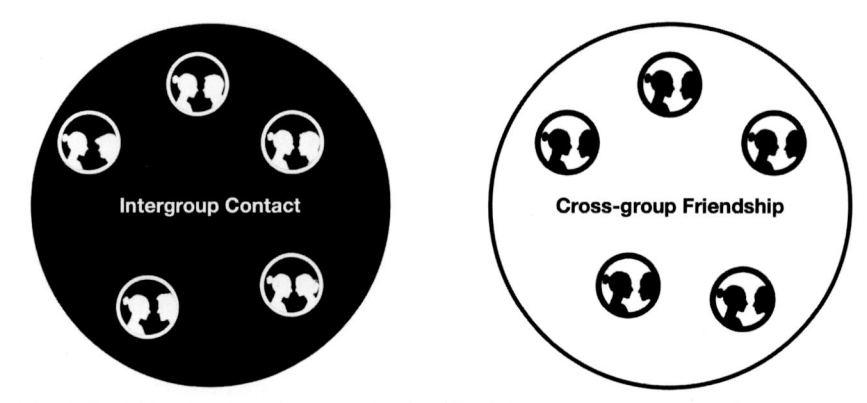

Fig. 3 Social interactions form the basis of both intergroup contact and cross-group friendship. Note: The circle on the left represents the construct of intergroup contact, and the circle on the right represents the construct of cross-group friendship. The smaller circles inside the larger circles represent social interactions as the basis for both intergroup contact and cross-group friendship. The difference between the intergroup interactions that comprise intergroup contact and the intergroup interactions that comprise cross-group friendship is that the intergroup interactions that comprise a cross-group friendship are repeated intergroup interactions with the same person.

to be a social interaction. Intergroup interactions can occur through any communication medium, including in-person or technology-mediated interactions (Harwood, 2021; White, Harvey, & Abu-Rayya, 2015). One of the most widely observed differences between social interactions with ingroup versus outgroup members is the presence of anxiety during intergroup interactions, termed "intergroup anxiety" (Stephan & Stephan, 1985).

We argue that both cross-group friendship and intergroup contact can be seen as collections of intergroup interactions (Fig. 3). Previously, we asserted that intergroup interactions are the basic unit of intergroup contact (MacInnis & Page-Gould, 2015; Page-Gould, 2012). This view incorporates the traditional treatment of intergroup contact as a quantity, with individual differences reflecting having "more contact" or "less contact." We take that idea one step further here by proposing that cross-group friendships are essentially comprised of repeated intergroup interactions with the same person. This assertion is an extension of the view that we know our friends through our social interactions with them (Lydon, Jamieson, & Holmes, 1997; Wilson, Harris, & Vazire, 2015). This formalization is helpful because social interactions are discrete events (e.g., they have start and end times), which makes it easier to reason about the relationship between cross-group friendship and intergroup contact.

If cross-group friendship and intergroup contact share the same basic components (i.e., multiple intergroup interactions), then we can use these components to understand how the constructs of intergroup contact and cross-group friendship relate to one another. The critical difference between the intergroup interactions that comprise intergroup contact and cross-group friendship in Fig. 3 is the familiarity of the interaction partners. In intergroup contact (Panel A), the intergroup interactions include all the interactions that occur with any person of a given social identity, both strangers and familiar outgroup members. In cross-group friendship (Panel B), all social interactions are repeated interactions with the same person. The intergroup interactions involved in a cross-group friendship would necessarily be present in and subsumed by the intergroup interactions that comprise a person's intergroup contact. We argue that the interplay of these *repeated* intergroup interactions leads to the emergence of a cross-group friendship. As an emergent entity, the cross-group friendship is more than a linear combination of the component intergroup interactions.

In the absence of intergroup interaction, there is no intergroup contact and no cross-group friendship. If you do not have intergroup interaction, then you do not have a cross-group friendship. So, you cannot have a cross-group friendship without first having intergroup contact. Cross-group friendship is not an inevitable outcome of intergroup contact, however.

2. Intergroup contact

Throughout this chapter, we treat intergroup contact as a given state of the social environment, both rhetorically and formally. Every human has multiple intersecting identities. So, in a certain sense, intergroup contact is inevitable. It would be anomalous for two interaction partners to be identical across all possible social identities. Within the context of research on intergroup contact, then, research tends to focus on social interactions where the differences in social identities reflect an asymmetry in societal power, privilege, and oppression, such as interracial contact (Paluck, Green, & Green, 2019; Pettigrew & Tropp, 2006).

Intergroup contact research has a long history that extends into policy (Pettigrew & Tropp, 2005). Intergroup contact researchers directly impacted legislation in the United States through the Society for the Psychological Study of Social Issues (SPSSI; Hartung, 2004). Both intergroup contact researchers and SPSSI rightfully take pride in the role that the contact hypothesis played in desegregating schools in the United States Brown vs. Board of

Education ruling of 1954 (e.g., Benjamin & Crouse, 2004; Pettigrew, 2011). At the time, the interest in intergroup contact was driven by the need to ameliorate the great disparities caused by segregation in the US (e.g., Clark, Chein, & Cook, 2004). Once desegregation began occurring, the field began to focus on the relationship between intergroup contact and prejudice and this focus remains despite various calls to focus on other outcomes (e.g., Christ & Wagner, 2013; Paluck, Porat, Clark, & Green, 2020; Paolini et al., 2021; Pettigrew & Tropp, 2006).

2.1 The linear model of intergroup contact

A major focus of intergroup contact research is whether prejudice increases or decreases with contact. Using the modeling tools most accessible, everyone looked for the linear relationship between contact and prejudice (Eq. 1). What does this choice to look for a linear relationship mean?

$$Prejudice_i = Default\ Bias + Contact\ Effect * Intergroup\ Interactions_i \qquad (1)$$

Viewing intergroup interactions as the unit of intergroup contact, we quantify intergroup contact as the count of intergroup interactions that one person has with members of a particular outgroup across their lifespan (*Intergroup Interactions_i*). This count starts at zero (i.e., birth until the first intergroup interaction) and increments up by one with every intergroup interaction, all the way to infinity (i.e., as long as you are alive, you could always have one more intergroup interaction).

In a linear model, the contact effect is the incremental change in prejudice after each subsequent social interaction. An intercept is the expected value of the dependent variable when all independent variables equal zero. In Eq. (1), the intercept is represented by "Default Bias," and it represents a person's prejudice before they have any intergroup contact (i.e., prejudice when intergroup contact count $= 0$). A slope weights the independent variable to match the size of the relationship between the independent and dependent variables. In Eq. (1), the slope is the linear "contact effect" as the field has modeled it.

What is the linear contact effect? A massive meta-analysis found that the effect size for the relationship between intergroup contact and prejudice[a]

---

[a] Table 1 in the Pettigrew and Tropp (2006) meta-analysis provides the estimates from a number of different ways that the intergroup contact effect could be calculated. Since we were looking for a point of reference for our arguments here, we selected the estimate of the contact effect that best matched our conceptualization of intergroup contact, which is the estimate of the correlations between intergroup contact and prejudice at the level of the test (Tests → All tests → Random, Table 1, p. 756).

is small but reliable, $r=-0.214$, 95% CI $[-0.20, -0.22]$ (Pettigrew & Tropp, 2006). A recent meta-analysis focused on experiments found a similar but smaller effect size, $r=-0.191$, 95% CI $[-0.115, -0.267]$ (converted from Cohen's d and with sign reversed, incorporating different coding of prejudice; Paluck et al., 2019, p. 20). These estimates (e.g., linear contact effect$=r=\sim 57680-0.21$) are the same in absolute value as the average effect sizes found in social psychology, $|r|=0.21$ (Richard, Bond Jr., & Stokes-Zoota, 2003).

Linear models are powerful tools, but their use affects how we characterize a phenomenon. The primary question asked by the linear model was, "Is this relationship negative, positive, or null?" This question is about direction, and it does not reference the *rate* of change. A linear model assumes a constant relationship.

Fig. 4 depicts a person's intergroup interactions across their life. A linear contact effect implies the prejudice shift from a person's 1st to 250th intergroup interaction (Bias$_1$) is 1/3 the magnitude change between their 250th and 1000th interaction (Bias$_2$). If the contact effect is linear, then more contact will continually improve a person's egalitarianism because the relationship is constant in magnitude. In a linear model of intergroup contact, there is no specific number of intergroup interactions that equate to a desired state of egalitarianism. The message that more contact is better may be generally and mildly true, but it is a race with no finish line.

2.2 The asymptotic model of intergroup contact

We proposed that this linear contact effect does not manifest but instead acts as an asymptote that observed data should approach as intergroup interactions increase (the "asymptotic model" of intergroup contact; MacInnis & Page-Gould, 2015). As the number of intergroup interactions approaches infinity, the impact of intergroup interactions on prejudice stabilizes into the construct generally sought as "intergroup contact" (i.e., Eq. 2). At smaller numbers, the

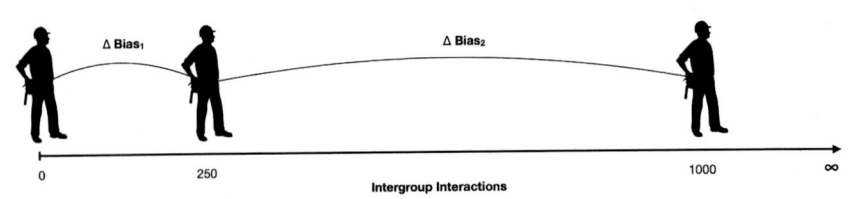

Fig. 4 Implications of a linear contact effect.

effect of contact should take a curvilinear form, where each intergroup interaction has the potential to make a strong impact on prejudice.

$$\lim_{\text{Intergroup Interactions}\rightarrow+\infty} f\left(\textit{Intergroup Interactions}\right) = \textit{Intergroup Contact} \quad (2)$$

Logically, we began by thinking about intergroup interactions as the components of intergroup contact. Intergroup interactions are discrete events that are usually observable. They range from zero to infinity. A theory that explains intergroup contact must then consider the effect of intergroup interactions on prejudice across the full range that intergroup interactions can take. This led us to define intergroup contact as the limiting function of intergroup interactions on prejudice (Eq. 2) as intergroup interactions extend to infinity. When researchers talk about the contact effect, they mean a stable, small relationship between intergroup interactions and prejudice. This limiting function is a linear asymptote. The observable relationship approaches linearity but never achieves it.

Thinking about intergroup contact in this way led us to use Eq. (1) to plot an oblique asymptote representing the stabilization of intergroup contact effects within a person (Fig. 5, black dashed line). By thinking about intergroup contact in this way, we can apply a known mathematical equation for a curved line that approaches an oblique asymptote. Eq. (3) shows that equation adapted to the relationship between intergroup interactions and prejudice.

$$\textit{Prejudice} = \frac{\textit{Contact Effect} * \textit{Interactions}^2 + \textit{Default Bias} + \textit{Contact Effect} * \textit{Interactions} + \textit{Rate}}{\textit{Interactions} - 1}$$

$$(3)$$

Compare Eq. (1) and Eq. (3). *Prejudice, Interactions, Default Prejudice,* and *Contact Effect* mean the same things in both equations, although the function that combines them is different. *Default Prejudice* is a person's starting level of *Prejudice* when *Interactions* are zero. *Contact effect* is the slope of the oblique asymptote that the curved line approaches. Therefore, the linear contact effect best captures the relationship between *Interactions* and *Prejudice* in later interactions.

We would say that a person crosses a "contact threshold" when the curved line becomes effectively parallel to the oblique asymptote. The speed with which this occurs is adjusted by the one new parameter in the asymptotic model (Eq. 3) relative to Eq. (1): *Rate.* Rate acts as a single value in the asymptotic model, but it is multidetermined. Factors like the quality of

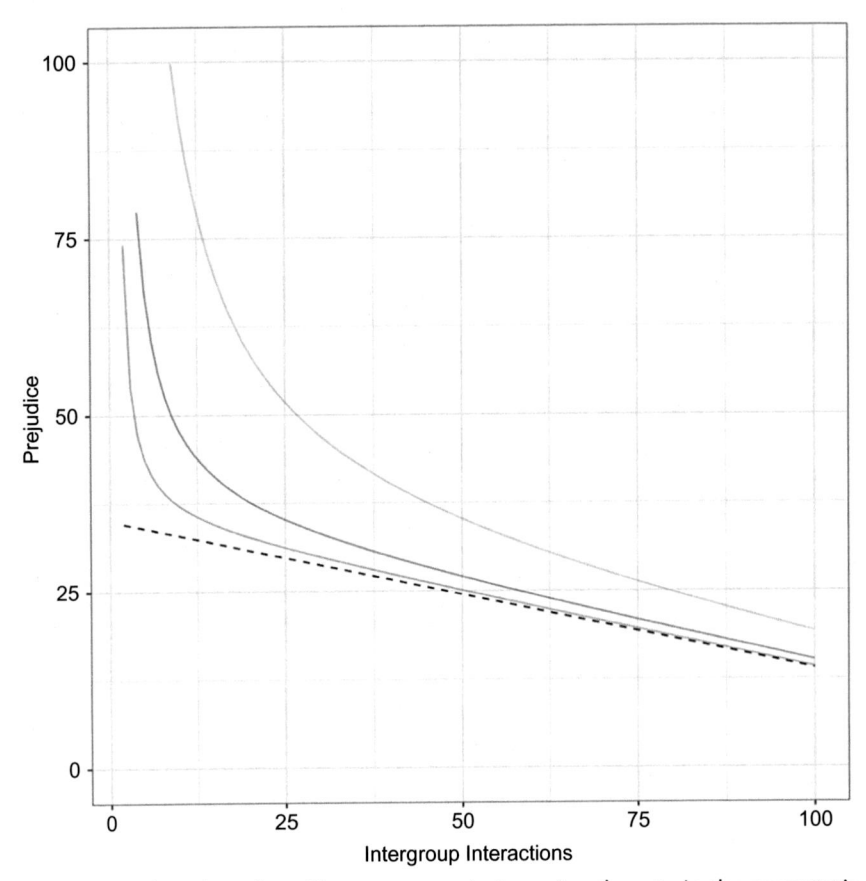

Fig. 5 Example trajectories of intergroup contact, varying the rate in the asymptotic model. Note: The asymptotic model is visualized here. The dashed line is the asymptote of the asymptotic model. It is the linear contact effect. For this visualization, the *contact effect* was held constant at the effect size estimated by Pettigrew and Tropp (2006), $r = -0.21$. The three curved lines represent the trajectories of prejudice for three different people as they have more intergroup interactions. All three lines have the same value for the *contact effect* parameter but nonetheless different *rate* parameters in the asymptotic model (Eq. 4).

intergroup interactions and the time intervals between them will play into *rate*, along with many other factors (MacInnis & Page-Gould, 2015). The rate parameter creates a bottleneck, then, through which the information from multiply deterministic factors is represented and can affect intergroup experience.

The asymptotic model implies a number of things for intergroup contact. Most clearly, the asymptotic model predicts that early intergroup interactions, far away from infinity, would not show a linear relationship with prejudice. Over the course of the initial intergroup interactions, the relationship between the amount of contact and prejudice is nonlinear and the rate of change is highest. The asymptotic model defines initial intergroup interactions as relatively volatile. Nonetheless, they hold more weight for the shape of individual trajectories. The asymptotic model suggests that early interactions play a greater role in contact processes than later intergroup interactions. Each subsequent interaction has slightly less of an impact on prejudice than the one that came before it, until eventually the impact of intergroup interactions achieves a steady state that infinitely approaches linearity.

An important feature of the asymptotic model is that this model is irrelevant before the first intergroup interaction. The denominator of Eq. (3) subtracts one from the count of intergroup interactions. This action in the denominator builds in the reduction in impact of later interactions while also creating a vertical asymptote at the first intergroup interaction a person ever has with someone with a particular social identity. The asymptotic model makes no predictions for this first intergroup interaction. The asymptotic model only applies once first contact between groups has occurred.

Relatedly, *default prejudice* is a person's prejudice toward a social identity prior to their first intergroup interaction with people with that identity. As in Eq. (1), the *default prejudice* parameter in Eq. (3) is the value of the dependent variable (*prejudice*) when *intergroup interactions* equals zero. However, the denominator term makes it so that the asymptotic model is not realized until at least the second intergroup interaction with people of a particular social identity. These features of the asymptotic model suggest that a person's "default" prejudice toward a social identity is defined by the amalgamation of their experiences prior to the moment of gaining direct knowledge through intergroup interaction. Note that, if *default prejudice* took a negative value in the asymptotic model, it would represent having an affinity for a social outgroup prior to intergroup interaction with people from that group.

The asymptotic model does not abandon the idea of a linear contact effect, rather it subsumes it. The linear contact effect is the asymptote itself, and its slope is coded into the model with the *contact effect* parameter in Eq. (3). The estimate of this slope tells us the direction and magnitude of the contact effect. Perhaps one of the greatest strengths of the asymptotic model over the linear model is its ability to account for contact to both improve and worsen prejudice. The direction and magnitude of the *contact effect* represents a person's general trajectory of prejudice with increased familiarity.

2.2.1 Intergroup contact can worsen prejudice

The asymptotic model allows for intergroup contact to worsen prejudice. That is, the overall trajectory of contact can be positive (i.e., increasing prejudice with more intergroup interactions). It is self-evident that sometimes intergroup contact leads to intense prejudice. War does not occur between groups that never met. A violent hate crime requires intergroup interaction. We thus view it as important for any model of intergroup contact to be able to accommodate cases where intergroup contact leads to prejudice, including extreme prejudice. Two components of the asymptotic model allow prejudice to worsen: The contact effect and the rate parameter.

In the asymptotic model, the *contact effect* is assumed to differ between people and between different social group pairings. Holding the social group constant (e.g., people who live with chronic pain), then different people would show different contact effects toward the group of people who live with chronic pain, mostly decreasing prejudice but some making no difference. Focusing on within-person differences in prejudice toward different groups, the asymptotic model should be a little different for each intergroup context that is relevant to a person's lived experiences. The example of people who live with chronic pain leads into how the contact effect could vary within a person and between social groups: Living with chronic pain is a more private condition than visible social group memberships, like those based on skin color. Moreover, the sociohistorical context of the intergroup interaction (e.g., Reicher, 2004; Trawalter, Bart-Plange, & Hoffman, 2020) would factor into both the rate parameter *and* the default prejudice that a person feels toward a particular social group. Given the myriad individual and societal factors that affect the rate parameter *and* the default prejudice, the asymptotic model must apply with unique parameters to each intergroup context, personalized to each individual. We can refine the asymptotic model presented in MacInnis and Page-Gould (2015) to incorporate the level at which each parameter in the model operates (Eq. 4).

$$Prejudice_{ijk} = \frac{Contact\ Effect_{jk} * Interactions_{ijk}^2 + Default\ Bias_{jk} + Contact\ Effect_{jk} * Interactions_{ijk} + Rate_{jk}}{Interactions_{ij} - 1}$$

(4)

In Eq. (4), there are 3 levels represented. The lowest level is the level of the intergroup interaction, *i*. The asymptotic model is supposed to be applied with each intergroup interaction as the unit of contact, and thus the interaction level is represented in the model itself. The second level is the social group, *j*, with whom a person, *k*, is interacting. This allows people to vary from each other, k, but also for contact to have different effects on prejudice toward different social groups, j, across i interactions with that social group. All other parameters in Eq. (4) mean the same as Eq. (3). Please note that Eq. (4) is an amendment to the equation that we originally introduced (cf., MacInnis & Page-Gould, 2015), arising in part from our computational approaches to theory development, which we describe in the next section.

If the core research question entertained by intergroup contact researchers has been, "Do intergroup interactions make prejudice better or worse and by how much?" then the asymptotic model allows a broader set of questions to be asked like, "Which intergroup interactions make whose prejudice better or worse, towards whom, by how much, and how long does it take for maximal improvement?" All parameters generated for the asymptotic model will have expected values that answer these questions. For example, if we want to know the linear contact effect for a given group, $Contact\ Effect_j$, is the expected value (average) of each person's trajectory of change in prejudice as a function of their intergroup interactions with a particular outgroup, i ($Contact\ Effect_{jk}$), across all people, k. The asymptotic model allows intergroup contact to behave differently in different intergroup contexts. The asymptotic model represents a psychological process that we expect to apply to every intergroup context relevant to a person's life. We represent this formally with Eq. (4).

Interactions with cross-group friends are subsumed by the asymptotic model. The intergroup interactions that serve as input to the asymptotic model include interactions with both known and unknown, close and non-close others. The quality of the intergroup interactions that constitute one person's intergroup experiences with a particular social group is represented with the rate parameter. The rate parameter mostly affects the speed with which the impact of intergroup interactions hit their point of minimum return. However, as we will argue later in the chapter, cross-group friendship emerges as something more than just a collection of intergroup interactions. Thus, while the asymptotic model incorporates contact with cross-group friends, cross-group friendships go beyond what can be characterized by the asymptotic model.

2.2.2 Implications of the asymptotic model

A significant benefit of creating a formal model of intergroup contact is that it makes it easier to explore the theoretical implications with computational tools. In the case of our interest in social interaction, an *agent-based model* (ABM) is an ideally matched computational tool for theory development. An ABM allows researchers to define different agents who live in a virtual environment (Grimm et al., 2010). ABM provide a powerful way to explore the predictive space of theoretical models, because researchers control (a) the behavior of agents; (b) the characteristics of agents; (c) features of the environment. It is then possible to explore how the system changes when starting values of the environmental parameters are systematically varied (e.g., to explore the influence of an environmental factor on the system) or when environmental parameters are suddenly shifted after the system had started (e.g., to explore environmental shocks to the system). In what follows, we describe some of the insights and predictions gained from using an ABM to explore the asymptotic model (Miller, MacInnis, & Page-Gould, 2021).

We created an ABM to test the asymptotic model, where each agent represented a person. The simulated universe of the ABM mimicked an urban environment by randomly distributing agents with a higher probability of being in the middle of the space than along the perimeter. The agents walked around this space, occasionally entering the same space as other agents and then choosing to interact with them or not. If the agents did interact with each other, then this interaction had a particular quality ranging from positive to negative. The intergroup nature of the ABM was applied by modeling contact between agents with different religious beliefs, using an interface to public data that allows for agents in an ABM to have evidence-based, representative characteristics of the real population (Miller & Cupchik, 2016). All agents were assigned values of default prejudice against religious outgroups that varied normally around an average value. An agent's current prejudice level decreased their likelihood of initiating intergroup interactions and contributed negatively to the quality of intergroup interactions. The published linear contact effect of $r = -0.21$ was used for the contact effect in our ABM, although any value could be used in the model. The ABM universe advanced in discrete steps, where every step represented 1 day. We simulated 5 years.

What did the agents do each day? On each step, agents first turned in a random direction. Then, they maybe moved a small distance, depending on random noise. If their new location was an adjacent patch to the location of another agent, then there would be the potential for the two agents to interact with each other. Not all agents who occupied adjacent locations interacted. If the proximal agent had a different religion, then the agent's prejudice reduced the likelihood they would interact. If a social interaction occurred, then it had a certain positive or negative quality ("valence"). We simulated the positive or negative valence of social interactions, using numbers from our past daily experience studies to estimate that approximately

81% of social interactions were positive (i.e., non-conflict interactions in Page-Gould, 2012). For interactions between agents with the same religion, the quality of social interactions was set around this expected value plus random noise. For intergroup interactions, the quality of social interactions was set around this expected value, but it was down-weighted by the prejudice of each agent before also having a random noise element added.

The quality of intergroup interactions had some effect on prejudice levels. Drawing from work on the valence of intergroup contact (Paolini, Harwood, & Rubin, 2010), we estimated that positive intergroup interactions would improve prejudice by half as much as negative intergroup interactions would worsen prejudice. We coded the ABM such that the valence of interactions with ingroup members made no impact on an agent's prejudice for that step—although it is conceivable that interactions with ingroup members could alter prejudice (e.g., Wright, Aron, McLaughlin-Volpe, & Ropp, 1997; Zhou, Page-Gould, Aron, Moyer, & Hewstone, 2019). This series of behaviors occurred in steps, and we could chart agents' trajectories across time.

Fig. 6 shows what happened with agents' prejudice over the simulated 5-year period. The count of intergroup interactions is represented on the

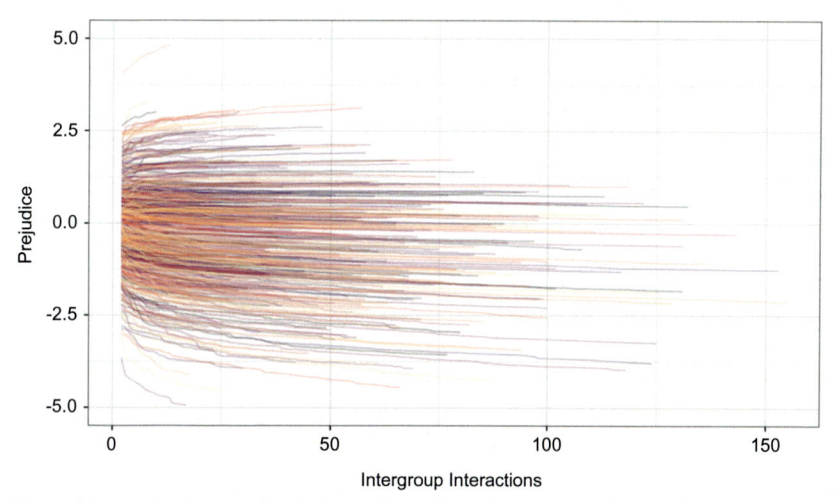

Fig. 6 Individual agents prejudice as a function of their intergroup interactions. Note: Each line represents the dynamic prejudice levels of the individual agents, as they interacted with religious outgroup members over time. Note that the time in between each intergroup interaction is not constant either within a person nor between them (i.e., the time between two subsequent intergroup interactions could be the equivalent of 10 min or 10 days).

horizontal axis. Agent prejudice is represented on the vertical axis, with zero representing the average prejudice for all agents in the ABM (i.e., negative values represented being relatively less prejudiced than the average person in the "society," but could still represent prejudice against outgroup members, in an absolute sense). Each line tracks individual agents' prejudice over time. The line colors were varied to help visually differentiate between individual trajectories.

Focusing on individual outcomes, the ABM shows us a few things. Looking at Fig. 7, there were two ways in which more intergroup interactions did not equate to less prejudice. Certainly, we see that some agents' trajectories are positive (Fig. 7, Panel A), meaning that the effect of contact was to worsen those agents' prejudice. Almost all these agents began with average levels of default prejudice, although one agent whose prejudice worsened began with relatively less prejudice than their society's average prejudice. We consider it a feature of the asymptotic model that we can incorporate that phenomenon.

The second thing we learned is more subtle. Notice the longest lines are in the middle of the cloud (Fig. 6). This means that the most intergroup interactions were experienced by agents who had stabilized around a slightly below-average level of prejudice. When we focus on the agents that had

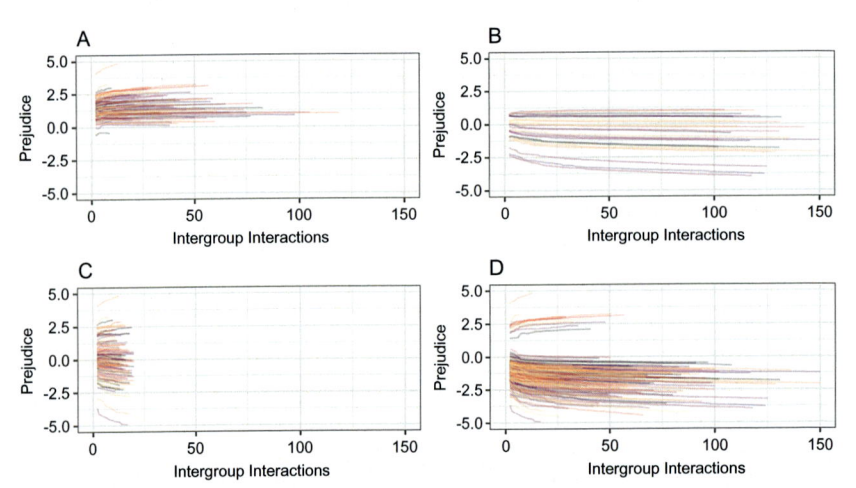

Fig. 7 Subsets of agents that illustrate behavior. Note: Each panel contains a subset of the individual agent lines from Fig. 6. Panel (A) shows only agents who increased in prejudice with contact. Panel (B) shows only agents who had at least 100 intergroup interactions. Panel (C) shows only agents who had less than 20 intergroup interactions. Panel D shows only agents who changed by half a standard deviation or more in prejudice.

at least 100 intergroup interactions (Fig. 7, Panel B), we see that the early rate of change relates to the steepness of the longer-term trajectory. The agents with the most intergroup interactions also generally had negative or neutral trajectories (i.e., more contact was generally good for reducing prejudice). Conversely, looking at agents that had less than 20 intergroup interactions (Fig. 7, Panel C), all directions are observed.

Although it looks visually like the agents who begin at either extreme of prejudice had steep slopes and fewer intergroup interactions, this is a bit of an illusion given the density of agent prejudice around average prejudice (Fig. 7, Panel C). Fig. 7, Panel D shows the trajectories for agents who showed a half a standard deviation or more change in prejudice as a function of intergroup contact. Focusing on the agents who changed the most from intergroup interactions suggests that it is not the *amount* of intergroup contact that matters, as the total number of intergroup interactions varies quite a bit among these agents. Instead, given our simple model, the only other terms that could affect these agents' prejudice would be the quality of the intergroup interactions and random Gaussian noise. The Gaussian noise term allows for individual intergroup interactions to randomly have more or less of an impact on agent prejudice than the model would otherwise predict. We infer that one way that contact may elicit egalitarianism without a lot of contact is when an early intergroup contact experience is particularly high quality and somewhat randomly impacts prejudice more than normal. Given that prejudice then plays back into the system by affecting the likelihood and quality of the next intergroup interaction, perhaps only a few very high quality intergroup experiences are sufficient to promote egalitarianism in a dynamic system.

Please note that these agents did not "stop" having intergroup interactions at a certain point. Rather, they had more ingroup interactions separating their intergroup interactions or they had less opportunity for social interaction, as a whole. Due to the way we set up our universe, this should have been true for extremely prejudiced agents but the opposite for agents who were extremely below-average in prejudice. Rather, this effect suggested to us that agents with fewer opportunities for intergroup interaction will have the greatest sustained impact of intergroup interactions over the course of their lives. However, if this model is true, it goes against what the linear model predicts for intergroup contact. The asymptotic model generates cases where agents with relatively little intergroup contact are the least prejudiced. Each intergroup interaction has a very positive impact on their prejudice levels, but those interactions are just few and far between. We also see that the number of intergroup interactions is greater for agents with lower-than-average prejudice.

Fig. 6 also emphasizes how important early intergroup interactions are for the personal development of prejudice. Some trajectories changed direction, but only in the initial interactions. Of course, this is not to say that a profound intergroup interaction cannot change someone's prejudice substantially. We did not include any shocks to the system in the ABM, but those shocks, fundamentally, occur. These external shocks can solidify and deepen friendships (Miller, Rozin, & Fiske, 1998) or destroy them (King & Sakamoto, 2015). For example, the sudden turn of geopolitical events like the eruption of a war or a severe famine can impact friendships at the individual level and intergroup relations at the societal level. There is evidence that climate change may have resulted in some of the earliest known human warfare (Crevecoeur, Dias-Meirinho, Zazzo, Antoine, & Bon, 2021), and we should expect similar shock events as the world heats. In the absence of such shocks, however, the first few intergroup interactions chart the course for that agent's intergroup contact.

Fig. 6 also illustrates the impact of prejudice prior to the first intergroup interaction ("default prejudice") on the system. Default prejudice negatively plays into the quality of the intergroup interactions, such that they were more likely to be negative—albeit, in the context of the default *social interactions* in this universe being generally positive, meaning most intergroup interactions were positive, even for relatively prejudiced agents. In turn, negative intergroup interactions worsened prejudice more than positive interactions improved it. Paired with increased avoidance of future intergroup interactions, agents who began with above-average prejudice were more likely to have trajectories where prejudice mildly increased with additional intergroup interactions. Nonetheless, many agents who began with above-average prejudice exhibited a negative contact effect, suggesting that there is value to intergroup contact for prejudiced people. The issue that intergroup contact is more likely to occur among people who needed it the least has been raised multiple times (Pettigrew & Tropp, 2013). The asymptotic model incorporates this feedback loop while still allowing for individual change across the span of default prejudice.

2.3 How do the processes of intergroup contact change with the environment?

An exciting feature of ABM is the ability to apply the asymptotic model at different levels of change. In ABM, it is common to conduct a sensitivity analysis to determine how sensitive agent behavior is to changes in the system parameters. Conceptually, we view the universe of our ABM to be a society. Thus, changing the parameters represents societies with different social norms. We simulated multiple societies, systematically varying the universe's default prejudice and the default positivity of social interactions. We viewed default prejudice as a cultural norm, specific to intergroup relations, and the default positivity of social interactions being a situational norm about the events of the interaction. Thus, the cultural norm was coded by varying default prejudice, but the situational norm was coded by shifting the average valence of all social interactions agents experienced positively or negatively. Within each combination, we simulated 500 societies.

The results of the sensitivity analysis are presented in Fig. 8. Within each panel, intergroup interactions are plotted on the horizontal axis and the average prejudice of agents in a given simulated society are on the vertical axis.

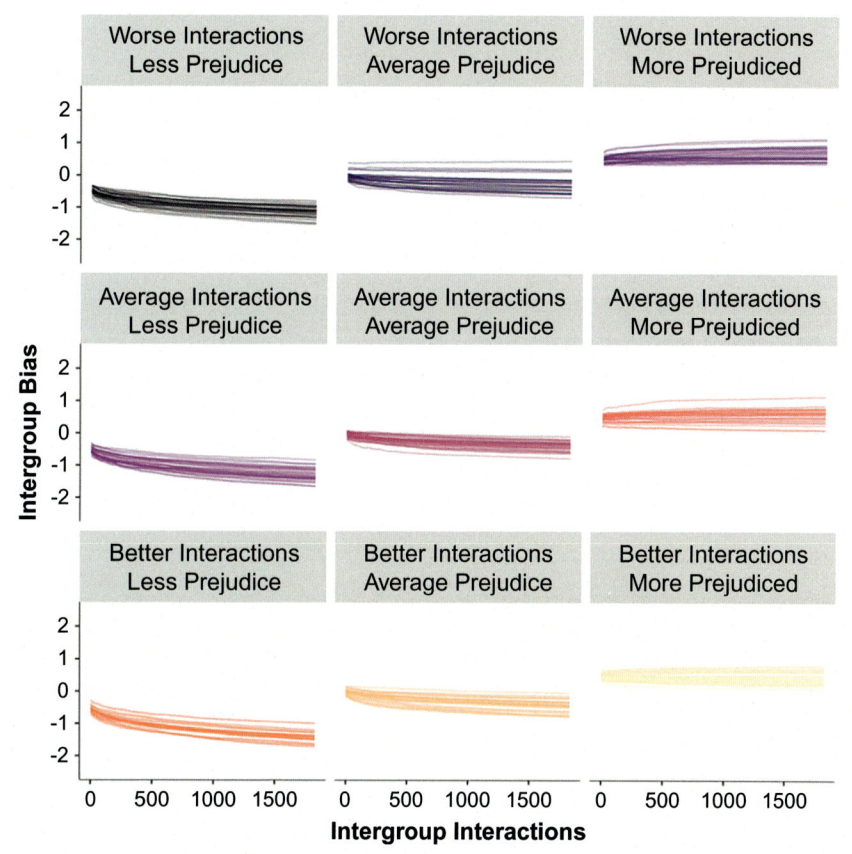

Fig. 8 Societal norms affect the result of contact. Note: Each line represents the average prejudice level of all agents in one society as a function of intergroup interactions. Each panel plots the simulation results from multiple societies that varied in cultural norms of default prejudice (columns shift right from less prejudice to more prejudice) and situational norms of social interaction positivity (rows shift from societies with less positive interactions in the top row to more positive interactions on the bottom row).

Each line represents the smoothed conditional means of all agents in one simulated society. The panels increase in default prejudice from left to right, and they improve in interaction quality from top to bottom. These plots are one level of scale above Fig. 6, as the data shown in Fig. 6 would be smoothed into one line in Fig. 8. Note that every society shown in Fig. 8 used the same linear contact effect estimated by Pettigrew and Tropp (2006) of $r = -0.21$. Despite this trajectory being used as the default, we see that simulated societies with cultural norms of greater prejudice and relatively worse quality social interactions reliably show that intergroup interactions worsen prejudice over time. When prejudice is high, even societies that had relatively better-quality social interactions, at best, showed a null relationship between intergroup contact and prejudice. In general, societies with situational norms for better quality social interactions had more beneficial contact effects.

Default prejudice made the biggest difference in both the absolute amount of prejudice and the direction of the contact effect. Recalling that default prejudice is defined as the prejudice a person has toward a social group before having any intergroup interactions with people from that group (i.e., prejudice = default prejudice when intergroup interactions = 0): The asymptotic model suggests that cultural norms of prejudice toward a particular group shape the efficacy of intergroup contact between members of that group before people even gain direct intergroup experience.

Altogether, the asymptotic model implies that the relationship between intergroup interactions and prejudice changes over the course of one's personal experiences with people with a particular social identity. The relationship between intergroup interactions and prejudice is initially volatile and eventually stabilizes. After that point, having more intergroup interactions may have negligible additional impact on prejudice. If the field of intergroup relations seeks to identify the pathway toward a stable state of global intergroup cooperation and thriving, then contact is simply the starting line. It is the first step beyond segregation. We need something else to move us forward from contact to cooperation.

2.4 Intergroup contact can only take us so far

The asymptotic model implies that the impact of intergroup contact on prejudice levels off. The inflection point when the observable relationship becomes effectively parallel to the asymptote is the contact threshold, after which we would say a person "has contact" and expect to see some behavioral phenomena covary with that state. However, the asymptotic model implies that there are not many intergroup gains to be won from intergroup interactions after that point.

Intergroup contact is necessary but not sufficient for intergroup cooperation. Helms and colleagues (Helms, 1984; Helms & Carter, 1990) viewed White racial identity as developing toward stages of an autonomous, egalitarian identity or a reintegrated, racist identity. They viewed intergroup contact as the first stage of this process, no matter which direction the person went. Helms and colleagues describe how it can appear positive for a while for a White person to have intergroup contact but no meaningful intergroup relationships, but that state will break down when a negative intergroup experience inevitably occurs. This is a particular problem because intergroup interaction also provides the opportunity for intergroup conflict (Page-Gould, 2012). As depicted in Fig. 9, the more close cross–ethnic friends people had (left box), the more conflicts they reported with people of other ethnicities in over a 10-day period (right box) *because* people with close cross–ethnic friends have many more cross–ethnic interactions (top/middle box). That is, contact provides opportunity for conflict. Helms and colleagues argue that interracial conflict can be a fork in the road for the development of White racial identity. Interracial conflict is an event that can lead toward "reintegration" or internalized racism if the person gets defensive or threatened. If the person is

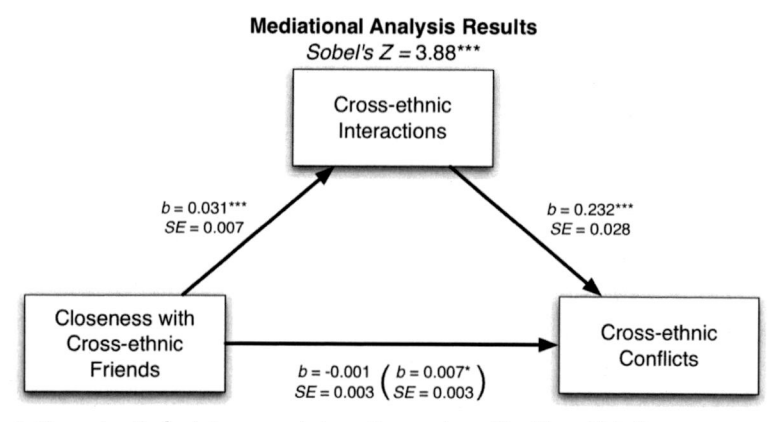

Fig. 9 Opportunity for intergroup interaction and conflict. Note: This figure appeared in Page-Gould (2012). Self-reported closeness with cross-ethnic friends (left box) predicted more cross-ethnic conflicts in daily life over a 10-day period (right box; statistical estimates in parentheses along the bottom arrow). However, this effect was erased when the total number of cross-ethnic interactions (top box) was included in the model. This suggests that cross-ethnic friendship provides the opportunity for more intergroup conflict because of more intergroup interaction.

resilient to the conflict, then their White racial identity further develops toward autonomy, because they learned and grew from the interracial conflict. Taken together, prolonged, non-close contact includes elements that may lead to worse attitudes (e.g., increased likelihood of intergroup conflict) without the mitigating elements that promote resilience (i.e., cross-group friendship).

This is where meaningful relationships matter. Interpersonal closeness involves a psychological merging of the Self with another person, including the extension of self-serving biases and equitable resource allocation (Aron et al., 1991). When that closeness develops in a cross-group friendship, we associate both personal and social characteristics of our friend's social identity with the Self (Page-Gould, Mendoza-Denton, et al., 2010). This merging of the Self with another person has unique relevance to intergroup relations (Page-Gould & Mendoza-Denton, 2011; Page-Gould, Mendoza-Denton, et al., 2010). For example, White Americans are more likely to engage in collective action for non-dominant group members as a function of perspective-taking and collective emotions (Mallett, Huntsinger, Sinclair, & Swim, 2008; Tropp & Uluğ, 2019). Intergroup contact is necessary for cross-group friendship, but cross-group friendship is something much more than intergroup contact.

3. Cross-group friendship

To disentangle cross-group friendship from intergroup contact, we must take a step back and separate the superordinate classes to which cross-group friendship and intergroup contact belong. Cross-group friendship is a specific type of interpersonal relationship. Intergroup contact is a specific type of social interaction. We can understand the difference between cross-group friendship and intergroup contact by understanding the difference between interpersonal relationships and social interactions.

Social interaction is a prerequisite for a relationship. For example, if an emotional bond exists in the absence of social interaction, it is considered a "parasocial relationship" (Schiappa, Gregg, & Hewes, 2005). Thus, social interaction is necessary for an interpersonal relationship to exist. We have no interpersonal relationships with "strangers." We can interact socially with strangers, however. Every interaction partner can be a stranger once. Assuming they were noticed the first time, then that same interaction partner is familiar to you during repeated social interactions. The earliest moment that an interpersonal relationship can develop is when an initial social interaction between strangers leads to a subsequent social interaction.

Traditionally defined, an interpersonal relationship is an affiliation between two people marked by psychological closeness (Clark & Lemay Jr., 2010). A friendship is a specific type of interpersonal relationship involving platonic intimacy and strong cooperative norms. Repeated social interactions are the field within which relationships can grow. In turn, relationships provide opportunity for social interactions to occur, fueling relationship development. If you have a relationship with someone, the affiliation amplifies the frequency of social interactions with that person. Experiences in these social interactions will vary from one event to the next. With every repeated social interaction, your mental representation of the other person grows in complexity.

3.1 Cross-group friendships are emergent processes of repeated intergroup interactions

We propose that cross-group friendships emerge from the interplay of repeated social interactions with the same person. Intergroup interactions are the mechanism through which societal level intergroup relations and our cross-group relationships affect daily experience. Psychologically, the complexity of encoding and storing information from repeated social interactions can lead to the emergence of a cross-group friendship between two or more people. We know the neurocognitive processes of organizing experiences within one social interaction are dynamic and nonlinear (Andrews-Hanna, Saxe, & Yarkoni, 2014; Barnett et al., 2020), thus incorporating knowledge across repeated interactions is necessarily more complex. Every new interaction with a cross-group friend can change the relationship and non-linearly adds to the web of experiences to cognitively integrate. The relationship may emerge as a way of mentally representing another person's repeated presence in your social world.

3.1.1 Where do cross-group friendships and intergroup interactions reside psychologically?

We believe complexity arises from the intrapersonal process of memory consolidation (e.g., Andrews-Hanna et al., 2014). This explanation positions cross-group friendship as existing psychologically within the individual. Thus, two people in a relationship can have "different" relationships or differentially perceive the presence or nature of the relationship. However, the relationship arises from the shared experiences of repeated social interactions, including dyadic interactions and group interactions.

We linger on this idea in this section because it helps explain some commonly reported phenomena in intergroup contact (e.g., secondary transfer effects, identity salience) and cross-group friendship research. Sometimes these phenomena are treated like methodological artifacts when they are perhaps a behavioral manifestation of the social psychological process being studied. For example, the perception of a friendship existing within each friend's mind allows for friendship nominations to be unreciprocated at a higher rate with cross-race friends than with same-race friends (Hallinan & Williams, 1987; Moody, 2001). By positioning interpersonal relationships psychologically as an individual experience, "non-reciprocated" friendship nominations are expected, as are differing reports of friendship quality. No individual friend can be considered the authority on the friendship.

Similarly, while social interactions are mostly objective, discrete events, whether a social interaction is perceived to be an intergroup interaction depends on each person's perception of differences in social identities with their interaction partner. Situating the "intergroup" quality of an interaction at the individual level allows for one person in a social interaction to perceive it as an intergroup interaction and their partner to perceive it as an ingroup interaction. It also allows for both people engaged in a social interaction to perceive it as an ingroup interaction and a third-party observer to perceive it as an intergroup interaction. All people can perceive the social interaction differently, if the intergroup quality of an interaction is an individual-level process. If all people can perceive the interaction differently, then their behavior will be consistent with their individual perceptions.

People behave as if they do not always expect their partner to perceive social interactions similarly to themselves. This is apparent in research on intergroup interactions in the context of non-visible identities (e.g., sexual orientation). Our work shows that there are both individual differences and identity-based differences in how much people feel they could conceal their social identities from other people (Le Forestier, Page-Gould, Lai, & Chasteen, 2020, 2022). These choices have interpersonal consequences, because revealing non-visible identities earlier in an intergroup interaction with a stranger had a positive impact on the quality of the intergroup interaction (e.g., MacInnis & Hodson, 2015). Both of these processes are predicated on the possibility that one member of a social interaction can know about a difference in social identity that their partner does not know. People do perceive some identities to be more concealable than others (Le Forestier et al., 2022). Thus, situating these processes as psychologically intrapersonal allows for discrepancies in perception like this at the dyadic level.

Situating intergroup interactions in the individual also allows for social interactions for which the social identities of interaction partners are unknown (e.g., interacting with a stranger online). In the modern world, many social interactions occur in which partners' various social identities are unknown. Thus, it is apparent that people can engage in social interactions without knowledge of their partner's social identities.

Situating intergroup interactions psychologically within the individual also allows for meta-perceptions of whether the other person perceives the social interaction as an intergroup interaction. One person's perception of the social interaction could be shifted by a realization that their partner was paying attention to a social identity that they did not think was meaningful. In this example, the person's perception would not be shifted by suddenly realizing they were in an intergroup interaction but rather by realizing their partner is affected by their social identity. If the perception of the intergroup interaction exists at the individual level, then this type of disagreement is easily explained. By contrast, if we view the "intergroup" quality to be an objective characteristic of the social interaction, then partner disagreement would be viewed as a methodological problem.

Situating both the situation and the friendship in the mind of the individual further provides an explanation for why intergroup contact with one outgroup seems to have a weaker, but positive, relationship with prejudice toward other outgroups that were not represented in the intergroup interaction, termed "secondary transfer effects" (Boin et al., 2021; Lolliot et al., 2013; Pettigrew, 2009). In our framework, the social interaction is the objective event and whether it is an "intergroup interaction" is a variable feature of the event, depending on how the interaction is perceived. If these processes are intraindividual, then individual differences in secondary transfer effects should map onto how closely different social identities are associated. Consistent with this idea, associating many social identities with each other ("social identity complexity") is a key mechanism of secondary transfer effects (Schmid, Hewstone, & Tausch, 2013; Vezzali, Di Bernardo, Cocco, Stathi, & Capozza, 2021). Each person associates social groups with each other to different degrees (i.e., within-person variance), and so you should see different degrees to which intergroup interactions with one outgroup would predict changes in prejudice toward another outgroup when you try to amalgamate across people's secondary transfer effects.

Viewing the "intergroup" quality of a social interaction as an intrapersonal perception also helps organize a long-standing debate in intergroup contact about the salience of social identities during intergroup contact.

Some theorists argued that social identities should be minimized during a social interaction to maximize the quality of the social interaction (Brewer & Miller, 1984). By reducing the salience of differing social identities, factors that can lead intergroup interactions awry like intergroup anxiety would not be relevant and the interaction partners could focus on each other as individuals. In contrast, other theorists argue that an intergroup interaction will not impact intergroup relations unless the intergroup nature of the interaction is emphasized (Brown & Hewstone, 2005; Voci & Hewstone, 2003). That is, they argue that intergroup contact only affects intergroup relations to the degree that people realize they are interacting with an outgroup member.

We view identity salience as an intrapersonal process that is relevant to an interpersonal event. This view is consistent with both sides of the identity salience debate. We go one step further to say that identity salience, as a perception that arises from an intrapersonal psychological process, is the only thing that makes a social interaction an intergroup interaction. If a social interaction is not perceived as an intergroup interaction, then it is not an intergroup interaction. Our reading of the identity salience debate is that all parties view the intergroup nature of a social interaction as being positioned at the dyadic level. The interaction is externally classified as being an intergroup interaction and then the people involved in the interaction are more or less aware of the intergroup interaction. As we noted, people belong to multiple social groups and they rarely, if ever, interact with someone who is aligned on all aspects of identity. What matters psychologically about an intergroup interaction (i.e., any downstream attitudes, behaviors, or cognitions) is triggered by the individual perception of the intergroup interaction. A joint perception of the intergroup interaction by both partners is not required. One person could walk away from a social interaction having perceived it as an intergroup interaction and another could walk away having perceived it as an ingroup interaction, and the impact of the same interaction on each of them would be driven by their individual perceptions.

3.1.2 Dyadic and group friendships

We focus here on dyadic relationships as basic units of all cross-group friendships, but more than two people could have a group friendship. Take a hypothetical example of 3 people who took a class together and became friends by regularly getting coffee together after class. The group of people, together, have a group friendship. The group friendship emerges from the experiences the three of them have together while interacting as a group.

If the three people never interacted in subgroups of two, we would consider the friendship to be truly triadic, without dyadic subcomponents. A dyadic friendship could form from the group friendship if two friends had a social interaction without the third friend. Psychologically, those two friends would each have mental representations for their dyadic friendship with each other and their group friendship with the third. The representations for the dyadic and group friendships would be intertwined, yet have distinct properties because they emerged from different social interactions.

3.2 Implications of emergence

Several implications follow from viewing cross-group friendships as emerging from repeated intergroup interactions. Intergroup interaction is positioned as the foundation of cross-group friendship, consistent with our initial arguments (e.g., Fig. 3). If so, then intergroup interactions provide input to cross-group friendships. Therefore, features of social interactions that differ between ingroup and intergroup interactions form the building blocks of the cross-group friendship. The way two people treat each other in these interactions shapes the relationship as a whole.

Our framework is consistent with seminal work on the processes of developing cross-race friendships (Shelton, Trail, West, & Bergsieker, 2010). This work showed that the intimacy of cross-race friendships develops through the same interpersonal processes as same-race friendships, specifically through mutual self-disclosure and responsiveness during intergroup interactions. Important to our argument, Shelton and colleagues emphasized that the intergroup context of interracial interactions and cross-race friendships introduces features like prejudice that present unique barriers to cross-race friendships (e.g., Shelton & Richeson, 2006a, 2006b).

If friendships emerge from the complexity of cognitively organizing experiences across repeated social interactions, cross-group friendships specifically emerge from the interplay of experiences across repeated intergroup interactions. Situational features with particular relevance to intergroup interactions should also be particularly relevant to cross-group friendship more so than to other relationships.

One feature of social interactions that is particularly relevant in intergroup interactions is the prejudice of each interaction partner. Each person in an intergroup interaction can be more or less prejudiced, including non-prejudiced, toward the social identities of the other person. If Person A is prejudiced against Person B, then that same prejudicial attitude would exist when Person A interacts with an ingroup member (Person C), but it would be less cognitively accessible during those ingroup interactions. Person A's prejudices would be more relevant to their behavior when socially interacting with Person B than with Person C because Person B is perceived to have an identity that is the target of Person A's prejudicial attitude. Person B's presence should activate the prejudice in Person A's mind, but Person C's presence would not. If prejudice is uniquely relevant to intergroup interactions, then we expect it to be uniquely relevant to the cross-group friendships that may arise from intergroup interactions. Indeed, we know that one interaction partner's prejudice levels predict their partner's liking in cross-group but not same-group interactions (Shelton, Richeson, Salvatore, & Trawalter, 2005).

At more extreme ends of prejudice, this variable may affect ingroup interactions as well as intergroup interactions. For example, we expect that most people would be affected by a visible tattoo of a hate symbol, even if their group is not the target of the symbol. When witnessing the use of a racial slur about an outgroup, people showed physiological patterns consistent with orienting response to the racist behavior (i.e., they paid attention to the slur) and were even more likely to choose to work with the person who made the racist slur instead of the person who was the target of it (Karmali, Kawakami, & Page-Gould, 2017). If a same-group friendship developed with someone that had this type of tattoo, that friendship would fundamentally be shaped by prejudice because it would have emerged in the context of its expression. Viewing relationships as complex adaptive systems allows for specific features of social interactions to impact the emergent friendship in this way. The example here of expressing hate symbols among ingroup members is meant to demonstrate that anything that affects social interactions that friends have will also play a part in the emergent friendship. Most of the time, however, we expect that factors that are particularly relevant to intergroup interactions are more likely to occur in cross-group friendships than same-group friendships.

3.3 Cross-group friendships show sensitivity to initial conditions

Early intergroup interactions have more impact on a cross-group friendship than later social interactions. A hallmark of complex adaptive systems is a sensitivity to initial conditions. Applied to cross-group friendship, this would mean that the first few intergroup interactions with someone make a greater difference in the development of a cross-group friendship than later intergroup interactions. Other researchers have noted that friendship is sensitive to starting conditions (DeScioli & Kurzban, 2011). For example, the propinquity effect shows that your *opportunity for social interaction* predicts friendship formation, even if that opportunity is incidental (Festinger, Schachter, & Back, 1950). These processes also appear to be present in the case of cross-group friendship.

Shelton, West, and Trail (2010) directly observed the shifting impact of social interactions on feelings about a potential new cross-group friend. Same-race and cross-race roommates completed diary surveys every night just over 2 weeks when they were first getting to know each other. Experiences between same-race and cross-race roommates diverged around the middle of the second week of interacting with each other. Among cross-race roommates, White roommates concerns about prejudice seemed to "leak" to their ethnic minority roommates during the early intergroup interactions. Around the tenth day, ethnic minority students paired with a White roommate began showing divergent patterns of anxious behaviors. When White roommates were very concerned about being viewed as prejudiced, their ethnic minority roommates showed increasing numbers of anxious behaviors, beginning in the second week. To the contrary, ethnic minority students paired with a White roommate without this self-focused concern showed a marked decline in anxious behaviors after the tenth day. Altogether, behavior during initial interactions predicted the relationship trajectory.

The sensitivity of chaotic systems to initial conditions provides an explanation for why cross-group friendships are rarer than they should be statistically (e.g., Blum, 1985). Indeed, strong counter-selection effects occur prior to when a cross-group friendship can start. These counterselection effects can overpower the self-organizing processes of cross-group friendship. For example, we stated earlier that a relationship cannot exist in stranger interactions. Nonetheless, most of what we know about intergroup interactions comes from first-time meetings between strangers (MacInnis & Page-Gould, 2015). We know that people expect these interactions to be bad (Mallett, Huntsinger, et al., 2008), are more likely to experience anxiety in them (Stephan & Stephan, 1985; West, Shelton, & Trail, 2009), and expend more mental effort (Richeson & Shelton, 2007; Richeson & Trawalter, 2005). All these things lead to avoidance of future interactions (Butz & Plant, 2011; Shelton, Richeson, & Vorauer, 2006; Trawalter et al., 2009). Thus, while there may be processes that propel people toward cross-group friendship, other processes push people in the other direction. If a relationship requires repeated intergroup interactions to form, as we have argued here, then experiences in intergroup interactions between strangers may be breaking the development of these relationships before they form (Vorauer & Sakamoto, 2006).

3.4 Cross-group friendships are self-organizing

Self-organizing systems regulate themselves toward their emergent states (i.e., from repeated intergroup interactions to cross-group friendship) through processes that feedback into themselves ("feedback loops"). Specifically, we believe that humans have innate processes that drive us toward affiliation, particularly with those who are different from us in interesting ways or in ways that otherwise require our attention. Reflections of these processes can be seen in basic processes like the orienting response that draws attention based on stimulus novelty (Sokolov, 1963). Specific to relationships, self-expansion theory states that humans have a basic motivation to expand the self-concept through close relationships with people who seem able to maximize our self-growth, like people with different social identities (Aron, Steele, Kashdan, & Perez, 2006; Wright, Aron, & Tropp, 2002).

If cross-group friendship represents an adaptive process, then we should see feedback loops that promote the emergence of these friendships. Indeed, our work has identified these feedback loops at two time points in the development of cross-group friendships (Fig. 10). In the earliest intergroup interactions in which a friendship is forming, physiological processes that are general to social interactions promote affiliation (Danyluck & Page-Gould, 2019). These affiliative processes may be amplified by optimal distinctiveness (Danyluck & Page-Gould, 2018). Similarly, the biggest behavioral changes may occur for people who are initially the most

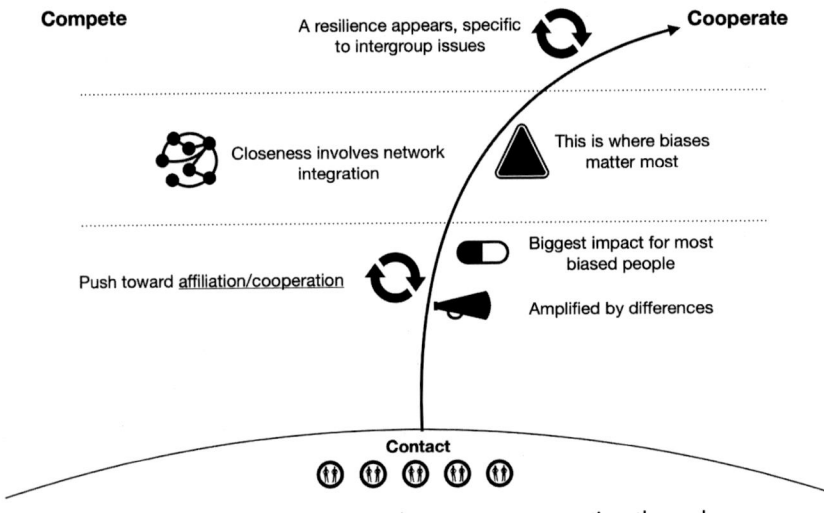

Fig. 10 Path from intergroup contact to intergroup cooperation through cross-group friendship.

prejudiced (Page-Gould, Mendoza-Denton, & Tropp, 2008; Hodson, Harry, & Mitchell, 2009). After a cross-group friendship has solidly emerged, these relationships and their intergroup benefits may be maintained through processes that promote resilience to negative intergroup interactions (Page-Gould, 2012; Page-Gould, Mendes, & Major, 2010). In between these two stages, however, there may be a particularly vulnerable point for cross-group friendships, where self-organizing processes may have the hardest time overcoming counterselection effects.

Fig. 10 depicts the path from intergroup contact (base) to intergroup cooperation (upper right corner) through friendship (arrow). Our research on cross-group friendship suggests three phases in cross-group friendship formation: (1) An initial phase involves processes that promote the development of cross-group friendship; (2) An intermediate phase where cross-group friendships may face particular barriers; (3) An established phase involves the long-term maintenance of the cross-group friendship. We now detail our work relevant to each phase.

3.4.1 Initial interactions: Physiological processes related to affiliation

We endorse the view that social interactions are a primary medium through which people experience the social world (e.g., Cantor & Kihlstrom, 1987). As demonstrated by the ABM exploring the asymptotic model, situational norms for behavior in social interactions, in general, can have specific impact on the intergroup benefit of intergroup interactions. Thus, global social interaction processes help us understand intergroup interactions. Social interactions among strangers help us understand the early formation of cross-group friendship, with an interest on what elicits a subsequent interaction.

3.4.1.1 Stress and social interactions

As we argue here, a cross-group friendship only has the potential to form when an intergroup interaction goes from an initial interaction between strangers to a repeated interaction with a newly-familiar outgroup member. One of the biggest barriers to the positive development of friendship across repeated intergroup interactions appears to be intergroup anxiety (e.g., Shelton, West, & Trail, 2010). More generally, intergroup anxiety is one of the most reliable differences found between ingroup and intergroup interactions.

We were interested in how the development of friendship during intergroup interactions affected physiological stress responses during intergroup interactions. Latinx and White participants were randomly assigned to same-ethnicity or cross-ethnicity pairs and completed a series of friendship-building tasks together over the course of 3 weeks (Page-Gould et al., 2008). As shown in Fig. 11, prejudiced participants exhibited adverse stress reactivity during the first cross-ethnic interaction, but this stress response was absent in subsequent intergroup interactions with the same interaction partner. As shown in Fig. 12, in the 10 days following the final friendship-building task, prejudiced participants (black bars) who made a new cross-ethnic friend in the lab (left bars) initiated more intergroup interactions in daily life than their counterparts who made a same-ethnic friend in the lab (right bars). Given the experimental assignment to make a same-ethnicity or cross-ethnicity friend, this study gave us the ability to say that friendly intergroup interactions

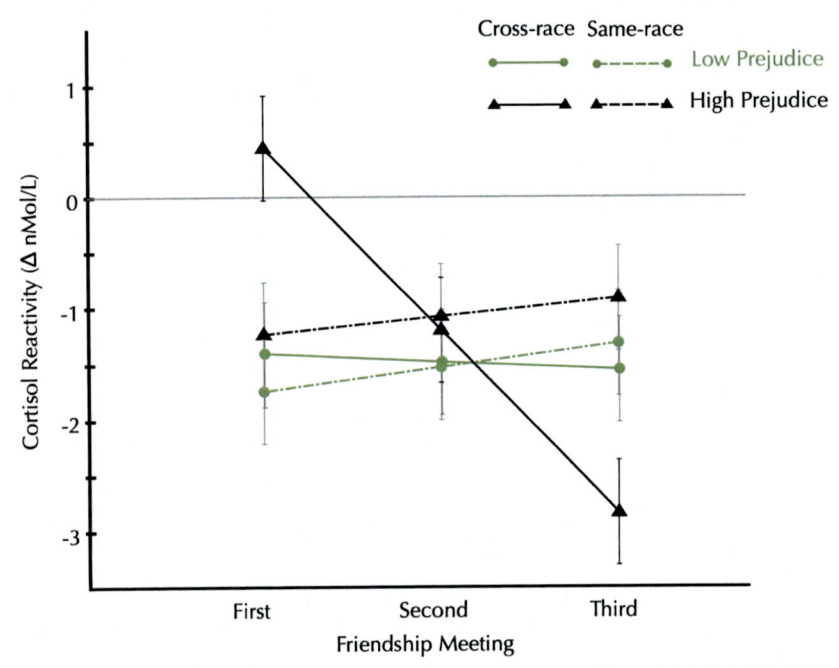

Fig. 11 Stress reactivity while making new same-ethnicity and cross-ethnicity friends in the lab. Note: This figure originally appeared in Page-Gould et al. (2008). Changes in the stress hormone, cortisol, during a social interaction from before the interaction are plotted on the vertical axis. The zero value represents no change. The horizontal axis depicts the progression of time across three friendship meetings. Dashed lines plot cortisol reactivity among participants paired with a same-race partner and the solid lines represent cortisol reactivity among participants paired with cross-race partners. The green lines depict participants who were low in prejudice (1 *SD* below the average prejudice of their ethnic ingroup) and the black lines depict participants who were high in prejudice (1 *SD* above the average prejudice of their ethnic ingroup).

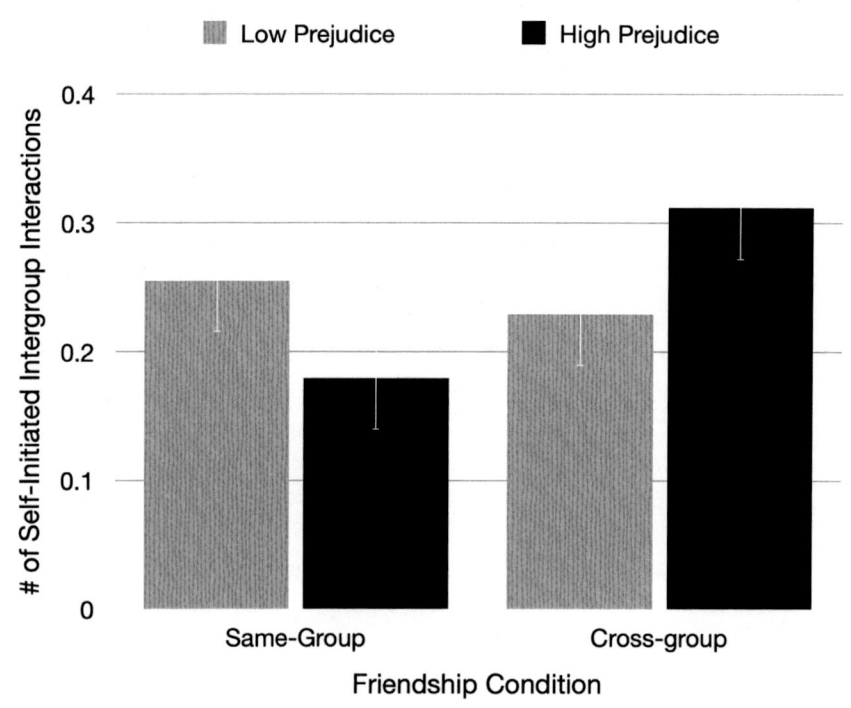

Fig. 12 Initiation of intergroup interactions after making a new cross-ethnic friend. Note: This figure originally appeared in Page-Gould et al. (2008). The number of intergroup interactions that participants reported initiating in the intermediate time period (10 days) after making a new friend in the lab are modeled as a function of initial prejudice (low prejudice, gray bars = − 1 SD from the mean; high prejudice, black pars = + 1 SD from the mean) and whether the new friendship was a same-ethnicity (left bars) or cross-ethnicity (right bars) friendship.

reduce stress during intergroup interactions. Moreover, it seemed that cross–group friendship had the biggest impact on the most prejudiced people.

3.4.1.2 Physiological synchrony

Given our declaration that repeated interactions are the field for close relationships, we are particularly interested in processes of affiliation during initial interactions with strangers that may lead to a second interaction. We became fascinated by a physiological phenomenon in social interactions known as physiological synchrony. Physiological synchrony refers to the synchronization in time of the physiological systems of two or more distinct organisms. Among humans, physiological synchrony can be observed across many different physiological systems, including both the sympathetic and parasympathetic branches of the autonomic nervous system (Danyluck & Page-Gould, 2019; Levenson & Ruef, 1992) and the central nervous system (Wheatley, Kang, Parkinson, & Looser, 2012).

Physiological synchrony is not necessarily prosocial, but we believe it reflects the relevance of another person in the moment. Some of the earliest research on physiological synchrony observed that it was stronger among friends than neutral acquaintances but strongest during social interactions with people who were explicitly disliked (Kaplan, Burch, & Bloom, 1964). We argued previously that physiological research on intergroup processes generally reveals a pattern of *inattention* to outgroup members, but not any biologically based inability to treat each other humanely (Page-Gould & Danyluck, 2016). From the perspective of psychophysiology, prejudice is a question of how much a person pays attention or looks away. Our view supports and is supported by work on intersectional invisibility (Mohr & Purdie-Vaughns, 2015), the goal relevance of other people (Neel & Lassetter, 2019), and coalitional cognition (Cikara, 2021). Viewing physiological synchrony as a correlate of attentional processes during social interactions, we see physiological synchrony as one of many feedback loops that promote initial affiliation.

In our lab experiments, we deconstructed aspects of social interactions to observe when physiological synchrony occurs. In one situation (Danyluck & Page-Gould, 2019), we matched people into same-gender pairs and varied two dimensions of the social situation: Participants were randomly assigned to talk to each other or not talk other during a 5-min period where they were both engaged in a knot-tying task. The reward structure of the knot-tying task was also manipulated to be cooperative (i.e., rewards given for collective performance) or competitive (i.e., rewards given for relative individual performance). This design allowed us to disentangle the roles of direct interaction versus shared presence and the coalitional context of the interaction on physiological synchrony.

We observed physiological synchrony in the sympathetic (Fig. 13, Panel 1) and parasympathetic (Fig. 13, Panel 2) nervous systems in all conditions. The middle row of Fig. 13 shows what physiological synchrony in each branch looks like. While the physiological responses of participant pairs were generally synchronized across conditions, the different contexts elicited different degrees of physiological reactivity across the sympathetic and parasympathetic nervous systems. The greatest sympathetic increases occurred in the cooperative talking condition (Fig. 13, Panel 1C) and the greatest parasympathetic reactivity occurred in the competitive talking condition (Fig. 13, Panel 2C). It should be noted that the average parasympathetic

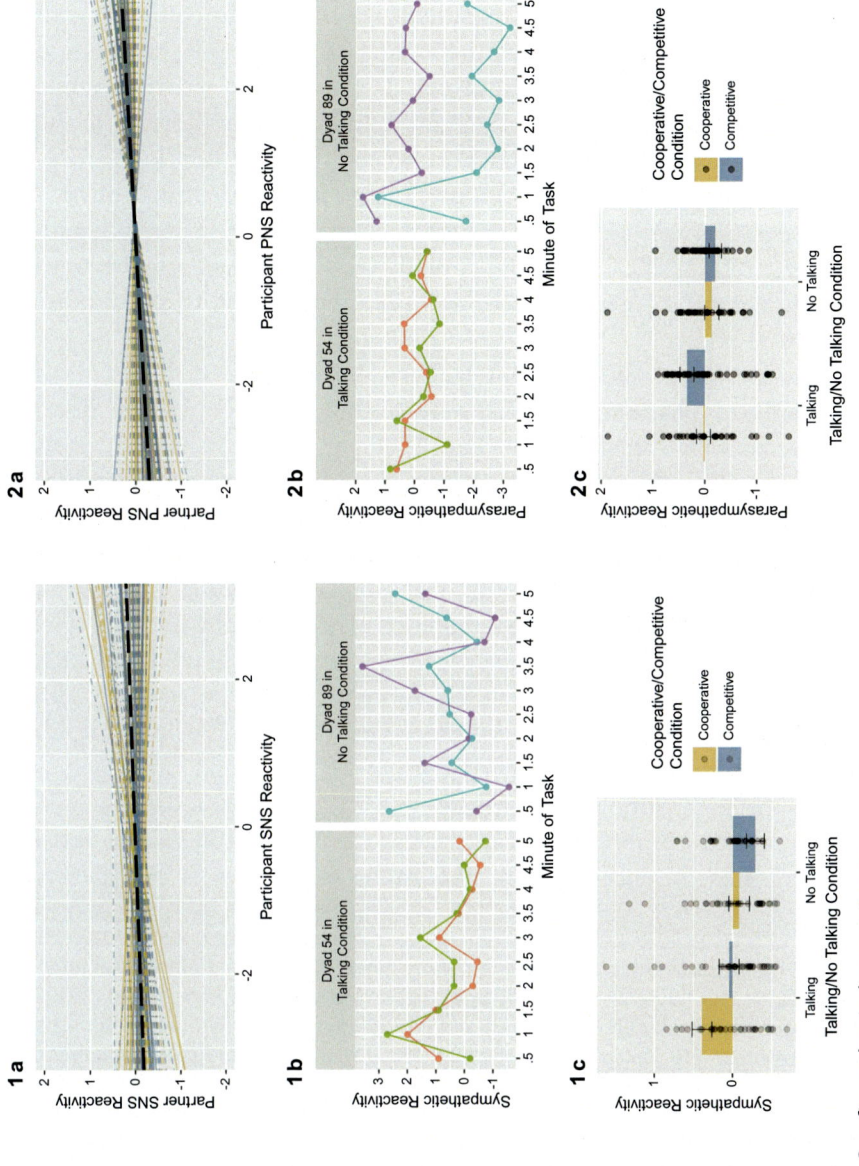

Fig. 13 See figure legend on next page.

response in the cooperative talking condition was an increase in parasympathetic activity from baseline, as parasympathetic increases are associated with processing complex stimuli in the environment and parasympathetic decreases are associated with focused attention (Porges & Raskin, 1969). Patterns of sympathetic and parasympathetic reactivity in the condition with no talking were more consistent with focusing on the task (i.e., decreases in parasympathetic activity, no great change in sympathetic activity). While physiological synchrony was present and unmodulated by features of the social situation, there were differences between participant pairs in the magnitude and direction of their synchrony. That is, some participant's physiological responses were synchronized with their interaction partners, but with an inverse relationship. The more strongly and concordantly interactions were physiologically synchronized, the more they tended to show other affiliative responses.

Now specific to intergroup interactions, we investigated the processes that amplified physiological synchrony during intergroup interactions. We systematically varied whether East Asian and South Asian participants spent time writing about conflict or harmony between the two social groups and the groups' similarities or dissimilarities. Supporting both self-expansion theory (Aron et al., 1991) and optimal distinctiveness theory (Leonardelli, Pickett, & Brewer, 2010), we found that emphasizing group dissimilarity prior to the intergroup interaction amplified concordant physiological synchrony. Again and specifically in intergroup interactions, we found that physiological synchrony was generally related to desire to interact with the partner in the future (Danyluck & Page-Gould, 2018). We infer that this physiological synchrony is amplified by group differences and thus may specially promote the formation of friendship across group boundaries.

We must take a moment to acknowledge the many barriers to the initial attraction phase. Concerns about confirming stereotypes of one's social

---

Fig. 13 Physiological synchrony in the autonomic nervous system during social interactions. Note: This figure was originally published in Danyluck and Page-Gould (2019). Physiological synchrony (Rows A and B) and physiological reactivity (Row C) during a social interaction are plotted for the sympathetic (Panel 1, left) and parasympathetic (Panel 2, right) branches of the Autonomic Nervous System. Physiological synchrony was present across all conditions. Row (A) plots slopes for each participant pair that capture how strongly the partners' physiological responses covaried with one another. Row (B) plots physiological reactivity as the task for two example dyads in each type of social interaction condition (talking on the left and no talking on the right). Row (C) shows physiological reactivity across all conditions.

identity create barriers to cross-ethnic friendship formation for both ethnic minority and White participants (Shelton et al., 2006). People overestimate the amount of friendship interest they express to outgroup members, and this misperception leads to a misunderstanding that inhibits interest in cross-group friendship (Vorauer & Sakamoto, 2006). Even before an intergroup interaction, people expect to experience more negative emotions like anxiety during intergroup interactions than they actually experience (Mallett, Wilson, & Gilbert, 2008). In some cases, like cross-gender friendship, there are strong cultural beliefs about whether it is even possible for people with different gender identities to be friends and not also romantic partners (e.g., George, Adalikwu-Obisike, Boyko, Johnson, & Boscanin, 2014), that could pose major social barriers to cross-group friendship formation. Ultimately, people have more ingroup friends than cross-group friends (Page-Gould, 2012; Tuch, Sigelman, & MacDonald, 1999), so we want to emphasize that any processes that encourage intergroup affiliation are fighting against strong counterselection effects in the environment.

3.4.2 Intermediate interactions: Threats to stability

The greatest threats to the stability of cross-group friendships seem to come during an intermediate stage. Cross-group friendships are more likely to dissolve during the first few months than same-group friendships, and this appears to be related to cross-group friends being more likely to be social isolates in a friendship network (Aboud & Sankar, 2007). That is, a person's cross-group friends are less likely to be known by same-group friends (Stark, 2020). Friendships between friends of friends is called "triadic closure." Triadic closure is considered important to the balance and maintenance of a friendship, but large-scale sociometric studies show that triadic closure is less common for cross-race friends (Moody, 2001). We sought to understand this process.

Given what was known about cross-group friendship stability and the reduced triadic closure for cross-group friendships, we hypothesized that cross-group friends would be less likely than same-group friends to be present during group interactions with friends (Harris & Page-Gould, 2021). We had abductively hypothesized from the reduced integration of cross-group friends in social networks that people were interacting with cross-group friends during one-on-one interactions.

We examined this question by asking people to report every activity they had over the previous week with friends (Harris & Page-Gould, 2021). When focusing on the level of the activity, we found that the number of friends in an activity *increased* the likelihood that a cross-ethnic friend was present. Same-ethnicity friends were more likely to be involved in one-on-one interactions than cross-ethnic friends, and this suggests cross-group friends may be missing out on opportunities for intimacy like self-disclosure.

Since cross-group friends were more likely to be present in group friend interactions, we became curious about these group interactions. We explored the diversity of the interactions. That is, are cross-group friends typically the only solo cross-group friend in a group interaction or are group interactions involving cross-group friends typically more diverse? We explored the diversity of these group interactions by determining the proportion of other same- and cross-group friends that were present during group interactions. We found that cross-group friends were much less likely to be involved in primarily same-group social interactions and that cross-group friends were much more likely to be present in social interactions that involved other cross-group friends.

We view this process as both a positive, relationship-maintaining process and a barrier to the establishment of long-standing cross-group friendship. On the one hand, it is likely that cross-group friends feel more comfortable when they are not the only cross-group friend among the friends present, for example, because being the only person with a particular identity in a social interaction can heightened identity threat in those social interactions (Inzlicht & Ben-Zeev, 2000). However, this would inhibit people's knowledge of their same-group friends' cross-group friends, which would reduce the positive impact of things like extended contact through knowledge of friends' contact (Stark, 2020; Zhou et al., 2019). Triadic closure is also thought to buffer against friendship dissolution because the loss of one tie affects other ties (Aboud & Sankar, 2007). Thus, understanding the process of network integration of cross-group friends is fundamental to understanding why these friendships are less likely to persist in this intermediate stage.

To better understand the experience of introducing new cross-ethnic friends to pre-existing same-group friendships, we induced same- and cross-ethnic friendships between East Asian and South Asian students over two lab sessions and then randomly assigned them to bring an existing same-ethnicity friend to the lab for a third lab session (i.e., an introduction to their new lab friend; MacInnis & Page-Gould, 2020). Students who made a cross-ethnic friend in the lab exhibited greater sympathetic stress responses when introducing this new cross-ethnic friend to an existing same-ethnicity friend than did students who were introducing a new same-ethnicity friend to an existing friend. Students interacting with a cross-ethnic friend for a third time without bringing a preexisting friend showed similar levels of stress to the participants introducing same-ethnicity friends. Desire for ongoing contact with the lab friend was lowest among participants who introduced a new cross-ethnic friend to an existing same-ethnicity friend. Interestingly, desire was highest among participants who interacted with a cross-group partner without another friend present. The experimental nature of the design suggests that both the ethnicity of the new lab friend and the introduction to an existing friend impacted stress responses and desire for future interactions.

Altogether, we believe that people find it stressful to introduce new cross-ethnic friends to same-ethnicity friends. Perhaps the way that cross-group friendships continue to grow and form is by integration with other cross-group friends and eventually introducing *same-group* friends to cross-group friends through group friend activities where multiple cross-group friends are present.

3.4.3 Established friendship interactions: Maintenance processes

Once a person establishes a few close friendships with outgroup members, we see processes that seem to promote the maintenance of cross-group friendships. We view this as a particular resilience to negative intergroup experiences. What would resilience look like? We would not expect to see a regression toward more prejudiced attitudes or behavior after intergroup conflict if a person were resilient to negative intergroup experiences. A resilient stress profile would show acute responses to negative intergroup experience that involve the fast, strong mobilization of the stress systems paired with rapid recovery after the stressor was removed (Page-Gould & Akinola, 2015). In the asymptotic model, however, even negative intergroup interactions should not matter much after enough intergroup interactions have occurred.

We followed people's social interactions for 10 days in an ethnically diverse setting, with an interest in initiation of intergroup interactions after intergroup conflicts. As shown in Fig. 14, people who did not have many cross-ethnic friends were likely to initiate no interethnic interactions on the day after an intergroup conflict. People with many close cross-ethnic friends did not show this avoidance-like behavior after interethnic conflict, being just as likely to initiate interethnic interactions after conflict as after no conflict (Page-Gould, 2012). We found that people with close cross-ethnic friends were more likely to seek social support from outgroup members after a cross-ethnic conflict, which accounted for the reduction in post-conflict avoidance.

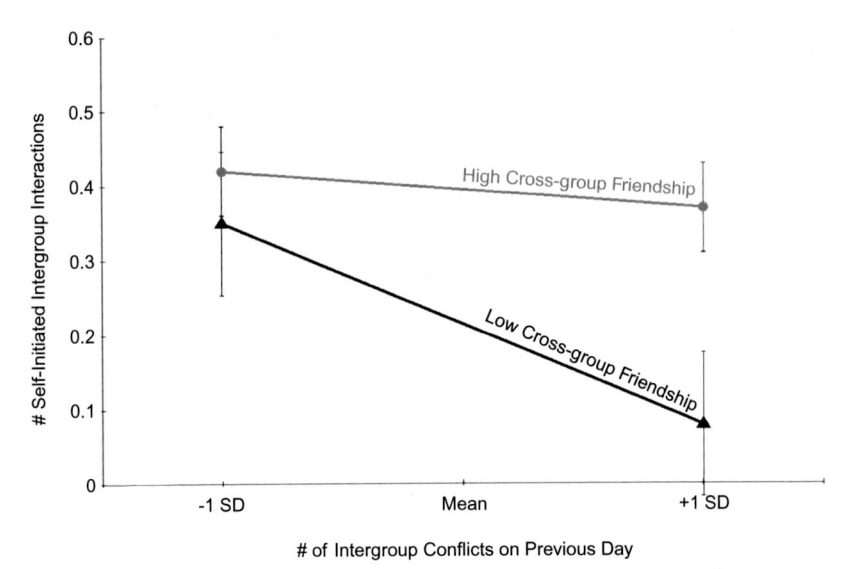

Fig. 14 Initiation of intergroup interaction as a function of cross-group friendship and intergroup conflict. Note. This figure was originally published in Page-Gould (2012). The number of intergroup interactions expected on average each day are plotted on the vertical axis. The number of intergroup conflicts on the previous day are reported as a continuous variable ranging from low (−1 SD from mean) to high (+1 SD to mean), as it was possible for participants to have more than 1 intergroup conflict in a day. The flat green line shows that people with close cross-group friends initiate approximately the same amount of intergroup interactions, irrespective of their recent intergroup conflicts. The black line that slopes down shows how people with few cross-group friends avoid intergroup interactions the day following intergroup conflict.

The study we just described tracked real intergroup interactions as they occurred in daily life. We also studied the impact of negative intergroup interactions on post-interaction physiological recovery (Page-Gould, Mendes, & Major, 2010). We induced stress during same-race and cross-race interactions among Black and White adults, using a social stressor called the Trier Social Stress Test (Kirschbaum, Pirke, & Hellhammer, 1993). The success of the social stressor was confirmed by the fact that all participants exhibited increases in physiological stress responses across both the sympathetic and hypothalamic adrenal medullary stress axes during the stressful social interactions. However, participants whose stressful interaction was in a same-race context recovered physiologically (i.e., returned to baseline) from the stress responses within 5 min of the end of the social interaction (Fig. 15). Participants who experienced a stressful cross-race interaction were less likely to recover immediately after the stressful interaction. Only participants with

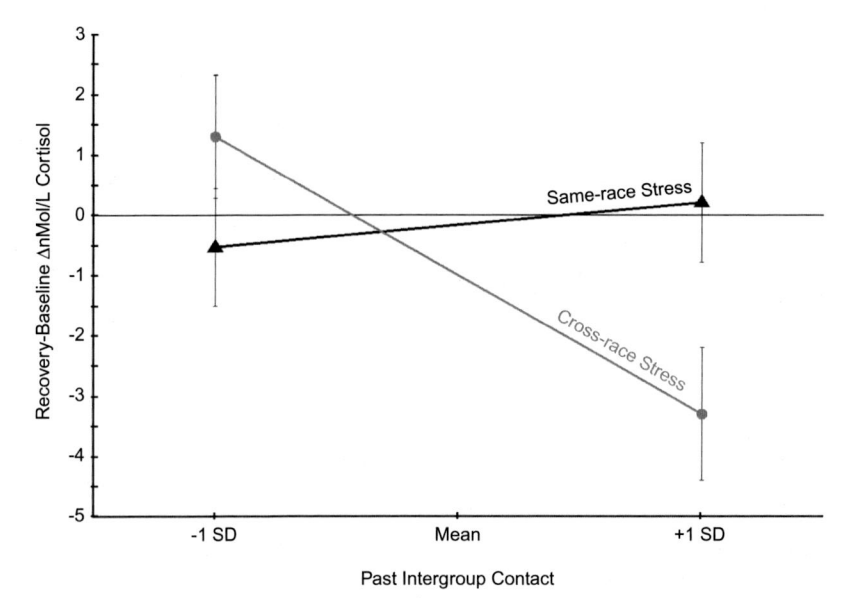

Fig. 15 Physiological recovery (return to baseline) following stressful social interactions. Note: This figure was originally published in Page-Gould, Mendes, and Major (2010). Differences between post-stressor and pre-stressor (baseline) values of the stress hormone, cortisol, following a stressful intergroup interaction are plotted on the vertical axis. The zero value represents return to baseline, which is considered physiological recovery for cortisol. Values below zero also represent post-stressor recovery of cortisol. Values above zero represent persistent stress responses (i.e., no recovery). Past intergroup contact is plotted along the horizontal axis. All participants recovered promptly after a stressful same-race interaction (black line), but only participants with relatively high past intergroup contact recovered promptly from the stressful cross-race interaction (green line).

high-quality intergroup contact recovered from a stressful intergroup interaction similarly to a stressful ingroup interaction.

These findings suggest that people with high-quality intergroup experiences like cross-group friendships develop a resilience to negative intergroup experiences. This process certainly helps to maintain friendships, when cross-group friendships likely involve various misunderstandings that are unique to the intergroup context, such as differences in perceptions of racialized social issues like cultural appropriation (Mosley & Biernat, 2021). We know that these issues are not always successfully navigated (e.g., Holoien, Bergsieker, Shelton, & Alegre, 2015). However, cross-group friendship seems to accompany a decreased association of outgroup members with rejection and intergroup anxiety (Barlow, Louis, & Hewstone, 2009; Page-Gould & Mendoza-Denton, 2011), and releasing these concerns was related to being more interested in engaging in discussions of racial issues in addition to prejudice (Barlow et al., 2009). Altogether, cross-group friendship appears to provide people with the psychological resilience and genuine concern needed for intergroup reconciliation.

We do not wish to make light of the unequal nature of barriers to cross-group friendship. These relationships may not be equally safe for all members of the friendship. In the context of cross-race friendships, majority-group members (White Americans) exhibited less understanding of cross-race friends than minority-group members, even among established cross-race friendships (Holoien et al., 2015). This process converges with other work showing that some members of racial minority groups may not feel as comfortable disclosing personal information to White friends (Shelton & Richeson, 2006a, 2006b).

Returning to Fig. 3, we view the components of cross-group friendship and intergroup contact as being the same: Intergroup interactions are the units of intergroup contact and cross-group friendship. When repeated intergroup interactions occur, there is the potential for a cross-group relationship to emerge. If the emergent relationship involves platonic feelings of closeness and affiliation, it would be a cross-group friendship. As we argued for relationships generally, this emergent cross-group friendship is a real thing. It has properties that are not ascribable to either person who is a part of the relationship nor to any particular social interaction. If cross-group friendships are emergent entities of repeated intergroup interactions, then the emergence implies that cross-group friendships are adaptive.

4. Why study cross-group friendship from the perspective of intergroup relations?

Think of living humans, at the broadest scope, as comprising the human community that matters right now. Is our community moving toward intergroup cooperation? The arguments laid out here present cross-group friendships as emergent processes that serve the necessary function of facilitating intergroup cooperation within our species. Cross-group friendships appear to be self-promoting through feedback loops in the initial and established phases of friendship development. Affiliative processes are amplified in intergroup interactions during the early stages and resilience to negative intergroup interactions appears in the later stages. The feedback loops support and promote these relationships. If cross-group friendships are complex adaptive systems, then their existence suggests that intergroup cooperation is one optimal state of intergroup relations.

So, what are we, as the field of intergroup relations, trying to achieve? Intergroup researchers frequently contrast intergroup cooperation with intergroup competition, implying that the human community's stable state is one of these two options. We add that intergroup predation has been institutionalized throughout human history (e.g., feudalism, colonialism, slavery, genocide), despite being considered fringe and extreme at the individual level of scale.

Pioneers of intergroup relations disagreed on the psychological sources of racism. W. E. B. Du Bois argued that the history of interracial predation created a psychological need for racial prejudice in dominant group members to justify their collective injustices (Gaines Jr. & Reed, 1995), coining the term "whiteness" to describe the psychological and behavioral outcomes of benefiting from systemic racism (Du Bois, 2014). W. E. B. Du Bois's ideas went underground while Gordon Allport's idea that racism is a universal construct propagated (Gaines Jr. & Reed, 1994). Many institutions in North America exhibit evidence of systemic anti-Black racism, such as the health (Onyeador et al., 2020), education (Warikoo, Sinclair, Fei, & Jacoby-Senghor, 2016), legal (Hunt & Maeder, 2017), and economic (Kraus, Onyeador, Daumeyer, Rucker, & Richeson, 2019) systems. If Du Bois's ideas are correct, then intergroup contact, as an intervention, singularly addresses the systemic racism of segregation policies—only one of many systems in which racism is embedded. Intergroup contact is necessary, because segregation is untenable. But, intergroup contact addresses only one part of a multifaceted problem, so contact was never able to be a complete solution. Psychologically, the processes of intergroup contact seem orthogonal to the roots of racism theorized by Du Bois.

Therefore, should we view intergroup contact as a prejudice reduction tool or a fundamental component of the social field? Paluck and colleagues (2021) emphasized that most prejudice interventions, including intergroup contact, move an individual person's prejudice levels only a small amount. They give the example of a typical change of 8 points on a 100-point scale of prejudice (Fig. 16). Paluck and colleagues suggest we should move beyond the focus on prejudice as an outcome. Many intergroup contact researchers already responded by identifying pathways through which intergroup contact can inform public policy (Paolini et al., 2021). A central message of this chapter is that we need to treat intergroup contact as a given. Assuming most adults have had enough intergroup interactions to have leveled off in the asymptotic model, then even a sudden increase of intergroup interactions with strangers should not have a major impact on prejudice, at least not in the absence of external shocks to the system.

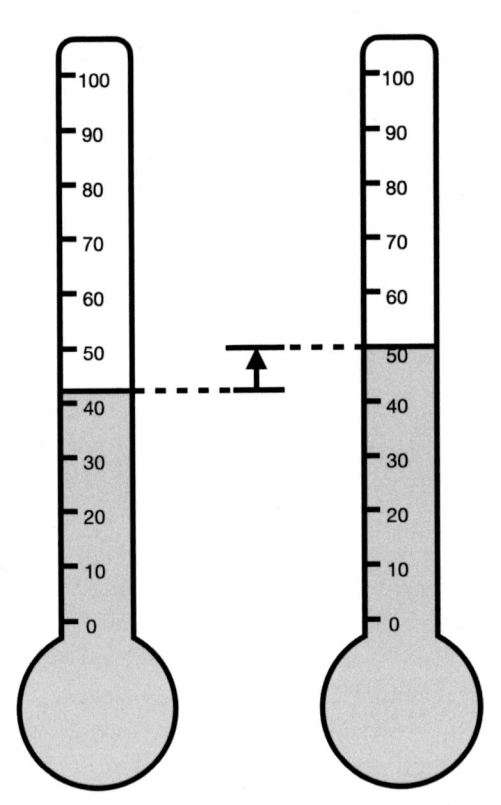

Fig. 16 Average change in prejudice from social psychological interventions. Note: Imagine these thermometers represent feelings of warmth toward a particular social group, which is a common measure of prejudice (less warmth represents more prejudice). The feeling thermometer on the left represents warmth toward the social group before intervention, and the feeling thermometer on the left represents warmth toward the social group after the intervention. The vertical arrow between them depicts the magnitude of the change that is typically seen from prejudice reduction interventions. *This figure is adapted from the meta-analysis and example provided in Paluck, E. L., Porat, R., Clark, C. S., & Green, D. P. (2020). Prejudice reduction: Progress and challenges.* Annual Review of Psychology, 72, 533–560.

In contexts where segregation is still formally or informally enforced, contact interventions are relevant and likely fundamental.

In contrast, we believe cross-group friendship is something special. To the extent that cross-group friendships *do* reduce prejudice, this likely occurs through the self-organizing and adaptive processes of the friendship system. Friendships can become strong alliances and intimate relationships (DeScioli & Kurzban, 2009), and they are self-defining (Aron et al., 1991; Page-Gould, Mendoza-Denton, et al., 2010). Scaling up, when cross-group friendships comprise diverse relationship and support networks, they may disrupt processes of systemic racism that transfer through all-White friendship networks (Feagin, 2020). Cross-group relationships make us care about each other and treat each other well (e.g., Gaither & Sommers, 2013; Page-Gould & Danyluck, 2016; Page-Gould, Mendoza-Denton, et al., 2010). Cross-group friendships foster beliefs about fairness and equity (Graham, Munniksma, & Juvonen, 2014; Roberts, Williams, & Gelman, 2017). It drives people with power to engage in collective action to share that power (Tropp & Barlow, 2018; Tropp & Uluğ, 2019). The power of cross-group friendship is that people care about their friends. However, these positive outcomes should only occur to the degree that inequalities and power differences in the relationship are recognized and condemned, and not all cross-group friendships go well.

As a complex adaptive system, cross-group friendship *is* intergroup cooperation at the individual level of scale. Cross-group friendships do not so much impact intergroup relations as they are a part of intergroup relations. Each emergent cross-group friendship is unique and dynamically changes with each new social interaction the friends have. More broadly and taken together, all types of cross-group relationships—from friendships to coworkers to enemyships—reflect the current intergroup zeitgeist. Scaling down, intergroup interactions comprise and dynamically shape intergroup processes at the intraindividual level of everyday experience. The intergroup relations approach to studying cross-group friendship, then, should be on figuring what makes cross-group friendships strong coalitions. Understanding how cross-group friendships promote thriving at the individual level may provide us with a pattern for reconciliation and cooperation at the societal level.

References

Aboud, F. E., & Sankar, J. (2007). Friendship and identity in a language-integrated school. *International Journal of Behavioral Development, 31*, 445–453.

Allport, G. W. (1954). *The nature of prejudice*. Addison-Wesley.

American Psychological Association. (n.d.). Just-world hypothesis. In APA dictionary of psychology. Retrieved January 19, 2021, from https://dictionary.apa.org/social-interactions.

Andrews-Hanna, J. R., Saxe, R., & Yarkoni, T. (2014). Contributions of episodic retrieval and mentalizing to autobiographical thought: Evidence from functional neuroimaging, resting-state connectivity, and fMRI meta-analyses. *NeuroImage, 91*, 324–335.

Aron, A., Aron, E. N., Tudor, M., & Nelson, G. (1991). Close relationships as including other in the self. *Journal of Personality and Social Psychology, 60*, 241–253.

Aron, A., Steele, J. L., Kashdan, T. B., & Perez, M. (2006). When similars do not attract: Tests of a prediction from the self-expansion model. *Personal Relationships, 13*, 387–396.

Barlow, F. K., Louis, W. R., & Hewstone, M. (2009). Rejected! Cognitions of rejection and intergroup anxiety as mediators of the impact of cross-group friendships on prejudice. *British Journal of Social Psychology*, *48*, 389–405.

Barnett, A. J., Reilly, W., Dimsdale-Zucker, H., Mizrak, E., Reagh, Z., & Ranganath, C. (2020). Organization of cortico-hippocampal networks in the human brain. *BioRxiv, 2020*(06), 09.142166.

Benjamin, L. T., & Crouse, E. M. (2004). The American Psychological Association's response to Brown v. Board of Education: The case of Kenneth B. Clark. In G. Philogène (Ed.), *Decade of behavior. Racial identity in context: The legacy of Kenneth B* (pp. 231–253). Clark: American Psychological Association.

Blum, T. C. (1985). Structural constraints on interpersonal relations: A test of Blau's macrosociological theory. *American Journal of Sociology*, *91*, 511–521.

Boin, J., Rupar, M., Graf, S., Neji, S., Spiegler, O., & Swart, H. (2021). The generalization of intergroup contact effects: Emerging research, policy relevance, and future directions. *Journal of Social Issues*, *77*, 105–131.

Brewer, M. B., & Miller, N. (1984). Beyond the contact hypothesis: Theoretical perspectives on desegregation. In N. Miller, & M. B. Brewer (Eds.), *Groups in contact: The psychology of desegregation* (pp. 281–302). Orlando, FL: Academic Press.

Brown, R., & Hewstone, M. (2005). An integrative theory of intergroup contact. *Advances in Experimental Social Psychology*, *37*, 255–343.

Butz, D. A., & Plant, E. A. (2011). Approaching versus avoiding intergroup contact: The role of expectancies and motivation. In L. R. Tropp, & R. K. Mallett (Eds.), *Moving beyond prejudice reduction: Pathways to positive intergroup relations* (pp. 81–98). American Psychological Association.

Cantor, N., & Kihlstrom, J. F. (1987). *Personality and social intelligence*. Englewood Cliffs, NJ: Prentice-Hall.

Chaitin, G. J. (1992). Information-theoretic incompleteness. *Applied Mathematics and Computation*, *52*, 83–101.

Christ, O., & Wagner, U. (2013). Methodological issues in the study of intergroup contact: Towards a new wave of research. In G. Hodson, & M. Hewstone (Eds.), *Advances in intergroup contact* (pp. 233–261). Psychology Press.

Clark, M. S., & Lemay, E. P., Jr. (2010). Close relationships. In S. T. Fiske, D. T. Gilbert, & G. Lindzey (Eds.), Handbook of social psychology (p. 898–940). John Wiley & Sons, Inc.

Cikara, M. (2021). Causes and consequences of coalitional cognition. *Advances in Experimental Social Psychology*, *64*, 65–128.

Clark, K. B., Chein, I., & Cook, S. W. (2004). The effects of segregation and the consequences of desegregation A (September 1952) social science statement in the Brown v. Board of Education of Topeka Supreme Court Case. *American Psychologist*, *59*, 495–501.

Crevecoeur, I., Dias-Meirinho, M. H., Zazzo, A., Antoine, D., & Bon, F. (2021). New insights on interpersonal violence in the late Pleistocene based on the Nile valley cemetery of Jebel Sahaba. *Scientific Reports*, *11*, 1–13.

Danyluck, C., & Page-Gould, E. (2018). Intergroup dissimilarity predicts sympathetic covariation and friendship interest within cross-group dyads. *Journal of Experimental Social Psychology*, *74*, 111–120.

Danyluck, C., & Page-Gould, E. (2019). Social and physiological context affects the meaning of physiological synchrony. *Scientific Reports*, *9*, 8222.

Davies, K., Tropp, L. R., Aron, A., Pettigrew, T. F., & Wright, S. C. (2011). Cross-group friendships and intergroup attitudes: A meta-analytic review. *Personality and Social Psychology Review*, *15*, 332–351.

Demir, M., & Özdemir, M. (2010). Friendship, need satisfaction and happiness. *Journal of Happiness Studies*, *11*, 243–259.

DeScioli, P., & Kurzban, R. (2009). The Alliance hypothesis for human friendship. *PLoS One*, *4*, e5802.

DeScioli, P., & Kurzban, R. (2011). The company you keep: Friendship decisions from a functional perspective. In J. I. Krueger (Ed.), *Social judgment and decision making* (pp. 209–225). New York: Psychology Press.

Du Bois, W. E. B. (2014). In H. L. Gates Jr., (Ed.), *Black reconstruction in America (The Oxford WEB Du Bois): An essay toward a history of the part which black folk played in the attempt to reconstruct democracy in America*. Oxford University Press.

Feagin, J. R. (2020). *The White racial frame: Centuries of racial framing and counter-framing* (3rd). Routledge.

Festinger, L., Schachter, S., & Back, K. (1950). *Social pressures in informal groups: A study of human factors in housing*. Harper.

Fletcher, A. C., Rollins, A., & Nickerson, P. (2004). The extension of school-based inter- and intraracial children's friendships: Influences on psychosocial well-being. *American Journal of Orthopsychiatry*, *74*, 272–285.

Gaines, S. O., Jr., & Reed, E. S. (1994). Two social psychologies of prejudice: Gordon W. Allport, W.E.B. Du bois, and the legacy of Booker T. Washington. *Journal of Black Psychology*, *20*, 8–28.

Gaines, S. O., Jr., & Reed, E. S. (1995). Prejudice: From Allport to DuBois. *American Psychologist*, *50*, 96–103.

Gaither, S. E., & Sommers, S. R. (2013). Living with an other-race roommate shapes Whites' behavior in subsequent diverse settings. *Journal of Experimental Social Psychology*, *49*, 272–276.

George, D., Adalikwu-Obisike, J., Boyko, J., Johnson, J., & Boscanin, A. (2014). Harry and Sally revisited: The influence of spirituality and education on sexual tension in cross-sex friendships in secular and Christian universities. *Journal of Research on Christian Education*, *23*, 70–94.

Graham, S., Munniksma, A., & Juvonen, J. (2014). Psychosocial benefits of cross-ethnic friendships in urban middle schools. *Child Development*, *85*, 469–483.

Grimm, V., Berger, U., DeAngelis, D. L., Polhill, J. G., Giske, J., & Railsback, S. F. (2010). The ODD protocol: A review and first update. *Ecological Modelling*, *221*, 2760–2768.

Hallinan, M. T., & Williams, R. A. (1987). The stability of students' interracial friendships. *American Sociological Review*, *52*, 653–664.

Harris, K., & Page-Gould, E. (2021). *Activities with friends*. Manuscript in Preparation.

Harris, K., & Vazire, S. (2016). On friendship development and the big five personality traits. *Social and Personality Psychology Compass*, *10*, 647–667.

Hartung, U. (2004). Research into the effects of segregation and its role in Brown vs. Board of Education. *International Journal of Public Opinion Research*, *16*, 88–90.

Harwood, J. (2021). Modes of intergroup contact: If and how to interact with the outgroup. *Journal of Social Issues*, *77*, 154–170.

Hatfield, E., Utne, M. K., & Traupmann, J. (1979). Equity theory and intimate relationships. In R. L. Burgess, & T. L. Huston (Eds.), *Social exchange in developing relationships* (pp. 99–133). New York: Academic Press.

Helms, J. E. (1984). Toward a theoretical explanation of the effects of race on counseling a Black and White model. *The Counseling Psychologist*, *12*, 153–165.

Helms, J. E., & Carter, R. T. (1990). Development of the White racial identity attitude scale. In J. E. Helms (Ed.), *Black and White racial identity: Theory, research, and practice* (pp. 66–80). Westport, CT, USA: Greenwood Press.

Hodson, G., Harry, H., & Mitchell, A. (2009). Independent benefits of contact and friendship on attitudes toward homosexuals among authoritarians and highly identified heterosexuals. *European Journal of Social Psychology*, *39*, 509–525.

Holoien, D. S., Bergsieker, H. B., Shelton, J. N., & Alegre, J. M. (2015). Do you really understand? Achieving accuracy in interracial relationships. *Journal of Personality and Social Psychology, 108,* 76–92.

Hunt, J. S., & Maeder, E. M. (2017). Without justice for all: An ethnic-minority psychology perspective on bias in the criminal justice and legal system. In A. M. Czopp, & A. W. Blume (Eds.), *Social issues in living color: Challenges and solutions from the perspective of ethnic minority psychology: Societal and global issues* (pp. 243–274). Praeger/ABC-CLIO.

Inzlicht, M., & Ben-Zeev, T. (2000). A threatening intellectual environment: Why females are susceptible to experiencing problem-solving deficits in the presence of males. *Psychological Science, 11,* 365–371.

Kaplan, H. B., Burch, N. R., & Bloom, S. W. (1964). Physiological covariation and socio-metric relationships in small peer groups. In P. H. Leiderman, & D. Shapiro (Eds.), *Psychobiological approaches to social behavior* (pp. 92–109). Stanford, CA, US: Stanford University Press.

Karmali, F., Kawakami, K., & Page-Gould, E. (2017). He said what? Physiological and cognitive responses to imagining and witnessing outgroup racism. *Journal of Experimental Psychology: General, 146,* 1073–1085.

King, R. U., & Sakamoto, I. (2015). Disengaging from genocide harm-doing and healing together between perpetrators, bystanders, and victims in Rwanda. *Peace and Conflict: Journal of Peace Psychology, 21,* 378–394.

Kirschbaum, C., Pirke, K. M., & Hellhammer, D. H. (1993). The 'Trier social stress test'—A tool for investigating psychobiological stress responses in a laboratory setting. *Neuropsychobiology, 28,* 76–81.

Kraus, M. W., Onyeador, I. N., Daumeyer, N. M., Rucker, J. M., & Richeson, J. A. (2019). The misperception of racial economic inequality. *Perspectives on Psychological Science, 14,* 899–921.

Le Forestier, J. M., Page-Gould, E., Lai, C. K., & Chasteen, A. L. (2020). Concealability beliefs facilitate navigating intergroup contexts. *European Journal of Social Psychology, 50,* 1210–1226.

Le Forestier, J. M., Page-Gould, E., Lai, C. K., & Chasteen, A. L. (2022). Subjective identity concealability and the consequences of fearing identity-based judgment. *Personality and Social Psychology Bulletin.* https://doi.org/10.1177/01461672211010038. In press.

Leonardelli, G. J., Pickett, C. L., & Brewer, M. B. (2010). Optimal distinctiveness theory: A framework for social identity, social cognition, and intergroup relations. *Advances in Experimental Social Psychology, 43,* 63–113.

Levenson, R. W., & Ruef, A. M. (1992). Empathy: A physiological substrate. *Journal of Personality and Social Psychology, 63,* 234–246.

Levin, S., Van Laar, C., & Sidanius, J. (2003). The effects of ingroup and outgroup friendships on ethnic attitudes in college: A longitudinal study. *Group Processes & Intergroup Relations, 6,* 76–92.

Lolliot, S., Schmid, K., Hewstone, M., Al Ramiah, A., Tausch, N., & Swart, H. (2013). Generalized effects of intergroup contact: The secondary transfer effect. In G. Hodson, & M. Hewstone (Eds.), *Advances in intergroup contact* (pp. 81–112). Psychology Press.

Lydon, J. E., Jamieson, D. W., & Holmes, J. G. (1997). The meaning of social interactions in the transition from acquaintanceship to friendship. *Journal of Personality and Social Psychology, 73,* 536–548.

MacInnis, C. C., & Hodson, G. (2015). The development of online cross-group relationships among university students: Benefits of earlier (vs. later) disclosure of stigmatized group membership. *Journal of Social and Personal Relationships, 32,* 788–809.

MacInnis, C. C., & Page-Gould, E. (2015). How can intergroup interaction be bad if intergroup contact is good? Exploring and reconciling an apparent paradox in the science of intergroup relations. *Perspectives on Psychological Science, 10,* 307–327.

MacInnis, C. C., & Page-Gould, E. (2020). *An experimental test of social network integration on the continuation of new cross-group friendships*. Manuscript in preparation.

Mallett, R. K., Huntsinger, J. R., Sinclair, S., & Swim, J. K. (2008). Seeing through their eyes: When majority group members take collective action on behalf of an outgroup. *Group Processes & Intergroup Relations, 11*, 451–470.

Mallett, R. K., Wilson, T. D., & Gilbert, D. T. (2008). Expect the unexpected: Failure to anticipate similarities leads to an intergroup forecasting error. *Journal of Personality and Social Psychology, 94*, 265–277.

Manson, S. M. (2001). Simplifying complexity: A review of complexity theory. *Geoforum, 32*, 405–414.

Miller, I. D., & Cupchik, G. C. (2016). A synthetic world population for agent-based social simulation. In *Proceedings of the 4th collective intelligence conference,* New York, NY, USA. https://doi.org/10.6084/m9.figshare.3427460.

Miller, I. D., MacInnis, C. C., & Page-Gould, E. (2021). *Explaining intergroup contact*. Manuscript in preparation.

Miller, L., Rozin, P., & Fiske, A. P. (1998). Food sharing and feeding another person suggest intimacy; two studies of American college students. *European Journal of Social Psychology, 28*, 423–436.

Mitchell, M. (2009). *Complexity: A guided tour*. New York, NY, US: Oxford University Press.

Mohr, R. I., & Purdie-Vaughns, V. (2015). Diversity within women of color: Why experiences change felt stigma. *Sex Roles, 73*, 391–398.

Moody, J. (2001). Race, school integration, and friendship segregation in America. *American Journal of Sociology, 107*, 679–716.

Mosley, A. J., & Biernat, M. (2021). The new identity theft: Perceptions of cultural appropriation in intergroup contexts. *Journal of Personality and Social Psychology, 121*, 308–331.

Nagamuthu, C., & Page-Gould, E. (2017). Competition between female friends. In M. L. Fisher (Ed.), *The Oxford handbook of women and competition* (pp. 133–146). New York, NY, US: Oxford University Press.

Neel, R., & Lassetter, B. (2019). The stigma of perceived irrelevance: An affordance-management theory of interpersonal invisibility. *Psychological Review, 126*, 634–659.

Norton, B. G., & Ulanowicz, R. E. (1994). Scale and biodiversity policy: A hierarchical approach. In F. B. Samson, & F. L. Knopf (Eds.), *Ecosystem management* (pp. 424–434). New York, NY: Springer.

Onyeador, I. N., Wittlin, N. M., Burke, S. E., Dovidio, J. F., Perry, S. P., Hardeman, R. R., & van Ryn, M. (2020). The value of interracial contact for reducing anti-black bias among non-black physicians: A cognitive habits and growth evaluation (CHANGE) study report. *Psychological Science, 31*, 18–30.

Page-Gould, E. (2012). To whom can I turn? Maintenance of positive intergroup relations in the face of intergroup conflict. *Social Psychological and Personality Science, 3*, 462–470.

Page-Gould, E., & Akinola, M. (2015). Incorporating neuroendocrine methods into intergroup relations research. *Group Processes & Intergroup Relations, 18*, 366–383.

Page-Gould, E., & Danyluck, C. (2016). The biological perspective on intergroup relations. In E. Harmon-Jones, & M. Inzlicht (Eds.), *Social neuroscience: Biological approaches to social psychology*. New York, NY, US: Taylor & Francis.

Page-Gould, E., Mendes, W. B., & Major, B. (2010). Intergroup contact facilitates physiological recovery following stressful intergroup interactions. *Journal of Experimental Social Psychology, 46*, 854–858.

Page-Gould, E., & Mendoza-Denton, R. (2011). Friendship and social interaction with outgroup members. In L. R. Tropp, & R. Mallett (Eds.), *Beyond prejudice reduction: Pathways to positive intergroup relations* (pp. 139–158). Washington, DC: APA Books.

Page-Gould, E., Mendoza-Denton, R., Alegre, J. M., & Siy, J. O. (2010). Understanding the impact of cross-group friendship on interactions with novel outgroup members. *Journal of Personality and Social Psychology, 98*, 775–793.

Page-Gould, E., Mendoza-Denton, R., & Tropp, L. R. (2008). With a little help from my cross-group friend: Reducing anxiety in intergroup contexts through cross-group friendship. *Journal of Personality and Social Psychology, 95*, 1080–1094.

Palombit, R. A., Seyfarth, R. M., & Cheney, D. L. (1997). The adaptive value of "friendships" to female baboons: Experimental and observational evidence. *Animal Behaviour, 54*, 599–614.

Paluck, E. L., Green, S. A., & Green, D. P. (2019). The contact hypothesis re-evaluated. *Behavioural Public Policy, 3*, 129–158.

Paluck, E. L., Porat, R., Clark, C. S., & Green, D. P. (2020). Prejudice reduction: Progress and challenges. *Annual Review of Psychology, 72*, 533–560.

Paolini, S., Harwood, J., & Rubin, M. (2010). Negative intergroup contact makes group memberships salient: Explaining why intergroup conflict endures. *Personality and Social Psychology Bulletin, 36*, 1723–1738.

Paolini, S., Hewstone, M., Cairns, E., & Voci, A. (2004). Effects of direct and indirect cross-group friendships on judgments of Catholics and Protestants in Northern Ireland: The mediating role of an anxiety-reduction mechanism. *Personality and Social Psychology Bulletin, 30*, 770–786.

Paolini, S., White, F. A., Tropp, L. R., Turner, R. N., Page-Gould, E., Barlow, F. K., & Gómez, Á. (2021). Intergroup contact research in the 21st century: Lessons learned and forward progress if we remain open. *Journal of Social Issues, 77*, 11–37.

Pettigrew, T. F. (1998). Intergroup contact theory. *Annual Review of Psychology, 49*, 65–85.

Pettigrew, T. F. (2009). Secondary transfer effect of contact: Do intergroup contact effects spread to noncontacted outgroups? *Social Psychology, 40*, 55–65.

Pettigrew, T. F. (2011). SPSSI and racial research. *Journal of Social Issues, 67*, 137–149.

Pettigrew, T. F., & Tropp, L. R. (2005). Allport's intergroup contact hypothesis: Its history and influence. In J. F. Dovidio, P. Glick, & L. A. Rudman (Eds.), *On the nature of prejudice: Fifty years after Allport* (pp. 262–277). Malden, MA, US: Blackwell Publishing.

Pettigrew, T. F., & Tropp, L. R. (2006). A meta-analytic test of intergroup contact theory. *Journal of Personality and Social Psychology, 90*, 751–783.

Pettigrew, T. F., & Tropp, L. R. (2013). *When groups meet: The dynamics of intergroup contact.* New York, NY, US: Psychology Press.

Porges, S. W., & Raskin, D. C. (1969). Respiratory and heart rate components of attention. *Journal of Experimental Psychology, 81*, 497–503.

Reicher, S. (2004). The context of social identity: Domination, resistance, and change. *Political Psychology, 25*, 921–945.

Richard, F. D., Bond, C. F., Jr., & Stokes-Zoota, J. J. (2003). One hundred years of social psychology quantitatively described. *Review of General Psychology, 7*, 331–363.

Richeson, J. A., & Shelton, J. N. (2007). Negotiating interracial interactions: Costs, consequences, and possibilities. *Current Directions in Psychological Science, 16*, 316–320.

Richeson, J. A., & Trawalter, S. (2005). Why do interracial interactions impair executive function? A resource depletion account. *Journal of Personality and Social Psychology, 88*, 934–947.

Roberts, S. O., Williams, A. D., & Gelman, S. A. (2017). Children's and adults' predictions of black, white, and multiracial friendship patterns. *Journal of Cognition and Development, 18*, 189–208.

Schiappa, E., Gregg, P. B., & Hewes, D. E. (2005). The parasocial contact hypothesis. *Communication Monographs, 72*, 92–115.

Schmid, K., Hewstone, M., & Tausch, N. (2013). Secondary transfer effects of intergroup contact via social identity complexity. *British Journal of Social Psychology, 53*, 443–446.

Schneider, B. H., Woodburn, S., del Toro, M. D. P. S., & Udvari, S. J. (2005). Cultural and gender differences in the implications of competition for early adolescent friendship. *Merrill-Palmer Quarterly, 51,* 163–191.

Shelton, J. N., & Richeson, J. A. (2006a). Interracial interactions: A relational approach. *Advances in Experimental Social Psychology, 38,* 121–181.

Shelton, J. N., & Richeson, J. A. (2006b). Ethnic minorities' racial attitudes and contact experiences with white people. *Cultural Diversity and Ethnic Minority Psychology, 12,* 149–164.

Shelton, J. N., Richeson, J. A., Salvatore, J., & Trawalter, S. (2005). Ironic effects of racial bias during interracial interactions. *Psychological Science, 16,* 397–402.

Shelton, J. N., Richeson, J. A., & Vorauer, J. D. (2006). Threatened identities and interethnic interactions. *European Review of Social Psychology, 17,* 321–358.

Shelton, J. N., Trail, T. E., West, T. V., & Bergsieker, H. B. (2010). From strangers to friends: The interpersonal process model of intimacy in developing interracial friendships. *Journal of Social and Personal Relationships, 27,* 71–90.

Shelton, J. N., West, T. V., & Trail, T. E. (2010). Concerns about appearing prejudiced: Implications for anxiety during daily interracial interactions. *Group Processes & Intergroup Relations, 13,* 329–344.

Sokolov, E. N. (1963). Higher nervous functions: The orienting reflex. *Annual Review of Physiology, 25,* 545–580.

Stark, T. H. (2020). Indirect contact in social networks: Challenging common interpretations of the extended contact hypothesis. *Group Processes & Intergroup Relations, 23,* 441–461.

Stephan, W. G., & Stephan, C. W. (1985). Intergroup anxiety. *Journal of Social Issues, 41,* 157–175.

Trawalter, S., Bart-Plange, D. J., & Hoffman, K. M. (2020). A socioecological psychology of racism: Making structures and history more visible. *Current Opinion in Psychology, 32,* 47–51.

Trawalter, S., Richeson, J. A., & Shelton, J. N. (2009). Predicting behavior during interracial interactions: A stress and coping approach. *Personality and Social Psychology Review, 13,* 243–268.

Tropp, L. R., & Barlow, F. K. (2018). Making advantaged racial groups care about racial inequality: Intergroup contact as a route to psychological investment. *Current Directions in Psychological Science, 27,* 194–199.

Tropp, L. R., & Uluğ, O. M. (2019). Are white women showing up for racial justice? Intergroup contact, closeness to people targeted by prejudice, and collective action. *Psychology of Women Quarterly, 43,* 335–347.

Tuch, S. A., Sigelman, L., & MacDonald, J. A. (1999). The polls-trends: Race relations and American youth. *Public Opinion Quarterly, 63,* 109–148.

Van Laar, C., Levin, S., Sinclair, S., & Sidanius, J. (2005). The effect of university roommate contact on ethnic attitudes and behavior. *Journal of Experimental Social Psychology, 41,* 329–345.

Van Rooij, I., & Wareham, T. (2008). Parameterized complexity in cognitive modeling: Foundations, applications and opportunities. *The Computer Journal, 51,* 385–404.

Veniegas, R. C., & Peplau, L. A. (1997). Power and the quality of same-sex friendships. *Psychology of Women Quarterly, 21,* 279–296.

Vezzali, L., Di Bernardo, G. A., Cocco, V. M., Stathi, S., & Capozza, D. (2021). Reducing prejudice in the society at large: A review of the secondary transfer effect and directions for future research. *Social and Personality Psychology Compass, 15,* e12583.

Voci, A., & Hewstone, M. (2003). Intergroup contact and prejudice toward immigrants in Italy: The mediational role of anxiety and the moderational role of group salience. *Group Processes & Intergroup Relations, 6,* 37–54.

Vorauer, J. D., & Sakamoto, Y. (2006). I thought we could be friends, but... systematic miscommunication and defensive distancing as obstacles to cross-group friendship formation. *Psychological Science, 17*, 326–331.

Warikoo, N., Sinclair, S., Fei, J., & Jacoby-Senghor, D. (2016). Examining racial bias in education: A new approach. *Educational Researcher, 45*, 508–514.

West, T. V., Shelton, J. N., & Trail, T. E. (2009). Relational anxiety in interracial interactions. *Psychological Science, 20*, 289–292.

Wheatley, T., Kang, O., Parkinson, C., & Looser, C. E. (2012). From mind perception to mental connection: Synchrony as a mechanism for social understanding. *Social and Personality Psychology Compass, 6*, 589–606.

White, F. A., Harvey, L. J., & Abu-Rayya, H. M. (2015). Improving intergroup relations in the internet age: A critical review. *Review of General Psychology, 19*, 129–139.

Wilson, R. E., Harris, K., & Vazire, S. (2015). Personality and friendship satisfaction in daily life: Do everyday social interactions account for individual differences in friendship satisfaction? *European Journal of Personality, 29*, 173–186.

Wright, S. C., Aron, A., McLaughlin-Volpe, T., & Ropp, S. A. (1997). The extended contact effect: Knowledge of cross-group friendships and prejudice. *Journal of Personality and Social Psychology, 73*, 73–90.

Wright, S. C., Aron, A., & Tropp, L. R. (2002). Including others (and groups) in the self: Self- expansion and intergroup relations. In J. P. Forgas, & K. D. Williams (Eds.), *The social self: Cognitive, interpersonal and intergroup perspectives* (pp. 343–363). Philadelphia: Psychology Press.

Wright, S. C., Brody, S. A., & Aron, A. (2005). Intergroup contact: Still our best hope for reducing prejudice. In C. S. Crandall, & M. Schaller (Eds.), *The social psychology of prejudice: Historical perspectives* (pp. 115–142). Lawrence, KS, US: Lewinian Press.

Zhou, S., Page-Gould, E., Aron, A., Moyer, A., & Hewstone, M. (2019). The extended contact hypothesis: A meta-analysis on 20 years of research. *Personality and Social Psychology Review, 23*, 132–160.

CHAPTER TWO

Construal of power as opportunity or responsibility

Annika Scholl[a,*], Naomi Ellemers[b], Daan Scheepers[c], and Kai Sassenberg[a,d]
[a]Leibniz-Institut für Wissensmedien, Tübingen, Germany
[b]University of Utrecht, Utrecht, The Netherlands
[c]Leiden University, Leiden, The Netherlands
[d]University of Tübingen, Tübingen, Germany
[*]Corresponding author: e-mail address: a.scholl@iwm-tuebingen.de

Contents

Abstract

Powerholders make decisions that impact not only their own situation, but also the outcomes of those who depend on them. The implications of being in power have been studied in a multitude of research: Social power is known to foster goal striving and to change interpersonal behavior. Yet, prior work has also yielded quite opposing effects of high as compared to low power (e.g., more but also less sensitivity toward others). One aspect that can resolve these inconsistencies is that power does not necessarily mean the same to everyone who experiences it. People can construe (i.e., appraise) high power differently—as an opportunity to freely "make things happen" and/or as a responsibility to "take care of things." How one's own power is construed, in turn, moderates the effects of power. The present chapter introduces this theoretical idea on the construal of power and summarizes results from a program of research on it, including its outcomes, preconditions, and a theoretical framework. The chapter integrates prior opposing findings and highlights how a multidimensional approach to power considering the construal of power can contribute to a better understanding of how the powerful behave—but also what makes them more likely to recognize the responsibility that power affords.

"The price of greatness is responsibility."

(Winston Churchill)

"With great power comes great responsibility."

(Stan Lee, Spiderman)

The concept of social power has been intriguing journalists, practitioners, and scientists for several decades (see Galinsky, Rucker, & Magee, 2015, for an illustration of the rise of publications). Indeed, how those high in power behave (e.g., make decisions, weigh risks, or take information into account on how to proceed) impacts not only themselves, but also many others—be it civilians in society, employees in an organization, children at school, or patients in a hospital, to name just a few. Accordingly, understanding the effects of social power is important for many domains in which people (or groups) collaborate or simply interact.

Social power implies asymmetric control over one's own and others' outcomes (e.g., valued resources such as time, money, or appreciation; Fiske & Berdahl, 2007). Being high in power (e.g., as a politician, professor, or manager) provides relative independence; being low in power means that one's outcomes largely depend on the powerholder(s). Research in social psychology so far has mostly focused on how experiencing high (rather than low) power impacts downstream responses.

A multitude of work on this topic has shown how social power fosters goal striving and changes interpersonal behavior (for reviews see Galinsky et al., 2015; Guinote, 2017; Tost, 2015). Across studies and labs, however, the findings show some inconsistent patterns; this inconsistency suggests that it is not adequate to assume unconditional main effects of social power. Regarding many outcomes, research documented contradictory effects. First, on the one hand, social power was found to predict less compassion toward others (Van Kleef et al., 2008); on the other hand, power was also shown to heighten sensitivity to others' feelings (Schmid Mast, Jonas, & Hall, 2009). Second, power led to selfish withholding of resources from others in some studies (e.g., Galinsky, Gruenfeld, & Magee, 2003; Maner & Mead, 2010), whereas in other work, power promoted fair resource sharing (De Cremer & van Dijk, 2008; Galinsky et al., 2003). As a third example, powerholders often seem to judge others superficially, to objectify others (e.g., Fiske, 1993; Goodwin, Gubin, Fiske, & Yzerbyt, 2000; Gruenfeld, Inesi, Magee, & Galinsky, 2008; Guinote & Phillips, 2010), or even to dehumanize them (Gwinn, Judd, & Park, 2013); conversely, powerholders were also shown to individuate others more carefully (compared to the powerless, e.g., Overbeck & Park, 2001, 2006).

How can we explain and resolve these seemingly contradictory effects? One way to explain these effects from a methodological perspective is that many studies so far have used *one-factorial* designs; that is, prior studies compared the impact of high as compared to low power (and sometimes a control condition with equal power; Galinsky et al., 2015; Guinote, 2017; Schaerer, du Plessis, Yap, & Thau, 2018). As such, social power has typically been treated as a *monolitic* concept. A crucial difference that has not been systematically considered yet is that social power does not mean one-and-the-same thing to everyone who experiences it.

Going beyond, we propose that powerholders can appraise—that is, cognitively construe—power in at least two different ways (Sassenberg, Ellemers, & Scheepers, 2012; Scholl, 2020). Powerholders can construe power as providing an *opportunity* to freely "make things happen" during goal striving—such as in case of a manager recognizing the freedom to freely make investment decisions for clients; yet, powerholders can also construe that very same power as a *responsibility* to "take care of things" that only they can manage during goal striving—as in case of the manager handling clients' retirement funds, or a school teacher dealing with students' education. How power is construed, in turn, should influence the outcomes of power, over and above simply being high (versus low) in power per se. Doing so, we argue that how people respond to power does not only depend on their level of power (e.g., whether they have elevated power or not), but also on how they *construe* power (i.e., recognize what power implies).

This chapter introduces this theoretical idea on the psychological construal of power and summarizes results from a program of research on it. Below, we first (1) define construal of power as opportunity or responsibility. We then (2) summarize recent research on how construal changes specific outcomes of power. Subsequently, we turn to (3) the preconditions that determine when power is construed especially as responsibility (rather than opportunity, as the likely default in Western societies). Finally, we (4) outline avenues for the future and a theoretical framework that connects to self-regulation (e.g., self-regulatory state; Kruglanski et al., 2000) and the perspective of those low in power (e.g., Schaerer et al., 2018).

In doing so, the present work addresses the call that "researchers should mind the differences between structural and *psychological* power in theorizing [...]" (Tost, 2015; *p.* 52; emphasis added; see also Gawronski & Brannon, 2020) and that "future research needs to build models and theories that take into account the *meanings attached to power*" (Galinsky et al., 2015; *p.* 447; emphasis added). This endeavor goes beyond prior work with the aims to integrate prior at times opposing findings and to illustrate how a multi-dimensional approach (considering the *construal* of power) can contribute to a better understanding of the effects of high power.

1. What does it mean to construe power as opportunity or responsibility?

Experiencing social power is associated with a sense of control and, thus, with the feeling to have the means to achieve goals (Fiske & Berdahl, 2007; Guinote, 2007a). Yet, even when keeping the level of power high, a person can appraise this relative outcome control in fundamentally different ways—as opportunity or as responsibility.

The most common notion is that people appraise elevated power as an *opportunity* to "make things happen." This construal provides a great amount of freedom and makes salient all the different possibilities on the way to goal attainment (Sassenberg et al., 2012; Sassenberg, Ellemers, Scheepers, & Scholl, 2014; Scholl, Ellemers, Sassenberg, & Scheepers, 2015). Powerholders who construe power as opportunity, per definition, feel liberated and enabled to do whatever they find important to reach the current agenda. Consider the example of bank managers making decisions about their company's investments. The managers' investment decisions affect their own, but also customers' outcomes. Construing power as opportunity, these managers consider themselves free to follow (their own, the company's or their clients') ideas, to make decisions, and to pursue visions.

Yet, a person may also appraise that same high power as a *responsibility* to "take care of things." In this case, the privilege of having control is seen as entailing commitment to goal achievement (De Wit, Scheepers, Ellemers, Sassenberg, & Scholl, 2017; Sassenberg et al., 2012; Scholl, Sassenberg, Scheepers, Ellemers, & De Wit, 2017). Per definition, powerholders construing power as responsibility feel driven to do what is needed and committed to take care of things that only they can do (due to this asymmetric control)—similar to the idea of "noblesse oblige" (e.g., Vanbeselaere, Boen, Van Avermaet, & Buelens, 2006). Consider the above example of the bank managers, construing their high-power position as responsibility. The managers making decisions would now experience that, because they are in power, *they* are the ones assigned with tasks that "nobody else can do"; they see themselves as enabled and obliged to complete these tasks.

In sum, we propose that people can construe one-and-the same (experience of) power as opportunity and/or as responsibility—be it in case of our bank managers example, or in case of teachers at school, professors at university, leaders of a political party, or CEOs in an organization. Just like the bank managers, teachers may sometimes understand their power and freedom to decide on topics, establish rules for class, and grade students' projects according to specific criteria as an *opportunity* that they can do all these things freely. At other times, teachers may understand their power as *responsibility*, for instance, needing to make sure that their class successfully completes the course program.

As these examples illustrate, the way a person construes power can *vary*—it is not fixed for a person or specific position but can change depending on the characteristics of the situation. A specific powerholder may, in general, have a strong tendency towards either construal or both. Notwithstanding, specific situations may make each construal more likely (see Section 3). Conceptually speaking, both states of construal are not different poles of one dimension, but rather distinct (or slightly correlated) dimensions. Especially in real life, both may go together—such that reflecting about their powerful position, people might realize both the opportunities and the responsibilities that it provides (e.g., a professor might see both the opportunity to lecture on topics the professor finds interesting and the responsibility to educate the students in their class). Yet, in a concrete situation, a powerholder will likely focus primarily on one of those aspects, rather than construing power simultaneously as responsibility and opportunity.

To be able to examine the specific implications of these two states of construal and how they differ, the focus in this chapter and the studies reported herein is on the *comparison* between these two: opportunity vs responsibility. This allows for a clear description of the effects of both types of construal and a clear investigation of how construal influences the conjoint role of power and goal content in predicting goal-directed outcomes.

Importantly, construing power differently does not mean sensing more or less power. Construal as opportunity or responsibility is not assumed and more importantly also not found to elicit differences in the *amount* of power a person experiences (for empirical evidence see, e.g., De Wit et al., 2017; Sassenberg et al., 2012; Scholl, De Wit, et al., 2018, which will be summarized with the respective studies below). Similarly, although some examples above for illustrative purposes may have suggested so, different construals per definition do not systematically concern different *tasks*. Rather, construal is equally applicable to, for instance, the tasks of making decisions, ensuring success, or instructing and evaluating those with less power (Scholl, De Wit, et al., 2018). In a nutshell, construing power differently simply refers to the cognitive *appraisal* of one's high-power role; it implies appraising this asymmetric control in a specific way—not more, and not less.

2. Construing power differently alters powerholders' behavior

The way in which a powerholder (generally or in a specific situation) construes power will likely affect the way how this person will think, feel, and behave—that is, the outcomes of power. In this section, we briefly integrate central theoretical ideas on how (construal of) power affects outcomes before we introduce and connect experimental and field findings that highlight the implications of power construed as responsibility or opportunity. Fig. 1 provides an overview of the empirical findings integrated here (i.e., as outcomes of power construal) and in Section 3 (as predictors of power construal).

2.1 A selective view on standard approaches to power: Power fosters goal striving

To derive predictions on the outcomes of construal, we build upon three established power theories (Guinote, 2007a; Keltner, Gruenfeld, & Anderson, 2003; Magee & Smith, 2013). These propose that social power influences goal striving via several routes. Emphasizing power-holders' independence, Keltner et al. (2003) proposed that elevated power activates the approach system, promoting a focus on rewards and facilitating action; in

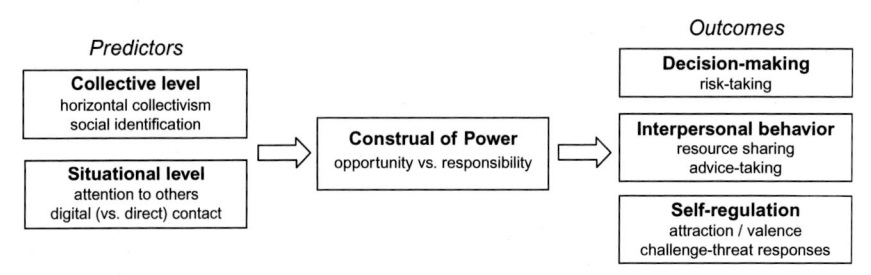

Fig. 1 Overview of empirical findings on predictors and outcomes of construal of power.

contrast, low power activates the inhibition system, inducing a focus on threats and punishments, and inhibiting action.

As a more nuanced elaboration of the power-approach model, a second theoretical perspective, the Situated Focus Theory of Power (Guinote, 2007a), suggests that the independence of power-holders enables them to more exclusively focus on a focal goal (or salient constructs more generally) than the powerless—meaning that the powerful better recognize and adapt to what is needed to reach their goal in a given situation; in contrast, powerless people will be more distracted by goal-irrelevant cues, as they focus also, for instance, on how others evaluate them (see Guinote, 2007c). Finally, as a third approach the Social Distance Theory (Magee & Smith, 2013) suggests that power increases (perceived) social distance, enabling people to mentally represent a goal at higher (abstract) levels and to focus on what they can do to reach it.

All three approaches converge regarding the notion that high (vs low) power enables people to better focus on and more efficiently pursue their focal goal. Substantial evidence supports this position (for summaries, see Galinsky et al., 2015; Guinote, 2017). Compared to those with low power, powerholders were found to better attend to the goal at hand (Guinote, 2007b, 2008; Schmid, Kleiman, & Amodio, 2015), to take the next steps more promptly toward a goal (Galinsky et al., 2003; Guinote, 2007c), and employ various strategies to reach it (Guinote, Judd, & Brauer, 2002). Powerholders are also more sensitive to information about goal progress and the appropriateness of goal-directed means (Scholl & Sassenberg, 2014a, 2015), more easily shield distractions or obstacles (Guinote, 2007b; Whitson et al., 2013), and are often more effective in reaching an activated goal than those with low power (Lammers, Dubois, Rucker, & Galinsky, 2013), to list some exemplary outcomes.

Moreover, evidence suggests that powerholders also behave towards *others* in a goal-focused way—often with the downstream consequence of neglecting the situation of those lower in power, for example, being less responsive to other people (Hogeveen, Inzlicht, & Obhi, 2014), showing stereotyping or objectification as goal-related means (Fiske, 1993; Gruenfeld et al., 2008; Guinote & Phillips, 2010), or ignoring others' advice or suffering (See, Morrison, Rothman, & Soll, 2011; Tost, Gino, & Larrick, 2012; Van Kleef et al., 2008). Notwithstanding the convergence of these findings, there is also evidence on the powerful showing the opposite pattern of responses, namely, showing more individuation or fairness than those with lower power (De Cremer & van Dijk, 2008; Overbeck & Park, 2001, 2006). This inconsistency points toward the need for additional theorizing to be able to explain these differential outcomes.

2.2 How construal of (high) power may affect the outcomes of power

We argue that the effects of high power documented in the above studies are specific to a construal as *opportunity* but become less likely under a construal as responsibility. The heightened (asymmetric) control powerholders have, together with a construal as opportunity, provide ideal conditions for goal pursuit. Under a construal as opportunity, powerholders' thoughts can center directly on goal-directed information (e.g., which resources are available or what outcome value can be achieved with a goal). Powerholders here will likely adopt a relatively narrow focus on the goal at hand—striving to move on towards goal attainment by showing behavior that is directly aimed at goal achievement. Because construal as opportunity is the likely default in Western cultures (in which much power research was conducted; see Section 3; see also Torelli & Shavitt, 2010), this construal may be the driver for many known effects of high power.

According to our reasoning, however, it is also possible to construe one's power as responsibility. Powerholders here feel obligated and committed not only to achieve the focal goal, but also to live up to the concerns created by the position they have. This construal likely prompts powerholders to deliberate more and consider aspects beyond the specific goal at hand—such as the relevance of the goal itself, whether relevant demands or standards are met, whether one is making progress, and whether there is a benefit from goal achievement (for oneself and/or others). Under this construal, powerholders might very well show behavior that is not only goal-directed, but also reflects fulfilling additional criteria (e.g., demands or standards). As such, we propose that the construal of power affects the outcomes of power.

Proposition 1. *People construing their power as opportunity show thoughts and behavior that reflect an approach that directly focuses on the achievement of the focal goal; by contrast, powerholders construing their power as responsibility show thoughts and behavior that reflect a broader, more deliberative approach during goal pursuit.*

We will now consider evidence from our research and studies from other labs that support this for a wide range of outcomes, ranging from (1) decision-making to (2) interpersonal behavior and (3) self-regulation (for an overview, see Fig. 1).

2.3 Decision-making: Construal alters powerholders' risk-taking

Powerholders' ability to focus on the goal is known to affect the way they make decisions during goal striving. For instance, the powerful are quicker to act than the powerless (e.g., Galinsky et al., 2003; Guinote, 2007c; Scholl & Sassenberg, 2014b), persist longer (Guinote, 2007c), and more promptly make a first offer in a negotiation (often affording them better deals; Magee, Galinsky, & Gruenfeld, 2007). Furthermore, powerholders limit their level of forethought before making a decision or solving a task (What would happen if...?), unless doing so is clearly beneficial for reaching the goal (Scholl & Sassenberg, 2015). Finally, powerholders are more ready to ponder what they could have done differently when a decision turns out to be wrong (i.e., after failure; Scholl & Sassenberg, 2014a).

One exemplary, well-established finding in research on decision-making is that powerholders are usually more willing than those with lower power to take risks during goal striving (neglecting potential dangers if they fail when their position is stable; Anderson & Galinsky, 2006; Maner, Gailliot, & Butz, 2007). However, this effect should depend on their construal of power: Powerholders who construe power as *opportunity* likely act in a narrowly focused way in favor of directly taking the next step toward a goal—which likely includes concentrating on potential payoffs and taking risks. For instance, a bank manager construing power as opportunity may feel relatively free to take a chance and make a risky investment. In contrast, powerholders construing power as *responsibility* might be more concerned about which criteria need to be considered (beyond goal progress, e.g., organizational interests or others' outcomes), which should result in less risk-taking. In our example, the manager construing power as responsibility may be more hesitant to take a risk as this manager considers whether doing so would contribute to the company's success, but also fulfill clients' interests.

A study by Anderson and Galinsky (2006, Study 4) yielded initial support for this idea on a correlational level. The authors manipulated power (high vs low) via recall of a high- or low-power situation and then assessed risk-taking tendencies in a scenario. As predicted, power promoted risk-taking; more importantly, however, additional analyses for the high-power condition suggested that the more high-power participants wrote about the responsibilities they had experienced in the recalled situation (without being explicitly asked to do so), the less willing they were to take a risk. In short, responsibility negatively correlated with risk-taking among high-power participants—here conceptualized as risky sexual behavior that could negatively affect themselves and others. This initial finding suggests that the extent to which people may have construed power as a responsibility moderated the standard effect that power promotes risk taking.

Scheepers, De Wit, Ellemers, Sassenberg, and Scholl (2020) experimentally tested the hypothesis that powerholders will be less inclined to take risks when they are *asked* to focus on the responsibilities, rather than the opportunities that power entails (i.e., adopt a specific construal of power). In a first study, a sample of managers were asked to contemplate and write about their own power position either in terms of the *responsibilities* (e.g., being responsible for their personnel, making sure that things go well) or the *opportunities* (e.g., the possibility to delegate tasks, to set out the general strategy). To measure risk-taking, the manager then completed the BART (balloon analogue risk task, Lejuez et al., 2002), for which they were asked to pump-up (fictitious) balloons on their computer screen. The goal was pumping-up each balloon as much as possible without making it explode. For each "pump" on a balloon (vs exploding balloon), participants received (vs lost) tokens. The number of exploded balloons served as validated measure of risk-taking (Lejuez et al., 2002). As hypothesized, managers as real powerholders in the responsibility (vs opportunity) condition took less risks during the first blocks.

In another study, the researchers replicated this result under more controlled conditions in the lab. This experiment implemented a 2 (power: high vs low) × 2 (construal: opportunity or responsibility) design. As such, it (1) included low-power conditions to be able to contrast these to the two high-power conditions; furthermore, this study (2) assessed people's subjective sense of power to show that the responsibility manipulation does not lower the level of experienced power (which was indeed not the case). Specifically, checks on subjectively sensed power neither yielded an effect of nor interaction with construal of power—but only a main effect of high vs low power. Accordingly, the construal manipulation did not change the amount of power that people experienced, but only the way said power was construed.

For this study, a sample of undergraduates completed a study on the computer in private cubicles involving a construal mindset manipulation in a sports scenario (following Sassenberg et al., 2012) and two tasks. The first task on social decision-making was a "delta game," on which they either received either high or low power. The delta game includes an allocator who makes an offer and a recipient who can either accept of refuse said offer. All participants were allocators and divided several tokens between themselves and the (imaginative) recipient. To manipulate social power, we specified a specific delta value which determines the consequences when the recipient decides to reject the offer. The delta value for participants in the high-power condition was 0.90; this means that if the recipient rejects the offer, allocators still receive 90% of the tokens that they had allocated to themselves. The delta value for those in the low-power condition was 0.00; this means that if the recipient rejects the offer, neither the recipient nor the allocator would receive any tokens. Participants did the allocator-delta task once. After their offer, they proceeded to the second task (and were informed they would later receive feedback on whether their offer was accepted).

The second task measured risk-taking again using the BART. Results showed that in the high-power condition, risk-taking was lower in the responsibility than in the opportunity condition; the way the power role was construed did not impact responses of participants in the low power condition. As such, the results replicated and extended Study 1.

Because the first two studies relied on relatively small sample sizes, a third study replicated the findings with a more substantial sample via implementing a low power condition (where power was not framed in any particular way), a "high power as opportunity" condition and a "high power as responsibility" condition. Participants were said to work with another person on a dyadic gambling task. A resource allocation of tokens would take the form of a "dictator game" where one person (the high-power person) would be the allocator and the other participant (the low power person) the recipient. In the "high power as opportunity" condition, it was stressed that the allocator would have the "opportunity and freedom" to make the allocations. In contrast, in the "high power as responsibility" condition, participants read that the allocator would have the "task and responsibility" to make the allocations. Risk-taking was measured using the Cambridge gambling task (Rogers et al., 1999). Again, those in the "high power-opportunity" condition took more risks than those in both the "high power as responsibility" condition and the low power condition; the latter conditions did not differ. Interestingly, the effect was stronger on the riskier subset of trials.

Together, these findings offer evidence that whether powerholders do promptly make a decision and take risks depends on how they construe power. Those construing power as responsibility seemed less willing to take risks than those construing power as opportunity. This finding can be interpreted to indicate that the former made powerholders focus not only on prompt goal attainment, but also to consider demands and standards along the way (e.g., if the decision does contribute to goal attainment).

Additional evidence was obtained with a group task in the lab. Here, we assessed powerholders' willingness to make risky decisions in a business setting (here, operationalized in terms of promotion- vs prevention-oriented choices; Scheepers, Ellemers, & Sassenberg, 2013): Results showed that powerholders made less risky choices when they had something to lose (i.e., belonged to a high-status group, where feelings of *responsibility* were particularly strong) than when they had nothing to lose (i.e., belonged to a group already low in status). Importantly, however, this effect did only occur when it was stressed beforehand that the powerholder would be held accountable (i.e., "responsible") for the outcomes of the group, and the effect disappeared (and tended to reverse) when the powerholder would *not* be held accountable. Again, these findings show that responsibility (made explicit or subjectively experienced) lowers powerholders' tendency to take risks.

2.4 Interpersonal behavior: Construal of power alters selfishness and advice-taking

Beyond decision-making, how people construe power likely also impacts their interpersonal behavior. The outcomes of power with regard to behavior toward others are manifold; for instance, power can lead to more selfish behavior—such as telling others what to do (Kipnis, 1972), attributing collective success to oneself (Lammers & Burgmer, 2019), withholding information (to protect one's power; Maner & Mead, 2010), or taking more from a common public good (but also contributing more to it under specific circumstances; De Cremer & van Dijk, 2008; Galinsky et al., 2003). We argue that such effects depend on power construal. Construing power as opportunity enables powerholders to narrowly focus on the goal at hand (see Proposition 2)—which may often come with the downstream effect of overlooking other aspects (e.g., the welfare and fair share of those lower in power). In contrast, construing power as responsibility should enable the powerful to take other aspects (e.g., people's situation) into account, which likely often results in less selfish behavior.

Though not directly addressing differences in the construal of power, a first set of findings from De Cremer and van Dijk (2008) offers evidence in line with this idea. More specifically, this work outlined the relevance of responsibility for lowering powerholders' selfishness. The researchers found (in Study 2) that powerholders behaved more selfishly in sharing resources than followers. However, this was only the case under conditions in which they seemed to experience low responsibility (because they had been appointed to their leader role by the experimenter); this was not the case when powerholders reported experiencing responsibility (i.e., when they thought they had been elected to their position by followers). Moreover, a follow-up study in this line of research (Study 3) tested the effects of power on selfishness when "responsibility" was made salient (compared to a control condition). Results showed that when responsibility was not made salient, those elected powerholders (who had already experienced high responsibility before) again shared more resources than appointed powerholders (who experienced low responsibility). Yet, when responsibility was made salient, both groups of powerholders showed low selfishness and shared an equally high number of resources. Across the board, this research suggests that being made aware of responsibility mitigated powerholders' selfishness.

Testing the role of both states of construal more directly, the research by Scheepers et al. (2020) mentioned above also demonstrated that construing power as opportunity (vs responsibility) resulted in less fairness toward others. This was the case both for selfishness measured on a dictator game (credits shared with the other person; see DeCelles, DeRue, Margolis, & Ceranic, 2012; Forsythe, Horowitz, Savin, & Sefton, 1994; Fowler & Kam, 2007) and measured on a delta game (measuring offers made to the other person). For both paradigms, powerholders construing power as opportunity were more selfish than those construing power as responsibility (and those with low power, irrespective of the activated construal mindset). In sum, these studies provide evidence for the central role of construal of power for predicting powerholders' (lower or higher) selfishness.

Moving beyond the domain of social decision-making, in other work, we examined a less direct way of "taking care of others," namely, the extent to which powerholders consider and value others' input. Powerholders can be overly confident (Fast, Gruenfeld, Sivanathan, & Galinsky, 2009) and often disregard others' opinions (Galinsky, Magee, Gruenfeld, Whitson, & Liljenquist, 2008)—which can mean that they rely on themselves to promptly reach a goal and disregard advice along the way (Briñol, Petty, Valle, Rucker, & Becerra, 2007; Fast et al., 2009; Pitesa & Thau, 2013; See et al., 2011; Tost et al., 2012). Again, we assumed that this tendency to disregard advice may be specific to construing power as opportunity rather than responsibility: When construing power as responsibility (vs opportunity), powerholders likely hesitate more to take the next step toward a goal without considering all information available (like when taking risks). These powerholders will attach more value to other people's input, contributing to powerholders' own advice-taking.

A set of studies tested this idea (De Wit et al., 2017). Study 1 was a field study. We investigated how leaders' construal of their own formal power position at work predicts the level of advice-taking (as rated by their subordinates, to overcome same-source common method bias). Leaders indicated how they *construed* their power at work and how powerful they felt at work in their supervisor–subordinate relationship. Their subordinate(s) answered items on their respective supervisor's advice-taking. All indicators were measured. Results showed that construal of power predicted advice-taking, moderated by sensed power: Leaders sensing relatively high power seemed to take less advice under a construal as opportunity (rather than responsibility), as predicted. In contrast, for leaders sensing low power, their advice-taking did not depend on construal of power. In other words, leaders sensing high (rather than low) power did seem to take less advice—but only so when they construed power as opportunity, not when they construed power as responsibility. These findings yielded first correlational evidence from two sources that the "effect" of power on advice-taking depends on construal; and vice versa, that for construal to play a role, leaders do need to sense a certain level of power.

To allow for clearer conclusions, Study 2 took an experimental approach in the field, with leaders from Chile and the Netherlands. Among these powerholders, we primed the salience of (a) opportunities or (b) responsibilities. To do so, participants contemplated how their own power role provides either. We also included (c) a high-power control condition in which neither construal was primed to see which construal(s) may drive the effects (i.e., whether powerholders' "default" tendency would be to construe power as opportunity or as responsibility). We then assessed their actual advice-taking on a subsequent task. Finally, we assessed confidence in their judgments on the advice-taking task as potential mediator.

To make their power salient, all leaders were first asked to briefly describe how their job position provided them with power (i.e., control over others' outcomes). As first part of the advice-taking task, they then completed three estimation tasks (e.g., estimating the costs of an expensive vacation in the Dominican Republic). This task assessed their *initial* estimations. Afterwards, we manipulated construal; participants were asked to recall and recount a recent high-power experience at work in which they (a) had felt a *responsibility* towards other (less powerful) people or (b) had felt certain *opportunities;* in (c) the control condition, they simply recalled and described their last working day. Once the manipulation was completed, participants returned to the three estimation tasks: they saw their initial estimations again plus an estimation from an "expert" on the respective topic. Based on this "expert estimation," they now had the option to revise their estimations (i.e., accept or reject this expert advice) and give a final estimation. This served to measure advice-taking. Finally, they indicated their subjective confidence in their final estimations.

Results indicated that, as hypothesized, participants in the responsibility condition accepted more advice than those in the opportunity and control condition (with no difference between the latter two conditions). Accordingly, opportunity seemed to be the "default" construal in this study (as it was more similar to the control condition than responsibility). Condition did not affect the level of confidence in estimations. As such, this study experimentally replicated findings with a sample of working professionals in high-power roles. The effect did not seem to be driven by lower confidence (measured after the final estimations, potentially reflecting the result of post-decisional rationalization).

Study 3 tested the predictions once again in a more controlled lab experiment and assessed confidence both before and after the final estimation, but also the perceived value of advice and competitiveness as potential mediators. In addition, we assessed the subjective level of power to rule-out that the construal manipulation changes the level (rather than construal) of power are given; this was, indeed, not the case. Participants learned that they would perform a decision-making task with another person (a confederate) under time pressure. After briefly meeting the confederate, each person (confederate and participant) entered their private cubicle; they received all instruction on a computer screen. They learned that they would complete three estimation tasks (same as in Study 2) in their dyad, and that the best performing dyad would win a bonus. One person in each dyad would be the "team captain" (determining the final solution; high-power role), the other person would be the "advisor" (providing advice to the captain; low-power role). After a short task to legitimize power role assignment, all participants learned that they were the (high-power) "team captain," and the confederate was their "advisor."

Construal was manipulated via the high-power role description: The text highlighted especially the opportunity or responsibility (or neither in the control condition) of their role. Then, they performed three estimation tasks (see Study 2). The confederate gave them personalized, but content-wise standardized feedback on each initial estimation via the webcam interface. Again, the confederate's advice reflected the objectively correct solution. Participants then had the chance to revise their three initial estimations as indicator of advice-taking. They indicated their confidence (also after the initial estimation), the perceived value of the advice, and their own competitiveness at this moment.

As in Study 2, high-power participants more readily accepted the confederate's advice when they were in the responsibility-construal condition (as compared to both the opportunity-construal and the high-power control condition; the latter two did not differ). Construal neither affected the level of confidence (neither before nor after the advice was given), nor their competitiveness. However, the perceived value of the advice was supported as mediator: Those construing power as responsibility (compared to the other two conditions) perceived greater value in the advice, which in turn predicted more advice-taking. Importantly, additional checks on subjectively sensed power demonstrated that across high-power conditions, participants experienced the same level of high power. This result rules out a potential alternative explanation of the findings that construing power as responsibility might simply make people experience less power.

Taken together, three studies in the field and in the lab supported the idea that construal of power alters powerholders' tendency to accept (or rather disregard) advice—as one exemplary form of interpersonal behavior. High-power people were more likely to accept advice (both on an "objective" task and as rated by subordinates) when construing their power as responsibility, as compared to opportunity or a high-power control condition. The last study showed that powerholders construing power as responsibility considered others' input as more valuable and, therefore, accepted more advice. Interestingly, across Studies 2 and 3, the pattern of the (standard) high-power control condition was more similar to the opportunity than the responsibility condition; this clearly suggests that construal as opportunity was the likely "default" construal of power (at least in the context of the mostly Western samples considered here). To conclude, this set of findings demonstrates that construal of power substantially alters effects of (high) power on interpersonal behavior—namely, in a way that suggests that powerholders take more aspects (input from others) into account when construing power as responsibility (vs opportunity or when no specific construal is activated).

2.5 Self-regulation: Construal alters motivational states and physiological responses

Notably, our theoretical argument builds upon the idea that a construal as opportunity enables people to feel free and to focus (only) on the focal goal at hand, whereas a construal as responsibility should also raise awareness of other relevant criteria (e.g., standards or demands; see Proposition 1). The previous sections provided evidence for this idea in terms of decision-making (e.g., willingness vs reluctance to take risks), selfishness, and advice-taking. The informative value of these outcomes notwithstanding, one can argue that these findings do not directly test and, thus, not yet support the idea of responsibility raising awareness of demands (as compared to opportunity). In the following, we address this question more directly by presenting evidence on (a) the attractiveness of power (construed as opportunity vs responsibility) and (b) the physiological correlates of power construal (which directly result from the evaluation of demands against resources; Blascovich, 2008).

Regarding the attractiveness of power, for a long time, the general idea in the power literature has been that high power is (often) attractive to possess because it provides many resources, and little demands to fulfill. Supporting this idea, for instance, we found in two studies that (a) experiencing a lack of resources (i.e., being in a motivational state of threat, rather than challenge) or (b) striving for using resources for self-fulfillment (i.e., in a promotion, rather than prevention focus) leads people to find high power especially attractive (and low power particularly unattractive; Sassenberg, Jonas, Shah, & Brazy, 2007; Sassenberg & Scholl, 2013; Scholl, Sassenrath, & Sassenberg, 2015). In line with our basic argument, however, this effect should especially apply to power construed as opportunity—less so for power construed as responsibility (as the latter is associated with resources, but also greater demands to fulfill).

Sassenberg et al. (2012) investigated this in a set of four experiments. Construal of power was primed again using the sports scenario already described above. Participants imagined having the high-power role of a member of an organizational committee for a sports event. As part of this role, they would decide about the implementation of 12 measures (e.g., whether extensive security checks should be performed on site—which would diminish the danger of terrorist attacks but would also complicate athletes' preparations). To manipulate the construal of this high-power role, participants then judged these 12 measures while adopting a specific focus on opportunity vs responsibility. In the construal-as-opportunity condition, participants judged each measure regarding its contribution to the events' success. In contrast, in the construal-as-responsibility condition, participants judged whether each measure constitutes an ethically responsible action.

As indicators for the outcome attraction of power, we included self-reports (e.g., the attractiveness of a group high and a group low in power) as well as an implicit measure of the evaluation of power via a lexical decision task (Sassenberg et al., 2007). Across studies, we found that (although both construals produced the same level of perceived power), high power construed as responsibility was less attractive to possess than high power as opportunity (especially for those with a promotion focus striving for self-fulfillment). This pattern shows that the attraction of power critically depends on how people construe power; more importantly, however, it also provides evidence in line with the idea that people might associate power as responsibility with greater demands (that are less attractive to fulfill).

Beyond the impact of construal on attractiveness of power, we also investigated the physiological correlates of construal of power as an indicator of the perception of demands (relative to resources). Prior work has shown that high (vs low) power typically boosts well-being (Kifer, Heller, Perunociv, & Galinsky, 2013) and lowers stress (Akinola & Mendes, 2014; Mehta & Josephs, 2010; Scheepers, De Wit, Ellemers, & Sassenberg, 2012; Wirth, Welsh, & Schultheiss, 2006). This response is likely due to the greater resources that high power provides—both on the objective level (see definition of social power; e.g., Fiske & Berdahl, 2007), but also on the subjectively perceived level (e.g., Fast et al., 2009; Scholl & Sassenberg, 2014a). Yet, if construal as responsibility (vs opportunity) raises awareness of potential demands, then this pattern should change; it should be more pronounced for high power as opportunity, but less so for power as responsibility (with potentially more stress responses in the latter case). We tested this to provide direct evidence for the role of demands in driving the effects of construal.

To be more precise, we focused on threat-challenge responses as captured by the biopsychosocial model of threat and challenge (Blascovich, 2008). The basic idea of the model is (building upon the transactional stress model; Lazarus & Folkman, 1984), that people respond to potentially stressful situations based on their evaluation of available demands against resources. In face of a stressful situation (so-called motivated performance situations, such as taking a test or giving a speech), people evaluate the perceived situational demands "('Is the situation stressful?'; e.g., the difficulty of a task) against their perceived personal resources ('Can I cope?'; e.g., their skills, abilities). If resources match or outweigh demands, this results in a challenge motivational state (I can cope); if resources fall short of the perceived demands, then a threat state occurs (I cannot cope)."

This state becomes evident in a specific pattern of cardiovascular responses (i.e., how efficiently oxygenated blood is transported during task performance) that predicts subsequent performance (Behnke & Kaczmarek, 2018; Blascovich, Seery, Mugridge, Norris, & Weisbuch, 2004; Hase, O'Brien, Moore, & Freeman, 2018; Scholl, Moeller, Scheepers, Nuerk, & Sassenberg, 2017; Seery, Weisbuch, Hetenyi, & Blascovich, 2010). Accordingly, if construal affects the awareness of demands, then it should result in a different cardiovascular pattern: A construal as responsibility (vs opportunity or a high-power control condition) should lead to more threat/less challenge.

We tested this hypothesis in four studies (Scholl, De Wit, et al., 2018). A first experiment sought to rule-out that the effects we may find apply to construal of any role (also a low-power role) as opportunity vs responsibility; accordingly, we manipulated construal (responsibility vs opportunity) and power (low vs high) orthogonally. This allowed us to test the idea that construal of high power (but not low power) as responsibility leads to more threat and less challenge than high power as opportunity. An undergraduate sample completed a simulated business situation, in which participants were told they would make investments in manager-assistant dyads. They were either the assistant making suggestions (low power) or the manager making final decisions (high power) of a well-known investment firm that was now about to reinvest a large amount of money; this reinvestment was presented either as a great opportunity (to increase their clients' funds, to boot the firm's income) or responsibility (to secure their clients' funds and retirement savings, to meet the firm's corporate social responsibility). They were now about to solve two rounds of investments with feedback, received some basic stock information, and solved a practice trial of an investment. Afterwards, we assessed their subjective level of threat and challenge for the upcoming task, as well as perceived resources and demands for exploratory purposes. Participants also completed a power manipulation check. Just as in previous studies, only a main effect of power (no effects of and no interaction with construal) on subjective sense of power was observed. Accordingly, the construal manipulations did not alter how powerful participants felt.

Results yielded no main effects but supported the predicted interaction of power and construal on relative challenge: High-power participants with an opportunity construal reported relatively more challenge than high-power participants with a responsibility construal; the reverse was the case for low-power people, who reported more relative challenge under a responsibility than an opportunity construal (see Fig. 2). An exploratory mediation analysis suggested that these effects were explained by a higher demands-to-resources ratio for high (but not low) power as opportunity (vs responsibility). Accordingly, results provided first evidence that (1) construal of high power changes the level of challenge versus threat (potentially resulting from the evaluation of demands against resources), (2) that perceived demands may explain this, and (3) that the effects of construal are specific to high power. A second experiment replicated these effects of high power for a task unrelated to the power role (i.e., a subsequent IQ-Test).

To go beyond self-self-report, two additional experiments tested how high power as opportunity vs responsibility (vs either a high- or a low-power control condition) affected cardiovascular indicators of threat and challenge—as a more objective, "online" measurement of the actual

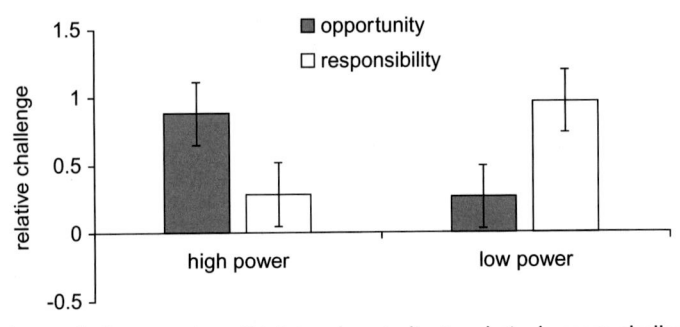

Fig. 2 Relative challenge ratings (higher values indicate relatively more challenge) as a function of Construal × Power. *From Scholl, A., De Wit, F. R. C., Ellemers, N., Sassenberg, K., Fetterman, A. K., & Scheepers, D. (2018). The burden of power: Construing power as responsibility (rather than as opportunity) alters threat-challenge responses.* Personality and Social Psychology Bulletin, 44(7), 1024–1038 (Experiment 1a), Copyright © 2018 SAGE *Publications. doi: https:/doi.org/10.1177/0146167218757452.*

responses people show while solving a stressful task (making estimations or giving a speech into the video camera; Blascovich & Tomaka, 1996; Blascovich, 2008; see also Scheepers et al., 2012). In both studies, participants received a high (or low) power role that was framed in terms of either opportunities or responsibilities; in the last study, there was also a control condition in which (high) power was not framed in any particular way.

In one study (Experiment 2 in the original paper, see Fig. 3), participants were asked to recall an incidence in which they had had high power and this power had meant having either responsibilities or opportunities, or they were asked to recall an incidence in which they had low power. Subsequently, participants were asked to deliver a speech into the web camera, a task that could be appraised as either a threat or a challenge. While doing so, we assessed cardiovascular responses, as compared to baseline responses, which were recorded during a rest period. In the other study (Experiment 3 in the paper), participants received a high-power role—framed either as carrying responsibility, opportunity, or highlighting neither. The procedure was the same as reported above for advice-taking; a team captain (high power role, which was always the participant) made initial estimations then presented these to the advisor (confederate,

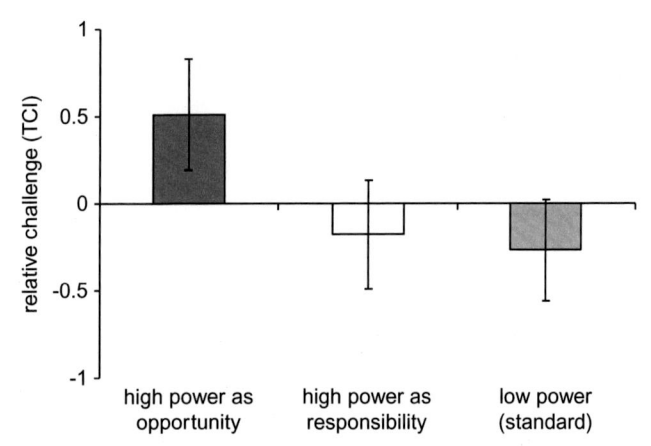

Fig. 3 Relative challenge as a function of Construal of High Power and Power. TCI—threat-challenge index; higher values indicate relatively more challenge and lower values indicate relatively more threat; controlled for speech preparation time. *From Scholl, A., De Wit, F. R. C., Ellemers, N., Sassenberg, K., Fetterman, A. K., & Scheepers, D. (2018). The burden of power: Construing power as responsibility (rather than as opportunity) alters threat-challenge responses.* Personality and Social Psychology Bulletin, 44(7), 1024–1038 (Experiment 2), Copyright © 2018 SAGE Publications. doi: https://doi.org/10.1177/0146167218757452.

low-power role), received advice, and could revise, make, and finally present the final decision. While performing these estimation tasks, we again assessed their cardiovascular responses (as cardiovascular indicators of threat and challenge).

In both studies, we found that cardiovascular responses reflected more relative challenge in the high-power-as-opportunity than in the high-power-as-responsibility condition; the pattern of those in the high-power-as-opportunity condition was similar to those in the high-power-control condition (highlighting no specific construal); again, this suggests that construal as opportunity was the default construal in our (Dutch) sample. Interestingly, the cardiovascular responses of those in the high-power-as-responsibility condition were like those in the low-power condition (see Fig. 3)—even though the former reported feeling more powerful than the latter (and as powerful as those in the high-power-as-opportunity condition). This suggests that powerholders construing power as responsibility likely experience the same level of resources as those construing power as opportunity; but the former are in addition also more aware of demands to fulfill, resulting in a lower challenge and stronger threat response (like those low in power, who perceive low resources and high demands). Again, manipulation checks demonstrated that manipulating the way people construed high power did not change the level of power they experienced, ruling out this potential alternative explanation for the results.

In sum, construal as responsibility (vs opportunity) makes high power less attractive to possess in the first place, and it changes the physiological responses people show while performing a potentially stressful task: Those construing their power as responsibility showed relatively less challenge (and more threat) than those construing their power as opportunity—likely due to the greater awareness of demands to fulfill in the former case.

2.6 Conclusions about the outcomes of construal

As the reviewed findings show, construal is clearly important to understand the implications of power—be it regarding decision-making, interpersonal behavior, or self-regulation. The work presented here demonstrates, in line with prior findings from other labs, that power can evoke different types of outcomes (e.g., more or less selfishness or risk-taking)—and how powerholders themselves construe their power provides a useful means to understand and explain these differential and at times contradictory outcomes.

3. When is power construed as opportunity or responsibility?

Being aware of the impact of different construals on subsequent behavior and self-regulation ultimately raises the question: When does a construal as responsibility (or opportunity) become more likely? In other words, what are the preconditions of construing power more as responsibility (or more as opportunity)?

Earlier work on power has acknowledged differences in how people take up their role of power but has attributed this to individual difference variables. Along this line, prior evidence suggested that powerholders' personal values or orientations (e.g., Chen, Lee-Chai, & Bargh, 2001; Côté et al., 2011; DeCelles et al., 2012; Gordon & Chen, 2013) play a role in shaping the outcomes of power. Accordingly, it may well be that these relatively stable predictors influence the way in which powerholders typically construe their power.

Going beyond such comparatively stable aspects, we specifically sought to investigate the role of the (often more flexible) social context. This approach highlights that situational factors can make a difference, which also offers opportunities for interventions (e.g., to implement power roles in a way to support a specific type of leadership, such as more "responsible" leader behavior). In this section, we thus outline the role of predictors of construal of power, especially as responsibility, as the type of construal than seems *not* to be the default in Western cultures (e.g., De Wit et al., 2017; Scholl, De Wit, et al., 2018; Torelli & Shavitt, 2010).

When are power-holders more likely to construe power either way? As introduced before, we define a construal as opportunity as being aware of the possibilities to "make things happen" along the way to goal attainment, whereas construing power as responsibility means being aware of the obligation and privileges that power provides to "take care of things" (e.g., make decisions) that other people lower in power cannot do. Based on these definitions, we argue that the social context can make a specific goal salient (which powerholders construing power as opportunity will focus more on). Importantly, however, the social context can also make the implications of one's power for people who will be afflicted by one's behavior salient, which should promote a construal as responsibility.

The social context can (generally or in a specific situation) make such implications more salient, for instance, when the far-reaching outcomes of a decision for others (or even oneself) are highlighted or the consequences for others become salient (for a similar argument see Zhong, Magee, Maddux, & Galinsky, 2006). Becoming aware of implications of their behavior, powerholders should come to realize that their behavior has consequences beyond the goal at hand for those lower in power, people working in the same organization, or even themselves, facilitating a construal as responsibility. Accordingly, we argue that:

Proposition 2. *If the broader implications of one's behavior are not made salient, power is more likely to be construed as opportunity; once such implications do become salient, power is more likely to be construed as a responsibility.*

We now turn to these predictors, starting with the broadest level of culture.

3.1 Culture as predictor of construal: Collectivist values in cultures

The broadest factor that might render different implications of power salient is embedded in human culture. Cultures attach importance to specific values (e.g., Triandis & Gelfand, 1998) and define how people distinguish their own value preferences from those that characterize other cultures. Consequently, cultural values can determine how people assign meaning to power (i.e., how they construe power on a cognitive level).

One exemplary set of values that may shape construal of power is *individualism* vs *collectivism*. These cultural differences impact on how people define the self—namely, as being more or less independent of (rather than being interdependent with) others. Most cultures value both independence and interdependence (Jansz, 1991), but cultures can put more or less emphasis on either. Western cultures typically view the self as being independent. Eastern cultures, besides valuing individualism, see the self primarily as being interconnected with others. Such feelings of interconnection especially distinguish those in influential (powerful) positions from influential individuals in more independent cultures (Miyamoto et al., 2018). Accordingly, in cultures that view the self as being *interdependent*, people may develop a general awareness of implications of their actions. Thus, they may tend to develop an understanding of power as responsibility (see also Torelli & Shavitt, 2010). In sum, in these cultures, the implications of one's behavior for others should be generally salient. In contrast, in cultures viewing the self as being relatively *independent*, people may develop such a tendency to a lesser extent, facilitating a construal as opportunity.

Indeed, cultural values do seem to influence how people appraise power. Torelli and Shavitt (2010) demonstrated that (vertical) individualism (i.e., a striving to distinguish oneself from others and to gain status via competition) is associated with construing power in personalized, potentially opportunity-related ways; in contrast, (horizontal) collectivism (i.e., emphasizing common goals, but not submitting to an authority) rather predicts construing power in terms of responsibility for taking care of others. Additionally, Zhong et al. (2005, as cited in Zhong et al., 2006) asked participants to complete a reaction time task to assess the association strength of the word "power" with targets representing "responsibility" (e.g., duty, obligation) or "entitlement" (e.g., deserve, earn). Participants from (individualistic) Western cultures associated power more with "entitlement"—potentially indicative of construal as opportunity; in contrast, participants from (collectivistic) Eastern cultures associated power more with "responsibility"—as indicative of construal as responsibility.

Similarly, even within the same cultural context, individuals who prioritize different values differ in how they construe power. A study conducted in our lab showed that, within a Western (German) sample of undergraduates, individualist values predicted greater perceived opportunity in a high-power role ($r(143) = 0.31$, $P < 0.001$, but not greater perceived responsibility ($r(142) = 0.07$, $P = 0.422$); in contrast, collectivist values predicted greater perceived responsibility ($r(142) = 0.28$, $P = 0.001$, and also opportunity, $r(143) = 0.24$, $P = 0.004$; Scholl & Sassenberg, 2021, unpublished data).

To conclude, we argue that cultural values emphasizing collectivism, face, honor, or other aspects (e.g., long-term orientation) make implications of power differentials for others or oneself salient. As a result, the more a culture emphasizes (or a person values) relational aspects beyond individualism, the more it may facilitate construal as responsibility. Conversely, the more a culture or person focuses solely on individualistic values and independence, the more likely it is that individuals construe power as opportunity.

3.2 Group-level predictors of construal: The example of social identification

Beyond culture, group-level factors can make the implications of one's actions salient and thereby influence the construal of power. In a specific social context, a person can either view the self as independent from others (e.g., in case of a salient personal identity)—such as when group membership is not very relevant or when individually competing with others in the group (e.g., for a promotion in the workplace). In contrast, a person can view the self primarily in terms of the connections to others. This is the case when a shared social identity is salient (Tajfel & Turner, 1986) and/or situational factors make powerholders aware that they belong to the same social category or organization as those with lower power.

Accordingly, one important group-level factor that likely influences construal of power is social identification: The more value people attach to a group that they belong to (i.e., the stronger their social identification)—the more they are motivated to engage in favor of that group. People here shift their concept of "self" from a personal identity ("I," differentiating oneself from others as an individual person) to a *social* identity ("we," considering oneself as belonging to a joint group). This shift means that this person's personal interests move to the background, while the implications for the group and its members become the main focus (Brewer, 1979; Ellemers, 2012; Tajfel & Turner, 1986; Turner, Hogg, Oakes, Reicher, & Wetherell, 1987). As the Situated Focus Theory suggests (Guinote, 2007a), especially those high in power respond to this greater salience of implications (more so than those low in power). Accordingly, we predicted that powerholders (as compared to those with lower power) should more likely recognize their responsibility when they strongly (as compared to weakly) identify with the group (e.g., people of their generation) to which they and the powerless (e.g., "subordinates") belong.

Two studies tested this predicted interplay between power and social identification on perceived responsibility (as an indicator of construal as responsibility; Scholl, Sassenberg, Ellemers, Scheepers, & De Wit, 2018). Study 1 was an online study for which leaders (as real-life powerholders) reported their subjectively experienced power at work, their social identification with the organization, and their level of perceived responsibility (and opportunity) towards others when making decisions at work in their role. Study 2 then tested the predictions in a more controlled environment, experimentally manipulating power (high vs low) and identification (high vs low).

Results for the field study (Study 1) yielded the expected power-by-identification interaction on responsibility. When leaders were strongly identified with their organization, a stronger sense of being in power correlated with a stronger perceived responsibility; conversely, when leaders were weakly identified with the organization, a stronger sense of social power predicted less perceived responsibility. An additional analysis on "attitudes towards power misuse" (toward own ends) yielded a similar interaction: The greater experienced power was, the more favorable leaders reported being toward power misuse toward their own ends—but only when being weakly, not when being strongly identified with their organization. Thus, in this first field-study we found that identification predicted perceived responsibility among leaders who feel powerful.

To replicate these findings experimentally, Study 2 manipulated social identification (high vs low) and power (low vs high) orthogonally. To manipulate level of identification, participants were asked to recall an experience with an ingroup they belonged to (i.e., their generation of "young people") that had made them happy (high identification) or angry (low identification) to belong to said group (see Kessler & Hollbach, 2005). Afterwards, they were told they would collaborate with a person from that ingroup in a manager-assistant dyad. Here, they were either the manager (high power) or assistant (low power) of an art gallery; before starting their task of organizing an art exhibition together, participants indicated the responsibility (and opportunity) they perceived for their respective partner, which served as our measure of power construal. They also completed a power manipulation check, which yielded a power main effect, as intended, but no effects of or interaction with social identification.

The main results of Study 2 revealed the expected interaction (see Fig. 4): High-power people perceived greater responsibility than low-power people in the high-identification condition (but less so in the low identification condition). Exploratory results on perceived opportunity only yielded a main effect of high (vs low) power. Accordingly, power increased the level of perceived opportunity and the level of perceived responsibility—but the latter was more strongly so when identification was high (rather than low).

Taken together, these findings illustrate and support the role of group-level predictors for power construal. Similar effects may occur for other factors on this level—including, for instance, group norms in an organization that include the expectation that powerholders should use their power for others' benefit (see Tost & Johnson, 2019).

3.3 Situational predictors of construal: Salience of others

At the most concrete level, a specific social situation can make implications of one's actions salient. For instance, a concrete situation can be structured in a way that consequences are salient (e.g., when powerholders are made aware of potential power or status loss in case of a wrong decision).

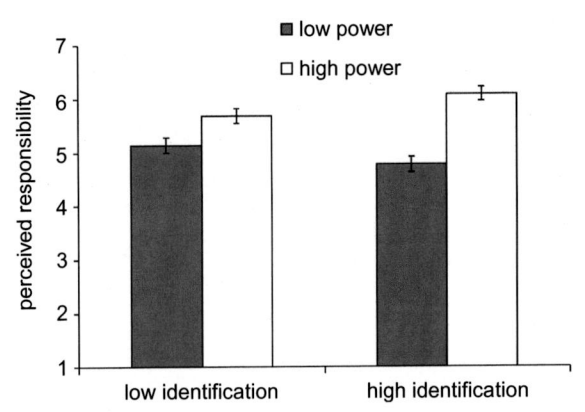

Fig. 4 Perceived responsibility as a function of Social Identification × Power. Copyright © 2017 John Wiley and Sons, The British Psychological Society. *Reproduced with permission from Scholl, A., Sassenberg, K., Ellemers, N., Scheepers, D., & De Wit, F. R. C. (2018). Highly identified power-holders feel responsible: The interplay between social identification and social power within groups.* British Journal of Social Psychology, *57, 112–129 (Study 2).*

Alternatively, the situation may cause other people more generally to become more salient (e.g., when powerholders have close contact with others). In such situations, the powerholder faces a situation in which implications of their behavior are salient, which may facilitate a construal as responsibility.

Indeed, some research findings suggest that powerholders feel more responsible when other people's contribution to one's powerful role becomes salient (i.e., among leaders who were elected by followers, rather than appointed by the experimenter; De Cremer & van Dijk, 2008). Moreover, two sets of findings from our lab directly tested and supported the role of salient others more generally. To do so, a first set of studies sought to make (implications for) others more or less salient by manipulating the extent of direct (face-to-face or digital) contact power holders anticipated to have with those depending on them. In the second set of experiments, we made others more or less salient by drawing the attention of research participants (prior to the assignment of power) either to others or to the self.

Specifically, Scholl, Sassenberg, Zapf, and Pummerer (2020) examined the role of type of contact in powerholders' construal of power—to make implications of one's behavior (here, for others) more or less salient. Digital contact (vs face-to-face contact) with others often implies less social presence of (i.e., greater experienced distance from) interaction partners (e.g., Kiesler, Siegel, & McGuire, 1984; Nielsen, 2017; Sassenberg, Boos, & Rabung, 2005). Accordingly, the mere anticipation of having solely digital, rather than face-to-face, contact with others should make implications of one's actions for others less salient. Accordingly, we predicted that when those high in power anticipate (direct) face-to-face contact, they should experience more responsibility for others than those low in power; yet, the impact of power on the experience of responsibility should be less pronounced when anticipating (indirect) digital contact—because in the latter case, other people and implications of one's behavior for them should be less salient, in the sense of "out of sight, out of mind."

Study 1 manipulated power (high vs low) and anticipated contact (digital vs face-to-face) among employees in a work context; Study 2 used the same procedure for a sample of undergraduates. Participants in both studies imagined working as assistants making suggestions (low power) or as managers making final decisions and evaluating their assistant (high power) in a firm. To allow them to engage with their role, they completed a set of tasks (e.g., evaluating their office decoration, finding their office on a floor plan, etc.). In this task their office reflected their power role, with a large, single office for the manager and a smaller, shared office for the assistant (see Inesi, Botti, Dubois, Rucker, & Galinsky, 2011).

To manipulate anticipated type of contact, participants learned that they would organize an event together with their manager or assistant, respectively, whose office was in another building. They either read that their collaboration would take place via digital means (digital contact condition) and saw a set of tools they would be able to use (e.g., telephone, e-mail); or they read that their collaboration would be face-to-face in a meeting room and saw a set of tools to use there (e.g., a flipchart, a laser pointer). To encourage participants to anticipate the situation as vividly as possible, they wrote down a few notes on how they would organize the collaboration under these conditions. Afterwards, we assessed the level of perceived responsibility (and opportunity) study participants anticipated feeling for their assistant/ manager, respectively, during the collaboration. This served as indicator for construal of power differentials as responsibility (or as opportunity).

Results supported the main prediction: Powerholders anticipating face-to-face contact experienced more responsibility than powerholders anticipating digital contact (and compared to both low power conditions, with digital or face-to-face contact; see Fig. 5). As was the case in prior studies, the experience of opportunity was only found to depend on the degree of

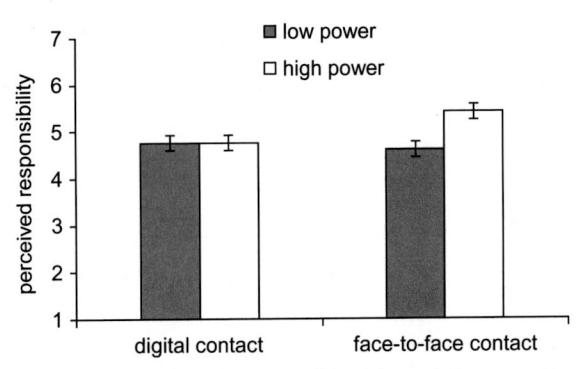

Fig. 5 Perceived responsibility as a function of Anticipated Contact × Power. Copyright © 2020 Elsevier Ltd. *Reproduced with permission from Scholl, A., Sassenberg, K., Zapf, B., & Pummerer, L. (2020). Out of sight, out of mind: Power-holders feel responsible when anticipating face-to-face, but not digital contact with others. Computers in Human Behavior, 112, Article 106,472 (Study 2).*

power: high power led to seeing more opportunity than low power. As such, the results suggest that concrete aspects of the social context—such as the type of contact people anticipate—might make (implications for) others more or less salient and influence the way how those in power construe their power (as responsibility).

In another set of studies (Scholl, Sassenberg, et al., 2017), we directly manipulated the salience of others. The basic idea was to draw powerholders (and powerless people's) attention directly to another person (rather than the self) and examine whether this would foster responsibility. In three studies, we asked people first to focus their attention on the self (recalling a personal positive event and answering questions on the consequences for them) or on another person they knew (recalling a positive event that this person had experienced and answering questions on the consequences for him/her). Afterwards, they received either a high or low power role; in two experiments, this was an assigned role as organizer of a sports event (Experiment 1, only high–power role) or as manager or assistant in a firm (Experiment 2; same as above; adapted from Inesi et al., 2011). In the final experiment (Experiment 3), we used a more subtle manipulation (adapted from Weick & Guinote, 2010) in which people evaluated other people's creative ideas from an alleged creativity contest and learned that their evaluations would be included in the final decision (high power) or would not have an impact on the final decision of determining the winner (low power).

After completing these manipulations, we assessed perceived responsibility (and in some studies we also examined additional outcomes, such

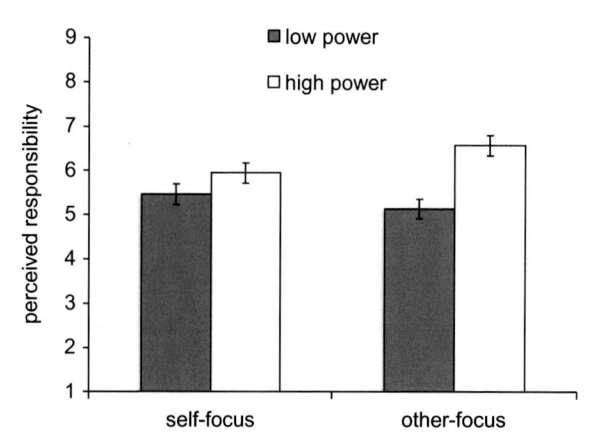

Fig. 6 Perceived responsibility as a function of Attentional Focus × Power. Copyright © 2016 John Wiley and Sons, The British Psychological Society. *Reproduced with permission from Scholl, A., Sassenberg, K., Scheepers, D., Ellemers, N., & De Wit, F. R. C. (2017). A matter of focus: Power-holders feel more responsible after adopting a cognitive other-focus, rather than a self-focus.* British Journal of Social Psychology, *56, 89–102 (Experiment 2).*

as opportunity, objectification, closeness to the other person, etc.). We predicted that high-power people (compared to low-power people) would perceive more responsibility after having focused their attention on another person, but not after having focused their attention on the self. Results supported this line of reasoning (see Fig. 6). That is, we found evidence that even this relatively subtle manipulation of the salience of (implications for) others can influence the extent to which powerholders construe their power as responsibility.

3.4 Conclusions about the predictors of construal

The results of the studies reviewed here show that contextual features on three different levels are relevant to the way powerholders construe their position. Characteristics at the cultural (or interindividual), group context, and situational level can (potentially interactively) influence how likely people are to be aware of different implications of a high-power position. In addition to considering opportunities to achieve the goal at hand, these factors also impact on the likelihood that they consider the broader implications of their behavior. We have seen that this can foster responsibility construal among the powerful. When studying power, it is thus important to examine the extent to which the context at hand does or does not make salient the broader implications of power—which will likely bring powerholders to construe their power primarily as opportunity or responsibility, respectively. Studies using different types of paradigms and measures offer evidence that cultural values, group identification and salience of others' outcomes invite a responsibility construal among the powerful.

On a cautionary note, we need to acknowledge that much of this research examined perceived social responsibility among the powerful—that is, responsibility for taking care of others. Though this work is clearly informative regarding designing interventions to foster responsibility, it is still unclear if these effects are also (partly) driven by salient social goals (i.e., reflect the goal content of benefitting others, not only a specific construal). As a result, future research should investigate more predictors of construal to disentangle them more clearly from the type of goal (e.g., individual, task, or social goal) that people pursue (see Scholl, 2020). We discuss this possibility in more detail in Section 4.

In sum, we argue and show that psychological construal processes— which also depend on situational features—guide the way in which powerholders exercise their power. This is an important advance beyond prior work that has attributed differences in how people respond to high power mainly to more *stable* individual differences. The insight that *situational* features foster a different construal of power, and hence invite a different response of those in power, provides very practical steppingstones; these may be used for interventions to foster responsibility among those wielding power in organizations and society.

4. Future directions for studying power construal

In this final section, we seek to (1) link our research to more general self-regulatory processes which underlie a variety of important social phenomena (e.g., locomotion and assessment mode; Kruglanski et al., 2000; implemental and deliberative mindsets; Gollwitzer, Heckhausen, & Steller, 1990); this allows us to extend the explanatory scope and substantiate our model while also outlining potential avenues for the future to study how exactly construal may shape subsequent outcomes. We then (2) connect construal of power (especially as responsibility) to other approaches to responsible power use, and leadership, before we (3) integrate our reasoning and findings into a model, especially outlining the potentially moderating role of which type of goal a person pursues (i.e., goal content). Finally, we (4) discuss practical advantages and disadvantages of either construal in terms of practical implications, and (5) outline the implications of our analysis from the perspective of those with lower power.

4.1 Linking construal to self-regulatory mechanisms

So far, we have linked construal of power to a number of outcomes (decision-making, interpersonal behavior, and self-regulation in terms of threat challenge responses). A question that remains, however, is by which means construal shapes such outcomes of power—in other words, what are the mechanisms driving these effects? Here, we propose that powerholders' self-regulatory state may represent a primary pathway through which salience of opportunity/responsibility impacts on downstream responses of powerholders.

When powerholders construe power as an opportunity to achieve goals they value, they will likely apply strategies that directly aim at making progress (moving on) toward these goals. Such a self-regulatory state is referred to as *locomotion mode* in Regulatory Mode Theory (Kruglanski et al., 2000). In this state, people strive to get things done and act toward the goal without much consideration of their surroundings or of alternative goals or means (Kruglanski, Orehek, Higgins, Pierro, & Shalev, 2010; Kruglanski et al., 2000). This self-regulatory state also relates to what is referred to as an *implemental mindset* in goal striving (Gollwitzer et al., 1990). This term indicates that, rather than contemplating the appropriateness of their goal, people's thoughts focus on the question how to implement the next steps toward the goal.

These self-regulatory states, in turn, promote those types of outcomes that reflect people's striving for such goal progress—similar to the outcomes we expected and found for power as opportunity: For instance, a locomotion state promotes hastened movement, improved performance on many tasks by increasing the tendency to "do something," and tempting people to consider less information (Kruglanski et al., 2000). Studies have documented that people in an implemental state are oriented toward goal-directed action (Taylor & Gollwitzer, 1995), have a relatively narrow attention focus (Büttner et al., 2014), and show a relatively low openness to alternatives (see Gollwitzer & Kinney, 1989; Heckhausen & Gollwitzer, 1987) while being confident to succeed (Gollwitzer & Kinney, 1989; Taylor & Gollwitzer, 1995). Very similar effects have been shown in cases where high power is likely to be construed as opportunity. For instance, as long as responsibility is not made salient, the powerful are typically more ready to act, focused on goal-relevant information, and show higher confidence (e.g., Galinsky et al., 2003; Guinote, 2007a, 2007b, 2007c; See et al., 2011; Tost et al., 2012). The observation of these parallel effects suggests there may be a link between construal as opportunity and self-regulatory states and outcomes that characterize locomotion.

In contrast, we argue that construing power as responsibility—and thus feeling committed to live up to standards created by this privilege should reflect a different type of self-regulation (and outcomes). Powerholders here may apply strategies aimed at assessing what to do and trying to "do things the right way." Such a self-regulatory state is referred to as *assessment mode* (Kruglanski et al., 2000), in which people critically evaluate and compare options of goals or means to choose the best one before starting to act. This state also relates to a so-called *deliberative mindset* (Gollwitzer et al., 1990), in which people compare goals and possible actions while weighing the expected consequences of each.

The self-regulatory state of assessment and deliberation (just as a construal as responsibility) benefits goal-directed outcomes that are not only oriented toward attaining the goal but aim to fulfill additional demands or criteria along the way. Assessment is known to be associated with relatively more critical thinking and considering more information. This typically also results in the experience of more stress (e.g., in case of ambiguity), while taking into account what is considered important or "right" by others. For instance, people in an assessment state have been found to accept the potential risk of procrastination or not getting started in the first place (see Kruglanski, Pierro, & Higgins, 2015; Pierro et al., 2008; Pierro, Giacomantonio, Pica, Kruglanski, & Higgins, 2011). They also tend to prefer leadership that considers formal standards and/or others' welfare beyond the goal at hand (see Kruglanski, Pierro, & Higgins, 2007; Orehek, Fitzsimons, & Kruglanski, 2014), and typically develop a relatively realistic view of action-outcome expectancies (Gollwitzer & Kinney, 1989). Similarly, a deliberative state has been found to promote a relatively broad focus of attention. For instance, deliberation allows for the evaluation of potential achievements and consequences of goal attainment, and openness to all incoming information (compared to locomotion or an implemental state; Büttner et al., 2014; Gollwitzer & Kinney, 1989; Heckhausen & Gollwitzer, 1987; Taylor & Gollwitzer, 1995). These outcomes match behavior known for powerholders who construe power as responsibility (e.g., less attractiveness of power, less challenge; Sassenberg et al., 2012; Scholl, De Wit, et al., 2018; higher openness to information; De Wit et al., 2017).

In addition to noting these parallels, we have also conducted a series of studies to obtain more direct evidence on the relation between locomotion versus assessment and situational construal (Scholl, Wenzler, Ellemers, Scheepers, & Sassenberg, 2021). Across seven data sets we noted that, independently of their power, people's perceived responsibilities correlate positively with assessment—and more strongly so than opportunities do. At the same time, perceived opportunities correlate positively with locomotion (while perceived responsibilities do so less strongly). This further supports our reasoning and sets the stage for additional empirical tests of the link between these two literatures. Taken together, results so far suggest that construal of power can be connected to specific strategies that people can follow to strive for the achievement of salient goals and important outcomes. As such, future research might elaborate on this connection between the construal of power and self-regulatory strategies. This would not only advance our understanding of the mechanisms bringing about the effects of construal, but also offers possibilities for a broader connection between these distinct areas of inquiry.

4.2 Connecting power construal to prior conceptualizations of responsibility

To understand the potential implications (and benefits) of the proposed framework, it is crucial to reconnect our propositions not only to previous empirical results, but also to prior theoretical approaches on power and responsibility. We are certainly not the first to propose that power can be associated with different meanings and, especially, with responsibility (for an overview, see Table 1).

Some previous approaches focused on why people may want to obtain power in the first place and suggested that responsibility may play a role. McClelland (1985) and Winter (1991, 1992) suggested that people strive to attain power either (1) to reach personal goals (i.e., influence others, gain impact etc.; McClelland, 1985; Winter, 1991, 1992) or (2) to reach social goals (i.e., to benefit or understand others; McClelland, 1985; Winter, 1992). While the latter was connected to responsibility, a key difference to our current analysis is that these accounts focus on why a person wants to attain power in the first place, while we address how people come to construe power once they have it.

Addressing the latter aspect, some prior approaches have also examined how people exercise (rather than construe) power once they have it (e.g., De Hoogh & Den Hartog, 2008; Torelli & Shavitt, 2010; Tost, 2015; Zhong et al., 2006). These all note that people can associate power either with (1) personal goals (i.e., benefit the self), or (2) social goals (i.e., benefit other people). For instance, Torelli and Shavitt (2010) suggested that people can differ in the specific beliefs, attitudes, goals, and behaviors they hold about

Table 1 Construal of power and its similarities and differences to related concepts

	Construal of power	Power motives	Power conceptualization	Network of power-related concepts	Ethical leadership
Source	The current framework	McClelland (1985) and Winter (1992)	Torelli and Shavitt (2010) and Zhong et al. (2006)	Tost (2015)	De Hoogh and Den Hartog (2008)
Question	What does power *mean*?	*Why* do people strive to attain power?	What *should* people *do* with power?	What do people *associate* with power?	What *does* a person do with power?
Focus on	Appraisal	Motives	Attitudes	Associations	Behaviors
Treated as	Trait or situationally activated	Trait predictor (interpersonal)	Trait predictor (intercultural)	Activated by stable predictors (culture, gender, etc.)	Behavioral outcome (leadership style)
Main idea	People can cognitively *appraise* power differently Motives, goals, behaviors not part of the definition; both construals can refer to self- and/or other-oriented concerns	People strive to *attain* power for different reasons Clear link either to selfish motives (gain impact) or other-oriented motives (benefit others)	People *associate goals & attitudes* with power Clear link either to selfish goals (attain prestige) or other-oriented goals (benefit others)	People *associate* concepts with power in a *cognitive network* Clear link either to selfish (agentic) or other-oriented (communal) behavior	People show more or less ethical *behavior* when being in power Is evident in clear behavioral outcomes (e.g., benevolence, fairness toward subordinates)

and associate with power (see also Zhong et al., 2006); accordingly, people may understand power in "personalized terms" (associate it with personal goals) or "socialized terms" (associate it with collective goals). Along a similar line, Tost (2015) suggested that experiencing power in organizational contexts may evoke a sense of social liberation or social responsibility; the latter, then, is defined as a "feeling of obligation to act in ways that *benefit others*" (Tost, 2015; *p.* 46; emphasis added).

Finally, leadership research also acknowledged the importance of responsibility among the powerful to ensure the functioning of hierarchies (which commonly denoted under the term "ethical leadership"). This field considers responsibility as a multidimensional concept that is defined via specific outcomes: "that a person 'means it', feels an inner obligation to do what is known to be right, is dependable and can be 'counted upon'" (De Hoogh & Den Hartog, 2008; *p.* 299), is "honest, trustworthy, fair, and caring" (Brown, Trevino, & Harrison, 2005, *p.*120) and refrains from performing any evil acts against others (Brown et al., 2005; Kanungo, 2001). In sum, these approaches suggest that people associate power with different (selfish or other-beneficial "responsible") goals and behave accordingly.

In contrast, we propose that power can be seen as responsibility and/or as opportunity. This is distinct from prior approaches, in that construal explicitly refers to the way powerholders, on the cognitive level, appraise power. Is it (only) the control over valued resources (i.e., their freedom) that they perceive, or are they also mindful and aware of the responsibilities bound to their position? In practice, these two types of construal may often relate to either self- or other-beneficial goals, beliefs, attitudes, or behaviors (as suggested by earlier approaches).

Importantly, however, self- vs other-directed goals, etc. are *not*, per definition, part of the concept of construal. Construing power as opportunity can be associated with a self-oriented agenda (striving freely toward personal gain), an other-oriented agenda (freely bringing organizational or team goals forward), or even a task-oriented agenda (making progress on an individually performed task). In parallel, construing power as responsibility can be associated with an other-oriented agenda (taking care of team success), a self-oriented agenda (keeping up one's own well-being as a leader), or a task-oriented agenda (making sure that this task is completed). Of course, this distinction of which type of goal people seek to achieve is clearly important. Yet, when it comes to the definition of construal of power as responsibility and opportunity, we regard the type of goal as being orthogonal to this conceptualization of construal. Rather, we integrate goal content together with power construal into a framework described in the following.

4.3 Toward a theoretical framework

As noted from the outset, previous work on power yielded partly contradictory findings. We observed that power lowers compassion (Van Kleef et al., 2008), but heightens interpersonal sensitivity (Schmid Mast et al., 2009). Likewise, power leads to selfish (e.g., Galinsky et al., 2003; Maner & Mead, 2010), but also to fair behavior (De Cremer & van Dijk, 2008; Galinsky et al., 2003). And power tempts people to disregard others (e.g., Fiske, 1993; Goodwin et al., 2000; Gruenfeld et al., 2008; Guinote & Phillips, 2010), but also to carefully attend to others (e.g., Overbeck & Park, 2001, 2006).

We proposed that considering the construal of power constitutes one way to explain these contradictory findings. We argued that in many cases, lower sensitivity and more selfishness among the powerful will occur when power is construed as opportunity—but less so when power is construed as responsibility. We reviewed a program of research that offers direct evidence for this reasoning and documents predicted outcomes (e.g., selfishness; Scheepers et al. (2020); considering others' input; De Wit et al., 2017. Indeed, other studies have also shown less selfish, "corrupted" behavior among the powerful when exposed to a manipulation that explicitly mentioned powerholders' responsibility to take care of others (e.g., Schmid Mast et al., 2009; Study 1). We argue this may have facilitated a construal of power as responsibility (rather than the "default" construal as opportunity).

4.3.1 The role of goal content

Notwithstanding these results, to fully understand the outcomes of power across different contexts, it is important to consider the type of goal as an additional aspect that may direct people's concerns to different aspects of their power position. Theoretical approaches to power suggest that social power will enable people to better focus on and engage on behalf of a specific goal. As a corollary of this idea, the type of goal in focus (i.e., which end-state the power holder seeks to achieve) needs to be considered beyond the construal of power. The goal content may be self-oriented (e.g., a personal goal to further one's career, outperform others, or reduce personal workload), other-oriented (e.g., to promote team performance, help others, or contribute to others' welfare), or simply task-oriented (e.g., to complete the task or identify the best decision without considering immediate benefits for oneself or others; see also Scholl, 2020). Which type of goal people pursue depends on multiple factors, such as the organizational mission, individual preferences, task instructions, or situational affordances (e.g., Cantor, 1994; Gibson, 1977). Like a signpost giving directions, the type of goal (goal content) predicts relevant foci during goal striving (e.g., selfish, prosocial, or task-related thoughts, feelings, and behaviors). High as compared to low power should simply boost this relation (via enhanced goal focus).

Going beyond this approach, we have argued that construal of (high) power matters for (a) how much powerholders will focus on the goal at hand (or also consider additional demands), and (b) potentially, which self-regulatory strategies they will apply on the way during goal striving. Integrating these ideas into a common framework (see Fig. 7) suggests that goal content (i.e., the type of goal in focus) will determine people's thoughts, actions, and feelings during goal striving, and that social power boosts this relation via improved goal focus. Yet, this moderating effect for high power critically depends on how this power is construed (as responsibility or opportunity) and potentially which self-regulatory strategies may follow from this construal.

Accordingly, both goal content and the construal of power may conjointly influence outcomes among the powerful—such as their behavior toward others, or their likelihood to reach the goal. Interestingly, this means that two powerholders focusing on the same type of goal may show different goal-directed outcomes (because they construe their power differently). Vice versa, two powerholders focusing on different types of goals may show similar goal-directed outcomes (because they construe their power similarly).

To give a few (nonexhaustive) examples: Powerholders who construe power as opportunity and strive toward a social goal (e.g., high status for the team) likely share much information with the team members—just like powerholders construing power as responsibility—just because doing so helps them to make progress toward said goal. Likewise, even powerholders who construe power as responsibility may keep important resources to themselves—just like those construing power as opportunity—when a personal goal is activated and doing so allows them to take additional demands into account (e.g., making a good impression on other powerholders by proving that they are resourceful). Taking a reverse perspective, one can thus also conclude that powerholders helping team members may do so, for instance, (i) because these powerholders construe power as responsibility to take care of things (including team members' situation), (ii) because these

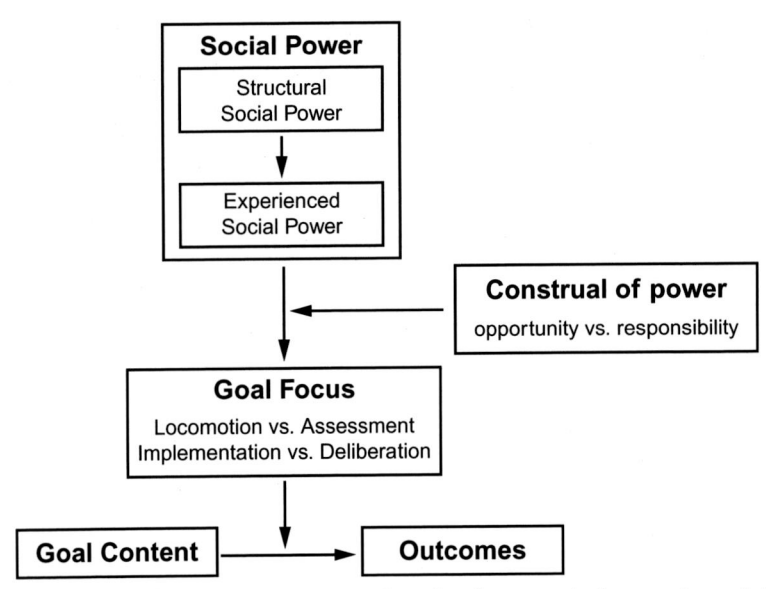

Fig. 7 Theoretical framework integrating the role of construal of power in explaining how type of goal (goal content), power, and construal of power predict goal-directed outcomes.

powerholders construe power as opportunity to make things happen and helping others does ensure goal progress, or (iii) because they follow an activated social goal (under either construal).

4.3.2 The role of structural and subjectively experienced power

Finally, the relation of objective and subjective power (as well as construal of power) deserve closer inspection. As outlined in the very beginning of the chapter, a person can objectively have (structural) power (e.g., as part of a leadership position) and/or subjectively experience power (e.g., in a specific situation). These two are most likely linked to each other, such that objective power facilitates subjective feelings of power and may, thereby, predict behavioral outcomes of power.

This reasoning is in line with prior findings (e.g., Anderson & Berdahl, 2002) that social power exerts its effects via the subjective experience of power, and it also fits prior approaches on how disentangle power on an objective and subjective level (Tost, 2015; here referred to as structural vs psychological power). To take a broader perspective, this general idea can be integrated with the functional-cognitive framework (e.g., De Houwer, 2011). In terms of this framework, objective power is an aspect of the environment that influences behavioral outcomes (functional level of analysis), whereas subjectively experienced power represents a mental construct that explains how objective power may affect these behavioral outcomes (cognitive level of analysis).

Importantly, taking the construal of power into account suggests that subjective power alone is likely insufficient to understand the effects of structural power on behavioral outcomes (at the functional level). Rather, we would argue that how people construe the power they experience needs to be considered as another important variable at the cognitive level.

To conclude, both construal of power (among the powerful) and goal content likely play a role and need to be taken into account when trying to understand the implications of power for goal striving across different situations. Our reading of prior work is that it often focused on social power in the lab and/or concerned individually performed tasks (i.e., likely making an individual or task goal salient) without directly taking the goal content and/or construal into account. Accordingly, more studies are needed to disentangle the effects of construal under clearly defined (different) types of goals.

4.4 Practical advantages and disadvantages of either construal

From a practical point of view, our framework raises the question of which construal may be more effective for organizations, leaders, followers, and all these parties in the long run. Note that any answer to this question ultimately depends on "normative" assumptions about what constitutes desired behavior; providing such answers is not in the realm of empirical social psychology. Still, we discuss several potential assumptions that could be of interest from an applied point of view.

On the one hand, it is typically important for powerholders (e.g., in organizations) to be successful and move forward toward goal attainment; on the other hand, powerholders also need to carefully consider other aspects around them (e.g., their subordinates' situation or organizational requirements) to secure support from others, to motivate subordinates, and to adapt to an organizations' potentially changing requirements. How might they balance these diverging concerns, and how may the two types of construal relate to this in the long run?

4.4.1 Potential implications of construal as opportunity

Construing power as opportunity—and being in a locomotion regulatory state—may result in prompt goal progress that benefits oneself (e.g., success under a salient personal goal), even at other people's potential costs or disadvantage—which may make those lower in power feel overlooked, lowering satisfaction and contributing to distress and willingness to quit (e.g., Tepper, 2000). Hence, in the absence of counterveiling forces, construing power as opportunity in combination with personal goals may harm interpersonal relationships and undermine followers' support. Yet, power as opportunity can also result in goal progress that benefits others—for instance, when achieving a social goal promotes others' welfare. Beyond this, construing power as opportunity may prove beneficial for a powerholder's own success—because this powerholder likely stays focused on the goal (rather than being "distracted"). This could benefit others in the long run, even independently of the specific type of goal in focus: In work settings, goal progress often not only benefits the powerholders, but their team and organization could also benefit from it (e.g., gain prestige).

4.4.2 Potential implications of construal as responsibility

Construing power as responsibility—and being in an assessment regulatory state—can enable powerholders to make well considered decisions, to consider multiple relevant aspects (e.g., up- and downsides of a decision for themselves, for others, and the organization), and prevent ill-considered actions. Accordingly, powerholders construing power as responsibility may typically take extra care to consider all information and interests, which can contribute to performance and others' welfare. These benefits notwithstanding, power as responsibility could have its costs for the powerholder. In extreme cases, these powerholders may never cease to weigh options and consider countless criteria beyond the goal at hand to "make everyone happy." This strategy may slow down decision-making, distract from the goal, and limit success in reaching it. Moreover, doing so can make a powerholder appear indecisive, frustrate followers (Webb, Coleman, Rossignac-Milon, Tomasulo, & Higgins, 2017), and ultimately undermine performance.

Finally, extensively figuring out how to do things the right way may be stressful for the powerholder. Indeed, people in an assessment mode typically find decision-making very stressful, as they are afraid to make the wrong decision (Chen, Rossignac-Milon, & Higgins, 2018). This idea resonates with our findings that construal as responsibility (vs opportunity) can induce physiological threat (rather than challenge; Scholl, De Wit, et al., 2018). This suggests that these powerholders likely experience more stress, which in the long run is also linked to lower performance and health (Behnke & Kaczmarek, 2018; Blascovich, 2008).

In sum, one construal should not generally be considered a "better" way to reach goals and ensure good collaboration than the other. Accordingly, from a practical point of view, combining "pros and cons" of each construal may be ideal. Mirroring this idea, approaches on locomotion and assessment suggest that neither regulatory state is generally (i.e., across contexts) better than the other. Rather, to be effective, a person needs to be able to show both types of regulatory states (Kruglanski et al., 2010). One possibility to do so would be by switching easily and flexibly between construals as a powerholder. In some situations (e.g., when quick decisions need to be made), a construal as opportunity can be preferred. In other contexts (e.g., when decisions require carefully weighing complex information against each other and taking long-term consequences into account), powerholders should be able to switch to recognizing their responsibility. We are not aware of any research on the ability to switch construals; accordingly, this idea clearly remains to be tested in the future.

4.5 Expanding perspectives: The view of the powerless and their power construal

Finally, we need to recall that social power is about a social relation between at least two parties—one having high, one having low(er) power. Although some studies presented here also address those low in power, this chapter did focus on the powerful and how they construe high power. Yet, one may just as well wonder about the perspective of those low in power: One interesting aspect here is whether and how those with low power depending on the powerful recognize these powerholders' construal of power (and potentially the type of goal being pursued).

After working together for some time, powerholders may have clearly communicated how they see their power (e.g., to set the work climate in their team). Even if they have not done so explicitly, those with less power (e.g., followers) may over time have come to develop a relatively valid understanding of their powerholder's characteristic (goal content and) construal from observing powerholders. This understanding may help the powerless anticipate and make sense out of powerholders' behaviors. If, for example, subordinates recognize how their leader construes power, this may influence their professional relationship. A match between power-holders' construal (and regulatory state) and subordinates' regulatory state may prove effective and reinforce each other in many cases—because, for example, a powerholder striving to "move on" may be more motivating for a subordinate with the same regulatory tendency, and vice versa (rather than who tries to "do things right" and carefully assess every step; see Sassenberg & Hamstra, 2017). Similar assumptions may apply for a match of goal content.

Another intriguing possibility, for which we are not aware of any systematic research yet, is whether the powerless can construe their own low-power position differently—as providing them (despite their low control) with some opportunity or responsibility. Our framework so far focused on the construal of power among the powerful. We did so because, for one, research so far largely focused on those high in power (often treating those low in power as a comparison group, e.g., Schaerer et al., 2018); accordingly, most of the evidence so far builds upon those high (vs low) in power. Second, the behavior among those high in power (and their construal) often has more immediate consequences for a wide range of people as compared to the behavior of those lower in power. Notwithstanding, it would be highly interesting to focus more on the powerless in future research on power (construal). One can imagine that powerless people construing their position as providing them with some opportunities could see this as a chance to prove themselves as they hope to gain more control over time—at least if they do perceive some opportunities and manage to stay focused on the goal. Similarly, powerless people construing their position as entailing some responsibility could see this as a dilemma between feeling responsible to contribute, but not being able to influence too much; alternatively, they could see this as a chance to enjoy their limited responsibility and let others handle those things they have little control over.

Indeed, findings about challenge-threat responses (Scholl, De Wit, et al., 2018; Experiment 1a) suggest that the effects of construal might reverse for those low (vs high) in power: Responsibility (vs opportunity) lowered challenge among the powerful, whereas responsibility (vs opportunity) promoted challenge among the powerless. These speculations offer interesting questions for future research, also in response to recent calls to focus more on the perspective of those with lower power (Schaerer et al., 2018).

5. Conclusion

To conclude, this chapter proposed that to understand the role of power for goal striving, it is essential to consider how powerholders appraise power (and accordingly how they likely strive to achieve said end-state), and potentially also the type of goal in focus. Specifically, we suggested powerholders construing power as opportunity will focus on and move toward the goal at hand, whereas powerholders construing power as responsibility will take additional demands and concerns (beyond the goal) into account, potentially refraining from action until having secured that they can do things "the right way." Empirical evidence from prior work clearly supports the role of power construal for decision-making, interpersonal behavior, and self-regulation. Moreover, we identified factors at the cultural, group, and situational level that serve to predict construal of power—outlining possible ways how to understand or foster the preconditions under which each construal becomes more likely across different contexts. Notwithstanding this emerging evidence, several further questions remain to be addressed in the future—starting with a direct and thorough test of the interplay between construal and goal content in guiding goal striving among those low and high in power. Doing so enables us to gain a comprehensive understanding of when and why powerholders may be more effective in reaching goals, as well as, for instance, the extent to which they consider not only their own, but also other people's welfare.

Acknowledgments

This research reported here was supported by a Wrangell fellowship granted to Annika Scholl by the European Social Fund and by the Ministry of Science, Research, and the Arts Baden-Wuerttemberg, and by a DFG grant (SA 800/12-1) to Kai Sassenberg and Annika Scholl. The authors would like to thank Frank de Wit for his important input on earlier versions of this chapter.

References

Akinola, M., & Mendes, W. B. (2014). It's good to be the king: Neurobiological benefits of higher social standing. *Social Psychological and Personality Science*, *5*, 43–51.

Anderson, C., & Berdahl, J. L. (2002). The experience of power: Examining the effects of power on approach and inhibition tendencies. *Journal of Personality and Social Psychology*, *83*, 1362–1377.

Anderson, C., & Galinsky, A. D. (2006). Power, optimism, and risk-taking. *European Journal of Social Psychology*, *36*, 511–536.

Behnke, M., & Kaczmarek, L. D. (2018). Successful performance and cardiovascular markers of challenge and threat: A meta-analysis. *International Journal of Psychophysiology*, *130*, 73–79.

Blascovich, J. (2008). Challenge, threat, and health. In J. Y. Shah, & W. L. Gardner (Eds.), *Handbook of motivation science* (pp. 481–493). New York, NY: Guilford Press.

Blascovich, J., Seery, M. D., Mugridge, C. A., Norris, R. K., & Weisbuch, M. (2004). Predicting athletic performance from cardiovascular indexes of challenge and threat. *Journal of Experimental Social Psychology*, *40*, 683–688.

Blascovich, J., & Tomaka, J. (1996). The biopsychosocial model of arousal regulation. *Advances in Experimental Social Psychology*, *28*, 1–51.

Brewer, M. B. (1979). In-group bias in the minimal intergroup situation: A cognitive-motivational analysis. *Psychological Bulletin*, *86*, 307–324.

Briñol, P., Petty, R. E., Valle, C., Rucker, D. D., & Becerra, A. (2007). The effects of message recipients' power before and after persuasion: A self-validation analysis. *Journal of Personality and Social Psychology, 93*, 1040–1053.

Brown, M. E., Trevino, L. K., & Harrison, D. A. (2005). Ethical leadership: A social learning perspective for construct development and testing. *Organizational Behavior and Human Decision Processes, 97*, 117–134.

Büttner, O. B., Wieber, F., Schulz, A. M., Bayer, U. C., Florack, A., & Gollwitzer, P. M. (2014). Visual attention and goal pursuit deliberative and implemental mindsets affect breadth of attention. *Personality and Social Psychology Bulletin, 40*, 1248–1259.

Cantor, N. (1994). Life task problem solving: Situational affordances and personal needs. *Personality and Social Psychology Bulletin, 20*, 235–243.

Chen, S., Lee-Chai, A. Y., & Bargh, J. A. (2001). Relationship orientation as a moderator of the effects of social power. *Journal of Personality and Social Psychology, 80*, 173–187.

Chen, C. Y., Rossignac-Milon, M., & Higgins, E. T. (2018). Feeling distressed from making decisions: Assessors' need to be right. *Journal of Personality and Social Psychology, 115*, 743–761.

Côté, S., Kraus, M. W., Cheng, B. H., Oveis, C., Van der Löwe, I., Lian, H., & Keltner, D. (2011). Social power facilitates the effect of prosocial orientation on empathic accuracy. *Journal of Personality and Social Psychology, 101*, 217–232.

De Cremer, D., & van Dijk, E. (2008). Leader- -follower effects in resource dilemmas: The roles of leadership selection and social responsibility. *Group Processes & Intergroup Relations, 11*, 355–369.

De Hoogh, A. H. B., & Den Hartog, D. N. (2008). Ethical and despotic leadership, relationships with leader's social responsibility, top management team effectiveness and subordinates' optimism: A multi-method study. *The Leadership Quarterly, 19*, 297–311.

De Houwer, J. (2011). Why the cognitive approach in psychology would profit from a functional approach and vice versa. *Perspectives in Psychological Science, 6*, 202–209.

De Wit, F. R. C., Scheepers, D., Ellemers, N., Sassenberg, K., & Scholl, A. (2017). Whether power holders construe their power as responsibility or opportunity influences their tendency to take advice from others. *Journal of Organizational Behavior, 38*, 923–949.

DeCelles, K. A., DeRue, D. S., Margolis, J. D., & Ceranic, T. L. (2012). Does power corrupt or enable? When and why power facilitates self-interested behavior. *Journal of Applied Psychology, 97*, 681–689.

Ellemers, N. E. (2012). The group self. *Science, 336*, 848–852.

Fast, N. J., Gruenfeld, D. H., Sivanathan, N., & Galinsky, A. D. (2009). Illusory control: A generative force behind power's far-reaching effects. *Psychological Science, 20*, 502–508.

Fiske, S. T. (1993). Controlling other people. *American Psychologist, 48*, 621–628.

Fiske, S. T., & Berdahl, J. (2007). Social power. In A. W. Kruglanski, & E. T. Higgins (Eds.), *Social psychology: Handbook of basic principles* (2nd ed., pp. 678–692). New York, NY: Guilford Press.

Forsythe, R., Horowitz, J. L., Savin, N. E., & Sefton, M. (1994). Fairness in simple bargaining experiments. *Games and Economic Behavior, 6*, 347–369.

Fowler, J. H., & Kam, C. D. (2007). Beyond the self: Social identity, altruism, and political participation. *Journal of Politics, 69*, 813–827.

Galinsky, A. D., Gruenfeld, D. H., & Magee, J. C. (2003). From power to action. *Journal of Personality and Social Psychology, 85*, 453–466.

Galinsky, A. D., Magee, J. C., Gruenfeld, D. H., Whitson, J. A., & Liljenquist, K. A. (2008). Power reduces the press of the situation: Implications for creativity, conformity, and dissonance. *Journal of Personality and Social Psychology, 95*, 1450–1466.

Galinsky, A. D., Rucker, D. D., & Magee, J. C. (2015). Power: Past findings, present considerations, and future directions. In M. Mikulincer, P. R. Shaver, J. A. Simpson, J. F.

Dovidio, M. Mikulincer, P. R. Shaver, ... J. F. Dovidio (Eds.), *APA handbook of personality and social psychology, volume 3: Interpersonal relations* (pp. 421–460). Washington, DC: American Psychological Association.

Gawronski, B., & Brannon, S. M. (2020). Power and moral dilemma judgments: Distinct effects of memory recall versus social roles. *Journal of Experimental Social Psychology, 86.* Article 103908.

Gibson, J. J. (1977). The theory of affordances. In R. Shaw, & J. Bransford (Eds.), *Perceiving, acting and knowing: Toward an ecological psychology* (pp. 67–82). Hillsdale, NJ: Lawrence Erlbaum.

Gollwitzer, P. M., Heckhausen, H., & Steller, B. (1990). Deliberative vs. implemental mindsets: Cognitive tuning toward congruous thoughts and information. *Journal of Personality and Social Psychology, 59,* 1119–1127.

Gollwitzer, P. M., & Kinney, R. F. (1989). Effects of deliberative and implemental mind-sets on illusion of control. *Journal of Personality and Social Psychology, 56,* 531–542.

Goodwin, S. A., Gubin, A., Fiske, S. T., & Yzerbyt, V. Y. (2000). Power can bias impression processes: Stereotyping subordinates by default and by design. *Group Processes and Intergroup Relations, 3,* 227–256.

Gordon, A. M., & Chen, S. (2013). Does power help or hurt? The moderating role of self–other focus on power and perspective-taking in romantic relationships. *Personality and Social Psychology Bulletin, 39,* 1097–1110.

Gruenfeld, D. H., Inesi, M. E., Magee, J. C., & Galinsky, A. D. (2008). Power and the objectification of social targets. *Journal of Personality and Social Psychology, 95,* 111–127.

Guinote, A. (2007a). Behaviour variability and the situated focus theory of power. *European Review of Social Psychology, 18,* 256–295.

Guinote, A. (2007b). Power affects basic cognition: Increased attentional inhibition and flexibility. *Journal of Experimental Social Psychology, 43,* 685–697.

Guinote, A. (2007c). Power and goal pursuit. *Personality and Social Psychology Bulletin, 33,* 1076–1087.

Guinote, A. (2008). Power and affordances: When the situation has more power over powerful than powerless individuals. *Journal of Personality and Social Psychology, 95,* 237–252.

Guinote, A. (2017). How power affects people: Activating, wanting, and goal seeking. *Annual Review of Psychology, 68,* 353–381.

Guinote, A., Judd, C. M., & Brauer, M. (2002). Effects of power on perceived and objective group variability: Evidence that more powerful groups are more variable. *Journal of Personality and Social Psychology, 82,* 708–721.

Guinote, A., & Phillips, A. (2010). Power can increase stereotyping. *Social Psychology, 41,* 3–9.

Gwinn, J. D., Judd, C. M., & Park, B. (2013). Less power = less human? Effects of power differentials on dehumanization. *Journal of Experimental Social Psychology, 49,* 464–470.

Hase, A., O'Brien, J., Moore, L. J., & Freeman, P. (2018). The relationship between challenge and threat states and performance: A systematic review. *Sport, Exercise, and Performance Psychology, 8,* 123–144.

Heckhausen, H., & Gollwitzer, P. M. (1987). Thought contents and cognitive functioning in motivational versus volitional states of mind. *Motivation and Emotion, 11,* 101–120.

Hogeveen, J., Inzlicht, M., & Obhi, S. S. (2014). Power changes how the brain responds to others. *Journal of Experimental Psychology: General, 143,* 755–762.

Inesi, M. E., Botti, S., Dubois, D., Rucker, D. D., & Galinsky, A. (2011). Power and choice: Their dynamic interplay in quenching the thirst for personal control. *Psychological Science, 22,* 1042–1048.

Jansz, J. (1991). *Person, self, and moral demands.* Leiden: DSWO Press.

Kanungo, R. N. (2001). Ethical values of transactional and transformational leaders. *Canadian Journal of Administrative Sciences*, *18*, 257–265.

Keltner, D., Gruenfeld, D. H., & Anderson, C. (2003). Power, approach, and inhibition. *Psychological Review*, *110*, 265–284.

Kessler, T., & Hollbach, S. (2005). Group-based emotions as determinants of ingroup identification. *Journal of Experimental Social Psychology*, *41*, 677–685.

Kiesler, S., Siegel, J., & McGuire, T. W. (1984). Social psychological aspects of computer-mediated communication. *American Psychologist*, *39*, 1123–1134.

Kifer, Y., Heller, D., Perunociv, W. Q. E., & Galinsky, A. D. (2013). The good life of the powerful: The experience of power and authenticity enhances subjective well-being. *Psychological Science*, *24*, 280–288.

Kipnis, D. (1972). Does power corrupt? *Journal of Personality and Social Psychology*, *24*, 33–41.

Kruglanski, A. W., Orehek, E., Higgins, E. T., Pierro, A., & Shalev, I. (2010). Modes of self-regulation: Assessment and locomotion as independent determinants in goal pursuit. In R. H. Hoyle (Ed.), *Handbook of personality and self-regulation* (pp. 375–402). Malden, MA: Blackwell-Wiley.

Kruglanski, A. W., Pierro, A., & Higgins, E. T. (2007). Regulatory mode and preferred leadership styles: How fit increases job satisfaction. *Basic and Applied Social Psychology*, *29*, 137–149.

Kruglanski, A. W., Pierro, A., & Higgins, E. T. (2015). Experience of time by people on the go: A theory of the locomotion-temporality interface. *Personality and Social Psychology Review*, *20*, 100–117. https://doi.org/10.1177/1088868315581120.

Kruglanski, A. W., Thompson, E. P., Higgins, E. T., Pierro, A., Shah, J. Y., & Spiegel, S. (2000). To "do the right thing" or to "just do it": Locomotion and assessment as distinct self-regulatory imperatives. *Journal of Personality and Social Psychology*, *79*, 793–815.

Lammers, J., & Burgmer, P. (2019). Power increases the self-serving bias in the attribution of collective successes and failures. *European Journal of Social Psychology*, *49*, 1087–1095.

Lammers, J., Dubois, D., Rucker, D. D., & Galinsky, A. D. (2013). Power gets the job: Priming power improves interview outcomes. *Journal of Experimental Social Psychology*, *49*, 776–779.

Lazarus, A. L., & Folkman, S. (1984). *Stress, appraisal and coping*. New York: Springer.

Lejuez, C. W., Read, J. P., Kahler, C. W., Richards, J. B., Ramsey, S. E., Stuart, G. L., Strong, D. R., & Brown, R. A. (2002). Evaluation of a behavioral measure of risk taking: The balloon analogue risk task (BART). *Journal of Experimental Psychology: Applied*, *8*, 75–84.

Magee, J. C., Galinsky, A. D., & Gruenfeld, D. H. (2007). Power, propensity to negotiate, and moving first in competitive interactions. *Personality and Social Psychology Bulletin*, *33*, 200–212.

Magee, J. C., & Smith, P. K. (2013). The social distance theory of power. *Personality and Social Psychology Review*, *17*, 158–186.

Maner, J. K., Gailliot, M. T., & Butz, D. A. (2007). Power, risk, and the status quo: Does power promote riskier or more conservative decision making? *Personality and Social Psychology Bulletin*, *33*, 451–462. https://doi.org/10.1177/0146167206297405.

Maner, J. K., & Mead, N. L. (2010). The essential tension between leadership and power: When leaders sacrifice group goals for the sake of self-interest. *Journal of Personality and Social Psychology*, *99*, 482–497.

McClelland, D. C. (1985). *Human motivation*. Glenview, IL: Scott, Foresman.

Mehta, P. H., & Josephs, R. A. (2010). Testosterone and cortisol jointly regulate dominance: Evidence for a dual-hormone hypothesis. *Hormones and Behavior*, *58*, 898–906.

Miyamoto, Y., Yoo, J., Levine, C. S., Park, J., Boylan, J. M., Sims, T., et al. (2018). Culture and social hierarchy : Self- and other-oriented correlates of socioeconomic status across cultures. *Journal of Personality and Social Psychology*, *115*, 427–445.

Nielsen, M. I. S. (2017). Computer-mediated communication and self-awareness–a selective review. *Computers in Human Behavior, 76*, 554–560.

Orehek, E., Fitzsimons, G. M., & Kruglanski, A. W. (2014). *Moving on means leaving behind: How locomotors devalue support providers.* Pittsburgh, PA: University of Pittsburgh (Unpublished manuscript).

Overbeck, J. R., & Park, B. (2001). When power does not corrupt: Superior individuation processes among powerful perceivers. *Journal of Personality and Social Psychology, 81,* 549–565.

Overbeck, J. R., & Park, B. (2006). Powerful perceivers, powerless objects: Flexibility of powerholders' social attention. *Organizational Behavior and Human Decision Processes, 99*, 227–243.

Pierro, A., Giacomantonio, M., Pica, G., Kruglanski, A. W., & Higgins, E. T. (2011). On the psychology of time in action: Regulatory mode orientations and procrastination. *Journal of Personality and Social Psychology, 101,* 1317–1331. https://doi.org/10.1037/a0025943.

Pierro, A., Leder, S., Mannetti, L., Higgins, E. T., Kruglanski, A. W., & Aiello, A. (2008). Regulatory mode effects on counterfactual thinking and regret. *Journal of Experimental Social Psychology, 44,* 321–329.

Pitesa, M., & Thau, S. (2013). Compliant sinners, obstinate saints: How power and self-focus determine the effectiveness of social influences in ethical decision making. *Academy of Management Journal, 56,* 635–665.

Rogers, R. D., Owen, A. M., Middleton, H. C., Williams, E. J., Pickard, J. D., Sahakian, B. J., et al. (1999). Choosing between small, likely rewards and large, unlikely rewards activates inferior and orbital prefrontal cortex. *Journal of Neuroscience, 19,* 9029–9038.

Sassenberg, K., Boos, M., & Rabung, S. (2005). Attitude change in face-to-face and computer-mediated communication: Private self-awareness as mediator and moderator. *European Journal of Social Psychology, 35,* 361–374.

Sassenberg, K., Ellemers, N., & Scheepers, D. (2012). The attraction of social power: The influence of construing power as opportunity versus responsibility. *Journal of Experimental Social Psychology, 48,* 550–555.

Sassenberg, K., Ellemers, N., Scheepers, D., & Scholl, A. (2014). "power corrupts" revisited: The role of construal of power as opportunity or responsibility. In J.-W. van Prooijen, & P. A. M. van Lange (Eds.), *Power, politics, and paranoia: Why people are suspicious of their leaders* (pp. 73–87). Cambridge, UK: Cambridge University Press.

Sassenberg, K., & Hamstra, M. R. W. (2017). The intrapersonal and interpersonal dynamics of self-regulation in the leadership process. *Advances in Experimental Social Psychology, 55,* 193–257.

Sassenberg, K., Jonas, K. J., Shah, J., & Brazy, P. (2007). Why some groups just feel better: The regulatory fit of group power. *Journal of Personality and Social Psychology, 92,* 249–267.

Sassenberg, K., & Scholl, A. (2013). If I can do it my way…the influence of regulatory focus on job-related values and job selection. *Journal of Economic Psychology, 38,* 58–70.

Schaerer, M., du Plessis, C., Yap, A. J., & Thau, S. (2018). Low power individuals in social power research: A quantitative review, theoretical framework, and empirical test. *Organizational Behavior and Human Decision Processes, 149,* 73–96.

Scheepers, D., De Wit, F., Ellemers, N., & Sassenberg, K. (2012). Social power makes the heart work more efficiently: Evidence from cardiovascular markers of challenge and threat. *Journal of Experimental Social Psychology, 48,* 371–374.

Scheepers, D., De Wit, F., Ellemers, N., Sassenberg, K., & Scholl, A. (2020). *Conceptualizing social power as responsibility (instead of opportunity) reduces risk taking and self-interested decision-making.* Leiden University: Unpublished manuscript.

Scheepers, D., Ellemers, N., & Sassenberg, K. (2013). Power in group contexts: The influence of group status on promotion and prevention decision making. *British Journal of Social Psychology, 52,* 238–254.

Schmid, P. C., Kleiman, T., & Amodio, D. M. (2015). Power effects on cognitive control: Turning conflict into action. *Journal of Experimental Psychology: General, 144,* 655–663.

Schmid Mast, M., Jonas, K., & Hall, J. A. (2009). Give a person power and he or she will show interpersonal sensitivity: The phenomenon and its why and when. *Journal of Personality and Social Psychology, 97,* 835–850.

Scholl, A. (2020). Responsible power-holders: When and for what the powerful may assume responsibility. *Current Opinion in Psychology, 33,* 28–32.

Scholl, A., De Wit, F. R. C., Ellemers, N., Sassenberg, K., Fetterman, A. K., & Scheepers, D. (2018). The burden of power: Construing power as responsibility (rather than as opportunity) alters threat-challenge responses. *Personality and Social Psychology Bulletin, 44,* 1024–1038.

Scholl, A., Ellemers, N., Sassenberg, K., & Scheepers, D. (2015). Understanding power in social context: How power relates to language and communication in line with responsibilities or opportunities. In R. Schulze, & H. Pishwa (Eds.), *The exercise of power in communication. Devices, reception and reaction* (pp. 312–334). Hampshire: Palgrave Macmillan.

Scholl, A., Moeller, K., Scheepers, D., Nuerk, H.-C., & Sassenberg, K. (2017). Physiological threat responses predict number processing. *Psychological Research, 81,* 278–288.

Scholl, A., & Sassenberg, K. (2014a). Where could we stand if I had…? How social power impacts counterfactual thinking after failure. *Journal of Experimental Social Psychology, 53,* 51–61.

Scholl, A., & Sassenberg, K. (2014b). "while you still think, I already type": Experienced social power reduces deliberation during e-mail communication. *Cyberpsychology, Behavior and Social Networking, 17,* 692–696.

Scholl, A., & Sassenberg, K. (2015). Better know when (not) to think twice: How social power impacts prefactual thought. *Personality and Social Psychology Bulletin, 41,* 159–170.

Scholl, A., & Sassenberg, K. (2021). *Cultural values predict how people construe high social power.* Tuebingen: Leibniz-Institut fuer Wissensmedien (Unpublished manuscript).

Scholl, A., Sassenberg, K., Ellemers, N., Scheepers, D., & De Wit, F. R. C. (2018). Highly identified power-holders feel responsible: The interplay between social identification and social power within groups. *British Journal of Social Psychology, 57,* 112–129.

Scholl, A., Sassenberg, K., Scheepers, D., Ellemers, N., & De Wit, F. R. C. (2017). A matter of focus: Power-holders feel more responsible after adopting a cognitive other-focus, rather than a self-focus. *British Journal of Social Psychology, 56,* 89–102.

Scholl, A., Sassenberg, K., Zapf, B., & Pummerer, L. (2020). Out of sight, out of mind: Power-holders feel responsible when anticipating face-to-face, but not digital contact with others. *Computers in Human Behavior, 112.* Article 106472.

Scholl, A., Sassenrath, C., & Sassenberg, K. (2015). Attracted to power: Challenge/threat and promotion/prevention focus differentially predict the attractiveness of group power. *Frontiers in Psychology, 6.* Article 397.

Scholl, A., Wenzler, M., Ellemers, N., Scheepers, D., & Sassenberg, K. (2021). Just do it or do it right? How regulatory mode relates to perceived responsibility and opportunity in collaborations. *Personality and Individual Differences, 176* (Article 110776).

See, K. E., Morrison, E. W., Rothman, N. B., & Soll, J. B. (2011). The detrimental effects of power on confidence, advice taking, and accuracy. *Organizational Behavior and Human Decision Processes, 116,* 272–285.

Seery, M. D., Weisbuch, M., Hetenyi, M. A., & Blascovich, J. (2010). Cardiovascular measures independently predict performance in a university course. *Psychophysiology, 47,* 535–539.

Tajfel, H., & Turner, J. C. (1986). The social identity theory of intergroup behavior. In S. Worchel, & W. Austin (Eds.), *Psychology of intergroup relations* (pp. 7–24). Chicago: Nelson-Hall.

Taylor, S. E., & Gollwitzer, P. M. (1995). Effects of mindset on positive illusions. *Journal of Personality and Social Psychology, 69*, 213–226.

Tepper, B. J. (2000). Consequences of abusive supervision. *The Academy of Management Journal, 43*, 178–190.

Torelli, C. J., & Shavitt, S. (2010). Culture and concepts of power. *Journal of Personality and Social Psychology, 99*, 703–723.

Tost, L. P. (2015). When, why, and how do powerholders "feel the power"? Examining the links between structural and psychological power and reviving the connection between power and responsibility. *Research in Organizational Behavior, 35*, 29–56.

Tost, L. P., Gino, F., & Larrick, R. P. (2012). Power, competitiveness, and advice taking: Why the powerful don't listen. *Organizational Behavior and Human Decision Processes, 117*, 53–65.

Tost, L. P., & Johnson, H. H. (2019). The prosocial side of power: How structural power over subordinates can promote social responsibility. *Organizational Behavior and Human Decision Processes, 152*, 25–46.

Triandis, H. C., & Gelfand, M. J. (1998). Converging measurement of horizontal and vertical individualism and collectivism. *Journal of Personality and Social Psychology, 74*, 118–128.

Turner, J. C., Hogg, M. A., Oakes, P. J., Reicher, S. D., & Wetherell, M. S. (1987). *Rediscovering the social group. A self-categorisation theory.* Oxford, UK: Basil Blackwell.

Van Kleef, G. A., Oveis, C., Van Der Löwe, I., Luokogan, A., Goetz, J., & Keltner, D. (2008). Power, distress, and compassion: Turning a blind eye to the suffering of others. *Psychological Science, 19*, 1315–1322.

Vanbeselaere, N., Boen, F., Van Avermaet, E., & Buelens, H. (2006). The Janus face of power in intergroup contexts: A further exploration of the noblesse oblige effect. *The Journal of Social Psychology, 146*, 685–699.

Webb, C. E., Coleman, P. T., Rossignac-Milon, M., Tomasulo, S. J., & Higgins, E. T. (2017). Moving on or digging deeper: Regulatory mode and interpersonal conflict resolution. *Journal of Personality and Social Psychology, 112*, 621–641.

Weick, M., & Guinote, A. (2010). How long will it take? Power biases time predictions. *Journal of Experimental Social Psychology, 46*, 595–604.

Whitson, J. A., Liljenquist, K. A., Galinsky, A. D., Magee, J. C., Gruenfeld, D. H., & Cadena, B. (2013). The blind leading: Power reduces awareness of constraints. *Journal of Experimental Social Psychology, 49*, 579–582.

Winter, D. G. (1991). A motivational model of leadership: Predicting long-term management success from TAT measures of power motivation and responsibility. *The Leadership Quarterly, 2*, 67–80.

Winter, D. G. (1992). Responsibility. In C. P. Smith (Ed.), *Motivation and personality: Handbook of thematic content analysis.* Cambridge: Cambridge University Press.

Wirth, M. M., Welsh, K. M., & Schultheiss, O. C. (2006). Salivary cortisol changes in humans after winning or losing a dominance contest depend on implicit power motivation. *Hormones and Behavior, 49*, 346–352.

Zhong, C.-B., Magee, J. C., Maddux, W. W., & Galinsky, A. D. (2006). Power, culture, and action: Considerations in the expression and enactment of power in east Asian and Western societies. In Y.-R. Chen (Ed.), *Vol. 9. National Culture and groups (Research on Managing Groups and Teams)* (pp. 53–73). Emerald Group Publishing Limited: Bingley.

CHAPTER THREE

How disgust affects social judgments

Yoel Inbar[a],* and David A. Pizarro[b],*
[a]Department of Psychology, University of Toronto, Toronto, ON, Canada
[b]Cornell University, Ithaca, NY, United States
*Corresponding authors: e-mail address: yoel.inbar@utoronto.ca; dap54@cornell.edu

Contents

Abstract

The emotion of disgust has been claimed to affect a diverse array of social judgments, including moral condemnation, inter-group prejudice, political ideology, and much more. We attempt to make sense of this large and varied literature by reviewing the theory and research on how and why disgust influences these judgments. We first describe two very different perspectives adopted by researchers on why disgust should affect social judgment. The first is the *pathogen-avoidance* account, which sees the relationship between disgust and judgment as resulting from disgust's evolved function as a pathogen-avoidance mechanism. The second is the *extended disgust* account, which posits that disgust functions much more broadly to address a range of other threats and challenges. We then review the empirical evidence to assess how well it supports each of these perspectives, arguing that there is more support for the pathogen-avoidance account than the extended account. We conclude with some testable empirical predictions that can better distinguish between these two perspectives.

1. Introduction

Over the last 25 years, the emotion of disgust has attracted enormous interest from researchers studying moral and social judgment. This might seem unexpected for an emotion whose primary evolved function is thought to be the avoidance of pathogens and parasites, but many researchers have argued that the disgust response has come to play a much broader role than would be expected given its putative evolutionary function. Specifically, disgust seems to play an important role in a wide variety of social judgments. For instance, disgust has been argued to underlie moral condemnation, particularly of acts involving physical purity (such as violations of social norms regarding food, sexuality, or hygiene) or spiritual purity (such as failures of mental discipline or piety). Individual differences in how readily people experience disgust (i.e., *disgust sensitivity*) have been found to be related to a host of social judgments, including evaluations of groups perceived as sexually deviant, evaluations of specific practices (e.g., abortion, sexual promiscuity), and endorsement of broader ideologies (e.g., social traditionalism and political conservatism). This has led some researchers to argue that disgust may have been co-opted evolutionarily and now functions as a bona fide social/moral emotion that can be elicited by certain social behaviors even if they are entirely absent of any pathogen threats (Rozin & Haidt, 2013).

In recent years, however, several empirical and theoretical critiques of this perspective have emerged. For instance, some of the reported experimental effects of induced disgust on moral judgment have not been reproduced in direct replication attempts (e.g., Ghelfi et al., 2020; Johnson et al., 2016), and a meta-analysis of the effects of disgust inductions on moral judgments reported an average effect size that was statistically indistinguishable from zero after correcting for publication bias (Landy & Goodwin, 2015). In addition, some research has questioned the relationship between individual differences in disgust sensitivity and social judgments, suggesting that a greater tendency to experience disgust might simply be correlated with harsher judgments in general (as might be expected of any negative emotion). For instance, researchers have reported that disgust sensitivity, although correlated with harsher moral judgments, is also correlated with harsher judgments of non-moral violations of social conventions (Chapman & Anderson, 2014), and even with aesthetic judgments (Landy & Piazza, 2019). Against this backdrop of empirical skepticism, researchers have also pointed out that many of the theoretical claims regarding the relationship between disgust and judgment are vague enough that they can be construed in very different ways. For example, the general claim that there is a relationship between disgust and moral judgment can be interpreted to mean that immoral behavior evokes disgust (i.e., disgust as a consequence), or that disgust amplifies moral condemnation (i.e., disgust as an amplifier), or that it moralizes otherwise non-moral behaviors (i.e., disgust as moralizer)—but these claims are often treated interchangeably in the literature (Pizarro, Inbar, & Helion, 2011).

Here, we review the evidence for disgust as a cause of social judgments with an eye toward resolving some of the empirical and theoretical disputes that have arisen over the last 10 years. We focus largely on the evidence for disgust as a *cause*, rather than a *consequence*, of judgments. This is for two reasons: First, there is a recent comprehensive review of disgust as a consequence of perceived moral violations (Giner-Sorolla, Kupfer, & Sabo, 2018). Second, we believe that the more provocative theoretical claim is that some social and moral judgments result from disgust (rather than the reverse). This does not necessarily limit our review to experimental studies. Many correlational studies of disgust sensitivity as an individual difference assume that differences in disgust sensitivity cause differences in some downstream judgment, perhaps because more disgust-sensitive people respond to disgust elicitors more strongly. Moreover, although correlational studies obviously pose challenges for causal inference, it can also be problematic to draw causal inferences from experimental studies for a variety of reasons (e.g., experimental manipulations can affect more than just the variable or process of interest). Accordingly, we review both correlational and experimental studies here as long as they focus on disgust as a cause of judgments, rather than a consequence.

We also limit our review to social judgments, by which we mean moral evaluations of acts and actors, evaluations of social groups, beliefs about what behaviors or practices ought to be promoted or discouraged, and broader beliefs about how society is best organized. This is obviously a broad definition, and our intention was to be as inclusive as possible. In the case of some judgments that seemed on the border between social and non-social (e.g., beliefs about science and technology; see Section 5.2.5) we have erred on the side of inclusion. We have, however, excluded clearly non-social judgments and behaviors such as willingness to pay for consumer goods (e.g., Lerner, Small, & Loewenstein, 2004). Our focus on social judgment is largely driven by the fact that, for many non-social behaviors (such as the avoidance of objects associated with disgust), theoretical predictions of how disgust should influence judgment are straightforward (i.e., the avoidance of the contaminating object). It is less clear how and why an emotion that evolved to protect individuals from the physical threat of pathogens would influence judgments of moral wrongness or evaluations of entire social groups.

Finally, to better organize this very diverse literature, we have categorized the types of judgments putatively influenced by disgust into moral judgments (i.e., judgments about the morality or acceptability of specific acts) and other social judgments (e.g., liking or disliking some social group or practice, social values, and broader political ideologies). Within each of these domains, we separately assess the evidence from experimental studies (where disgust is induced extrinsically to the judgment being made) and correlational studies (where individual differences in disgust sensitivity are correlated with some judgment) and evaluate consistency between them.

Before reviewing the empirical literature, we will first describe two broad theoretical views about the nature and origins of disgust, as we believe that understanding this debate is key to understanding the patterns that have emerged in empirical findings of the last 20 years. We will then explain how disgust is manipulated and measured, before finally reviewing the empirical evidence for disgust as a cause of social judgments.

2. Disgust and social judgment: Two theoretical perspectives

There is a long-running theoretical debate as to why disgust ought to be related to social judgments at all (see Table 1). On one view, which we call the *pathogen-avoidance* perspective, the influence that disgust might have on social judgment is a direct result of its evolved function as a pathogen-avoidance mechanism that mitigates pathogen and parasite threats. On this account, to the extent that, for example, inducing disgust causes increased prejudice toward some social groups, it is the result of disgust activating an evolved pathogen-avoidance mechanism that responds to certain kinds of outgroups that historically posed a greater risk of transmitting contagious diseases. On the second account, which we refer to as the *extended disgust* perspective, disgust has expanded to serve *social* functions (likely on top of

Table 1 Comparing the pathogen-avoidance and extended perspectives on the relationship between disgust and social judgments.

Disgust	Pathogen-avoidance perspective	Extended disgust perspective
Core domain	Disease avoidance	Many social threats and challenges (symbolic or concrete)
Primary elicitors	Pathogen threats	Pathogen threats, reminders of animal nature, moral violations, inappropriate sexual partners
Influence on social judgments	Only when pathogen threats are involved	For many social/moral norm violations
Origins	Pathogen-avoidance adaptations	Preadaptation of (oral) pathogen-avoidance response

its evolved function as a pathogen-avoidance mechanism, although not necessarily). On this perspective, although the original function of disgust may have been to keep us free from physical contamination, it now underlies social judgments that are not even distantly related to pathogen avoidance. So, for example, inducing disgust might cause prejudice toward some outgroups because disgust functions to enforce social group boundaries and hierarchies.

The pathogen-avoidance perspective has its origins in evolutionary psychology (Curtis, de Barra, & Aunger, 2011; Lieberman & Patrick, 2014; Oaten, Stevenson, & Case, 2009), whereas the most prominent extended account of disgust has its origins in social and moral psychology (Haidt, McCauley, & Rozin, 1994; Rozin, Haidt, & McCauley, 1999; Rozin, Haidt, & McCauley, 2008, 2009). Researchers in different areas have sometimes tacitly accepted the premises of one or the other perspective (or some of both) without clearly distinguishing their different premises and empirical implications. Next, we turn to a more detailed description of these two approaches (Table 2).

2.1 Disgust as pathogen avoidance

There is a surprising amount of consensus among emotion researchers that disgust evolved as an adaptation to disease threats. Cross-culturally, there appear to be a set of common disgust elicitors that strongly suggest disgust evolved to mitigate pathogen risks by motivating the avoidance of pathogen-rich stimuli (Curtis et al., 2011; Oaten et al., 2009). These elicitors include body products

Table 2 Summary of reviewed research on relationships between induced disgust or disgust sensitivity and social judgment.

Citation	Primary finding(s)
Effects of induced disgust on moral judgment	
Białek et al. (2021)	Exposure to a noxious odor did not affect moral judgments in two experiments, and self-reported disgust had inconsistent relationships with moral judgments across the two studies
Cameron et al. (2013)	Exposure to disgusting images did not affect moral judgments, except for those chronically (Study 1) or situationally (Study 2) lower in "emotion differentiation," for whom viewing disgusting images caused harsher moral judgments
Eskine et al. (2011)	Tasting a bitter drink caused harsher moral judgments compared to tasting a sweet or neutral drink
Ghelfi et al. (2020)	A large-scale (n = 1137) replication of Eskine et al. (2011) that found no reliable effect of bitter vs. sweet vs. neutral drink on moral judgments
Horberg et al. (2009)	Viewing a disgusting film clip (vs. a sad clip) caused greater condemnation of purity-related moral violations and greater praise of purity-related moral virtues. There was no effect for judgments of non-purity violations/virtues
Johnson et al. (2016)	Recalling and writing about a disgusting experience (vs. recalling and writing about the events of the previous day in Study 1 and no recall task in Study 2) did not cause harsher moral judgments overall. There was also no moderation of the disgust manipulation by individual differences in "private body consciousness"
Jylkkä et al. (2021)	Viewing disgusting images (Study 1) and film clips (Study 2) did not cause harsher moral judgments (vs. neutral images/clips)
Landy and Goodwin (2015)	Meta-analysis of 50 experiments inducing disgust and measuring moral judgments. Overall, there is a small effect of disgust ($d = 0.11$) which is not significantly different from zero ($d = -0.01$) after statistically correcting for publication bias
Sanyal et al. (2021)	Viewing disgusting (vs. frightening or neutral) images caused slightly more negative evaluations of some biotechnologies, but this effect was not significant after correcting for multiple comparisons
Sato and Sugiura (2014)	Writing about a disgusting (vs. neutral) experience made moral judgments more severe only for participants who scored low on the "acting with awareness" subscale of the Five Facet Mindfulness Questionnaire

Schnall et al. (2008)	Exposure to a disgusting odor (vs. no odor; Study 1), sitting at a messy desk (vs. a clean desk; Study 2), writing about a disgusting experience (vs. no writing; Study 3), and watching a disgusting film clip; (vs. sad or neutral clips; Study 4) led to harsher moral judgments. In Study 1, this was true for all participants, in Studies 2–4, it was true only for those dispositionally high in "private body consciousness"
van Dijke et al. (2018)	Two of the studies in this paper were experimental (Studies 2 and 4). In Study 2, imagining and writing about a disgusting situation (vs. a no-task control) did not affect moral judgments overall, but did interact with (manipulated) psychological distance from a moral violation only for purity-related moral judgments, such that the disgust induction caused harsher moral judgments only for psychologically distant purity-related violations. In Study 4, imagining and writing about a disgusting situation (vs. a no-task control) led to harsher purity-related moral judgments (but not harsher non-purity moral judgments), but this was not moderated by psychological distance
van Dillen et al. (2012)	One study in this paper compared induced disgust to a control condition (Study 1). In this study, reading disgusting sentences (vs. control sentences) caused harsher moral judgments of a hypothetical moral violation (keeping a lost wallet). In the disgust condition (but not the control condition), participants who were lower in attentional control as measured by performance on a Stroop task gave harsher moral judgments
Wheatley and Haidt (2005)	A post-hypnotic suggestion to "feel a sickening feeling" when reading a "trigger" word (either "take" or "often") caused harsher moral judgments when scenarios contained the trigger word in two studies

Relationships between disgust sensitivity and moral judgment

Chapman and Anderson (2014)	Two studies showed that individuals dispositionally high in disgust sensitivity rated moral and conventional violations as more wrong than individuals low in disgust sensitivity, even when controlling for social conservatism, trait anger, and trait anxiety
Horberg et al. (2009)	In Study 3, trait disgust (but not trait anger or fear) predicted greater punishment for purity violations, and praise for purity virtues
Jones and Fitness (2008)	In one study, mock jurors higher in disgust sensitivity were more likely to favor conviction of a fictitious defendant. In another study, disgust sensitivity predicted judgments of culpability for crimes, longer prison sentences, and greater perceptions of crime in the community
Karinen and Chapman (2019)	A meta-analysis of six studies showing a positive relationship between disgust sensitivity and condemnation of nonpurity (i.e., harm) transgressions

Continued

Table 2 Summary of reviewed research on relationships between induced disgust or disgust sensitivity and social judgment.—cont'd

Citation	Primary finding(s)
Landy and Piazza (2019)	In four studies, disgust sensitivity was associated with harsher judgments of moral and conventional violations, as well as imprudent actions. Disgust sensitivity was also associated with competence judgments, aesthetic evaluations, and praise for positive moral acts
Wagemans et al. (2018)	In five studies, disgust sensitivity was more strongly correlated with moral condemnation of purity violations than with condemnation of transgressions in other moral domains

Effects of induced disgust on social judgments

Buckels and Trapnell (2013)	Induced disgust (via IAPS pictures) caused relatively stronger implicit associations between minimal outgroups and animals vs. minimal ingroups and humans, compared to induced sadness and neutral control groups
Cunningham et al. (2013)	Disgust induced with odor manipulations led to less positive evaluations of gay men and lesbians on a feeling thermometer
Dasgupta et al. (2009)	In Study 1, anger and disgust (induced via autobiographical recall) caused more positive implicit associations to minimal ingroups vs. outgroups. In Study 2, disgust (induced via autobiographical recall) increased implicit bias against outgroups associated with disgust (e.g., homosexuals), but anger did not. In Study 3, induced anger (but not disgust) increased implicit bias against outgroups associated with anger (e.g., Arabs)
Faulkner et al. (2004)	In two experiments, manipulating disease salience led to less positive attitudes toward foreign (but not familiar) immigrants and to greater endorsement of policies that would favor immigration of familiar vs. foreign people. However, it did not affect ratings of immigrants on many other evaluative attributes
Inbar, Pizarro and Bloom (2012)	Disgust induced with odor manipulation led to less positive evaluations of gay men (but not other social groups) on a feeling thermometer
Ji et al. (2019)	Across four studies, pathogen primes did not cause more negative evaluations of immigrants (although individual differences in pathogen disgust sensitivity were related to these evaluations)
Kiss et al. (2020)	A meta-analysis of 17 studies found a moderate effect of disgust sensitivity on evaluations of gay men, and a large effect of induced disgust on evaluations of gay men

Navarrete and Fessler (2006)	Participants who completed a disgust sensitivity scale as a disgust induction reported greater in-group favoritism (but not out-group derogation)
Shook and Oosterhoff (2020)	In two studies, induced disgust (via reading a disgusting story) did not affect self-reported political ideology

Relationships between disgust sensitivity and social judgments

Aarøe et al. (2017)	In four samples, disgust sensitivity was associated with greater opposition to immigration. In one U.S. sample, this relationship held for Middle Eastern but not European immigrants
Al-Shawaf et al. (2015)	Disgust sensitivity was associated with general food neophobia (i.e., reluctance to consume novel foods)
Billingsley et al. (2018)	Sexual disgust was associated with voting for Donald Trump and supporting the Republican party, but pathogen disgust was not related to these outcomes after controlling for pathogen disgust
Brenner and Inbar (2015)	In two studies in the Netherlands, greater disgust sensitivity was associated with greater anti-immigrant sentiment, sexual conservatism, and voting for a socially conservative party
Clay (2017)	In two studies, disgust sensitivity was associated with more negative attitudes toward vaccines
Clifford and Piston (2017)	Disgust sensitivity was associated with greater support for policies excluding homeless people from everyday life (e.g., banning panhandling)
Clifford and Wendell (2016)	Disgust sensitivity was associated with opposition to genetically engineered food and anti-vaccination beliefs
Crawford et al. (2014)	Disgust sensitivity was associated with more negative evaluations of groups seen as threatening traditional sexual morality, and with more positive evaluations of groups seen as upholding traditional sexual morality
Halstead and Lewis (2020)	Disgust sensitivity was associated with more opposition to GE food, but more *support* of gene editing in humans, both for treatment and enhancement

Continued

Table 2 Summary of reviewed research on relationships between induced disgust or disgust sensitivity and social judgment.—cont'd

Citation	Primary finding(s)
Hodson and Costello (2007)	Interpersonal disgust sensitivity was associated with more negative evaluations of foreigners and low-status social groups as well as higher social dominance orientation and right-wing authoritarianism
Inbar, Pizarro, and Bloom (2012), Inbar, Pizarro, Iyer, and Haidt (2012)	Disgust sensitivity was associated with self-reported conservatism across 121 countries, and was associated (at the state level) with a higher vote share for John McCain over Barack Obama
Inbar, Pizarro, and Bloom (2009)	Disgust sensitivity was associated with self-reported conservatism (Studies 1 and 2) and with more conservative positions on abortion and gay marriage (Study 2)
Inbar, Pizarro, Knobe, and Bloom (2009)	Disgust sensitivity was associated with rating encouraging same-sex couples to kiss in public as more intentional (Study 1), and with more negative implicit evaluations of gay men and lesbians (Study 2)
Ji et al. (2019)	Disgust sensitivity was associated with lower comfort with immigrants specifically from pathogen-rich ecologies, and with lower support for allowing individuals to immigrate (regardless of their origin)
Kahan and Hilgard (2016)	Disgust sensitivity was associated with seeing vaccines and GE food as more risky, but also with higher risk judgments of other hazards (e.g., carjackings and elevator accidents)
Karg et al. (2019)	In four studies, disgust sensitivity was associated with higher scores on the Domain-Specific Risk-Taking (DOSPERT) scale across five different risk domains
Karinen et al. (2019)	Disgust sensitivity was associated with anti-immigrant sentiment when an immigrant was described as not assimilating to US culture, but not when he was described as assimilating
Kempthorne and Terrizzi (2021)	Disgust sensitivity was associated with anti-vaccination attitudes
Kiss et al. (2020)	In a meta-analysis, disgust sensitivity was associated with more negative evaluations of gay men and lesbians (58 effects; average effect size $r = 0.31$)

Lieberman et al. (2012)	Disgust sensitivity was associated with more negative evaluations of obese people for women, but not men
Luz et al. (2019)	In a path model, the direct path between disgust sensitivity and self-reported flu vaccine uptake was positive, but the indirect effect via vaccine attitudes was negative
Olatunji (2008)	Disgust sensitivity was associated with discomfort with interpersonal contact with gay people; this was partially mediated by sexual conservatism and religiosity
Park et al. (2003)	Disgust sensitivity was associated with stronger implicit associations between disability and disease for Asian (but not white) Canadian undergraduates
Park et al. (2007)	Germ aversion (as measured by a subscale of the Perceived Vulnerability to Disease scale) was associated with disliking obese people
Scott et al. (2016)	Disgust sensitivity was associated with greater opposition to genetically engineered food
Shook et al. (2015)	In a latent variable model, the direct path between pathogen avoidance and political conservatism was significantly positive even when accounting for the (positive and significant) indirect path via sexual strategies
Tybur et al. (2010)	In three studies, there was no relationship between disgust sensitivity and self-reported political ideology
Tybur et al. (2015a)	In three studies, restrictive sexual strategies fully mediated the relationship between disgust sensitivity and political conservatism
Tybur et al. (2016)	In 30 countries, disgust sensitivity was associated with higher traditionalism but not with higher social dominance orientation
van Leeuwen et al. (2021)	In 31 countries, disgust sensitivity was associated with greater negativity towards gay men and lesbians, but also to other groups associated with violations of traditional sexual norms
Vanaman and Chapman (2020)	Disgust sensitivity was associated with greater support for policies restricting public bathroom access for transgender people
Wilks et al. (2019)	Disgust sensitivity was associated with opposition to lab-grown meat

and secretions (e.g., feces, urine, pus, blood); contaminated food (food with visible or olfactory indications of decay); and signs of disease (open wounds, boils, sores, coughing and sneezing). The subjective experience of disgust—a sensation of aversion, queasiness, and, in its strongest form, nausea and vomiting—also seems to reflect its evolved function. The facial expression most associated with disgust is a wrinkled nose, squinting eyes, a raising of the upper lip, and in extreme cases the protrusion of the tongue (Ekman & Friesen, 1971; Ekman, Friesen, & Hager, 2002). This facial expression may be functional, as the wrinkling of the nose protects against the entry of pathogens into the mucus membranes of the face (Susskind et al., 2008), and the gag reflex and protrusion of the tongue are mechanisms that serve to expel potential contaminants from the mouth (evidence, perhaps, that disgust has origins as protection from oral contamination and is closely associated with taste; Rozin, Haidt, & McCauley, 1999).[a]

Further evidence that disgust has evolved for pathogen avoidance comes from developmental and comparative research. Avoidance of certain disgust elicitors seems to emerge fairly early in development: 2- to 3-year-old children make disgust expressions at the smell of urine and feces and are reluctant to touch filthy socks (although less so than older children or adults; Stevenson, Oaten, Case, Repacholi, & Wagland, 2010). As children develop and need to make more choices for themselves, the range of disgust elicitors expands. For example, many young children (1.5- to 2-year-olds) will willingly consume imitation dog feces, whole dried fish, and dried grasshoppers, whereas older children refuse these foods (Rozin, Hammer, Oster, Horowitz, & Marmora, 1986).

Some non-human animals also appear to show evolutionary precursors of disgust in their avoidance of pathogens and parasites. Mandrills will avoid grooming individuals who show signs of parasite infestation and will selectively avoid their feces (Poirotte et al., 2017). Cats and mice will likewise avoid conspecifics showing olfactory evidence of disease (Kavaliers & Colwell, 1995). Chimpanzees and bonobos also avoid feces and other body products, particularly feces-contaminated food (Sarabian, Belais, & MacIntosh, 2018).

Researchers taking a pathogen-avoidance perspective on disgust often see it as part of a broader "behavioral immune system," a system of behaviors

---

[a] There is also evidence of a secondary facial expression reliably associated with disgust: a "sick" face, that involves a raised upper lip and a dropped jaw (Yoder, Widen, & Russell, 2016).

hypothesized to have evolved to reduce the risk of exposure to disease (Faulkner, Schaller, Park, & Duncan, 2004; Murray & Schaller, 2016; Park, Faulkner, & Schaller, 2003; Schaller & Duncan, 2007; Schaller & Park, 2011). Some theorists see disgust and the behavioral immune system as the same thing (e.g., Lieberman & Patrick, 2014), but we believe that there are important reasons to distinguish between the two. While disgust is an affective state (it feels like something), behaviors considered part of the behavioral immune system need not entail any such affective state. In non-human animals, for example, behaviors such as avoidance of infected conspecifics, grooming or cleaning, and avoidance of waste products are considered part of the behavioral immune system (Murray & Schaller, 2016), but researchers do not generally think that there is a subjective feeling of disgust that motivates these behaviors in animals. In humans, broad social orientations such as conformity (Murray, Trudeau, & Schaller, 2011) and collectivism (Clay, Terrizzi, & Shook, 2012) have been argued to be influenced by the behavioral immune system. Although some researchers have argued that disgust may facilitate the *development* of these social orientations (Schaller, 2014), no one thinks that (for example) any particular decision to agree with what your neighbors think is motivated by disgust. In addition, research on the behavioral immune system has typically focused on the measurement and manipulation of disease threats, which may or may not induce disgust (e.g., photos of skin lesions may be disgusting, but a passage of text describing the risk of getting ill is not). We view the pathogen-avoidance account of disgust as an approach that is consistent with disgust being part of a larger behavioral immune system, but that focuses on the affective response that is traditionally referred to as disgust.

In sum, the pathogen-avoidance account views disgust as an emotional response whose core domain is avoiding exposure to disease. On this view, while disgust may influence any number of judgments, it is primarily (if not exclusively) elicited by pathogenic threats. As such, it makes a clear set of predictions regarding the role of disgust in social judgment: Disgust should influence social judgments specifically when pathogen threats are involved. So, for example, moral judgments of acts that entail physical pathogenic threats (such as certain sexual acts) would likely to be influenced by disgust, whereas moral judgments of behaviors that do not contain any pathogen threats would not be. This approach stands in contrast to the approach we turn to next, which has dominated work on disgust within moral psychology in the last two decades.

2.2 Extended disgust

The second perspective, which we call the *extended* view of disgust, posits that the nature and function of disgust are much broader. We use the term "extended" to describe this approach because theorists adhering to it do not see the evolved function of disgust as limited to protection against threats of physical contamination, but also as addressing a range of other threats and challenges. These could be symbolic (e.g., coping with death anxiety and sanctioning violations of social or moral "purity"; Rozin et al., 2008; Rozin & Haidt, 2013) or more concrete (e.g., avoiding inappropriate sexual partners and condemning moral violations; Tybur & de Vries, 2013). According to these accounts, disgust has expanded its role in humans through a process of preadaptation, by co-opting the disgust emotion that evolved for pathogen avoidance to serve a completely different function: that of regulating behavior in completely novel (i.e., non–pathogenic) social domains. The most influential example of this perspective is summarized nicely by Rozin and Haidt (2013, p. 367):

> *"On this account, the elicitors of disgust expanded by preadaptation, but the outputs—expressive, physiological, and behavioral—were generally conserved. These included contamination sensitivity and a motivation to cleanse, avoid, or expel the contaminant. The elicitors expanded from a food rejection system related to pathogen avoidance to avoidance of reminders of humans' animal nature, especially death, and then on to some aspects of the moral domain."*

Similarly, the philosopher Dan Kelly has defended this view, which he calls the *Co-opt thesis*, and describes it as such: "[I]n the face of...adaptive pressures, disgust was recruited to perform several novel functions, and became implicated in the psychological systems underlying cognition of social norms and ethnic boundary markers" (Kelly, 2011, p. 118).

Importantly, this view offers a very different set of predictions for how disgust might cause social judgments. If disgust is evoked by reminders of our animal nature, it may underlie prejudice toward social outgroups who are dehumanized by being seen as more animal-like (Haslam, 2006). Likewise, if disgust is evoked not only by physical contamination but also by social disorder and spiritual impurity, disgust might underlie negative reactions to groups seen as spiritually tainted or socially threatening, entirely apart from any pathogen threats they might pose (e.g., Hodson & Costello, 2007). But at its broadest, the expanded view of disgust can be taken to predict that disgust can be evoked by the violation of nearly any social or moral norm.

Those adopting the expanded view generally also adopt the claims of the pathogen-avoidance view but offer a further distinction between "core disgust" and "moral disgust" (e.g., Rozin et al., 2008). Rozin first defined "core disgust" as an emotion of revulsion at the prospect of eating offensive substances (Rozin & Fallon, 1987; from Angyal, 1941), but the terms have come to be used by many researchers to refer to the broader distinction between physical disgust and the "moral" disgust that is proposed to be at work in sociomoral evaluations that do not involve core disgust elicitors. Moral disgust has been described variously as motivating the rejection of "certain classes of violators who are beyond redemption" (Rozin, Haidt, & McCauley, 1999, p. 436) and as responding to contamination of the body and soul (Graham, Haidt, & Nosek, 2009). Importantly, on this account, the set of emotional responses involved in core and moral disgust is hypothesized to be the same (as described above by Rozin & Haidt, 2013). People are thought to react with the same emotion to the smell of feces as they do to a person who has violated a moral rule that contains no physical disgust elicitor (such as violations of fairness in an economic game; Chapman, Kim, Susskind, & Anderson, 2009). As evidence for this two-tiered account of core and moral disgust characteristic of the expanded view, researchers have observed that individuals report feeling disgusted and make characteristic disgust facial responses to non-pathogenic moral violations (e.g., Chapman et al., 2009; Danovitch & Bloom, 2009).[b]

2.2.1 Criticisms of the extended perspective

The claim that disgust has come to be co-opted to be a sociomoral emotion has been questioned by researchers who have designed studies to specifically test this extended account of disgust. For instance, these researchers have argued that if the expanded account of disgust is correct and disgust has evolved to enforce sociomoral norms, one would expect that similar words for "disgust" across languages would encode for the emotional response to sociomoral violations as well as to pathogen threats. This is the case in English—English speakers often report being disgusted at a con artist who preys on the elderly, or on someone who has acted disloyally, for instance

---

[b] A somewhat different extended account of disgust was proposed by Tybur, Lieberman, and Griskevicius (2009), Tybur and de Vries (2013). According to this view, disgust has three separate functional domains: avoiding pathogen threats, avoiding inappropriate sexual partners (i.e., kin or partners with low mate value), and communicating and coordinating moral condemnation. Despite important differences from the account proposed by Rozin and colleagues, this account also proposes that moral violations elicit the same emotion that physical pathogen threats do.

(e.g., Rozin, Haidt, & McCauley, 1999, p. 436). There is also evidence that disgust language is used to describe a response to sociomoral evaluations across languages other than English as well (e.g., French, German, Hebrew; Rozin, Haidt, & McCauley, 1999). However, recent research has shown that there are many other languages for which disgust is used in a much narrower sense (i.e., only as a response to core disgust elicitors), leading researchers to conclude that the term "disgust" in English encodes for two very different kinds of emotional responses: the core disgust that arises from exposure to a pathogen threat, and something more akin to anger or moral disapproval (Gutierrez, Giner-Sorolla, & Vasiljevic, 2012). The term "grossed-out," on the other hand, describes the response to pathogens specifically, and appears to be a better translation of the term disgust across a variety of languages (Kollareth & Russell, 2017). Note that this is a problem not only for the interpretation of people's responses to specific sociomoral norm violations, but also for individual-difference measures such as the Three-Domain Disgust Scale (Tybur et al., 2009) which defines "moral disgust" as how disgusted people say they are by pathogen-free moral violations such as lying and cheating.

Another concern regards the kinds of moral violations the extended account would predict to be associated with disgust. At times, theorists defending the extended disgust account have argued that moral violations that include physical disgust elicitors are not a good test case for sociomoral disgust. For example, Rozin, Haidt, and McCauley (1999) write that "many of the most disgusting sociomoral violations appear to be disgusting because they involve aspects of core or animal-nature disgust (e.g., the sexual molestation of children, or brutal murders that involve mutilation or other body envelope violations)" (p. 436). They contrast these cases with sociomoral violations that have no obvious core disgust content, such as "hypocrisy, racism, betrayal, and disloyalty." However, research on the role of disgust in moral judgment has often focused on moral violations of "purity," that is, "acts that are disgusting or degrading to one's spiritual nature" (Haidt, Koller, & Dias, 1993, p. 614), and many of the purity violations used in these studies clearly include pathogen content (e.g., a man masturbating into a chicken carcass before cooking and eating it; Haidt et al., 1993). The inclusion of such pathogen-relevant content in these violations means their results cannot be taken as support for the extended view.

In fact, in research that has directly tried to test whether moral violations without core disgust elicitors evoke the same emotion that core disgust elicitors do, individuals do not appear to experience the same sort of disgust as they do in response to pathogen threats. For instance, in a cross-cultural study, Kollareth and Russell (2019) created a variety of scenarios that described a moral purity violation or a non-purity moral violation, and which contained either a pathogen elicitor or not. They found that while the term "disgust" was used by both American and Indian participants when reporting responses to purity and non-purity moral violations, the term "grossed-out" (which captures the emotion of core disgust more accurately) was only used in reporting responses to pathogen violations. In addition, ratings of immorality were not reliably related to core disgust, as would be predicted on the extended disgust account. Likewise, Royzman, Atanasov, Landy, Parks, and Gepty (2014) assessed responses to moral violations that involved pathogen threats vs. those that did not and showed that participants were not likely to report being grossed out, gagging, or losing their appetite for moral violations—features that would normally be present in a core disgust reaction. When given the option, people were also more likely to select the term "angry" than "grossed out" in response to non-pathogen moral violations as well as to select an "anger" face rather than a "disgust" face to describe their reactions to non-pathogenic moral violations.

In short, there is now a fair amount of evidence on the linguistic use of the term disgust that does not appear to support the extended view, which holds that the emotional response to moral violations is qualitatively identical to the core disgust response to pathogen threats. Rather, it appears as if, in some languages, the term disgust has simply come to be used in some situations as a metaphorical stand-in for an emotion that is closer to anger.

However, there are other potential sources of evidence that *could* provide support for the extended view, including evidence from the influence of disgust on social judgment. We will be reviewing the empirical literature with an eye toward this evidence. If, for instance, if it is the case that inducing disgust consistently makes people more condemning of (non-pathogenic) sociomoral violations, we would take this as evidence in favor of the extended view and against the more constrained pathogen-avoidance view. Similarly, if it is the case that individuals who are higher in disgust sensitivity tended to be consistently harsher in their judgments of (non-pathogenic) sociomoral violations (but not harsher for non-sociomoral violations), we would also consider this as evidence in favor of the extended view. This is one of the major goals of this review—to evaluate the patterns of empirical findings on the relationship between disgust and social judgment across studies that use a wide variety of methods to investigate this broad question. The next section reviews these methods.

3. The manipulation and measurement of disgust

3.1 Disgust manipulations

Experimental studies of the effects of disgust on judgment typically rely on disgust inductions that are independent from the judgment being measured (i.e., incidental affect manipulations; Loewenstein & Lerner, 2003). By inducing disgust with a stimulus that is independent of the judgment of interest, the effects of the emotion can be understood as a carry-over effect where the disgust aroused by the stimulus is (mis)attributed to the target of judgment (Clore, Gasper, & Garvin, 2001). This means that for the disgust induction to affect unrelated judgments, (1) the induction must evoke disgust; (2) disgust must persist and extend to the (unrelated) judgment task; and (3) participants must be unable to correct for their feelings of disgust when making their judgments.

Disgust inductions usually either directly expose participants to disgusting stimuli or ask participants to imagine or recall disgusting situations. In the direct-exposure category, visual inductions are most common (e.g., in a meta-analysis of effects of induced disgust on moral judgments, 35 of the 73 studies used visual inductions; Landy & Goodwin, 2015). Visual inductions are often short film clips (one popular clip, from the film "Trainspotting," depicts an addict digging through a dirty toilet bowl with his bare hands) or images, often from the International Affective Picture System (Lang, Bradley, & Cuthbert, 2005). Some direct-exposure inductions use other sensory modalities: chemical odorants that smell of feces or decay (e.g., Inbar, Pizarro, & Bloom, 2012), unpleasant tastes (e.g., Eskine, Kacinik, & Prinz, 2011; Ghelfi et al., 2020), or the sounds of vomiting (e.g., Seidel & Prinz, 2013). Some researchers have used multimodal inductions, such as asking participants to sit at a filthy desk to complete the study (Schnall, Haidt, Clore, & Jordan, 2008). For imagined-exposure inductions, participants might be asked to recall and write about a disgusting event they experienced (e.g., Schnall et al., 2008) or they might be asked to picture a novel disgusting experience (e.g., listening to a detailed story describing incest; Ottaviani, Mancini, Petrocchi, Medea, & Couyoumdjian, 2013).

There is also a heterogeneous category of less common disgust inductions. For example, Wheatley and Haidt (2005) selected highly hypnotizable participants, and, during hypnosis, gave them the post-hypnotic suggestion to feel "a brief pang of disgust" when reading an otherwise-innocuous word ("take" or "often") embedded in scenarios describing immoral behavior. Similarly, David and Olatunji (2011) paired disgusting images with an innocuous word ("part") during a training phase, and then embedded that word in scenarios describing immoral behavior. Subliminal priming has also occasionally been used. For example, Ong, Mullette-Gillman, Kwok, and Lim (2014) visually primed participants with a disgust face for 17 ms, preceded and followed by a masking stimulus to ensure that they could not be perceived consciously.

Unfortunately, it is not clear which types of inductions are most effective at creating the kinds of carry-over effects that researchers are usually trying to produce. In their meta-analysis, Landy and Goodwin (2015) found that gustatory and olfactory disgust inductions were more effective at changing moral judgments than other types, but this was based on only eight studies in that category. Elsewhere, Kiss, Morrison, and Morrison (2020) found no significant heterogeneity between different disgust inductions in their effects of attitudes toward gay men and lesbians, but this was based on only six studies. More research is needed to determine what disgust inductions, if any, consistently produce carry-over effects on judgment.

3.2 Measuring individual differences in disgust

There is some debate about the terminology that should be used to describe individual differences in disgust. Most researchers use "disgust sensitivity" and "disgust proneness" interchangeably to refer to individual differences in how frequently and intensely disgust is experienced. Some, however, have argued that this ought to be called "disgust propensity" and that "disgust sensitivity" should be used to refer to how *upsetting* people find the experience of being disgusted (but see Tybur & Karinen, 2018; van Overveld, de Jong, Peters, Cavanagh, & Davey, 2006). Without taking a side in this debate, we here use "disgust sensitivity" in the more common sense, to refer to individual differences in the frequency and intensity of disgust in response to disgust elicitors. For those interested in learning more about popular measures of disgust, there is a recent in-depth review (Tybur & Karinen, 2018).

3.2.1 Self-report measures of disgust sensitivity

Individual differences in disgust sensitivity have typically been measured using self-report scales. The two most common measures are the Disgust Scale-Revised (DS-R; Olatunji et al., 2007), and the Three Domain Disgust Scale (TDDS; Tybur et al., 2009). The DS-R is based on the original

Disgust Scale (Haidt et al., 1994), which used 32 items to measure eight theorized disgust domains: food, animals, body products, hygiene, envelope violations (i.e., blood and gore), death, sex, and magic (contagion based-magical thinking). (Note that these domains were derived from the extended account of disgust described in Section 2.2). Subsequently, the same authors developed the Disgust Scale 2 which reduced the number of domains to four: interpersonal disgust, core disgust, death/body envelope disgust, and sex disgust. This version of the scale was never peer-reviewed and its validity is therefore unknown, but it is used in some research conducted before the Disgust Scale-Revised was published.

The most current, best-validated, and widely-used version of the Disgust Scale is the Disgust Scale-Revised (Olatunji, Williams, et al., 2007). The original Disgust Scale did not perform well psychometrically, showing poor measurement model fit in confirmatory factor analyses and low internal reliability of the subscales ($\alpha s = 0.34$–0.64; Haidt et al., 1994), likely because each subscale consisted of only four items. The DS-R reduced the proposed factor structure to three: core (food, animals, and body products), contamination (germs and hygiene), and animal-reminder (which now only contains death, gore, and blood items). Compared to the original Disgust Scale, the 25-item revised version shows acceptable fit in confirmatory factor analyses and higher reliability of the subscales (Olatunji, Williams, et al., 2007; van Overveld, de Jong, Peters, & Schouten, 2011). It also shows convergent and discriminant validity with related measures including contamination fear, anxiety, and other trait disgust measures such as the Disgust Emotions Scale (DES; Kleinknecht, Kleinknecht, & Thorndike, 1997) and the Disgust Propensity and Sensitivity Scale-Revised (van Overveld et al., 2006).

The 21-item Three Domain Disgust Scale (TDDS; Tybur et al., 2009) also has a three-factor structure, but the factor content is quite different from that of the DS-R. All pathogen-relevant items (which ask about disgust in response to pathogen cues such as dog poop, body odor, or moldy food) compose a single "pathogen disgust" subscale. Two additional subscales assess moral disgust (the extent to which respondents say they are disgusted by non-pathogen-relevant moral transgressions such as lying and cheating) and sexual disgust (the extent to which respondents report disgust at sexual promiscuity, pornography, and oral/anal sex, among other practices). Like the DS-R, the TDDS has been shown to have good psychometric properties, and its three-factor structure fits well in confirmatory factor analyses. Nevertheless, the three subscales may not tap the same underlying emotional experience. Particularly for the moral disgust subscale, responses might also reflect more generic moral disapproval or negative affect, given the multiple meanings of "disgust" in English (Kollareth & Russell, 2017). Likewise, the TDDS sexual disgust subscale may tap sexual restrictiveness in addition to (or instead of) a genuine affective reaction; it correlates highly with other measures of sociosexuality (i.e., willingness to engage in commitment-free sex) and has often been used interchangeably with them (Tybur & Karinen, 2018).

Therefore, when using the TDDS researchers generally use only the pathogen subscale to measure "disgust sensitivity." When using the DS-R, researchers most commonly use the entire scale. We think that this is reasonable. Although the DS-R was derived from the extended disgust account and thus is not exclusively focused on pathogen-threatening stimuli, there are conceptual and empirical reasons to think that both the DS-R and the TDDS pathogen subscale measure sensitivity to pathogen threats. Conceptually, all the TDDS pathogen items and most of the DS-R items ask about pathogenic stimuli: decay, blood and body products, signs of disease, and so on. Empirically, the three DS-R factors are correlated strongly with each other ($rs = 0.66$–0.84; Olatunji, Lohr, Sawchuk, & Tolin, 2007, Olatunji, Williams, et al., 2007), and total DS-R scores are strongly correlated with the TDDS pathogen subscale ($r = 0.65$). In contrast, total DS-R scores correlate much more modestly with the TDDS sexual and moral disgust subscales ($rs = 0.38$ and 0.12 respectively; Tybur, Merriman, Hooper, McDonald, & Navarrete, 2010). Finally, meta-analyses (e.g., Terrizzi, Shook, & McDaniel, 2013) treat the DS-R and TDDS pathogen subscale interchangeably as measures of pathogen disgust. We will follow this practice and assume that the two scales measure roughly the same construct, although we will usually note when researchers use one or the other.

3.2.1.1 Behavioral validation of self-report measures

Disgust sensitivity as assessed by self-report is related, as one would expect, to behavioral avoidance of objects seen as unclean or contaminating. People higher in disgust sensitivity have been found to be more reluctant to touch used combs and floor cookies (Deacon & Olatunji, 2007), sterilized cockroaches and previously-worn fedoras (Rozin, Haidt, McCauley, Dunlop, & Ashmore, 1999), worms and moldy oranges (Olatunji, Lohr, et al., 2007), used tissues (Fan & Olatunji, 2013), and colostomy bags (Reynolds, McCambridge, Bissett, & Consedine, 2014). There is thus consistent evidence that people who say they are more disgust sensitive are more reluctant to touch disgusting items. One caveat is that all these studies used versions of the Disgust Scale. One study (Olatunji et al., 2012) that used the TDDS pathogen subscale found that it was not significantly associated with reluctance to touch a public toilet (although the relationship was directionally consistent).

3.2.2 Physiological measures of disgust sensitivity

Less commonly, researchers have assessed disgust sensitivity by measuring physiological reactivity to disgusting stimuli. Smith, Oxley, Hibbing, Alford, and Hibbing (2011), for example, measured skin conductance as participants viewed three disgusting images and computed the change from baseline skin conductance as an index of physiological reactivity. Aarøe, Petersen, and Arceneaux (2017) measured skin conductance as participants viewed six disgusting images and computed physiological reactivity as the average of the skin conductance from 1 to 15 s after stimulus onset across the six images. However, there seems to be mixed evidence for the relationship between physiological reactivity and self-reported disgust sensitivity. Smith et al. (2011) found that skin conductance was not correlated significantly with self-reported disgust sensitivity as measured by the DS-R, but Olatunji et al. (2012) found that skin conductance response when viewing five disgusting images was correlated with TDDS Pathogen disgust ($r = 0.34$; note that in this case skin conductance scores were adjusted for skin conductance at baseline).

We believe that these measures are promising but should be interpreted cautiously given the limited evidence of their validity and the fact that they have been computed in different ways by different research teams (see Flake & Fried, 2020).

3.3 Comparing induced disgust and disgust sensitivity

It is appealing to think that studies that induce disgust and those that measure disgust sensitivity are testing the same underlying process. That is, researchers may assume that by inducing disgust (vs. not) one can randomly assign participants to be more like people who are higher in disgust sensitivity (and are chronically more strongly and frequently disgusted). This logic is appealing, and in some cases it is surely reasonable. However, in other cases it may not be. As an analogy, imagine a "chronic thirst scale" that asks people to report how frequently and strongly they experience thirst. On some outcomes (e.g., current desire for a glass of water) one would expect people who score high on this scale to be like people who have been assigned to drink nothing for 6 h. However, this is not necessarily true for all outcomes associated with chronic thirst. For example, the chronically thirsty might support greater public drinking fountain availability, believe that retail stores should be legally required to offer shoppers water, support political parties who advocate for more public investment in water infrastructure, and so on. It is not obvious that someone who is only temporarily thirsty would shift their beliefs in this direction, because the relationship between *chronic* thirst and beliefs is the result of a longer and less direct causal chain established over time, and perhaps now supported by any number of related factual beliefs and moral commitments. As Hatemi et al. (2013, p. 281) put it, dispositional differences in emotion can "exert influence throughout one's life, including downstream preferences, and alter how one selects into and experiences specific environments." A very similar argument is made by Schaller (2014), who argues that disgust may lead to the adoption of broad social beliefs (such as a dislike of non-conformity) which are then activated and expressed without a subjective feeling of disgust.

The process comparability between induced disgust and disgust sensitivity might therefore depend on whether the dependent variable is more like the desire for a glass of water or more like support for societal thirst-reduction initiatives. This is partly a theoretical question, but there are also helpful empirical indicators. If induced disgust and disgust sensitivity generally show the same pattern of relationships with dependent variables, this should increase our confidence that the underlying processes are the same. If they do not show the same pattern of relationships, that should undermine our confidence. In the following sections, we examine the relationship between induced disgust and disgust sensitivity on the one hand, and moral judgments (Section 4) or social judgments (Section 5) on the other. We begin with the relationship between disgust and moral judgments.

4. Disgust and moral judgments

"Moral judgment" is notoriously a fuzzy category. In their review of moral disgust, Chapman and Anderson (2013) write that "there is as yet no consensus as to how morality should be defined" (p. 301). It can be challenging to cleanly distinguish moral from social judgments. Because morality is often about the regulation of behavior in others, many moral judgments are inherently social. In addition, there is a great deal of debate about whether the domain of morality is in any sense unified, with some researchers arguing that psychologists and philosophers have forced very different kinds of judgments into a general "moral" bucket with little justification (Parkinson et al., 2011).

Fortunately, for the purposes of this review we do not need to arrive at a definitive answer as to the difference between moral judgments and other social attitudes. Our goal is rather to organize the literature to reflect the way that researchers have most commonly divided up the conceptual territory. As such, when we discuss moral judgments, we mean expressions of (dis)approbation toward an individual or their action because of the perceived violation of a normative standard (i.e., a belief about how people ought to act). When we refer to social (and political) judgments we mean beliefs about social groups, what behaviors ought to be socially encouraged or discouraged, and how society is best organized. Of course, these categories are blurry around the edges. For example, a religious traditionalist who believes that homosexuality is sinful would likely view gay people as a group more negatively. This would also likely entail harsher moral judgments of a specific individual who has same-sex relationships, although in this case those moral judgments would be downstream of the broader belief about the sinfulness of homosexuality. Luckily, the distinction is generally less fuzzy in practice than in theory. Research on disgust and moral judgment tends to ask about moral transgressions that are not linked to any larger group membership, such as lying, cheating, or unusual sex. In contrast, research on disgust and social attitudes tends to ask about evaluations of groups, or support for specific laws and policies.

4.1 Effects of induced disgust on moral judgment

Research on the effects of induced disgust on moral judgment only began fairly recently, but it has expanded rapidly following several influential early studies. In one especially well-known set of studies (Wheatley & Haidt, 2005), highly hypnotizable participants were given post-hypnotic suggestions to feel disgusted in response to specific "trigger" words. Participants judged moral transgressions (e.g., a politician condemning corruption while secretly taking bribes) as more immoral when they were described in scenarios containing the trigger words, vs. in scenarios that contained neutral words (Wheatley & Haidt, 2005). Subsequent studies found that more commonplace disgust elicitors also led to harsher moral judgments. Participants who completed questionnaires next to a smelly trash can or at a messy desk rated practices ranging from consensual sex between first cousins to resume falsification as more immoral (e.g., Schnall et al., 2008), and participants who tasted a bitter drink subsequently rendered harsher moral judgments (on the same scenarios used by Wheatley & Haidt, 2005) compared to those who tasted a sweet drink or unflavored water (Eskine et al., 2011).

However, as this literature grew, so did the inconsistencies between findings. First, there has been little consistency as to whether the effects of disgust are specific to certain kinds of moral violations concerning "purity," or whether they influence judgments of moral violations more generally. Purity violations are defined as behaviors that are "disgusting or degrading to one's spiritual nature" (Haidt et al., 1993, p. 614) but have generally been operationalized as lack of physical cleanliness or non-traditional sexual practices. Some researchers have found effects of induced disgust on moral judgments only for violations of purity. For example, Horberg, Oveis, Keltner, and Cohen (2009) found that induced disgust increased condemnation of purity violations such as "keeping an untidy and dirty living space" and "being sexually promiscuous." Others, however, have found that disgust causes greater condemnation of all moral violations, whether they are purity-relevant or not (e.g., Schnall et al., 2008). One study even found that disgust led participants to condemn morally neutral behavior (a student council member choosing topics for discussion; Wheatley & Haidt, 2005).

A second inconsistency concerns the moderation of experimental disgust manipulations by individual differences. Some studies (e.g., Schnall et al., 2008, Studies 2 and 3) have found significant effects of disgust on moral judgment only for those who are chronically more focused on their internal physical states (i.e., people high in "private body consciousness," Miller, Murphy, & Buss, 1981). Others have found unmoderated main effects of disgust on moral judgment (Eskine et al., 2011; Horberg et al., 2009; Schnall et al., 2008, Study 1; Wheatley & Haidt, 2005). Taken together, these inconsistencies raise the concern that some of the initial findings of relationships between disgust and moral judgment might be false positives, especially because these studies are from an era in social psychology where sample sizes were small, p-hacking and selective publication were common, and direct replications were not (Nelson, Simmons, & Simonsohn, 2018). These concerns were a large part of the motivation for Landy and Goodwin (2015) to conduct a meta-analysis of the studies looking at the effects of induced disgust on moral judgment. Although they found a small aggregate effect of disgust on moral judgment ($d = 0.11$), it was not statistically distinguishable from zero when correcting for publication bias ($d = -0.01$). Even using the uncorrected effect size estimate, the studies in their analysis would have been dramatically underpowered, as 80% power to detect $d = 0.11$ in a two-group between-subjects design requires a total sample size of nearly 2600.

These conclusions have been contested (Schnall, Haidt, Clore, & Jordan, 2015) on the grounds that the effects of disgust on moral judgment might be moderated by other individual differences such as attentional control (van Dillen, van der Wal, & van den Bos, 2012), emotional differentiation (Cameron, Payne, & Doris, 2013), or mindfulness (Sato & Sugiura, 2014). However, research in the last few years has largely borne out the pessimistic case. As it has become easier to publish non-significant results, more researchers have reported finding null relationships between disgust and moral condemnation (Białek, Muda, Fugelsang, & Friedman, 2021; Jylkkä, Härkönen, & Hyönä, 2021; Sanyal, McAuliffe, & Curry, 2021). Furthermore, two large replication attempts of early and influential studies have failed to replicate the original results. The first was a multi-site direct replication of the finding reported in Eskine et al. (2011) that tasting a bitter liquid caused people to make harsher moral judgments. This replication attempt (Ghelfi et al., 2020) found a negligible effect of taste on moral judgments, despite having a much larger sample size ($N = 1137$) than the original ($N = 57$). Bayesian analyses showed that the observed effects were most consistent with the null hypothesis of no relationship between taste and moral judgments.

Another team (Johnson et al., 2016) attempted to replicate the finding that recalling a disgusting experience caused people high in private body consciousness (PBC) to make harsher moral judgments (Schnall et al., 2008, Study 3). Two large studies (combined $N = 1412$) found no significant main effects of disgust on moral judgments and no significant moderation by PBC. Again, Bayesian analyses showed that the observed effects were strongly consistent with the null hypothesis.

At the same time, new studies have been published proposing new moderators (e.g., psychological distance; van Dijke, van Houwelingen, De Cremer, & De Schutter, 2018). However, pre-registered replications of these moderations are lacking. Furthermore, a set of findings showing effects of disgust *only* when moderated by different individual differences is internally contradictory if each study finds the effect of disgust on judgments is only significant when moderated by a variable that the other studies did not measure. Thus, a literature showing many different moderated effects but few or no main effects should *reduce* our confidence rather than increase it. Without pre-registration, moderation allows analytic flexibility (if the unmoderated main effect is significant but the moderator is not, report the main effect; if the main effect is not significant but the moderation is, report the moderation), raising the likelihood of false-positive results (Gelman & Loken, 2014).

Our overall assessment of this literature is that, despite several initial positive results, there is not enough evidence to conclude that inducing incidental disgust leads to any change in moral judgments. Our conclusion is based on the meta-analysis of studies conducted up to 2014 (Landy & Goodwin, 2015), the negative results (including high-powered replication studies) published since then, and the lack of convincing pre-registered studies showing main effects of disgust or moderation by individual differences. This is obviously not to say that such evidence might not emerge in the future, only that it is currently lacking. We next turn to the research examining relationships between individual differences in disgust sensitivity and moral judgment.

4.2 Relationships between disgust sensitivity and moral judgment

There are a number of studies showing a relationship between greater disgust sensitivity and harsher moral judgments. As we will see, these findings are consistent enough that it is safe to conclude that there is some relationship between disgust sensitivity and judgments. The open question is how general this relationship is. Is disgust sensitivity associated preferentially with only certain kinds of moral judgments, with moral judgments overall, or even more broadly with non-moral interpersonal judgments? Overall, it seems that the evidence points to a broader relationship between disgust sensitivity and judgments than was initially believed.

In one set of studies, Jones and Fitness (2008) created ad hoc disgust scales by selecting items (8 items in Study 2; 13 items in Study 3) from the 32-item Disgust Scale ($\alpha s = 0.34-0.64$; Haidt et al., 1994). They found that participants scoring higher in disgust sensitivity were more likely to find a hypothetical defendant guilty in a mock-jury paradigm (Study 2) and were more likely to rate defendants described in four vignettes as more likely to be guilty (Study 3). Higher disgust sensitivity was also associated with rating four separate criminals (a con man, murderer, drunk driver, and drug trafficker) as more evil (Study 3). Overall, these studies lend moderate support for a link between disgust and moral judgment. The dependent variables are not all purely about moral judgment (i.e., a judgment of guilt can be the result of beliefs about facts rather than the moral badness of a behavior), but "evilness" can straightforwardly be interpreted as a judgment of bad moral character. The interpretability of these findings is somewhat lessened by the use of unvalidated ad hoc scales, but overall these studies provide some evidence of a link between disgust sensitivity and harsher moral judgment.

While the studies in Jones and Fitness (2008) suggest a broad relationship between disgust sensitivity and moral judgment, there is evidence pointing to a more specific relationship between disgust sensitivity and moral purity violations (behaviors that are "disgusting or degrading to one's spiritual nature"; Haidt et al., 1993, p. 614). Horberg et al. (2009) created an ad hoc three-item disgust sensitivity measure that asked participants to rate how frequently they felt "grossed out," "disgusted," and "repulsed." They found that scores on this measure were significantly associated with how much participants thought purity-violating behaviors should be punished (behaviors included "being sexually promiscuous," "buying music with sexually explicit lyrics" and "purposefully wearing unmatched clothing"), even when controlling for self-rated political ideology. Disgust sensitivity was not, however, associated with participants' desire to punish harm- or injustice-relevant behaviors (e.g., "kicking a dog that is blocking a doorway," "expecting to be given special rights or treatment"). However, there are some features that complicate the ability to interpret these results—the ad hoc disgust scale, the small sample (N = 88), and the oddness of asking liberal U.C. Berkeley undergraduates how much buying explicit music and wearing unmatched clothes should be punished.

More recent findings have called into question the idea that disgust sensitivity is exclusively associated with the evaluation of moral violations having to do with purity. Karinen and Chapman (2019) meta-analyzed six studies (total N = 1082) in which participants were asked to rate the moral wrongness of instances of mild-to-moderate harm (e.g., "a female student slaps another girl in the face"). No purity violations were included, nor did any scenarios contain physical disgust elicitors. Nonetheless, wrongness ratings were significantly associated (standardized $b = 0.22$) with disgust sensitivity as measured by the Disgust Scale-Revised.

In fact, it appears that disgust sensitivity is even associated with condemnation of non-moral behaviors. Chapman and Anderson (2014) examined the relationship between disgust sensitivity (as measured by the original Disgust Scale in Study 1 and the Disgust Scale-Revised in Study 2), wrongness ratings of moral violations (e.g., "a female student slaps another girl in the face"), and wrongness ratings of violations of social convention (e.g., "a student wears a t-shirt and jeans to school instead of the school uniform"). In both studies they found that higher disgust sensitivity was associated with greater wrongness ratings for both moral *and* conventional transgressions. In Study 2, these relationships held when controlling for social conservatism using a previously validated issue-based scale (Henningham, 1996).

While these findings are consistent with the claim that there is a relationship between disgust sensitivity and moral judgment, they call into question the claim that this relationship is specific to moral judgment (or to moral judgment only in the purity domain). Rather, they suggest that it may be a result of a broader relationship between disgust sensitivity and social judgment in general.

A further challenge to the claim that there is a special relationship between disgust sensitivity and moral judgment comes from a recent set of studies (Landy & Piazza, 2019), which found a relationship between disgust sensitivity (as measured by the TDDS pathogen subscale) and immorality ratings for not only moral and conventional violations, but also for imprudent behaviors (e.g., running in the rain). The authors also found that disgust sensitivity (this time measured with the DS-R) was also associated with lower judgments of the intelligence and competence of individuals engaging in imprudent behaviors (Study 2), and with more extreme judgments (positive or negative) of faces, landscapes, (painted) portraits, and abstract art.

There is, however, also strong evidence for *some* specificity in the relationship between disgust sensitivity and moral judgment. In five studies (one of which was pre-registered), Wagemans, Brandt, and Zeelenberg (2018) found that disgust sensitivity as measured by the DS-R was correlated more strongly with moral condemnations of violations of purity than with other moral violations (across the five studies, disgust sensitivity correlated with condemnation of purity violations at $r=0.40$ on average; correlations for the other violations ranged from rs of 0.07 to 0.27 depending on the domain). These studies drew moral violations from previously-validated vignettes based on Moral Foundations Theory (Clifford, Iyengar, Cabeza, & Sinnott-Armstrong, 2015), which operationalize moral purity as violations of sexual and food taboos. These items (e.g., "You see a story about a remote tribe eating the flesh of their deceased members"; "You see a woman having intimate relations with recently deceased loved one") clearly are descriptions of pathogen threats rather than conceptual or symbolic purity violations (e.g., disrespecting a sacred object).

What is to be made of the seeming inconsistencies across these studies, which all purport to have a similar aim (that of testing the relationship between moral judgment and disgust sensitivity)? Overall, the research with the strongest indicators of reliability (i.e., use of validated scales, large sample sizes, pre-registration) shows a relationship such that individuals higher in disgust sensitivity tend to make harsher moral judgments, but also tend to make harsher judgments of non-moral behaviors, suggesting that at least part of the DS-moral judgment relationship is due to a broader relationship between disgust sensitivity (or perhaps emotional reactivity in general; Landy & Piazza, 2019) and negativity in social judgment. However, it is interesting to note that the strongest evidence for specificity—that is, for selective affinity between disgust sensitivity and certain moral judgments (Wagemans et al., 2018)—comes from studies that have investigated judgments regarding behaviors that were specifically in the pathogen-threatening domains of food and sex.

4.3 Disgust and moral judgment: Summary

In Section 3.3 we asked whether induced disgust and disgust sensitivity might be similarly related to judgment. In the case of moral judgment, it seems that they are not. The evidence for *any* relationship between induced disgust and moral judgment is currently weak. As mentioned above, both a recent meta-analysis (Landy & Goodwin, 2015) and recent large-scale replication attempts (Ghelfi et al., 2020; Johnson et al., 2016) suggest that the effects of induced disgust on moral judgment are trivially small or null. The findings regarding the relationship between disgust sensitivity and moral judgment look quite different. Here, there are broad and replicable relationships, but they may not be specific to moral judgments per se (Landy & Piazza, 2019). The strongest evidence for specificity is for moral judgments of scenarios with clear pathogen content (e.g., cannibalism and necrophilia; Wagemans et al., 2018).

The simplest explanation for this pattern of results is that disgust does not directly affect moral judgment in the way that theorists initially claimed (Haidt, 2001). That is, there is currently not convincing evidence that people rely on an in-the-moment feeling of disgust to determine whether a behavior is immoral, or, if it is immoral, to determine how much it ought to be condemned. This does not mean that there is not a class of moral violations that may have *originally* become moralized because of their associations with pathogen risk (such as sexual and food taboos). But it does not appear that morally condemning these violations (or any others) results from feeling disgust in the moment.

The broad relationship between disgust sensitivity and moral, conventional, prudential, and aesthetic judgments is most plausibly due to a relationship between general negative emotional reactivity and disgust sensitivity (for example, Olatunji, Lohr, et al., 2007, Olatunji, Williams, et al., 2007 found the DS-R to correlate with state anxiety at $r=0.23$; Tybur & De Vries, 2013 found a correlation of $r=0.18$ between the TDDS pathogen subscale and HEXACO PI-R emotionality). Importantly, these results do not appear to offer support for the extended perspective on disgust, which would predict (1) a clear effect of induced disgust on moral judgment (or on moral judgments for non-pathogenic purity violations); and (2) a specific relationship between disgust sensitivity and moral judgment (or a more specific relationship between disgust sensitivity and moral judgments for non-pathogenic purity violations). There is greater support for the pathogen-avoidance account of disgust, which (definitionally) holds that more pathogen-sensitive people will react more strongly to pathogen threats—and would thus predict a specific relationship between disgust sensitivity and harsher judgments of behaviors with pathogen content (Wagemans et al., 2018).

5. Disgust and social judgments

We now turn to the literature on disgust's influence on social judgments, by which we mean beliefs about and evaluations of social groups, beliefs about what behaviors ought to be socially encouraged or discouraged, and broader beliefs about how society is best organized. We begin with the research examining the effects of induced disgust on social judgments.

5.1 Effects of induced disgust on social judgments
5.1.1 Sexual minorities
There is consistent evidence that many people report feeling disgusted by gay men and lesbians (Haidt, Rozin, McCauley, & Imada, 1997; Herek, 1993), and it is a common tactic for anti-gay rhetoric to appeal to themes of disgust, especially regarding sexual acts (Nussbaum, 2010). There is reason to believe that recruiting disgust to amplify anti-gay sentiment may be an effective strategy, given that the sexual domain is one in which pathogen concerns are active (Tybur, Inbar, Güler, & Molho, 2015a). This would also suggest that inducing disgust should be a particularly effective strategy for amplifying negativity toward *any* group of individuals who engage in non-traditional sexual acts (as defined by the majority), not just gay men and lesbians. However, most of the research looking at the relationship between disgust and evaluations of sexual minorities has focused on evaluations of gay men and lesbians.

For example, Dasgupta, Desteno, Williams, and Hunsinger (2009) found that, compared to a control group who viewed neutral images, participants who viewed disgusting images (e.g., a cockroach on a piece of food) subsequently showed more negative implicit evaluations of gay people relative to straight people on the Implicit Association Test (IAT; Greenwald, McGhee, & Schwartz, 1998). Similarly, Inbar, Pizarro, and Bloom (2012), Inbar, Pizarro, Iyer, and Haidt (2012) found that participants who were exposed to a noxious odor rated gay men less positively relative to straight men (vs. those who were not exposed to the odor), and Cunningham, Forestell, and Dickter (2013) found that participants who were exposed to a noxious odor (a chemical mixture described as "body odor") were less positive toward gay men less on both an explicit and an implicit measure.

These findings seem to represent consistent evidence for the claim that induced disgust leads to more negative evaluations of gay men and lesbians. However, the size of the effects across these studies varies widely. In their recent review of studies looking at the effects of induced disgust on attitudes toward gay people, Kiss et al. (2020) found six studies total with effect sizes ranging from $d = 0.16$ to 0.61.[c] It should be noted, however, that the total number of studies is small and that the authors might not have been able to locate all unpublished studies, despite making efforts to do so.

The evidence suggests that inducing disgust does not have a similar effect on evaluations of all social groups. To the extent that researchers have included other social groups in their studies, the effects of disgust appear to be specific to evaluations of gay men and lesbians. For instance, both Inbar, Pizarro, and Bloom (2012), Inbar, Pizarro, Iyer, and Haidt (2012), and Cunningham et al. (2013) included evaluations of other social groups in their studies (such as African-Americans and the elderly), and found that disgust manipulations did not affect those ratings. Similarly, Dasgupta et al. (2009) found that induced disgust affected implicit evaluations of gay men, but not implicit evaluations of African-Americans (whereas induced anger had the reverse effect).

5.1.2 Minimal outgroups

Evidence for the effects of induced disgust on evaluations of other social groups is generally less conclusive. As mentioned above, some studies looking at the effects of induced disgust on judgments about sexual minorities have used other social groups as controls and have failed to find any

---

[c] This range omits two very large effect sizes ($ds = 2.38$ and 3.76) that appear to be the result of a calculation error in Kiss et al. (2020). The average meta-analytic effect size when excluding those studies is $d = 0.44$.

effects on these judgments. There are, however, two experiments suggesting that inducing disgust might make people more negative toward outgroups in general. Buckels and Trapnell (2013) randomly assigned participants to view a slideshow of images that were either disgusting (e.g., a dirty toilet), sad (e.g., a young boy crying), or neutral (e.g., a lamp). All participants then completed a minimal-groups task in which they were informed that they were "overestimators" and that another group of participants (the outgroup) were "underestimators." In a subsequent IAT, participants who had seen the disgusting images showed stronger associations between ingroup members and "human" words (e.g., person, humanity, people) and outgroup members and "animal" words (e.g., pet, mongrel, critter) relative to the other two groups (i.e., those who had seen sad or neutral images). The authors used these findings to argue that inducing disgust caused outgroup dehumanization (although they acknowledged that because the IAT measures relative associations, part or all of the effect might be due to stronger associations between ingroup and human in the disgust condition).

Similary, Dasgupta et al. (2009, Study 1) induced disgust or anger with an autobiographical recall task. All participants then completed a minimal-groups task in which they were (falsely) told that they were "underestimators" or "overestimators." Compared to a control group who recalled a neutral event, both induced-disgust and induced-anger participants showed more positive implicit associations to the ingroup relative to the outgroup.

5.1.3 Immigrants and foreigners

Some researchers have argued that, given its role in motivating the avoidance of pathogens, disgust ought to play a role in motivating the avoidance of immigrants and foreigners. On this account, foreign (i.e., unfamiliar) groups inherently pose a greater disease threat, because they may carry pathogens from unfamiliar ecologies (Fincher & Thornhill, 2012; Thornhill, Fincher, & Aran, 2009). Disgust therefore ought to make people more negative toward these groups, just as it does toward sexual minorities. Consistent with this account, anti-immigrant rhetoric sometimes explicitly mentions threats of disease or likens immigrants to disease-carrying animals (Savage, 2007). However, although the assumption that non-local pathogens are more dangerous seems plausible, it has been contested by some researchers on the grounds that most pathogens are locally adapted and thus are *less* virulent to hosts not from the local ecology (de Barra & Curtis, 2012), and that pre-modern humans did not encounter others from radically different ecologies (van Leeuwen & Petersen, 2018).

While there is some experimental evidence for a link between disgust and anti-immigrant sentiment, the findings across studies are inconsistent. In one study, Navarrete and Fessler (2006) asked participants from the United States to provide ratings of (ostensibly) American and foreign essay writers (who wrote pro- and anti- US essays, respectively), either before or after they completed the DS-R. They found that participants who completed the DS-R before providing ratings rated the American writer more positively (and the foreign writer non-significantly more negatively), compared to participants who provided their ratings first and the DS-R second. The authors argued that in this study the DS-R served as a disgust induction, as it describes a variety of disgust elicitors (although they did not report a manipulation check). Similarly, Faulkner et al. (2004, Study 5), found that after viewing an informational slideshow about germs (vs. non-disgusting common hazards) Canadian participants were more supportive of allowing a familiar foreign group (Scots) to immigrate to Canada and less supportive of allowing an unfamiliar foreign group (Nigerians) to immigrate. There were, however, no significant effects of the manipulation for 18 other items pertaining to the two groups, including whether participants thought they would bring health problems or criminal problems into Canada, and ratings of the groups on attributes including "sanitary," "filthy," "hygienic," "clean," "dirty," "likeable," "hostile," and "trustworthy." A second study using the same manipulation (Study 6), found no effects on any ratings of Taiwanese people (familiar group) or Mongolians (unfamiliar group). Finally, Ji, Tybur, and van Vugt (2019) found no significant effects of induced disgust on anti-immigrant sentiment across four studies (total $N = 1849$), even though manipulation checks showed that the manipulations successfully induced disgust.

5.1.4 Induced disgust and social judgments: Interim conclusions

Overall, there is not consistent evidence that induced disgust causes greater negativity toward social groups other than sexual minorities. There are not many published studies on other groups, and the studies that do exist have shown mixed results or have assessed behaviors that are several steps removed from liking or disliking real social groups (e.g., implicit associations to minimal in- and outgroups). The strongest evidence is for a link between induced disgust and evaluations of gay people—and in several of these studies, researchers found that the effects of disgust were specific to gay people and did *not* extend to other social groups. As sexual behavior is clearly pathogen-relevant (Tybur et al., 2015a), whereas other social groups are less clearly pathogen-relevant, this pattern of results is most consistent with the pathogen-avoidance account of disgust (which would obviously predict the strongest relationship between disgust and evaluations of clearly pathogen-relevant groups). It is less consistent with extended accounts of disgust, which would predict a relationship between disgust and social groups defined much more broadly (e.g., Hodson & Costello, 2007). We next turn to the literature linking individual differences in disgust sensitivity to social judgments.

5.2 Relationships between disgust sensitivity and social judgments

5.2.1 Overall political ideology

A substantial body of research has linked disgust sensitivity (generally assessed using the Disgust Scale-Revised or the pathogen subscale of the Three Domain Disgust Scale) with an individual's overall political ideology (i.e., their description of themselves as liberal or conservative, or their political party identification). A relationship between disgust sensitivity and conservative/liberal self-placement was first documented by Inbar, Pizarro, and Bloom (2009), who found that disgust sensitivity—as measured by an unpublished short form of the Disgust Scale in Study 1 and by the 32-item Disgust Scale 2 in Study 2—was correlated with participants' rating of themselves as liberal vs. conservative on a single item in Study 1, and with a composite measure that asked participants to rate themselves as "liberal," "Democrat," "conservative" and "Republican" (on separate items) in Study 2. Tybur et al. (2010), however, reported a failure to replicate the relationship between pathogen disgust sensitivity and self-reported political orientation in a US undergraduate sample using both the DS-R and the TDDS. This led Inbar, Pizarro, and Bloom (2012), Inbar, Pizarro, Iyer, and Haidt (2012) to attempt to replicate their original finding from Inbar, Pizarro, and Bloom (2009) using a larger sample of about 25,000 US respondents and 5000 international respondents. In both the US and the international sample, they found the predicted relationship between disgust sensitivity (as measured by the DS-R) and ideology, with more disgust sensitive respondents rating themselves as more conservative on average. In the US sample, the correlation between disgust sensitivity and self-reported overall ideology was $r = 0.17$; effect sizes in the international sample were somewhat larger ($rs = 0.22$—0.33). In addition, the relationship between disgust sensitivity and ideology held when controlling for demographics including gender, age, education, and religiosity, as well as the Big Five personality traits (openness, conscientiousness, agreeableness, extraversion, and neuroticism). For the subset of participants who separately reported their political orientation in social, economic, and foreign-policy domains, the relationship with disgust sensitivity was stronger for social conservatism ($r = 0.20$) than for economic and foreign-policy conservatism ($rs = 0.09$ and 0.15, respectively). The larger effect size estimates for social conservatism are consistent with the findings reported in a meta-analysis that examined the relationship between measures of disgust sensitivity and social conservatism specifically. Depending on the meta-analytic model used, these effect size estimates ranged from $r = 0.23$ to $r = 0.31$ (Terrizzi et al., 2013).

There is thus consistent evidence across a wide set of studies for a moderately-sized relationship between disgust sensitivity and political ideology in the US and elsewhere, with individuals higher in disgust sensitivity showing the largest correlation with social conservatism (rather than conservatism regarding economic or foreign policy). Why does this relationship exist? For some theorists who hold an extended view of disgust, there is a broad compatibility between disgust as an emotion of rejection and contamination and support for intergroup hierarchies, derogation of groups and individuals seen as inferior, and a dislike of socially "deviant" groups that are seen as violating social norms and values (see Hodson & Costello, 2007). On this account, because all these ideological orientations are constituents of conservative ideology (Jost, Glaser, Kruglanski, & Sulloway, 2003), there is an emergent overall relationship between disgust sensitivity and ideology.

The pathogen-avoidance account of disgust sees the relationship between disgust sensitivity and ideology as more specific. On this account, many traditional norms in domains including food, sex, and hygiene likely evolved culturally to mitigate pathogen risks (e.g., favoring pathogen-mitigating methods of food preparation and storage, sexual restrictiveness, and specific purification and cleansing practices; Murray & Schaller, 2012; Schaller & Murray, 2008). Because food, sex, and body products are core disgust elicitors, those who are more disgust-sensitive should be more attracted to these traditional norms and values, which are often conceived of explicitly as helping individuals avoid contamination (Shweder, Much, Mahapatra, & Park, 1997). Therefore, on this account, the overall relationship between disgust sensitivity and political ideology (for example, self-description as liberal or conservative) is simply a downstream consequence of greater social traditionalism among the more disgust-sensitive.

To test one part of this explanatory account, Tybur et al. (2016) examined the relationship between disgust sensitivity (as measured by the TDDS pathogen subscale), traditionalism as measured by the six-item traditionalism subscale of the Authoritarianism-Conservatism-Traditionalism scale; (Duckitt, Bizumic, Krauss, & Heled, 2010) and social dominance orientation (SDO). Social dominance orientation is thought of as encompassing a competitive view of intergroup relations, a preference for group hierarchies, and prejudice toward other racial or ethnic groups (Pratto, Sidanius, Stallworth, & Malle, 1994). Across 30 nations, disgust sensitivity was correlated with greater traditionalism ($r=0.10$) but not higher SDO ($r=-0.06$). This pattern of results supports the narrower pathogen-avoidance account over broader extended accounts, which would plausibly have predicted a relationship between disgust sensitivity and both SDO and traditionalism. The pathogen-avoidance account would not, however, predict a relationship between SDO and disgust sensitivity.

Research on the relationship between disgust sensitivity and other intergroup judgments is also informative for distinguishing between these two accounts of disgust. We start with the research on the relationship between disgust and evaluations of sexual minorities.

5.2.2 Sexual minorities

As with induced disgust (see Section 5.1), some of the strongest evidence for a relationship between disgust sensitivity and social judgments is for evaluations of sexual minorities (particularly gay men and lesbians, but also bisexuals and transgender men and women). A relationship between attitudes toward sexual minorities and scores on the original Disgust Scale (Haidt et al., 1994) is somewhat tautological because that scale includes an item about homosexuality ("I think homosexual activities are immoral"). However, the Disgust Scale-Revised dropped all the sex items, and the pathogen subscale of the Three-Domain Disgust Scale does not contain any items concerning sex. As such, the relationships we describe here are not simply the result of content overlap between measures.

In one study, Olatunji (2008) found a correlation of $r=0.30$ between disgust sensitivity (as measured by the DS-R) and the Index of Attitudes Toward Homosexuals (Hudson & Ricketts, 1980), a 25-item measure assessing discomfort with interpersonal contact with gay people. Subsequent research found a similar relationship between disgust sensitivity and implicit evaluations: Inbar, Pizarro, and Bloom (2009), Inbar, Pizarro, Knobe, and Bloom (2009) found that greater disgust sensitivity (as measured by the Disgust

Scale 2 with the eight sex items removed) was correlated with scores on the gay-straight IAT (Nosek, Banaji, & Greenwald, 2006). The more disgust sensitive participants were, the more they had negative associations with gay men and lesbians as compared to heterosexuals (standardized $b = -0.30$).

In a recent meta-analysis, Kiss et al. (2020) analyzed 58 tests of the relationship between disgust sensitivity and evaluations of gay men and lesbians and estimated an overall effect size of $r = 0.31$. This aggregate effect size estimate is the average of studies using a heterogeneous mix of measures of disgust sensitivity so its magnitude may not be particularly interpretable, but overall it seems safe to say that disgust sensitivity is reliably related to negativity toward gay men and lesbians. There is evidence that this relationship extends to other sexual minorities including transgender men and women. For instance, Vanaman and Chapman (2020) found that greater disgust sensitivity (as measured by the pathogen subscale of the TDDS) was associated with greater support for requiring people to use public bathrooms that match their birth sex (that is, requiring transgender men and women to use bathrooms that do not match their felt/expressed gender identity).

Indeed, disgust sensitivity seems to be broadly related to evaluations of groups associated with sex. Crawford, Inbar, and Maloney (2014) found that disgust sensitivity (as measured by the DS-R) was associated not only with more negative ratings of "gay men and lesbians" and "pro-gay activists," but also with more negative ratings of other groups that participants rated as highly threatening to "traditional moral values about sex," (i.e., "young people who are sexually active," "pro-choice activists," and "feminists"). In addition, the degree to which social groups were rated as threatening or upholding sexual morality predicted the relationship between disgust sensitivity and evaluations of that group. Specifically, individuals higher in disgust sensitivity liked sexual morality-threatening groups less, but liked sexual morality-upholding groups (e.g., pro-life activists) more. This suggests that rather than resulting from specific features of certain groups (e.g., gay men, transgender women) the relationship between disgust sensitivity and evaluations of sexual minorities results from their association with sex in general, and thus their perceived threat to traditional sexual morality. While this study looked at participants from the US, there is evidence for a similar pattern worldwide in an unpublished analysis (van Leeuwen et al., 2021) of data originally collected by Tybur et al. (2016) from respondents in 31 countries. This dataset contained feeling thermometer ratings of gay men, lesbians, and three groups associated with sexual promiscuity and/or threats to traditional morality: atheists, prostitutes, and sexually promiscuous people. Across the

31 countries, disgust sensitivity (as measured by the TDDS pathogen sub-scale) was modestly but reliably associated with more negative ratings of gay men (male participants: $r=0.10$, female participants: $r=0.08$), and lesbians (male participants: $r=0.07$, female participants: $r=0.11$). However, the relationship between disgust sensitivity and ratings of other sexual morality-threatening groups was of a similar magnitude ($rs=0.07$–0.15). Decomposition analyses (Kohler, Karlson, & Holm, 2011) showed that once the relationship between disgust sensitivity and other groups was accounted for, the remaining relationship between disgust sensitivity and ratings of gay men/lesbians did not significantly differ from zero. Again, this suggests that the relationship between disgust sensitivity and evaluations of gay men and lesbians is due to their association with non-normative sex, and thus their perceived threat to traditional sexual morality.

Some researchers have even proposed that sexual conservatism might be the key component of traditionalism that explains the relationship between disgust sensitivity and political ideology (Tybur et al., 2015a). This is a more specific version of the pathogen–avoidance account outlined above, in that *sexual* traditionalism specifically is hypothesized to be the mediating variable between disgust sensitivity and overall ideology. In the research that first documented a relationship between disgust sensitivity and ideology, Inbar, Pizarro, and Bloom (2009) also asked participants about a range of political issues and found that disgust sensitivity correlated with more conservative positions on gay marriage and abortion but not with positions on other issues including affirmative action, gun control, or the death penalty (disgust sensitivity did correlate significantly with greater support for tax cuts, but given the other evidence we discuss this may be a false-positive). When controlling for the indirect path between disgust sensitivity, gay marriage and abortion attitudes, and overall ideology, the direct path between disgust sensitivity and overall ideology was no longer significant. The same idea was tested more systematically by Tybur et al. (2015a), who examined sexual restrictiveness (i.e., a preference for monogamy and aversion to sexual promiscuity). Using a path modeling approach and a variety of measures of disgust sensitivity, sexual restrictiveness, and conservatism, the authors found that once the indirect path between disgust sensitivity and conserva-tism via sexual restrictiveness was accounted for, the direct path from disgust sensitivity to conservatism did not differ significantly from zero. In other words, the relationship between disgust sensitivity and general conservatism was entirely accounted for by the relationship both had with sexually con-servative beliefs. Likewise, Billingsley, Lieberman, and Tybur (2018) found that sexual conservatism statistically explained the relationship between disgust sensitivity and voting intentions in the 2016 US Presidential election.

However, in our view, it is too early to close the book on a broader relationship between disgust sensitivity and political beliefs. Shook, Terrizzi, Clay, and Oosterhoff (2015) reported a study in which the direct path between disgust sensitivity and conservatism remained significant when controlling for sexual conservatism (but see Tybur, Inbar, Güler, & Molho, 2015b). Furthermore, researchers have reported associations between disgust sensitivity and evaluations of other groups that seem unlikely to result from shared variance with sexual conservatism.

5.2.3 Immigrants and foreigners

There is consistent evidence linking disgust sensitivity and anti–immigrant sentiment, although effect sizes are generally small to moderate. For example, in a sample of Canadian undergraduates, Hodson and Costello (2007) found that disgust sensitivity (as measured by the Disgust Scale 2) was related to more anti-immigrant beliefs ($r=0.25$) as measured by a version of the Modern Racism Scale (McConahay, Hardee, & Batts, 1981) adapted to measure anti-immigrant beliefs (e.g., "Immigrants are getting too demanding in their push for equal rights"). In a sample of American adults, Crawford et al. (2014) found that disgust sensitivity (as measured by the DS-R) was related to more negative feeling thermometer ratings of illegal immigrants ($r=-0.19$). Using a community sample in the Netherlands, Brenner and Inbar (2015) found that disgust sensitivity (as measured by the DS-R) was related ($r=0.15$) to more anti-immigrant sentiment using a 10-item set of statements related to immigration and Islam (immigrants to the Netherlands tend to be Muslim); e.g., "Immigrants are a threat to our society," "There are too many immigrants in the Netherlands, so sometimes I feel strange in my own country."

Though they are consistent, the generalizability of these results is hampered by the fact that researchers relied on non-representative convenience samples. Aarøe et al. (2017) addressed this shortcoming in two studies using nationally-representative samples in Denmark and the United States. In these studies, scores on the five-item contamination subscale of the DS-R (Studies 1 and 2) were associated with anti-immigrant sentiment as assessed by a six-item scale created by the researchers (for example "Immigrants improve American [Danish] society by bringing in new ideas and cultures"). In a separate (non-representative) sample of Americans, this relationship held when measuring disgust sensitivity using the pathogen subscale of the TDDS. These relationships were small (bs 0.10–0.13) but reliable even when controlling for demographic variables including age, gender, income, and race, as well as the "Big Five" personality factors. Finally, the authors also included a study using a Danish undergraduate sample in which disgust sensitivity was measured physiologically by measuring skin conductance response (SCR) when viewing six disgusting images. Higher SCR when viewing these images was again associated ($r = 0.24$) with higher anti-immigrant sentiment on the same six-item scale.

In a set of studies that directly tested the role of sexual conservatism, Ji et al. (2019) found that disgust sensitivity (as measured by the TDDS pathogen subscale) was associated with lower comfort with immigrants and greater likelihood of opposing their settling in the participant's community. These relationships largely held when controlling for sexual conservatism as measured by the TDDS sexual disgust subscale, particularly for immigrants said to come from Liberia (which at the time was suffering from an Ebola outbreak).

There are at least two reasons that disgust sensitivity might be related to discomfort with immigration and immigrants. The first is the hypothesis we outlined in Section 5.1.3, that foreign (i.e., unfamiliar) groups heuristically pose a greater disease threat, because they may carry pathogens from unfamiliar ecologies (Fincher & Thornhill, 2012; Thornhill et al., 2009), and that more disgust-sensitive people are reacting to this perceived threat. Another possibility is that immigrants are seen as threatening traditional norms and values (i.e., if they are seen as not assimilating and instead adhering to a different set of cultural norms), which are supported more by people who are more disgust sensitive. Indeed, questionnaire items such as "Immigrants improve society by bringing in new ideas and cultures" or "Immigrants are a threat to our society" (Aarøe et al., 2017; Brenner & Inbar, 2015) explicitly focus on threats to traditional norms and values. This reasoning would suggest that disgust sensitivity should predict negativity toward immigrants that do not assimilate to the local culture more so than toward those who do.

This question was tested by Karinen, Molho, Kupfer, and Tybur (2019), who examined whether the relationship between disgust sensitivity and anti-immigrant sentiment is moderated by whether immigrants are seen as assimilating to the host country's culture. In this study, the authors presented American participants with a scenario describing an immigrant who either assimilated to local (American) norms or did not. In addition, he was also described as having either high or low contact with native-born

Americans. Disgust sensitivity (as measured by the TDDS pathogen scale) was related to greater anti-immigrant sentiment when the immigrant was described as not assimilating but was unrelated to anti-immigrant sentiment when he was described as assimilating. Level of contact (high or low) between the immigrant and native-born Americans did not moderate the relationship between disgust sensitivity and anti-immigrant sentiment. These results suggest that when disgust sensitivity is related to negativity toward immigrants and immigration, it is because immigrants are seen as threatening traditional norms by not assimilating, and not because immigrants are seen as intrinsic pathogen risks (if this were the case, more contact ought to have resulted in a stronger relationship between disgust sensitivity and anti-immigrant sentiment).

Some apparently contradictory findings were reported by Aarøe et al. (2017), who found that describing a hypothetical immigrant as willing to learn English and committed to democracy and equal rights (vs. not) did not moderate the relationship between disgust sensitivity and negativity toward him. Karinen et al. (2019) suggest that the specific norms to which immigrants are assimilating may be important, and that the relationship between disgust sensitivity and anti-immigrant sentiment may be moderated specifically by perceived adherence to disgust-relevant social norms of food, sex, and hygiene.

5.2.4 Disease-associated groups

There is some research showing relationships between disgust and evaluations of social groups that appear visually non-normative, such as disabled or obese people. The theoretical explanation for this relationship is that unusual physical appearance is an intuitive disease cue, even if people know explicitly that most unusual-looking people (e.g., burn victims or amputees) pose no communicable disease risk. As disgust sensitive people are more attuned to pathogen cues, they may respond negatively to these cues even if they are invalid. Along these lines, Park et al. (2003) reported that among East Asian undergraduate participants in Canada, those who were more disgust sensitive (as measured by a version of the original Disgust Scale that underwent unspecified revisions) had stronger implicit associations between disability and disease. However, this result did not replicate in participants of European descent, and the decision to split the sample between East Asian and European participants may have been post-hoc.

In another set of studies, Lieberman, Tybur, and Latner (2012) found that disgust sensitivity as measured by the TDDS pathogen scale was associated with more negative evaluations of obese people, but only among women. Similarly, Park, Schaller, and Crandall (2007) found a relationship between negative evaluations of obese people and germ aversion, a subscale of the Perceived Vulnerability to Disease scale that taps concerns about contamination and contagion (e.g., "I'm comfortable sharing a water bottle with a friend;" "I don't like to write with a pencil someone else obviously chewed on."). The authors did not say whether they tested for moderation by participant gender (the sample was 73%—209/286—women).

Our assessment is that although they are suggestive, at present these results do not provide strong evidence for the hypothesized relationship between disgust sensitivity and evaluations of disabled or obese people. The strongest evidence for a relationship between disgust sensitivity and evaluations of disease-associated groups is for the homeless, who are often associated with pathogen cues (Clifford & Piston, 2017). In a national sample of 861 Americans surveyed as part of the 2014 Cooperative Congressional Election Study, the researchers found that more disgust-sensitive respondents were more supportive of policies excluding the homeless from public life (i.e., bans on panhandling and sleeping in public), especially when they had read a paragraph about homeless people that emphasized disgust cues (e.g., public urination and littering). There was, however, no relationship between disgust sensitivity and support for policies *helping* the homeless (e.g., subsidized housing). Thus, the relationship with disgust sensitivity was specific to policies that would minimize contact with homeless individuals.

5.2.5 Technology evaluations

Disgust sensitivity has also been linked to evaluations of technologies that do not involve clear pathogen threats. Several investigations have found that disgust sensitivity is associated with greater opposition to GE (genetically engineered) food (Clifford & Wendell, 2016; Scott, Inbar, & Rozin, 2016). This could be because people higher in disgust sensitivity dislike genetic engineering in general (perhaps because, consistent with the extended disgust account, it is seen as impure or unnatural). It is also possible that they are simply more wary of novel foods (this is consistent with both the extended and pathogen-avoidance accounts, as one of disgust's primary functions is to discourage oral incorporation of harmful substances). It seems that the balance of the evidence favors the latter possibility. First, higher disgust sensitivity is also associated with greater wariness of other novel foods, such as lab-grown meat (Wilks, Phillips, Fielding, & Hornsey, 2019), as well as with general food neophobia (Al-Shawaf, Lewis, Alley, & Buss, 2015). Second, Halstead and Lewis (2020) found that greater disgust sensitivity (as measured by the DS-R and the TDDS Pathogen subscale) was associated with opposition to GE food but with greater *support* of genetic engineering of humans, either to cure diseases or to enhance attributes such as strength or attractiveness. This was the case even when controlling for general risk aversion and neuroticism, along with individual differences including age, gender, race, education, and political ideology. Both these findings are more consistent with a link between disgust sensitivity and wariness of novel foods than with a more general dislike of genetic engineering by the disgust sensitive.

There is also some mixed evidence on the relationship between disgust sensitivity and vaccine opposition. Clifford and Wendell (2016) found an association between disgust sensitivity (as measured by the TDDS pathogen subscale) and anti-vaccine beliefs, although this was somewhat inconsistent across studies (the relationship between disgust sensitivity and vaccine negativity was significant in two studies but non-significant in another). Subsequently, other researchers have found small-to-moderate relationships between vaccine negativity or hesitancy and disgust sensitivity (Clay, 2017; Kempthorne & Terrizzi, 2021; Reuben, Aitken, Freedman, & Einstein, 2020), although some have also reported null relationships (Halstead & Lewis, 2020).

One possibility is that more disgust sensitive people may be more attuned to risks in general. As vaccine hesitancy is often assessed by asking about risks (e.g., risks of autism or long-term health consequences; Clifford & Wendell, 2016), a relationship between disgust sensitivity and vaccine hesitancy may be a specific example of this more general tendency. In an unpublished paper, Kahan and Hilgard (2016) asked people how much risk they thought each of a number of hazards posed to "human health, safety, or prosperity." They found that disgust sensitivity (as measured by the TDDS pathogen subscale) was associated with greater risk perceptions for vaccines ($r = 0.17$) but also with greater risk perceptions for many other hazards including carjackings ($r = 0.31$), mass shootings ($r = 0.30$) and elevator crashes in high-rise buildings ($r = 0.28$). Likewise, Karg, Wiener-Blotner, and Schnall (2019) found that disgust sensitivity (as measured by the DS-R) was associated with a broad measure of risk perceptions (Weber, Blais, & Betz, 2002) in multiple studies (rs ranged from 0.30 to 0.40).

If more disgust-sensitive people are more attuned to risk in general, they should also be more attuned to disease risks (which one would expect to be associated with more *positive* evaluations of vaccines). Some evidence consistent with this idea is reported by Luz, Brown, and Struchiner (2019), who used a path model to examine the relationships between disgust sensitivity, vaccine evaluations, and flu vaccine uptake (this was a self-reported binary variable: whether the respondent got a flu vaccine in the 2016 flu season). There was a significant indirect negative path between disgust sensitivity (as measured by the DS-R), vaccine evaluations, and flu vaccine uptake: Disgust sensitivity predicted greater vaccine negativity, which in turn predicted a lower probability of having received the flu vaccine. However, once this indirect path was modeled, the remaining *direct* path between disgust and vaccination was positive—that is, more disgust sensitive people were more likely to have been vaccinated.

5.3 Disgust and social judgments: Summary

Overall, there is consistent evidence for a relationship between disgust sensitivity and overall political ideology, evaluations of sexual minorities, and evaluations of immigrants and foreigners. The evidence when it comes to *induced* disgust is narrower. There is reasonably strong evidence that induced disgust causes more negative evaluations of gay men and lesbians, but the evidence when it comes to other groups is much less convincing. The simplest explanation for this is that induced disgust will shift judgments when the target of judgment evokes core disgust elicitors. Sex intrinsically entails core disgust elicitors, including close contact with others and exposure to their body products (Tybur et al., 2015a), and therefore judgments of groups defined by their sexual practices are affected by induced disgust. In terms of the analogy to chronic vs. induced thirst we proposed in Section 3.3, evaluations of sexual minorities are like desire for a glass of water: they are affected both by temporary changes in state and by trait differences. Other social beliefs and values—for example, overall political ideology or anti-immigrant sentiment—seem to be more like support for social thirst-reduction initiatives: they are the product of a longer and less direct causal chain, which means that they will not be affected by disgust inductions even though they are associated with individual differences in disgust sensitivity. Indeed, a recent registered report failed to find any effect of induced disgust on self-reported political ideology in two studies (Shook & Oosterhoff, 2020).

The most plausible intervening variable between disgust sensitivity and broader ideological commitments is social traditionalism—support for traditional cultural values. Most plausibly, the relationship between disgust and social traditionalism is the result of the pathogen-mitigating functions of some traditional values, which leads more disgust-sensitive individuals to find them more appealing. Adhering to traditional values, then, has downstream consequences including greater general conservatism, dislike of immigrant groups seen as threatening traditional cultural norms, and dislike of groups seen as threatening sexual morality.

If this view of the distinction between induced disgust and disgust sensitivity is correct, it has some interesting implications. The first is that induced disgust ought to shift attitudes toward other groups associated with primary disgust elicitors. For example, if a particular immigrant group is described as eating unusual foods or as violating cultural standards of hygiene, disgust inductions should lead to more negative evaluations of that group. The second implication is that the relationship between disgust sensitivity and evaluations of sexual minorities is over-determined, in that it is a product of both the association of sexual minorities with primary disgust elicitors and the fact that they are seen as threatening sexual morality. In theory, these two paths could be distinguished empirically by varying these characteristics experimentally, or by measuring and modeling each proposed path.

Finally, how are we to interpret the association between disgust sensitivity and evaluations of specific technologies? We believe that the most straightforward explanation is that more disgust-sensitive people are more reluctant to consume novel foods (consistent with avoidance of dangerous foods as one of the core functions of disgust) and are also generally more risk-averse. This suggests that researchers should be wary of over-interpreting a relationship between disgust sensitivity and evaluations of a specific technology, as this could simply be a consequence of greater general risk aversion. Ideally, researchers would control for risk aversion when studying the relationship between disgust and science and technology evaluations. Another possibility is to compare the size of the relationship between disgust sensitivity and evaluations of the focal technology to evaluations of technologies that theoretically should not be related to disgust.

 ## 6. Pathogen-avoidance and extended perspectives on disgust: Assessing the evidence

We began by describing two perspectives on how disgust might affect social judgments. The *pathogen-avoidance* perspective sees disgust as an emotion that motivates the avoidance of objects or entities that are likely to pose a risk of physical contamination. The *extended* perspective sees disgust as having expanded its functional domain beyond this, to many intra- and inter-personal challenges: mate selection, coordinating moral condemnation, managing one's fear of death, maintaining intergroup boundaries and hierarchies, guarding spiritual and physical purity, and more. We first described some preliminary evidence for and against these two perspectives, but one of the major goals of this chapter was to evaluate the empirical findings on the relationship between disgust and social judgment to see which perspective better fit the data.

We think that although the data are not perfectly consistent in their support of one perspective over the other, the general pattern is quite clear: The predictions generated by the extended account of disgust are the least likely to have robust support. This is particularly true of the many studies in moral psychology that aimed to show that incidental manipulations of disgust (that were independent of the judgment being made by participants) played a role in social and moral judgments regarding actions, individuals, or groups of people that were not also, to some degree, relevant to the pathogen-avoidance goals of core disgust. So, for example, there is simply not strong evidence that inducing disgust causes changes in moral judgment writ large (i.e., for moral violations that do not involve core pathogenic disgust elicitors). One explanation is that it is simply hard to induce disgust in a way that carries over to subsequent unrelated judgments. After all, this requires that the disgust induction is strong enough to change emotional states but also that participants misattribute some of their felt disgust to the focal judgment. However, there *do* seem to be reliable effects of induced disgust on evaluations of gay men and lesbians.

We do not want to overstate the case. There are relatively few studies showing this relationship, none of which were pre-registered, so it may be that later replication attempts do not find the same results. And there is not consistent evidence that induced disgust shifts evaluations of immigrants and foreigners, who some theorists have argued are associated with pathogen risks. However, for now it seems the strongest evidence for any effects of induced disgust is for evaluations of groups strongly associated with sex, which is inherently a pathogen-risky endeavor. This general pattern is also true of the correlational evidence. There is no strong evidence that disgust sensitivity is associated with greater moral harshness above and beyond its association with generally harsher judgments of even non-moral actions. There *is* convincing evidence that disgust sensitivity is associated specifically with moral violations with pathogen content, and—consistent with the experimental evidence—with evaluations of sexual minorities.

There is an ambiguity in some extended-disgust theorizing on the relationship between disgust and moral judgment that can make the evidence for it seem stronger than it is. One possible way to interpret the extended-disgust perspective is that it predicts that disgust ought to influence moral judgments in general; that disgust has expanded to become an emotion that serves to regulate the behavior of others in what is best described as the moral domain. We believe there is insufficient evidence for this claim—there are many cases in which disgust (either as an experimental induction or as an individual difference) seems to play no special role in moral judgment. Perhaps the more defensible interpretation of the expanded view is that disgust is only relevant for moral judgments of actions that violate some notion of "purity." However, we believe that this approach is problematic for different reasons. The term "purity" has been used in so many ways that it is hard to pin down exactly what this approach ought to predict. Researchers have at various times described as purity violations: sibling incest; sexual promiscuity; other weird sexual acts with no apparently direct harm (sex with chickens or with teddy bears on grandma's bed); keeping an untidy and dirty living space; purposefully wearing unmatched clothing; consuming drugs, alcohol, tobacco, meat, or foods deemed to be "unclean"; smearing cat feces on your arm; drinking spoiled milk; giving a homeless person a moldy sandwich; and a widow wearing jewelry too soon after her husband's death. Many acts that are described as purity violations do in fact involve pathogen threats (e.g., sexual behaviors, eating bad/rotten food, touching feces); others do not (e.g., wearing unmatched clothing or prematurely wearing jewelry); still others may or may not (e.g., keeping an untidy living space or recreational drug use).

One consequence of labeling such a heterogeneous set of behaviors as purity violations is that researchers sometimes include pathogen-relevant violations within a set of broader non-pathogen-relevant violations, and collapse these into the category of "purity violations." If disgust is shown to influence these, they can point to their findings as evidence that disgust has come to shape not just the avoidance of pathogens, but also responses to violations of moral purity. This, in turn, helps bolster the expanded view that disgust has become co-opted in the service of sociomoral regulation. More research is needed here, but to the extent that researchers have systematically separated pathogen-relevant content from these moral scenarios, it has become evident that disgust does not play the role predicted by the expanded account (e.g., Kollareth & Russell, 2019; Oaten et al., 2018).

The relationship between disgust sensitivity and a variety of social beliefs and values—beliefs about immigration, social traditionalism, and overall political ideology, among others—might seem to support the extended-disgust perspective. The choice between a right-wing vs. left-wing political party, for example, usually does not involve pathogen threats. However, there is convincing evidence that these attitudes and ideologies are down-stream of reactions to pathogen threats, and that social traditionalism—which seems to be the intervening variable between disgust sensitivity and a broad range of attitudes—can be a cultural adaptation to pathogen threats in the environment (see Schaller, 2014). So, like the research on purity violations, this research is less supportive of the extended-disgust perspective than it might at first seem.

A general challenge for the extended-disgust perspective is discriminant validity. Because the extended-disgust perspective predicts broad relation-ships between disgust and judgment, researchers must be careful to establish both that relationships exist where they should, but also that they don't where they should not. We have reviewed several cases in which not doing this would have made the evidence for the extended-disgust perspective look stronger than it is. For example, greater disgust sensitivity is associated with harsher judgments of many kinds of moral violations, which seemingly supports the extended-disgust perspective, but it is also associated just as strongly with harsher judgments of non-moral stimuli (Landy & Piazza, 2019). Likewise, disgust sensitivity is associated with greater perceived risks of vaccination, but also greater perceived risks associated with many other hazards including carjackings and elevator accidents (Kahan & Hilgard, 2016). This is just as much a concern with experimental studies as correla-tional ones. Induced disgust does not seem to reliably affect moral judg-ment, but if replicable effects were to be found, researchers would need to ensure that they were the result of disgust specifically, rather than of neg-ative affect. The same problem applies to judgments of social groups (where some researchers have in fact contrasted disgust with other negative emo-tions, see Dasgupta et al., 2009), or, indeed, to any other social judgment.

Conversely, an advantage of the pathogen-avoidance account is its spec-ificity; it not only seems to be able to provide a satisfactory explanation for the observed effects of disgust on judgment, but also of the *absence* of reliable effects for some targets. Indeed, the pathogen-avoidance perspective makes a clear set of predictions regarding what sorts of judgments ought to be influenced by disgust. For instance:

1. Groups that are either defined by acts that pose pathogen risks, or groups for which pathogen-risky behaviors are made salient in a study, should be

judged more harshly by individuals who are disgusted or individuals who are high in disgust sensitivity.

2. Social or moral norm violations that involve pathogen risks should be judged more negatively (and perhaps as more immoral, if they are viewed as a moral violation to begin with) by more disgust-sensitive people, and by people who are induced to feel temporarily disgusted. Induced and dispositional disgust should likewise correlate with seeing individuals who engage in pathogenic norm violations as worse people, with greater blame, and (within the constraints of societal norms) with harsher punishment of these individuals.

3. "Purity" violations as a category should not be responsive to dispositional or induced disgust, unless, again, those violations contain some element of pathogen risk. The use of these terms, however, sometimes includes acts that do not involve pathogenic risks of any kind (such as some violations of honor). For violations of these acts, we should see disgust play a much smaller role (if any) in influencing evaluations.

4. More disgust-sensitive people, and those who are temporarily disgusted, ought to object more to social practices or policies that are heuristically associated with pathogen risks. One example is drinking purified wastewater, which does draw greater objections from the disgust-sensitive (Rozin, Haddad, Nemeroff, & Slovic, 2015). There are many practices, from fecal transplants to eating horse meat, that we would expect to be similarly affected.

5. Disgust sensitivity and induced disgust should diverge in their effects when the judgment in question does not directly concern pathogen threats but is instead the result of a longer causal chain—for example, when disgust sensitivity is associated with political ideology via social traditionalism. In these cases, we would expect no effect of induced disgust (which is what the evidence generally shows). In terms of the analogy we proposed earlier, making people thirsty should not increase support for a political party that, among other things, supports more public drinking fountains.

We emphasize that these are just hypotheses (although some do have some evidence for them). We propose them not because we think that they are all necessarily true, but because they seem to be the sort of tests that would be most informative in further adjudicating between the different perspectives on disgust.

6.1 Conclusion

We have described two very different perspectives on disgust that posit very different explanations for its role in social judgments. In our view, the evidence currently supports the pathogen-avoidance account over the extended-disgust alternative, but the question is best settled by future research explicitly designed to differentiate the two perspectives.

References

Aarøe, L., Petersen, M. B., & Arceneaux, K. (2017). The behavioral immune system shapes political intuitions: Why and how individual differences in disgust sensitivity underlie opposition to immigration. *The American Political Science Review, 111*, 277–294.

Al-Shawaf, L., Lewis, D. M. G., Alley, T. R., & Buss, D. M. (2015). Mating strategy, disgust, and food neophobia. *Appetite, 85*, 30–35.

Angyal, A. (1941). Disgust and related aversions. *Journal of Abnormal and Social Psychology, 36*, 393–412.

Białek, M., Muda, R., Fugelsang, J., & Friedman, O. (2021). Disgust and moral judgment: Distinguishing between elicitors and feelings matters. *Social Psychological and Personality Science, 12*, 304–313.

Billingsley, J., Lieberman, D., & Tybur, J. M. (2018). Sexual disgust trumps pathogen disgust in predicting voter behavior during the 2016 U.S. presidential election. *Evolutionary Psychology, 16*, 1474704918764170.

Brenner, C. J., & Inbar, Y. (2015). Disgust sensitivity predicts political ideology and policy attitudes in the Netherlands: Disgust sensitivity predicts Dutch politics. *European Journal of Social Psychology, 45*, 27–38.

Buckels, E. E., & Trapnell, P. D. (2013). Disgust facilitates outgroup dehumanization. *Group Processes & Intergroup Relations, 16*, 771–780.

Cameron, C. D., Payne, B. K., & Doris, J. M. (2013). Morality in high definition: Emotion differentiation calibrates the influence of incidental disgust on moral judgments. *Journal of Experimental Social Psychology, 49*, 719–725.

Chapman, H. A., & Anderson, A. K. (2013). Things rank and gross in nature: A review and synthesis of moral disgust. *Psychological Bulletin, 139*, 300–327.

Chapman, H. A., & Anderson, A. K. (2014). Trait physical disgust is related to moral judgments outside of the purity domain. *Emotion, 14*, 341–348.

Chapman, H. A., Kim, D. A., Susskind, J. M., & Anderson, A. K. (2009). In bad taste: Evidence for the oral origins of moral disgust. *Science, 323*, 1222–1226.

Clay, R. (2017). The behavioral immune system and attitudes about vaccines: Contamination aversion predicts more negative vaccine attitudes. *Social Psychological and Personality Science, 8*, 162–172.

Clay, R., Terrizzi, J. A., Jr., & Shook, N. J. (2012). Individual differences in the behavioral immune system and the emergence of cultural systems. *Social Psychology, 43*, 174–184.

Clifford, S., Iyengar, V., Cabeza, R., & Sinnott-Armstrong, W. (2015). Moral foundations vignettes: A standardized stimulus database of scenarios based on moral foundations theory. *Behavior Research Methods, 47*, 1178–1198.

Clifford, S., & Piston, S. (2017). Explaining public support for counterproductive homelessness policy: The role of disgust. *Political Behavior, 39*, 503–525.

Clifford, S., & Wendell, D. G. (2016). How disgust influences health purity attitudes. *Political Behavior, 38*, 155–178.

Clore, G. L., Gasper, K., & Garvin, E. (2001). Affect as information. In J. P. Forgas (Ed.), *Handbook of affect and social cognition* (pp. 121–144). Lawrence Erlbaum Associates Publishers.

Crawford, J. T., Inbar, Y., & Maloney, V. (2014). Disgust sensitivity selectively predicts attitudes toward groups that threaten (or uphold) traditional sexual morality. *Personality and Individual Differences, 70*, 218–223.

Cunningham, E., Forestell, C. A., & Dickter, C. L. (2013). Induced disgust affects implicit and explicit responses toward gay men and lesbians. *European Journal of Social Psychology, 43*, 362–369.

Curtis, V., de Barra, M., & Aunger, R. (2011). Disgust as an adaptive system for disease avoidance behaviour. *Philosophical Transactions of the Royal Society of London. Series B, Biological Sciences, 366*, 389–401.

Danovitch, J., & Bloom, P. (2009). Children's extension of disgust to physical and moral events. *Emotion, 9*, 107–112.

Dasgupta, N., Desteno, D., Williams, L. A., & Hunsinger, M. (2009). Fanning the flames of prejudice: The influence of specific incidental emotions on implicit prejudice. *Emotion, 9*, 585–591.

David, B., & Olatunji, B. O. (2011). The effect of disgust conditioning and disgust sensitivity on appraisals of moral transgressions. *Personality and Individual Differences, 50*, 1142–1146.

de Barra, M., & Curtis, V. (2012). Are the pathogens of out-groups really more dangerous? *Behavioral and Brain Sciences, 35*, 85–86.

Deacon, B., & Olatunji, B. O. (2007). Specificity of disgust sensitivity in the prediction of behavioral avoidance in contamination fear. *Behaviour Research and Therapy, 45*, 2110–2120.

Duckitt, J., Bizumic, B., Krauss, S. W., & Heled, E. (2010). A tripartite approach to right-wing authoritarianism: The authoritarianism-conservatism-traditionalism model. *Political Psychology, 31*(5), 685–715. https://doi.org/10.1111/j.1467-9221.2010.00781.x.

Ekman, P., & Friesen, W. V. (1971). Constants across cultures in the face and emotion. *Journal of Personality and Social Psychology, 17*, 124–129.

Ekman, P., Friesen, W. V., & Hager, J. C. (2002). *Facial action coding system: The manual on CD ROM.* Salt Lake City: A Human Face.

Eskine, K. J., Kacinik, N. A., & Prinz, J. J. (2011). A bad taste in the mouth: Gustatory disgust influences moral judgment. *Psychological Science, 22*, 295–299.

Fan, Q., & Olatunji, B. O. (2013). Individual differences in disgust sensitivity and health-related avoidance: Examination of specific associations. *Personality and Individual Differences, 55*, 454–458.

Faulkner, J., Schaller, M., Park, J., & Duncan, L. (2004). Evolved disease-avoidance mechanisms and contemporary xenophobic attitudes. *Group Processes & Intergroup Relations, 7*, 333.

Fincher, C. L., & Thornhill, R. (2012). Parasite-stress promotes in-group assortative sociality: The cases of strong family ties and heightened religiosity. *The Behavioral and Brain Sciences, 35*, 61–79.

Flake, J. K., & Fried, E. I. (2020). Measurement Schmeasurement: Questionable measurement practices and how to avoid them. *Advances in Methods and Practices in Psychological Science, 3*, 456–465.

Gelman, A., & Loken, E. (2014). The statistical crisis in science. *American Scientist, 102*, 460–465.

Ghelfi, E., Christopherson, C. D., Urry, H. L., Lenne, R. L., Legate, N., Ann Fischer, M., Wagemans, F. M. A., Wiggins, B., Barrett, T., Bornstein, M., de Haan, B., Guberman, J., Issa, N., Kim, J., Na, E., O'Brien, J., Paulk, A., Peck, T., Sashihara, M., … Sullivan, D. (2020). Reexamining the effect of gustatory disgust on moral judgment: A multilab direct replication of Eskine, Kacinik, and Prinz (2011). *Advances in Methods and Practices in Psychological Science, 3*, 3–23.

Giner-Sorolla, R., Kupfer, T., & Sabo, J. (2018). What makes moral disgust special? An integrative functional review. In J. M. Olson (Ed.), *Vol. 57. Advances in experimental social psychology* (pp. 223–289). Elsevier.

Graham, J., Haidt, J., & Nosek, B. A. (2009). Liberals and conservatives rely on different sets of moral foundations. *Journal of Personality and Social Psychology, 96*, 1029–1046.

Greenwald, A. G., McGhee, D. E., & Schwartz, J. L. (1998). Measuring individual differences in implicit cognition: The implicit association test. *Journal of Personality and Social Psychology, 74*, 1464–1480.

Gutierrez, R., Giner-Sorolla, R., & Vasiljevic, M. (2012). Just an anger synonym? Moral context influences predictors of disgust word use. *Cognition & Emotion, 26*, 53–64.

Haidt, J. (2001). The emotional dog and its rational tail: A social intuitionist approach to moral judgment. *Psychological Review, 108*, 814–834.

Haidt, J., Koller, S. H., & Dias, M. G. (1993). Affect, culture, and morality, or is it wrong to eat your dog? *Journal of Personality and Social Psychology, 65*, 613–628.

Haidt, J., McCauley, C. R., & Rozin, P. (1994). Individual differences in sensitivity to disgust: A scale sampling seven domains of disgust elicitors. *Personality and Individual Differences, 16*, 701–713.

Haidt, J., Rozin, P., McCauley, C. R., & Imada, S. (1997). Body, psyche, and culture: The relationship between disgust and morality. *Psychology & Developing Societies, 9*, 107–131.

Halstead, I., & Lewis, G. J. (2020). Understanding opposition to human gene editing: A role for pathogen disgust sensitivity? *Politics and the Life Sciences: The Journal of the Association for Politics and the Life Sciences, 39*, 154–166.

Haslam, N. (2006). Dehumanization: An integrative review. *Personality and Social Psychology Review, 10*, 252–264.

Hatemi, P. K., McDermott, R., Eaves, L. J., Kendler, K. S., & Neale, M. C. (2013). Fear as a disposition and an emotional state: A genetic and environmental approach to out-group political preferences. *American Journal of Political Science, 57*, 279–293.

Henningham, J. P. (1996). A 12-item scale of social conservatism. *Personality and Individual Differences, 20*, 517–519.

Herek, G. M. (1993). Documenting prejudice against lesbians and gay men on campus: The Yale sexual orientation survey. *Journal of Homosexuality, 25*, 15–30.

Hodson, G., & Costello, K. (2007). Interpersonal disgust, ideological orientations, and dehumanization as predictors of intergroup attitudes. *Psychological Science, 18*, 1–8.

Horberg, E., Oveis, C., Keltner, D., & Cohen, A. (2009). Disgust and the moralization of purity. *Journal of Personality and Social Psychology, 97*, 963–976.

Hudson, W. W., & Ricketts, W. A. (1980). A strategy for the measurement of homophobia. *Journal of Homosexuality, 5*, 357–372.

Inbar, Y., Pizarro, D. A., & Bloom, P. (2009). Conservatives are more easily disgusted than liberals. *Cognition & Emotion, 23*, 714–725.

Inbar, Y., Pizarro, D. A., & Bloom, P. (2012). Disgusting smells cause decreased liking of gay men. *Emotion, 12*, 23–27.

Inbar, Y., Pizarro, D. A., Iyer, R., & Haidt, J. (2012). Disgust sensitivity, political conservatism, and voting. *Social Psychological and Personality Science, 3*, 537–544.

Inbar, Y., Pizarro, D. A., Knobe, J., & Bloom, P. (2009). Disgust sensitivity predicts intuitive disapproval of gays. *Emotion, 9*, 435–439.

Ji, T., Tybur, J. M., & van Vugt, M. (2019). Generalized or origin-specific out-group prejudice? The role of temporary and chronic pathogen-avoidance motivation in intergroup relations. *Evolutionary Psychology, 17*, 1474704919826851.

Johnson, D. J., Wortman, J., Cheung, F., Hein, M., Lucas, R. E., Donnellan, M. B., Ebersole, C. R., & Narr, R. K. (2016). The effects of disgust on moral judgments: Testing moderators. *Social Psychological and Personality Science, 7*, 640–647.

Jones, A., & Fitness, J. (2008). Moral hypervigilance: The influence of disgust sensitivity in the moral domain. *Emotion, 8*, 613–627.

Jost, J. T., Glaser, J., Kruglanski, A. W., & Sulloway, F. J. (2003). Political conservatism as motivated social cognition. *Psychological Bulletin, 129*, 339–375.

Jylkkä, J., Härkönen, J., & Hyönä, J. (2021). Incidental disgust does not cause moral condemnation of neutral actions. *Cognition and Emotion, 35*, 96–109.

Kahan, D. M., & Hilgard, J. (2016). *The impact of pathogen-disgust sensitivity on vaccine and gm food risk perceptions: Some evidence for skepticism.* Social Science Research Network. https://papers.ssrn.com/abstract=2891623.

Karg, S. T., Wiener-Blotner, A., & Schnall, S. (2019). Disgust sensitivity is associated with heightened risk perception. *Journal of Risk Research, 22*, 627–642.

Karinen, A. K., & Chapman, H. A. (2019). Cognitive and personality correlates of trait disgust and their relationship to condemnation of nonpurity moral transgressions. *Emotion, 19*, 889–902.

Karinen, A. K., Molho, C., Kupfer, T. R., & Tybur, J. M. (2019). Disgust sensitivity and opposition to immigration: Does contact avoidance or resistance to foreign norms explain the relationship? *Journal of Experimental Social Psychology, 84*, 103817.

Kavaliers, M., & Colwell, D. D. (1995). Odours of parasitized males induce aversive responses in female mice. *Animal Behaviour, 50*, 1161–1169.

Kelly, D. (2011). *Yuck! The nature and moral significance of disgust.* MIT Press.

Kempthorne, J. C., & Terrizzi, J. A. (2021). The behavioral immune system and conservatism as predictors of disease-avoidant attitudes during the COVID-19 pandemic. *Personality and Individual Differences, 178*, 110857.

Kiss, M. J., Morrison, M. A., & Morrison, T. G. (2020). A meta-analytic review of the association between disgust and prejudice toward gay men. *Journal of Homosexuality, 67*, 674–696.

Kleinknecht, R. A., Kleinknecht, E. E., & Thorndike, R. M. (1997). The role of disgust and fear in blood and injection-related fainting symptoms: A structural equation model. *Behaviour Research and Therapy, 35*, 1075–1087.

Kohler, U., Karlson, K. B., & Holm, A. (2011). Comparing coefficients of nested nonlinear probability models. *The Stata Journal, 11*, 420–438.

Kollareth, D., & Russell, J. A. (2017). The English word disgust has no exact translation in Hindi or Malayalam. *Cognition and Emotion, 31*, 1169–1180.

Kollareth, D., & Russell, J. A. (2019). Disgust and the sacred: Do people react to violations of the sacred with the same emotion they react to something putrid? *Emotion, 19*, 37–52.

Landy, J. F., & Goodwin, G. P. (2015). Does incidental disgust amplify moral judgment? A meta-analytic review of experimental evidence. *Perspectives on Psychological Science, 10*, 518–536.

Landy, J. F., & Piazza, J. (2019). Reevaluating moral disgust: Sensitivity to many affective states predicts extremity in many evaluative judgments. *Social Psychological and Personality Science, 10*, 211–219.

Lang, P. J., Bradley, M. M., & Cuthbert, B. N. (2005). *International Affective Picture System (IAPS): Affective ratings of pictures and instruction manual.* NIMH, Center for the Study of Emotion & Attention.

Lerner, J. S., Small, D. A., & Loewenstein, G. (2004). Heart strings and purse strings: Carryover effects of emotions on economic decisions. *Psychological Science, 15*, 337–341.

Lieberman, D., & Patrick, C. (2014). Are the behavioral immune system and pathogen disgust identical? *Evolutionary Behavioral Sciences, 8*, 244–250.

Lieberman, D. L., Tybur, J. M., & Latner, J. D. (2012). Disgust sensitivity, obesity stigma, and gender: Contamination psychology predicts weight bias for women, not men. *Obesity, 20*, 1803–1814.

Loewenstein, G., & Lerner, J. S. (2003). The role of affect in decision making. In R. Davidson, H. Goldsmith, & K. Scherer (Eds.), *Handbook of affective science* (pp. 619–642). Oxford University Press.

Luz, P. M., Brown, H. E., & Struchiner, C. J. (2019). Disgust as an emotional driver of vaccine attitudes and uptake? A mediation analysis. *Epidemiology and Infection, 147*, e182.

McConahay, J. B., Hardee, B. B., & Batts, V. (1981). Has racism declined in America? It depends on who is asking and what is asked. *The Journal of Conflict Resolution, 25*, 563–579.

Miller, L. C., Murphy, R., & Buss, A. H. (1981). Consciousness of body: Private and public. *Journal of Personality and Social Psychology, 41*, 397–406.

Murray, D. R., & Schaller, M. (2012). Threat(s) and conformity deconstructed: Perceived threat of infectious disease and its implications for conformist attitudes and behavior. *European Journal of Social Psychology, 42*, 180–188.

Murray, D. R., & Schaller, M. (2016). The behavioral immune system: Implications for social cognition, social interaction, and social influence. In J. M. Olson, & M. P. Zanna (Eds.), *Vol. 53. Advances in experimental social psychology* (pp. 75–129). Academic Press.

Murray, D. R., Trudeau, R., & Schaller, M. (2011). On the origins of cultural differences in conformity: Four tests of the pathogen prevalence hypothesis. *Personality and Social Psychology Bulletin, 37*, 318–329.

Navarrete, C. D., & Fessler, D. M. T. (2006). Disease avoidance and ethnocentrism: The effects of disease vulnerability and disgust sensitivity on intergroup attitudes. *Evolution and Human Behavior, 27*, 270–282.

Nelson, L. D., Simmons, J., & Simonsohn, U. (2018). Psychology's renaissance. *Annual Review of Psychology, 69*, 511–534.

Nosek, B. A., Banaji, M. R., & Greenwald, A. G. (2006). *Sexuality IAT stimulus materials.* Retrieved from http://implicit.harvard.edu.

Nussbaum, M. C. (2010). *From disgust to humanity: Sexual orientation and constitutional law.* Oxford University Press.

Oaten, M., Stevenson, R. J., & Case, T. I. (2009). Disgust as a disease-avoidance mechanism. *Psychological Bulletin, 135*, 303–321.

Oaten, M., Stevenson, R. J., Williams, M. A., Rich, A. N., Butko, M., & Case, T. I. (2018). Moral violations and the experience of disgust and anger. *Frontiers in Behavioral Neuroscience, 12*, 179.

Olatunji, B. O. (2008). Disgust, scrupulosity and conservative attitudes about sex: Evidence for a mediational model of homophobia. *Journal of Research in Personality, 42*, 1364–1369.

Olatunji, B. O., Adams, T., Ciesielski, B., David, B., Sarawgi, S., & Broman-Fulks, J. (2012). The three domains of disgust scale: Factor structure, psychometric properties, and conceptual limitations. *Assessment, 19*, 205–225.

Olatunji, B. O., Lohr, J. M., Sawchuk, C. N., & Tolin, D. F. (2007). Multimodal assessment of disgust in contamination-related obsessive-compulsive disorder. *Behaviour Research and Therapy, 45*, 263–276.

Olatunji, B. O., Williams, N. L., Tolin, D. F., Abramowitz, J. S., Sawchuk, C. N., Lohr, J. M., & Elwood, L. S. (2007). The disgust scale: Item analysis, factor structure, and suggestions for refinement. *Psychological Assessment, 19*, 281–291.

Ong, H. H., Mullette-Gillman, O. A., Kwok, K., & Lim, J. (2014). Moral judgment modulation by disgust is bi-directionally moderated by individual sensitivity. *Frontiers in Psychology, 5*. https://doi.org/10.3389/fpsyg.2014.00194.

Ottaviani, C., Mancini, F., Petrocchi, N., Medea, B., & Couyoumdjian, A. (2013). Autonomic correlates of physical and moral disgust. *International Journal of Psychophysiology, 89*, 57–62.

Park, J., Faulkner, J., & Schaller, M. (2003). Evolved disease-avoidance processes and contemporary anti-social behavior: Prejudicial attitudes and avoidance of people with physical disabilities. *Journal of Nonverbal Behavior, 27*, 65–87.

Park, J. H., Schaller, M., & Crandall, C. S. (2007). Pathogen-avoidance mechanisms and the stigmatization of obese people. *Evolution and Human Behavior, 28*, 410–414.

Parkinson, C., Sinnott-Armstrong, W., Koralus, P. E., Mendelovici, A., McGeer, V., & Wheatley, T. (2011). Is morality unified? Evidence that distinct neural systems underlie moral judgments of harm, dishonesty, and disgust. *Journal of Cognitive Neuroscience, 23*, 3162–3180.

Pizarro, D., Inbar, Y., & Helion, C. (2011). On disgust and moral judgment. *Emotion Review, 3*, 267–268.

Poirotte, C., Massol, F., Herbert, A., Willaume, E., Bomo, P. M., Kappeler, P. M., & Charpentier, M. J. E. (2017). Mandrills use olfaction to socially avoid parasitized conspecifics. *Science Advances, 3*, e1601721.

Pratto, F., Sidanius, J., Stallworth, L. M., & Malle, B. F. (1994). Social dominance orientation: A personality variable predicting social and political attitudes. *Journal of Personality and Social Psychology, 67*, 741–763.

Reuben, R., Aitken, D., Freedman, J. L., & Einstein, G. (2020). Mistrust of the medical profession and higher disgust sensitivity predict parental vaccine hesitancy. *PLoS One, 15*, e0237755.

Reynolds, L. M., McCambridge, S. A., Bissett, I. P., & Consedine, N. S. (2014). Trait and state disgust: An experimental investigation of disgust and avoidance in colorectal cancer decision scenarios. *Health Psychology, 33*, 1495–1506.

Royzman, E., Atanasov, P., Landy, J. F., Parks, A., & Gepty, A. (2014). CAD or MAD? Anger (not disgust) as the predominant response to pathogen-free violations of the divinity code. *Emotion, 14*, 892–907.

Rozin, P., & Fallon, A. E. (1987). A perspective on disgust. *Psychological Review, 94*, 23–41.

Rozin, P., Haddad, B., Nemeroff, C., & Slovic, P. (2015). Psychological aspects of the rejection of recycled water: Contamination, purification and disgust. *Judgment and Decision making, 10*, 50–63.

Rozin, P., & Haidt, J. (2013). The domains of disgust and their origins: Contrasting biological and cultural evolutionary accounts. *Trends in Cognitive Sciences, 17*, 367–368.

Rozin, P., Haidt, J., & McCauley, C. R. (1999). Disgust: The body and soul emotion. In T. Dalgleish, & M. J. Power (Eds.), *Handbook of cognition and emotion* (pp. 429–445). John Wiley & Sons, Ltd.

Rozin, P., Haidt, J., & McCauley, C. R. (2008). Disgust. In M. Lewis, J. M. Haviland-Jones, & L. F. Barrett (Eds.), *Handbook of emotions* (pp. 757–776). The Guilford Press.

Rozin, P., Haidt, J., & McCauley, C. R. (2009). Disgust: The body and soul emotion in the 21st century. In *Disgust and its disorders: Theory, assessment, and treatment implications* (pp. 9–29). American Psychological Association.

Rozin, P., Haidt, J., McCauley, C. R., Dunlop, L., & Ashmore, M. (1999). Individual differences in disgust sensitivity: Comparisons and evaluations of paper-and-pencil versus behavioral measures. *Journal of Research in Personality, 33*, 330–351.

Rozin, P., Hammer, L., Oster, H., Horowitz, T., & Marmora, V. (1986). The child's conception of food: Differentiation of categories of rejected substances in the 16 months to 5 year age range. *Appetite, 7*, 141–151.

Sanyal, M., McAuliffe, W. H. B., & Curry, O. S. (2021). Gross values: Investigating the role of disgust in bioethics. *Current Psychology*. https://doi.org/10.1007/s12144-021-01609-7.

Sarabian, C., Belais, R., & MacIntosh, A. J. J. (2018). Feeding decisions under contamination risk in bonobos. *Philosophical Transactions of the Royal Society of London. Series B, Biological Sciences, 373*, 20170195.

Sato, A., & Sugiura, Y. (2014). Dispositional mindfulness modulates automatic transference of disgust into moral judgment. *Shinrigaku Kenkyu: The Japanese Journal of Psychology, 84*, 605–611.

Savage, R. (2007). "Disease incarnate": Biopolitical discourse and genocidal dehumanisation in the age of modernity. *Journal of Historical Sociology, 20*, 404–440.

Schaller, M. (2014). When and how disgust is and is not implicated in the behavioral immune system. *Evolutionary Behavioral Sciences*, *8*, 251.

Schaller, M., & Duncan, L. A. (2007). The behavioral immune system: Its evolution and social psychological implications. In J. P. Forgas, M. G. Haselton, & W. von Hippel (Eds.), *Evolution and the social mind: Evolutionary psychology and social cognition* (pp. 293–307). Routledge/Taylor & Francis Group.

Schaller, M., & Murray, D. R. (2008). Pathogens, personality, and culture: Disease prevalence predicts worldwide variability in sociosexuality, extraversion, and openness to experience. *Journal of Personality and Social Psychology*, *95*, 212–221.

Schaller, M., & Park, J. H. (2011). The behavioral immune system (and why it matters). *Current Directions in Psychological Science*, *20*, 99–103.

Schnall, S., Haidt, J., Clore, G., & Jordan, A. (2008). Disgust as embodied moral judgment. *Personality and Social Psychology Bulletin*, *34*, 1096–1109.

Schnall, S., Haidt, J., Clore, G. L., & Jordan, A. H. (2015). Landy and Goodwin (2015) confirmed most of our findings then drew the wrong conclusions. *Perspectives on Psychological Science*, *10*, 537–538.

Scott, S. E., Inbar, Y., & Rozin, P. (2016). Evidence for absolute moral opposition to genetically modified food in the United States. *Perspectives on Psychological Science*, *11*, 315–324.

Seidel, A., & Prinz, J. (2013). Sound morality: Irritating and icky noises amplify judgments in divergent moral domains. *Cognition*, *127*, 1–5.

Shook, N. J., & Oosterhoff, B. (2020). Testing the effects of pathogen threat and sexual strategies on political ideology. *Politics and the Life Sciences*, *39*, 187–199.

Shook, N. J., Terrizzi, J. A., Clay, R., & Oosterhoff, B. (2015). In defense of pathogen disgust and disease avoidance: A response to Tybur et al. (2015). *Evolution and Human Behavior*, *36*, 498–502.

Shweder, R. A., Much, N. C., Mahapatra, M., & Park, L. (1997). The "big three" of morality (autonomy, community, divinity) and the "big three" explanations of suffering. In A. M. Brandt, & P. Rozin (Eds.), *Morality and health* (pp. 119–169). Taylor & Frances/Routledge.

Smith, K. B., Oxley, D., Hibbing, M. V., Alford, J. R., & Hibbing, J. R. (2011). Disgust sensitivity and the neurophysiology of left–right political orientations. *PLoS One*, *6*. https://doi.org/10.1371/journal.pone.0025552.

Stevenson, R. J., Oaten, M. J., Case, T. I., Repacholi, B. M., & Wagland, P. (2010). Children's response to adult disgust elicitors: Development and acquisition. *Developmental Psychology*, *46*, 165–177.

Susskind, J. M., Lee, D. H., Cusi, A., Feiman, R., Grabski, W., & Anderson, A. K. (2008). Expressing fear enhances sensory acquisition. *Nature Neuroscience*, *11*, 843–850.

Terrizzi, J. A., Shook, N. J., & McDaniel, M. A. (2013). The behavioral immune system and social conservatism: A meta-analysis. *Evolution and Human Behavior: Official Journal of the Human Behavior and Evolution Society*, *34*, 99–108.

Thornhill, R., Fincher, C. L., & Aran, D. (2009). Parasites, democratization, and the liberalization of values across contemporary countries. *Biological Reviews of the Cambridge Philosophical Society*, *84*, 113–131.

Tybur, J. M., & de Vries, R. E. (2013). Disgust sensitivity and the HEXACO model of personality. *Personality and Individual Differences*, *55*, 660–665.

Tybur, J. M., Inbar, Y., Aarøe, L., Barclay, P., Barlow, F. K., de Barra, M., Becker, D. V., Borovoi, L., Choi, I., Choi, J. A., Consedine, N. S., Conway, A., Conway, J. R., Conway, P., Adoric, V. C., Demirci, D. E., Fernández, A. M., Ferreira, D. C. S., Ishii, K., … Žeželj, I. (2016). Parasite stress and pathogen avoidance relate to distinct dimensions of political ideology across 30 nations. *Proceedings of the National Academy of Sciences of the United States of America*, *113*, 12408–12413.

Tybur, J. M., Inbar, Y., Güler, E., & Molho, C. (2015a). Is the relationship between pathogen avoidance and ideological conservatism explained by sexual strategies? *Evolution and Human Behavior*, *36*, 489–497.

Tybur, J. M., Inbar, Y., Güler, E., & Molho, C. (2015b). Pathogen disgust requires no defense: A response to Shook, Terrizzi, Clay, & Oosterhoff (2015). *Evolution and Human Behavior*, *36*, 502–504.

Tybur, J. M., & Karinen, A. K. (2018). Measurement and theory in disgust sensitivity. In V. Ziegler-Hill, & T. K. Shackleford (Eds.), *The SAGE handbook of personality and individual differences* (pp. 159–179). Sage Reference.

Tybur, J. M., Lieberman, D., & Griskevicius, V. (2009). Microbes, mating, and morality: Individual differences in three functional domains of disgust. *Journal of Personality and Social Psychology*, *97*, 103–122.

Tybur, J. M., Merriman, L. A., Hooper, A. E. C., McDonald, M. M., & Navarrete, C. D. (2010). Extending the behavioral immune system to political psychology: Are political conservatism and disgust sensitivity really related? *Evolutionary Psychology*, *8*, 599–616.

van Dijke, M., van Houwelingen, G., De Cremer, D., & De Schutter, L. (2018). So gross and yet so far away: Psychological distance moderates the effect of disgust on moral judgment. *Social Psychological and Personality Science*, *9*, 689–701.

van Dillen, L. F., van der Wal, R. C., & van den Bos, K. (2012). On the role of attention and emotion in morality: Attentional control modulates unrelated disgust in moral judgments. *Personality and Social Psychology Bulletin*, *38*, 1222–1231.

van Leeuwen, F., Inbar, Y., Petersen, M. B., Aarøe, L., Barclay, P., Barlow, F. K., de Barra, M., Becker, D. V., Borovoi, L., Choi, J. A., Consedine, N. S., Conway, J. R., Conway, P., Cubela Adoric, V., Demirci, E., Fernández, A. M., Ferreira, D. C. S., Ishii, K., Jakšić, I., … Tybur, J.M. (2021). *Disgust sensitivity relates to attitudes toward gay men and lesbian women across 31 nations*. (Manuscript submitted for publication).

van Leeuwen, F., & Petersen, M. B. (2018). The behavioral immune system is designed to avoid infected individuals, not outgroups. *Evolution and Human Behavior*, *39*, 226–234.

van Overveld, W. J. M., de Jong, P. J., Peters, M. L., Cavanagh, K., & Davey, G. C. L. (2006). Disgust propensity and disgust sensitivity: Separate constructs that are differentially related to specific fears. *Personality and Individual Differences*, *41*, 1241–1252.

van Overveld, M., de Jong, P. J., Peters, M. L., & Schouten, E. (2011). The disgust scale-R: A valid and reliable index to investigate separate disgust domains? *Personality and Individual Differences*, *51*, 325–330.

Vanaman, M. E., & Chapman, H. A. (2020). Disgust and disgust-driven moral concerns predict support for restrictions on transgender bathroom access. *Politics and the Life Sciences*, *39*, 200–214.

Wagemans, F. M. A., Brandt, M. J., & Zeelenberg, M. (2018). Disgust sensitivity is primarily associated with purity-based moral judgments. *Emotion*, *18*, 277–289.

Weber, E. U., Blais, A.-R., & Betz, E. (2002). A domain-specific risk-attitude scale: Measuring risk perceptions and risk behaviors. *Journal of Behavioral Decision Making*, *15*, 263–290.

Wheatley, T., & Haidt, J. (2005). Hypnotic disgust makes moral judgments more severe. *Psychological Science*, *16*, 780–784.

Wilks, M., Phillips, C. J. C., Fielding, K., & Hornsey, M. J. (2019). Testing potential psychological predictors of attitudes towards cultured meat. *Appetite*, *136*, 137–145.

Yoder, A. M., Widen, S. C., & Russell, J. A. (2016). The word disgust may refer to more than one emotion. *Emotion*, *16*(3), 301–308.

CHAPTER FOUR

Political ideology and social categorization

Chadly Stern*

University of Illinois, Urbana-Champaign, Champaign, IL, United States
*Corresponding author: e-mail address: chadly@illinois.edu

Contents

Advances in Experimental Social Psychology, Volume 65
ISSN 0065-2601
https://doi.org/10.1016/bs.aesp.2021.11.003

Abstract

Social categorization, the process of mentally placing others into a group, is a universal aspect of daily life. Researchers have long been interested in understanding the consequences of social categorization and have more recently turned their attention to determining the processes of how people categorize others into social groups. In this chapter, I present the efficient categorization framework (ECF), which integrates research in social cognition and political psychology to understand the role of a perceiver's political ideology (i.e., whether a person is more liberal or conservative) in social categorization processes. The ECF proposes that political conservatives prioritize efficient categorization—expending few cognitive resources to make a correct judgment—more so than do liberals. Drawing from this framework, I review evidence indicating that liberals and conservatives diverge in their beliefs about which strategies contribute to accurate social category judgments, as well as how they process available cues during social categorization. I also outline findings that highlight how ideological differences in the social categorization process contribute to evaluations, policy attitudes, and political behaviors. I discuss how the ECF gives novel insight into variability in social categorization processes and offers unique perspective into why liberals and conservatives commonly fail to see "eye-to-eye" in their perceptions of the world.

1. Political ideology and social categorization

People mentally organize the world into categories (Macrae & Bodenhausen, 2000). An individual might pass a person on the street and categorize them as Black, a woman, or elderly immediately and without any conscious intent. These categorization processes also frequently operate on a more explicit level. For example, a growing number of expectant parents throughout the world have begun holding "gender reveal parties" in which they announce their future child's biological sex to family and friends (Gieseler, 2019). Social categories are also integral to the political structure of societies, such as their critical role in various policies (e.g., affirmative action, Title IX) and foundational documents of a government (e.g., Amendments to the United States Constitution granting voting rights). In short, social categories are a fundamental aspect of human life.

Psychologists have long been interested in understanding how social category information (e.g., race, sex) shapes the inferences that people make about others (e.g., Allport, 1954; Devine, 1989; Gilbert & Hixon, 1991;

Macrae & Bodenhausen, 2000; Richeson & Shelton, 2007; Tajfel, 1981; Wilder, 1986). Applying category information (e.g., stereotypes) in judgments about individuals in large part stems from people first mentally placing others into social groups. For example, when a perceiver categorizes an individual as Black or as a woman the relevant category information becomes activated and subsequently guides judgments and behaviors.

Researchers have historically allocated considerably less attention to understanding how people categorize others into groups. For example, what information do perceivers rely on when categorizing a person's race or gender? How do perceivers process this information before reaching a final category judgment? There has also been less focus on how the categorization process itself might contribute to social evaluations and judgments. For example, how does the difficulty of the categorization process shape subsequent evaluations that perceivers form about targets? In recent years, however, there has been growing interest in examining these questions in order to provide a deeper understanding of social categorization (Freeman & Ambady, 2011; Freeman, Stolier, & Brooks, 2020; Johnson, Lick, & Carpinella, 2015; Kawakami, Amodio, & Hugenberg, 2017).

In this chapter, I describe how a person's political ideology (i.e., their degree of political liberalism versus conservatism) systematically contributes to social categorization processes, as well as subsequent evaluations, policy positions, and political behaviors that those categorization processes guide. Specifically, I introduce the efficient categorization framework (ECF; Fig. 1). The ECF presents an overarching framework for understanding how political ideology contributes to information processing during social categorization, and how those processes inform downstream evaluations

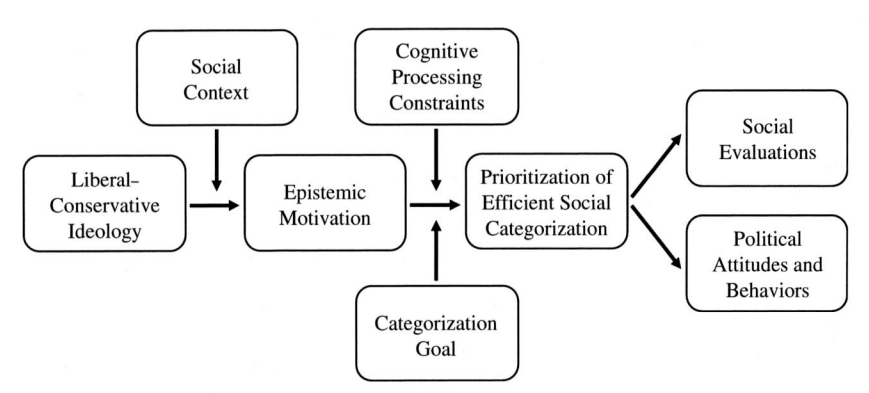

Fig. 1 The efficient categorization framework.

and judgments. The ECF outlines how ideological differences in preferred processing styles lead conservatives to more strongly prioritize efficient social categorization than do liberals, which in turn shapes evaluative and behavioral outcomes. The model integrates social cognitive research on categorization, evaluation, and person perception with political psychology research on worldviews and motivations. In doing so, the ECF highlights how incorporating theoretical frameworks from political psychology into classic models of social cognition can enrich our understanding of basic categorization processes.

In the sections that follow, I discuss in detail how a perceiver's political ideology corresponds to social categorization processes. First, I briefly outline relevant perspectives and important gaps in research examining the processes of social categorization. Next, I discuss the way in which political ideology is conceptualized and assessed in the ECF. I then explain the central premises of the ECF. For the remainder of the chapter, I summarize recent findings that support the premises and novel contributions of the framework.

2. Individual differences in the social categorization process

Researchers have used the term *categorization* to describe various forms of judgments (for a review, see Klapper, Dotsch, van Rooij, & Wigboldus, 2017). In this chapter, social categorization refers to the process by which perceivers apply a category label (e.g., Black, Muslim, straight) to a target person. Defining social categorization in this way aligns with conceptualizations where scholars have focused on the consequences of categorization (e.g., Grant & Holmes, 1981; Nicolas, de la Fuente, & Fiske, 2017), and also dovetails with discussions in intergroup research (Gaertner & Dovidio, 2000; Hewstone, Islam, & Judd, 1993; Kawakami et al., 2017; Tajfel & Turner, 1979). Thus, considering factors that contribute to variability in the process of applying category labels to targets allows for broad and direct connections with social judgment research.

Social categorization is a largely inescapable aspect of human cognition. Human categories are culturally constructed forms of group membership in which meaning has been attached to a physical, behavioral, or psychological aspect of a person. For example, the attachment of cultural meaning (e.g., stereotypes) to primary and secondary sex characteristics, skin tone, sexual attraction, and spiritual beliefs contribute to the social basis of sex, race, sexual orientation, and religion categories, respectively (Bem, 1993; Diamond, 2003; Eagly & Wood, 1999; Markus, 2008). The specific social groups that exist within categories vary across time and place (e.g., racial groups vary across cultures; Katz, 2007; Lopez, 1994; Lorber & Farrell, 1991). However, all human cultures and epochs have possessed social categories in some form (Cuddy et al., 2009; Sidanius & Pratto, 2001). Further, categorization based on some forms of group membership (e.g., race, sex, age) occurs without any conscious intent (Brewer, 1988; Fiske, 1998; Kogan, 1979; Taylor, Fiske, Etcoff, & Ruderman, 1978).

It is important to note that there are conditions under which some social category judgments can be altered or reduced. Providing a novel form of group membership (e.g., sports teams) overrides race, but not sex, categorization (Kurzban, Tooby, & Cosmides, 2001; Pietraszewski, Cosmides, & Tooby, 2014). Dependence on another person and explicit instructions to individuate targets also promote individuating- over category-based processing (Hugenberg, Miller, & Claypool, 2007; Neuberg & Fiske, 1987). Critically, however, highlighting one social category over another does not prevent social categorization from occurring; it simply shifts the focus of the categorization. Additionally, to the degree that individuation occurs, it is likely to be relatively targeted and brief. Overall, social categorization is pervasive and consequential in human interaction. It occurs across all known human cultures and in virtually every aspect of person perception and interpersonal interaction, essentially without exception.

Research suggests that situational contexts and individual differences among perceivers can independently and interactively contribute to how people process available information during social categorization (Freeman et al., 2020; Freeman & Ambady, 2011; Johnson et al., 2015). Scholars have identified several contextual features that modulate categorization. For example, feelings of economic scarcity shape racial categorization (Krosch & Amodio, 2014; Rodeheffer, Hill, & Lord, 2012), and inferred base rates from a social context shape categorization based on race, sexual orientation, and religion (Lick, Johnson, Rule, & Stroessner, 2019; Pauker, Carpinella, Lick, Sanchez, & Johnson, 2018).

Much less is known about the role of specific individual differences in shaping the categorization process. For example, random-effects modeling highlights that individual differences among people can contribute to impression formation (Hehman, Sutherland, Flake, & Slepian, 2017; Xie, Flake, & Hehman, 2019). This research points out that some traits differing between individuals seem to affect social judgment, but does not elucidate which specific traits and characteristics matter. Additionally, research that has examined the influence of specific individual differences has typically focused on traits that hold relevance only for a single social category, such as racial prejudice shaping how people process faces in terms of race (Blascovich, Wyer, Swart, & Kibler, 1997; Cassidy, Sprout, Freeman, & Krendl, 2017; Fazio & Dunton, 1997). The ECF contributes to developing a more comprehensive picture of how, when, and why a specific and relatively stable aspect of a perceiver—in this case, political ideology—can consistently correspond to social categorization processes across groups.

3. Conceptualizing and assessing political ideology

Ideologies are interrelated and shared sets of beliefs about how society and the world should be organized. One prominent way in which political ideology has been conceptualized is on a single dimension ranging from liberal/left to conservative/right (Jost, Federico, & Napier, 2009; Jost, Glaser, Kruglanski, & Sulloway, 2003). Drawing from this conceptualization, the ECF defines political ideology as the extent to which a person embraces conservative and right-wing beliefs that oppose novel change (or in some instances support reactive change) compared to liberal and left-wing beliefs that support novel change. Polarization between competing political ideologies has grown more extreme in recent years, and this increasing divide shows little sign of narrowing (Abramowitz, 2010; Iyengar, Lelkes, Levendusky, Malhotra, & Westwood, 2019; Pierson & Schickler, 2020). Due in part to these trends, there has been rapid growth in the amount of psychological research examining the antecedents and consequences of liberal-conservative ideology (e.g., Choma, Hanoch, Hodson, & Gummerum, 2014; Graham, Haidt, & Nosek, 2009; Jost, 2006; Jost, Nosek, & Gosling, 2008; Proulx & Brandt, 2017).

Scholars have produced various recommendations for how a person's political ideology can be most effectively assessed (for a review, see Stern & Ondish, 2019). One of the most common approaches, which I adopt in my research conducted in the United States, is the usage of a continuous single item with endpoint anchors of *very/extremely/strongly liberal* and *very/extremely/strongly conservative* (e.g., Graham et al., 2009; McAdams et al., 2008; Prusaczyk & Hodson, 2019). Measurement outside of the United States replaces the labels with *left* and *right* to account for cultural differences in political terminology (e.g., Malka, Soto, Inzlicht, & Lelkes, 2014), but these measures are often viewed as capturing the same underlying construct.

In the past, some social scientists rejected the idea that the average person could possess a stable and coherent political ideology (e.g., Converse, 1964; Lipset, 1960). Further, to the degree that the average person did hold some semblance of a consistent ideology, this worldview was presumed to result from simply adopting attitudes that political elites had bundled together (Rokeach, 1968). As a result of these arguments, some scholars continue to express doubt that political ideology can be assessed as a meaningful construct among average members of a society (Kalmoe, 2020; Kinder & Kalmoe, 2017). While any measurement system for an abstract construct is inherently imperfect, several findings support the perspective that political ideology can be effectively measured and utilized in psychological research.

First, most people report possessing a political ideology. For example, in a Pew Research poll, Americans were asked to report their ideology using a single item ranging *very liberal* to *very conservative*. Fewer than 10% of respondents indicated that they "don't know" what their ideology was (Pew Research Center, 2014). Second, when self-reported ideology (assessed via similar single-item measures) is compared to stances on various policy positions (e.g., abortion, environmental regulations), people report their ideology with a strong (although imperfect) degree of accuracy (Zell & Bernstein, 2014). Third, a single-item measure captures political ideology to a degree at least as strong as multi-item measures do. We (Axt & Stern, under review) found that a single-item measure of political ideology was associated with various criterion variables (e.g., voting behavior, policy positions) at a magnitude similar to (and sometimes greater than) multi-item scales of ideology, such as White, Kinney, Danek, Smith, and Harben's (2020) Resistance to Change-Beliefs Scale and van der Toorn, Jost, Packer, Noorbaloochi, and Van Bavel's (2017) measure of resistance to change. Fourth, for many people, political ideology tends to be relatively stable over time. For example, in one longitudinal study a single-item measure of political ideology was correlated at $r = .54$ over a nine-year period (Osborne & Sibley, 2020). Ideology will not be perfectly stable over time for various reasons (e.g., situational impacts on worldviews, measurement error), but observed correlations are comparable to those of other commonly assessed constructs in psychology (e.g., personality factors; Roberts & DelVecchio, 2000). Collectively, these findings lend considerable support to the idea that researchers have the ability to assess ideology and incorporate the construct into psychological theorizing.

4. Central premises

In this section, I outline the basic premises of the ECF. I also discuss alternative perspectives that are sometimes used to explain ideological differences and, separately, the social categorization process. I additionally summarize the factors that distinguish the ECF from alternative theoretical perspectives and highlight the novel contributions of the framework.

4.1 Ideological differences in epistemic motivation

The ECF begins with the premise that political ideology is associated with particular constellations of epistemic motivations. Political belief systems provide people with some degree of order, structure, and meaning to the complicated and ever-changing social, economic, and political landscape (Greenberg & Jonas, 2003; Lane, 1962). However, not all belief systems are associated with the same psychological motivations and goals. When assessed using self-report measures, we have found that people who are more politically conservative (versus liberal) indicate a greater desire for structure (Stern, 2019; Stern & Axt, 2020) and cognitive closure (Ruisch & Stern, 2021), and a higher intolerance for ambiguity (Stern & Axt, 2021). In contrast, people who are more liberal (versus conservative) report a greater desire to deliberate and engage in effortful thought (Hennes, Nam, Stern, & Jost, 2012; Stern & Axt, 2021).

In a recent meta-analysis, we (Jost, Sterling, & Stern, 2018) aggregated 181 samples with responses from over 133,000 people to examine ideological differences on various assessments of epistemic motivation. When relying on benchmarks that Cohen (1988) outlined for the interpretation of effect sizes, overall differences between liberals and conservatives ranged from relatively small to large ($|r|$s $= .07-.51$). The majority of average effect sizes were moderate in magnitude (see Fig. 2), indicating that conservatives display a greater preference for structure, order, and closure than do liberals.

Some researchers have challenged this interpretation of the findings. Specifically, they argue that ideological differences in self-reported epistemic motivation might not reflect genuine processing style differences between liberals and conservatives (e.g., Kahan, 2012; Van Hiel, Onraet, & De Pauw, 2010) or that the findings stem from scale items possessing political

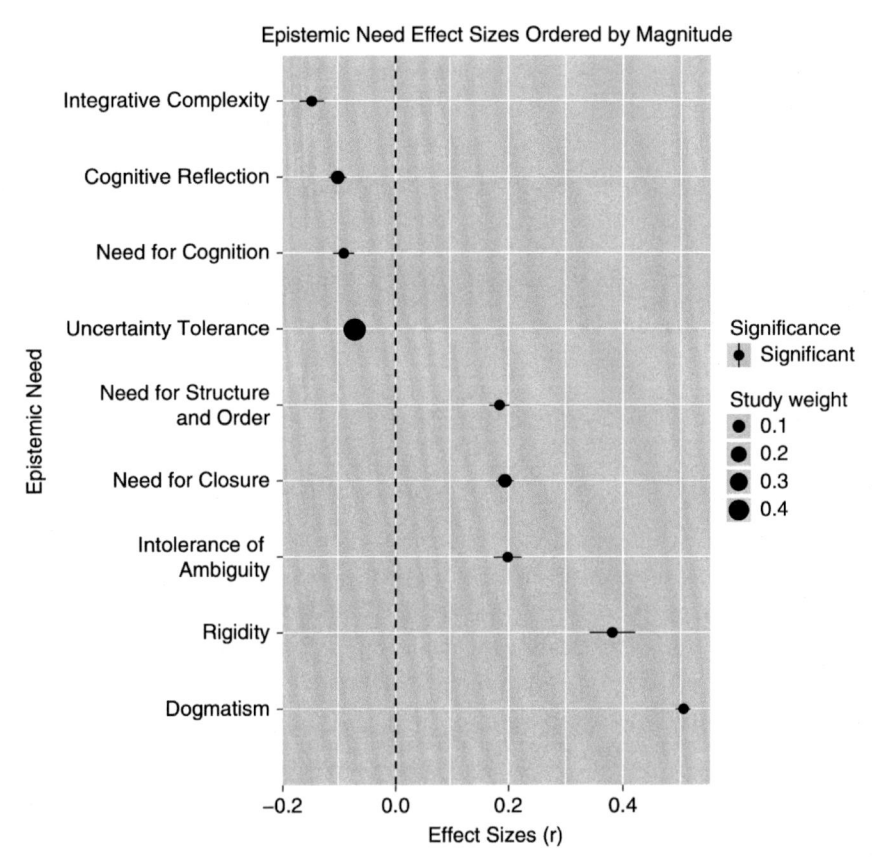

Fig. 2 Average relationships between ideology and epistemic motivation as reported in Jost et al. (2018). Positive effect sizes indicate that the motivation is stronger among conservatives, and negative effect sizes indicate that the motivation is stronger among liberals.

content (Conway III et al., 2016). Importantly, however, ideological differences also emerge on some more direct assessments of deliberative thought. The tasks that are utilized are also devoid of political content. For example, liberals (versus conservatives) considered more response possibilities before coming to a decision on a task (estimating the quantity of dots on a screen; Ruisch & Stern, 2021), and engaged in more exploration when forming attitudes about novel objects (i.e., beans; Ruisch, Shook, & Fazio, 2021; Shook & Fazio, 2009).

Relatedly, ideological differences emerge on some tasks that require effortfully overriding an automatic response. For example, the Cognitive Reflection Test (CRT) includes non-political questions such as: *A bat* *and ball cost $1.10 in total. The bat costs $1.00 more than the ball. How much does the ball cost?* (Frederick, 2005). The automatic response ($0.10) is incorrect, and individuals must engage in deliberation to reach the correct answer ($0.05). Liberals tend to perform slightly better on these types of measures capturing cognitive reflection than do conservatives (Jost et al., 2018). The Go/No-Go Association Task similarly requires individuals to consciously override an automatic response (Nosek & Banaji, 2001). Amodio, Jost, Master, and Yee (2007) examined whether liberals and conservatives would differ in performance on this task when stimuli were non-political. Half of participants were told to indicate a *Go* response when they were shown the letter *M* and to withhold a response (i.e., *No-Go*) when shown the letter *W*, whereas the other half of participants were given the opposite instructions. The authors found that liberals displayed greater accuracy on the No-Go trials than did conservatives. It is unlikely that liberals and conservatives differed in the prepotent response to respond *Go* for certain letters, given that the letters did not possess political value. As such, these findings suggest that liberals were more likely than conservatives to effortfully override the prepotent response. Overall, both self-report and behavioral measures on non-political tasks support the existence of ideological differences in epistemic motivation.

4.2 Ideological differences in prioritizing efficient categorization

The second premise of the ECF is that ideological differences in epistemic motivation lead conservatives to more strongly prioritize efficient categorization than do liberals. Generally speaking, efficiency includes both minimizing the inputs of a task and maximizing the outputs. In other words, efficiency is highest when the effort or resources expended on a task are low while also producing the strongest quality outcome (Farrell, 1957; Sickles & Zelenyuk, 2019).

In the ECF, the primary input of social categorization is defined as the amount of cognitive resources that people dispense when making a judgment. Humans possess a limited amount of time and cognitive resources. When people engage in a task that requires cognitive effort, they display reduced attention control (Garrison, Finley, & Schmeichel, 2019), disengage from expending additional cognitive effort (Lin, Saunders, Friese, Evans, & Inzlicht, 2020) and indicate a (small) preference for future tasks to be less difficult (Gieseler, Inzlicht, & Friese, 2020). Expending cognitive effort on a task also distracts from the completion of other endeavors, as the person is primarily attentive to the task at hand (Lavie, 2010). Allocating as few cognitive resources and little attention as possible to a task allows people to more readily spread their effort over a wider array of daily demands. Although a single category judgment is unlikely to consume a considerable amount of time and cognitive resources, people make a multitude of social category judgments over the course of a day. Focusing deeply on discerning the group membership of every person that one encounters or observes would consume cognitive resources and distract from engaging more broadly with the world. Thus, lower expense of cognitive resources during the process of social categorization constitutes greater efficiency of the input.

Some researchers have primarily attended to input when discussing cognitive efficiency (e.g., Andersen, Klatzky, & Murray, 1990; Hewstone, Hantzi, & Johnston, 1991; Wilder, 1986). However, both the input and output are necessary aspects. A student who quickly writes a term paper (low expense of effort) but receives a poor grade (low quality outcome) and a student who unnecessarily labors over a paper (high expense of effort) but receives a high grade (high quality outcome) would both be considered less efficient than a student who quickly writes a paper (low expense of effort) and receives a high grade (high quality outcome).

The ECF defines the quality of the output as the degree to which the social category judgment achieves a focal goal. What is the focal goal during social categorization? Several scholars have noted that people are primarily oriented toward making judgments that they feel are veridical perceptions of the world (e.g., Higgins, 2013; Kruglanski, 1989). The desire to make a correct judgment has, in particular, been viewed as an integral aspect of social categorization. For example, Higgins (2019) argues that "truth motivation is central to categorization" and that "the selected category must be experienced as reflecting the reality of what is being categorized" (p. 190). People are motivated to make accurate category judgments because doing so affords a functional advantage over making an incorrect judgment. Accurate social categorization facilitates effective pursuit of additional goals that perceivers find important. For example, making an accurate category judgment supports relationship and mating goals (Macrae, Alnwick, Milne, & Schloerscheidt, 2002; Rule, Rosen, Slepian, & Ambady, 2011), avoids backlash from a target (Bosson & Vandello, 2011; Buck, Plant, Ratcliff, Zielaskowski, & Boerner, 2013), and allows perceivers to more appropriately rely on broader forms of knowledge when making further inferences about a target person (Tajfel, 1981). Thus, the ECF assumes that making an accurate judgment is generally the focal goal during social categorization.

A judgment is accurate when it corresponds to the correct answer (Stern, West, & Schoenthaler, 2013; West & Kenny, 2011). In the case of social categorization, the correct answer to a judgment typically consists of targets self-identifying their group membership (e.g., Johnson, Gill, Reichman, & Tassinary, 2007; Rule, Garrett, & Ambady, 2010). While this is not a perfect index of the correct answer (e.g., a person might solely engage in same-sex sexual behavior but identify their sexual orientation as straight), self-reported group membership often corresponds to behavioral indicators of group membership (Ammerman, 2003; Chandra, Copen, & Mosher, 2013).

The ECF's overall definition of efficiency aligns with broader discussions in psychological research. For example, researchers have discussed cognitive efficiency as completing a higher number of correct responses on a task in a lower amount of time (Farmer, Cady, Bleiberg, & Reeves, 2000) and as accurately completing a task with the lowest amount of exertion from brain regions associated with planning (Rypma et al., 2006). Some social categorization research also tacitly weaves the accuracy of a judgment into its discussion of efficiency (Jung, White, & Powanda, 2019). The ECF makes this aspect of efficiency explicit. The ECF's definition of efficiency is also consistent with previous discussions of epistemic motivation, the underlying mechanism in the framework. For example, the epistemic motivation for structure concerns the extent to which people prefer for their environment to be organized and predictable (Neuberg & Newsom, 1993). Constructing a world in which there is a place for everything, and everything stays in its place, both preserves cognitive resources and ensures that quick judgments and decisions lead to the correct outcomes.

Collectively, the ECF argues that ideological differences in epistemic motivation lead conservatives (more so than liberals) to prioritize efficient categorization. In other words, conservatives more strongly prefer to rely on quick strategies that foster accurate judgments than do liberals. It is important to emphasize that the ECF assumes liberals and conservatives both intend to make accurate category judgments. However, differences in epistemic motivation lead liberals and conservatives to adopt divergent approaches to what they think will produce an accurate judgment. Throughout this chapter, I review research supporting the ECF. Specifically, I outline research indicating that conservatives are more likely than liberals to (a) believe that quick categorization strategies lead to accurate judgments, (b) rely on strategies that preserve cognitive resources when categorizing people into groups, (c) favor targets who facilitate efficient categorization, and (d) form political attitudes, intentions, and behaviors that are based on the idea that social category judgments can be made accurately through quick judgment strategies.

4.3 Alternative theoretical perspectives

Previous research has drawn from different theories and conceptual frameworks to make sense of patterns of social categorization. It is sometimes the case that researchers form predictions from theories that were broadly developed to explain patterns of intergroup behavior and that are subsequently applied to understand social categorization. As a result, the same social categorization patterns can sometimes be explained with multiple theoretical perspectives, especially when underlying mechanisms are not directly assessed (Ho, Kteily, & Chen, 2020). Political ideology is associated with various traits, attitudes, and motivations (Jost et al., 2009; Sibley, Osborne, & Duckitt, 2012). In turn, it is important to consider additional psychological constructs beyond those included in the ECF that could contribute to ideological differences in social categorization processes. Alterative (or additional) explanations for ideological differences can generally be placed under the umbrella of three different perspectives.

First, social dominance theory argues that people vary in the degree to which they are motivated to uphold group-based hierarchy (Pratto, Sidanius, Stallworth, & Malle, 1994). Stereotypes activated after social categorization (e.g., men are agentic and women are communal) provide culturally distributed information about whether a group's characteristics are considered "good" or "bad" in a society and what roles the person can fulfill (Fiske & Taylor, 2013). This information can be used to enforce group-based hierarchy (Czopp, Kay, & Cheryan, 2015; Oldmeadow & Fiske, 2007). Additionally, specific categorization patterns can reinforce hierarchy, such as when members of racial majority groups are more likely to categorize multiracial individuals as Black than White (Ho, Kteily, & Chen, 2017; Ho, Sidanius, Levin, & Banaji, 2011). Political ideology is associated with individual differences in social dominance orientation, such that conservatives report being more motivated to maintain group-based hierarchy than do liberals (Ho et al., 2015). Further, the motivation to oppress (versus support) members of marginalized groups has been used to explain ideological differences in behavior related to intergroup outcomes (Kteily, Rocklage, McClanahan, & Ho, 2019), and so could contribute to liberal-conservative differences in social categorization processes.

Second, social identity theory argues that people identify with social groups and will typically display a pattern of evaluations, judgments, and behaviors that favor the ingroup over the outgroup as a means of fostering a positive social identity (Abrams & Hogg, 1990; Tajfel & Turner, 1979). Social category memberships of perceivers contribute to patterns of category judgments. For example, people tend to have a more selective threshold for categorizing individuals as ingroup members than outgroup members (Knowles & Peng, 2005; Yzerbyt, Castano, Leyens, & Paladino, 2000). Liberals and conservatives differ on some demographic characteristics. People who identify as belonging to lower status groups (e.g., women, African-American individuals) report being more liberal than do individuals who identify with higher status groups (e.g., men, White individuals; Eagly, Diekman, Johannesen-Schmidt, & Koenig, 2004; Saad, 2019). Thus, social identities of perceivers could contribute to ideological differences in social categorization processes.

Third, the ideological conflict hypothesis argues that people evaluate groups more positively when they are perceived to (or actually) share their worldview (Brandt & Crawford, 2020). In other words, liberal perceivers hold more prejudice toward target groups perceived as conservative, whereas conservative perceivers show the opposite pattern. The hypothesis also argues that evaluative patterns emerge in a symmetrical manner, such that liberals and conservatives hold equally prejudicial views toward people who do not share their worldview. While the ideological conflict hypothesis has not been directly used to explain social categorization, prejudice toward a group can impact categorization patterns. For example, people who hold more anti-Semitic attitudes display a stronger response bias toward categorizing targets as Jewish (Himmelfarb, 1966) and are less accurate in their judgments concerning whether targets are Jewish or not (Andrzejewski, Hall, & Salib, 2009). Thus, prejudice toward certain groups could potentially contribute to ideological differences in some social category processes.

These theoretical perspectives have been generative in fostering discussions about intergroup relations and social categorization. However, they diverge from the ECF in the focus of what they have been used to explain. Specifically, as of to date these perspectives have been primarily used to make predictions about *directional patterns* of judgment, such as the conditions under which a multiracial person is more likely to be categorized as an outgroup (versus ingroup) member. These perspectives have also focused on how the categorization *judgment* satisfies particular psychological goals. For example, members of racial majority groups might categorize a multiracial target as Black (versus White) and in doing so satisfy a goal to reinforce racial hierarchy.

The ECF instead speaks to when and why people are expected to differentially *process* available information while making a social category judgment. The epistemic motivations that underlie the ECF are *non-directional* in nature. In other words, the ECF does not posit that epistemic motivations lead people to categorize targets in a specific way (e.g., Black or Jewish) because of the implications of that judgment for further behavior. Rather, the ECF focuses on how liberals and conservatives differentially process available information, and how this processing distinction leads to divergent category judgments and social evaluations.

It is worth noting that social judgments are generally derived from several psychological processes that operate in tandem (Higgins, 1998). In other words, multiple motivations and beliefs can simultaneously contribute to an outcome. Thus, even if these alternative perspectives were used to generate similar predictions about how liberals and conservatives process available information, the ECF posits that epistemic motivation will still play a distinct and independent role in shaping ideological differences in social categorization processes. When outlining supporting findings of the ECF in this chapter, I highlight how epistemic motivation uniquely contributes to observed findings.

5. Political ideology modulates categorization processes

In this section, I outline evidence supporting the ECF's proposal that conservatives more strongly prioritize efficient categorization than do liberals. I discuss findings indicating that liberals and conservatives diverge in the belief that cue reliance produces accurate category judgments, as well as how they process available cues when forming a category judgment. I also discuss the implications of these processes for both the degree to which liberals and conservatives think their category judgments are accurate as well as when they are actually accurate.

5.1 Beliefs about cue diagnosticity

Perceivers sometimes possess information that directly reveals a person's group membership. For example, a person might state their race on a social media page or their sexual orientation on a dating website. However, in most situations perceivers lack this type of information and instead make judgments indirectly through reliance on available cues. Cue diagnosticity concerns the extent to which the available information used to make a category judgment clearly signals one group membership over others. The cues that people use to make some social category judgements are highly diagnostic of group membership, in the sense that the cues strongly distinguish between groups. For example, people use skin tone and Afrocentricity of facial characteristics to categorize race (Blair, Judd, Sadler, & Jenkins, 2002; Maddox, 2004) and gender typicality to categorize sex (Johnson & Tassinary, 2005). The cues that people use to categorize other forms of group membership are less diagnostic, in the sense that the cues more weakly distinguish groups. For example, people use gender typicality in a person's face and gait to categorize sexual orientation (Freeman, Johnson, Ambady, & Rule, 2010; Johnson et al., 2007) and facial dominance to categorize political party membership (Rule & Ambady, 2010).

People's beliefs about categorization generally reflect these varying degrees of cue diagnosticity. People think that their judgments will be more accurate for categories that possess strongly diagnostic cues (e.g., race and sex) relative to those where cues are less diagnostic (e.g., sexual orientation; Lick & Johnson, 2014). Importantly, however, there is considerable variability among people in the degree to which they believe that they can render accurate category judgments from minimal cues (Rule, Ambady, Adams, & Macrae, 2008).

A perceiver's political ideology contributes to variability in beliefs about cue diagnosticity. Specifically, conservatives (versus liberals) more strongly believe that physical appearance cues can be used to accurately categorize group membership. In one study, we (Stern, West, Jost, & Rule, 2013; Study 3) asked participants the extent to which they possessed knowledge of and, separately, endorsed stereotypes about cues that could be used to categorize sexual orientation. For example, participants rated the degree to which gay men are more likely than straight men to have groomed eyebrows and styled hair. We found that liberals and conservatives did not differ in reported *knowledge* of the stereotypes. However, conservatives were more likely than liberals to *endorse* these stereotypes as being accurate. Additionally, this ideological difference was explained in part through liberals reporting a stronger desire to engage in deliberative thought than conservatives, which was measured with the need for cognition scale (Cacioppo & Petty, 1982). These patterns held when accounting for greater anti-gay prejudice among conservatives and greater contact with gay men among liberals, supporting the unique contribution of epistemic motivation. These findings indicate that liberals and conservatives are both *aware* of cues that could be used to quickly categorize group membership, but that conservatives more strongly *endorse* these cues as being diagnostic than do liberals.

Moving beyond specific cues, liberals and conservatives also diverge in their general beliefs that various social categories can be accurately gleaned from reliance on minimal cues. For example, Suzuki, Tsukamoto, and Takahashi (2019) found that people who endorsed more conservative (i.e., just world) beliefs scored higher on Livingston's (2001) Perceptual Reliance Index, which includes items assessing cue diagnosticity for various group memberships (e.g., *You can usually tell if a woman is a lesbian by her physical appearance.*). In a more systematic analysis, I (Stern, 2019; Study 2) asked participants to indicate the perceived diagnosticity of cues that could be used to categorize various groups: sex, race, sexual orientation, age, and religion. To do so, participants completed an adapted version of Lick and Johnson's (2014) Diagnosticity Scale. An example item includes: *A person's [insert social category] can largely be determined by their physical appearance.*

The correlation between ideology and the Diagnosticity Scale within each social category condition is presented in Fig. 3. Overall, conservatives were more likely than liberals to believe that cues are diagnostic, in the sense that group memberships can be accurately gleaned from minimal information. Additionally, the strength of the relationship between ideology

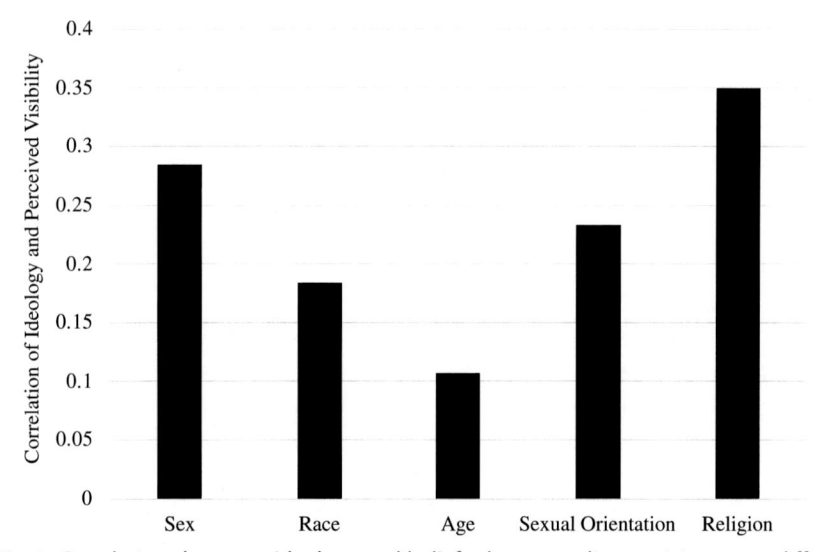

Fig. 3 Correlations between ideology and beliefs about cue diagnosticity across different social categories, as reported in Study 2 of Stern (2019). Positive correlations indicate that beliefs about cue diagnosticity are higher among conservatives (versus liberals).

and perceived cue diagnosticity did not consistently vary across the different categories, meaning that conservatives were more likely than liberals to believe that cues are diagnostic of group membership regardless of the actual degree of diagnosticity.

Given that social categories are culturally constructed, there is no "right" answer to the number of groups that compose a category. People also diverge in their views about how many groups exist within social categories (Morgenroth et al., 2021; Morgenroth & Ryan, 2021), which raises the question of whether ideological differences in cue diagnosticity are simply derived from beliefs about category breadth. Cues typically become less diagnostic, and group memberships harder to categorize, when there are more groups in a category (Chen & Hamilton, 2012; Ding & Rule, 2012). For example, categorizing a person's race is easier if the possible response options are *Black* and *White* compared to when the option *multiracial* is also provided. To determine whether liberals and conservatives differed in the perceived breadth of social categories, I (Stern, 2019) asked participants to indicate what group memberships they would provide to people on a survey (e.g., what options would they give people to report their race). Overall, liberals reported that social categories were composed of a larger number of groups than did conservatives. For example, conservatives were more likely to state that they would include only the options of *male* and *female* for the category *sex* whereas liberals often included more options. Statistically adjusting for ideological differences in perceived category breadth did not eliminate the relationship between ideology and perceived cue diagnosticity, ruling out these beliefs as a potential confound or "third variable."

In a subsequent study (Stern, 2019; Study 3), I examined whether a desire for efficient categorization contributed to ideological differences in beliefs about cue diagnosticity. Participants completed the Diagnosticity Scale and then reported their epistemic motivation through the Personal Need for Structure Scale (e.g., *I enjoy having a clear and structured mode of life*; Neuberg & Newsom, 1993) as well as their motivation to uphold group-based hierarchy through the SDO_7 scale (e.g., *An ideal society requires some groups to be on top and others to be on the bottom*; Ho et al., 2015). Consistent with past findings, conservatives reported a greater desire to achieve a sense structure in daily life and, separately, a stronger motivation to maintain hierarchy than did liberals. The motivation to achieve structure explained in part why conservatives were more likely than liberals to believe that cues were diagnostic of group membership, even when accounting for ideological differences in the desire to uphold hierarchy. These findings support the perspective that a desire to make efficient judgments contributes to why liberals and conservatives diverge in how strongly they believe that cues are diagnostic of group memberships.

5.2 Processing of cues during social categorization

In the absence of information that directly reveals a person's group membership, all categorization judgments occur under a degree of ambiguity. Some judgments require engaging with more uncertainty and ambiguity than do others. For example, a person who possesses a masculine gait, masculine facial characteristics, short hair, and facial hair will most likely be categorized as a man. However, a target person who possesses a masculine gait, feminine facial characteristics, long hair, and facial hair will less clearly signal a group membership and there will be greater variability among perceivers in their final judgments. Some social categories like sexual orientation and religion are also considered inherently ambiguous, because their defining features cannot be directly observed (i.e., sexual attraction and spiritual beliefs, respectively; Tskhay & Rule, 2013). The epistemic motivations on which liberals and conservatives differ revolve around reaching closure in the face of ambiguity and uncertainty. In turn, the ECF proposes that liberals and conservatives should be most likely to diverge in categorization processes when targets' group memberships possess some degree of ambiguity.

We (Stern et al., 2013; Study 1) examined whether ideological differences in beliefs about cues being diagnostic of group membership translated into how perceivers actually categorized others. Specifically, we investigated whether conservatives would be more likely than liberals to rely on physical appearance cues in the process of categorizing sexual orientation. Unless otherwise specified, when discussing separate effects among liberals and conservatives for the remaining studies reviewed in this chapter, *conservatives* refers to estimated effects at 1 standard deviation above (i.e., more conservative than) the sample ideology mean and *liberals* refers to estimated effects at 1 standard deviation below (i.e., more liberal than) the mean.

In the study, participants viewed facial photographs of White men and indicated whether they believed each man was gay or straight. They were given an unlimited amount of time to make their judgments. A separate set of raters indicated the extent to which the target men possessed gender typical facial characteristics. Overall, conservatives were more likely than liberals to rely on physical appearance cues to make sexual orientation judgments. Specifically, for conservative perceivers, lower gender typicality among targets was associated with a higher likelihood of categorizing targets as gay rather than straight. For liberal perceivers, however, there was no association between target gender typicality and sexual orientation judgments.

Categorization response times also suggested that liberals expended more cognitive resources than did conservatives during the judgment process. Greater time taken to make a judgment is commonly argued to reflect deliberation and expense of cognitive resources (e.g., Epley, Keysar, Van Boven, & Gilovich, 2004; Kleiman & Hassin, 2011; Lick & Johnson, 2013; Tamir & Mitchell, 2013). We found that liberals took more time to render sexual orientation judgments than did conservatives, suggesting that conservatives were more likely than liberals to make quick and low effort judgments predicated on physical appearance cues.

Because sexual orientation is inherently ambiguous when categorized from perceptual information, physical appearance cues stand as one of the few pieces of information on which individuals can rely. As previously reviewed, however, conservatives are more likely than liberals to believe that cues can be used to accurately categorize group membership regardless of the actual degree of diagnosticity (Stern, 2019). As a result, ideological differences are also expected to emerge when ambiguity arises within categories typically considered more obvious.

For example, when categorizing targets who are racially ambiguous people commonly rely on hypodescent, which is also known as the *one drop rule* (Peery & Bodenhausen, 2008). Hypodescent dictates that even a small number of cues suggesting racial minority group membership (e.g., relatively low levels of Afrocentric facial characteristics) are diagnostic of racial minority group membership (Banks & Eberhardt, 1998). Hypodescent has been historically used to subjugate African-Americans and maintain race-based economic inequality. However, relying on hypodescent also serves the epistemic goal of facilitating rapid social categorization. For example, hypodescent emerges in speeded categorization tasks where participants are required to make a judgment within 2500 milliseconds, suggesting that this judgment strategy unfolds relatively quickly (Ho et al., 2011). Hypodescent allows people to swiftly disambiguate the race of targets through relying on physical appearance cues and, as a result, expend low cognitive effort.

Krosch, Berntsen, Amodio, Jost, and Van Bavel (2013; Studies 1 & 2) examined whether political ideology would correspond to racial categorization under ambiguity. The researchers morphed "parent" faces of Black and

White men in a manner that created stimuli varying from 100% Black to 100% White in 10% intervals. As a result, some target stimuli were highly prototypical of a racial group whereas others were moderately or strongly ambiguous. Participants categorized these faces as White or Black. Through using this approach, the researchers were able to gauge the precise point at which people were more likely to categorize targets as Black than White. Overall, a higher degree of Afrocentricity in target faces was required among liberal (versus conservative) perceivers before targets were more likely to be categorized as Black (versus White). In other words, conservatives were more likely to engage in hypodescent than were liberals. Interestingly, conservatives' (i.e., estimated effects at two standard deviations more conservative than the sample mean) probability of categorizing targets as Black increased above chance before targets were 50% Black/ White. This categorization strategy ensured that conservatives could swiftly categorize targets as their racial ambiguity increased. Liberals (i.e., estimated effects at two standard deviations more liberal than the sample mean), however, were almost equally likely to categorize 50% Black/White targets as Black or White, suggesting that they more readily engaged with ambiguity to construct a category judgment.

The researchers also examined mechanisms that could account for ideological differences in hypodescent (Krosch et al., 2013; Study 2). They found that a greater desire to oppose equality in part explained the ideological difference, but need for structure (i.e., epistemic motivation) did not play an explanatory role. At first glance, these findings seem inconsistent with the ECF. However, results indicated that conservatives reported a stronger motivation for structure than did liberals, and need for structure was (nonsignificantly) associated with greater use of hypodescent ($r=-.13$). The researchers collected a sample size ($N=71$) in which moderate to large effect sizes could be detected. It is possible that the study simply did not possess enough statistical power to detect the smaller influence of epistemic motivation. Relatedly, other findings suggest that motivations guiding reliance on hypodescent might be highly sensitive to contextual factors. Chen, Kteily, and Ho (2019) reported that the motivation to uphold hierarchy was unrelated to how Asian Americans categorized White-Asian biracial targets. Ho, Sidanius, Cuddy, and Banaji (2013) also found that the motivation to uphold hierarchy was only related to hypodescent in categorizing a biracial target when White perceivers were first informed that African-Americans were a growing socioeconomic threat.

Based on these findings, the specific motivational reason(s) why political ideology is linked to hypodescent during racial categorization remains somewhat unclear. In the Unites States, and most places throughout the world, race operates as a social category is which inequality and discrimination are woven into the fabric of social, economic, and political life (Eberhardt, 2020; Markus, 2008; Payne, Vuletich, & Brown-Iannuzzi, 2019). As a result, various motivations and beliefs are implicated in race-based judgments (Ho et al., 2020). It is possible that mechanisms driving liberals and conservatives to diverge in the racial categorization process are highly context dependent. Alternatively, multiple motivations might simultaneously guide judgments and more highly powered studies are needed to estimate precise effect sizes. Despite the existence of this open question, the findings reviewed in this section collectively highlight that conservatives are more likely than liberals to process and utilize available cues in a manner that quickly resolves uncertainty about group membership.

5.3 Processing capability modulates the expression of ideological differences

How do liberals and conservatives come to diverge in their final category judgments? One possibility is that liberals and conservatives differ in their initial judgments and that liberals continue to deliberate on that judgment before coming to a final conclusion. For example, when presented with a photograph of a feminine man, conservative perceivers might make the initial assumption that the target person is gay whereas liberal perceivers make the judgment that he is straight. However, knowledge of stereotypes tends to be reflected in the information that is initially activated in a perceiver's mind (e.g., Devine, 1989). As previously reviewed, both liberals and conservatives possess knowledge about cues that could be used in categorization. Thus, the same category is likely to be activated upon perceiving cues from a target person, regardless of the perceiver's ideology. For example, perceiving a man with feminine physical characteristics is likely to activate the idea that the man could be gay to a comparable degree for liberals and conservatives. Overall, it is unlikely that differences between liberals and conservatives would emerge in initial category judgments.

We (Stern et al., 2013) reasoned that ideological differences were instead emerging because liberals were more likely than conservatives to adjust the initial judgments that came to mind. When an initial judgment clashes with a person's beliefs, there is an increased likelihood that they will consider changing that judgment (Skitka, Mullen, Griffin, Hutchinson, & Chamberlin, 2002). In the case of social categorization, an initial judgment based on stereotypical cues is more strongly misaligned with liberals' (versus conservatives') beliefs about the diagnosticity of cues. Overriding or changing an initial judgment often requires deliberation and effortful thought, especially when a specific task or stimulus has not been previously encountered (Epley et al., 2004; Tamir & Mitchell, 2013). For example, liberals are more likely than conservatives to adjust their initial judgments about people who appear responsible for a negative outcome (Skitka et al., 2002) and their assumptions about how widely their beliefs are shared with ingroup members (Stern & West, 2016). However, ideological differences in this adjustment process are reduced when deliberation is experimentally impaired, such as through cognitive load or time pressure (Skitka et al., 2002; Stern & West, 2016).

The ECF proposes that liberals and conservatives only diverge in social categorization processes when perceivers are able to engage in deliberation. In a subsequent study ((Stern et al., 2013); Study 2), we directly examined this prediction. Participants were again shown images of White men and indicated whether they believed each man was gay or straight. Additionally, participants were either assigned to complete the categorization task without any distractions or while under cognitive load (i.e., they were asked to remember a seven-digit alphanumeric code). Participants received unlimited time to make the category judgments.

We found that liberals and conservatives reported comparable degrees of distraction in the cognitive load (versus no load) conditions, but the manipulation more strongly affected liberals' (versus conservatives') judgments through impairing the ability to deliberate (Fig. 4). Specifically, among participants who made judgment without distraction (i.e., those not under cognitive load), conservatives were again more likely than liberals to rely on gender typicality cues to make sexual orientation judgments. However, when participants made judgments under cognitive load, liberals were just as likely as conservatives to categorize targets as gay (versus straight) as gender typicality decreased. In other words, liberals were more likely to rely on gender typicality cues in their final category judgments when they were under cognitive load compared to when they were able to deliberate. These judgment patterns suggest that initial category activation was comparable for liberals and conservatives, and that cognitive distraction prevented adjustment of those initial judgments. Liberals also took more time than conservatives to make a category judgment when undistracted, whereas liberals and conservatives took comparable amounts of time when under cognitive load. These findings collectively support the perspective that

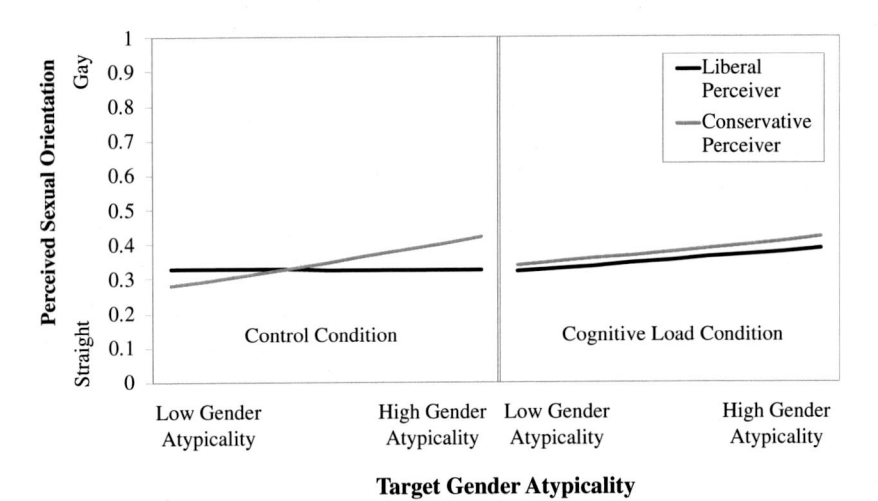

Fig. 4 Relationship between target gender atypicality (plotted at one standard deviation below and above the gender atypicality mean) and sexual orientation judgments among liberal and conservative perceivers (one standard deviation below and above the ideology mean, respectively), as a function of cognitive load condition. *Adapted from Study 2 of Stern, C., West, T. V., & Schoenthaler, A. (2013). The dynamic relationship between accuracy and bias in social perception research.* Social and Personality Psychology Compass, 7(5), 303–314.

conservatives are more likely than liberals to stick with an initial category judgment that is based on physical appearance cues and, as a result, make quicker judgments.

Ideological differences in judgment patterns held when accounting for greater anti-gay prejudice among conservatives and greater contact with gay men along liberals. These constructs also did not modulate how strongly people relied on gender typicality cues to make category judgments. How do we make sense of these findings in light of previous research linking prejudice to stereotype usage? For example, past work has documented that people low in prejudice are less likely to consciously use stereotypes to form judgments once targets have been categorized into a social group (Monteith, Sherman, & Devine, 1998; Monteith, Spicer, & Tooman, 1998).

I argue that there is a common distinction between stereotypes used for social categorization and stereotypes that are activated after a person has been mentally placed into a group. Information that becomes cognitively active after social categorization has frequently contributed to the stigmatization of minority groups, such as when people who are categorized as gay (versus straight) are subsequently viewed as promiscuous (Pinsof & Haselton, 2016), and people categorized as women (versus men) are viewed as lacking agency (Eagly, Nater, Miller, Kaufmann, & Sczesny, 2019; Haines, Deaux, & Lofaro, 2016). However, category stereotypes that are viewed as positive or flattering of a group (e.g., African-American individuals are better athletes than White individuals) generate less compunction in their usage than do stereotypes viewed as negative (Czopp et al., 2015; Kay, Day, Zanna, & Nussbaum, 2013). I posit that the stereotypical cues used to categorize group membership are often viewed in a less negative, and sometimes positive, manner. As a result, epistemic motivations might sometimes be prioritized over prejudice reduction motives during social categorization.

Two pieces of evidence support this argument, at least in the context of categorizing sexual orientation. First, both liberals and conservatives view cues used to categorize sexual orientation as being neutral (e.g., long eyelashes) or positive (e.g., clear skin) in valence (Stern et al., 2013). Second, manipulations that reduce concerns about expressing prejudice do not change the extent to which people rely on appearance cues to categorize sexual orientation. Previous research has found that when participants indicate what they believe other people feel, as opposed to what they personally think, there is reduced concern about appearing prejudiced in judgments (Devine & Elliot, 1995; Petsko & Bodenhausen, 2019). We (Spielmann & Stern, 2021) drew upon this paradigm and asked participants to categorize targets' sexual orientation either based on what the average person would say or what they personally think. Targets' gender typicality was associated with perceivers' sexual orientation judgments, and the manipulation did not change how strongly perceivers relied on gender typicality cues to make category judgments. These findings highlight why epistemic motivation might sometimes take priority over other constructs, such as prejudice, in guiding how liberals and conservatives process information and make category judgments.

5.4 Perceived and actual categorization accuracy

Using cues in one's environment to make rapid social inferences often leads to accuracy and, as a result, greater efficiency. For example, a person who categorizes an object with four legs, a seat, and a back, as a chair based solely on minimal information will more often than not correctly determine what the object is. Similar processes occur for perceptions of the social world, such that relying on cues to make low effort judgments often fosters accuracy. People are highly accurate in their judgments of race and gender when they rely on physical appearance information to render judgments

(Cutting, Proffitt, & Kozlowski, 1978; Hill, Bruce, & Akamatsu, 1995; Johnson & Tassinary, 2005). People's judgments of more ambiguous social categories are also relatively accurate (Tskhay & Rule, 2013). For example, gender typicality is associated with sexual orientation, such that gay and lesbian individuals display less gender typicality than do heterosexuals (Rieger, Linsenmeier, Gygax, Garcia, & Bailey, 2010). In turn, using gender typicality as a cue to infer sexual orientation allows for rapid and low effort judgments that are accurate at levels above chance (Freeman et al., 2010; Johnson et al., 2007; Rieger et al., 2010). Thus, relying on cues to make category judgments often generates some degree of accuracy.

Do differences in cue usage lead liberals and conservatives to diverge in the accuracy of their category judgments? On a subjective level, conservatives more strongly *believe* that their judgments are accurate than do liberals. In a series of studies (Stern, Ruisch, & Rule, under review), participants categorized various group memberships (e.g., race, sex, sexual orientation) from facial photographs. After making each judgment, they also indicated how confident they were that the judgment was accurate. Across the different category judgments, conservatives consistently reported greater confidence than did liberals.

There is reason to believe that people's beliefs about accuracy might not reflect reality. People generally possess poor insight into whether their category judgments are correct (e.g., Olivola, Eubanks, & Lovelace, 2014; Rule et al., 2008), and often fail to use information that would produce the most accurate category judgments (Olivola & Todorov, 2010). Some theorists have also noted that the ideology a person embraces can lead them to form a uniquely distorted understanding of the world. For example, philosopher Louis Althusser (1971, p. 52) argued that "ideology represents the imaginary relationship of individuals to their real conditions of existence." Similar ideas have been echoed in psychology (e.g., Jost, 1995; Jost & Banaji, 1994), suggesting a complex relationship between political ideology and categorization accuracy.

How do we determine when liberals and conservatives will differ in judgment accuracy? Understanding when perceivers are more (or less) likely to make accurate judgments necessitates the usage of paradigms in which there is both a correct answer to the judgment and that answer is available as a response option to participants. Obtaining stimuli in which there is a correct answer might pose a challenge when researchers examine perceptions of minority groups (e.g., multiracial individuals). However, using computer-generated faces produces findings that sometimes diverge from those of real target individuals (Gaither, Chen, Pauker, & Sommers, 2019), and a growing number of databases allow researchers to use stimuli in which the actual group membership of targets is known (e.g., Chen, Norman, & Nam, 2021; Ma, Kantner, & Wittenbrink, 2021). Paradigms that deviate from these criteria preclude the assessment of accuracy and actual judgment efficiency.

As noted above, perceivers can make accurate judgments through relying on cues (e.g., physical appearance) that allow them to correctly discriminate between possible category judgments. However, it is also possible that accuracy could occur through response biases in categorization. For example, some perceivers might display a response bias to categorize target's religion as Jewish (Allport & Kramer, 1946; Himmelfarb, 1966) or sexual orientation as straight (Lick & Johnson, 2016). Historically, researchers did not always account for response biases when discussing the accuracy of category judgments. In more recent years, though, researchers have begun to consistently conduct statistical models that account for response bias when estimating accuracy, such as signal detection (e.g., Rule & Ambady, 2008) and multi-level analyses (e.g., Johnson et al., 2007; Stern et al., 2013). Above chance accuracy consistently emerges in categorization judgments when accounting for response biases (Tskhay & Rule, 2013), which suggests that perceivers are utilizing cues to discriminate between category options.

For a perceiver to correctly discriminate between possible category judgments, there need to be available cues that are diagnostic of group membership *and* the perceiver must use that information in their judgments (Brunswik, 1955; Stern, West, & Schoenthaler, 2013; West & Kenny, 2011). Breakdown in either of these factors reduces judgment accuracy. Low effort category judgments are inaccurate when perceivers rely on cues that are undiagnostic of group membership (Freeman et al., 2010). Effortful deliberation also undermines accuracy when perceivers become less reliant on diagnostic cues (Ambady & Gray, 2002).

To the extent that cues possess an overwhelming degree of diagnosticity, conservatives—who are more reliant on the cues—would be expected to more effectively discriminate between the group memberships of targets than would liberals. However, cues are never perfectly diagnostic of group membership. For example, effect sizes of the relationship between sexual orientation and gender typicality in physical appearance range from moderate to large across samples (e.g., $r = .37–.61$; Freeman et al., 2010;

Stern et al., 2013). Additionally, even for categories where cues tend to be more diagnostic of group membership (e.g., sex, race), there is still variability across targets in strength of diagnosticity (Ma, Correll, & Wittenbrink, 2015). As a result, liberals and conservatives possess similar average degrees of accuracy in social category judgments. For example, Stern et al. (2013) assessed judgment accuracy through comparing perceivers' judgments of targets' sexual orientation to targets' self-reported sexual orientation. Liberals and conservatives displayed a comparable degree of overall accuracy in their judgments. Similarly, we (Stern et al., under review) also found no overall differences in how accurately liberals and conservatives could determine sex, race, and sexual orientation from facial photographs.

Rather than differing in overall accuracy, liberals and conservatives instead diverge in the types of targets for whom they are able to discern the correct group membership. Because conservatives more strongly rely on stereotypical cues to make final category judgments than do liberals, they are better able to discriminate between groups than are liberals when cues are diagnostic of group membership. However, liberals are better able to correctly discriminate between groups than are conservatives when cues are undiagnostic. We (Stern et al., 2013) found that when participants made judgments without distraction, conservatives were more accurate than liberals in categorizing stereotypical targets for whom cues were highly diagnostic (feminine gay men and masculine straight men), whereas liberals were more accurate than conservatives in categorizing counterstereotypical targets for whom cues were undiagnostic (masculine gay men and feminine straight men). When participants made judgments under cognitive load, however, liberals and conservatives did not diverge in their patterns of accuracy. Liberals and conservatives were both more accurate in categorizing stereotypical targets than counterstereotypical targets.

These findings highlight that neither liberals nor conservatives utilize a social judgment strategy that consistently produces more accurate category judgments. Although epistemic motivations lead conservatives (versus liberals) to more strongly prioritize efficient categorization and believe that reliance on cues reliably promotes accurate judgments, conservatives do not always display greater actual efficiency than liberals. Conservatives are more efficient than liberals when cues are highly diagnostic of group membership because they expend fewer cognitive resources and are more accurate in their judgments. However, conservatives are not more efficient than liberals when cues are low in diagnosticity because they are less accurate in categorizing those targets.

5.5 Summary

Previous research has noted that individual differences among perceivers can impact social categorization processes. The ECF outlines how political ideology plays a focal role in social cognitive processes and provides nuance in understanding the way in which people categorize others into groups. People who are politically conservative more strongly believe that physical appearance cues are diagnostic of group membership than do people who are liberal. Conservatives also more strongly rely on these cues to make category judgments than do liberals, but only when perceivers are able to engage in deliberative processing. Further, conservatives appraise their category judgments as being more accurate than do liberals. However, the reality is more complex. Conservatives achieve greater categorization accuracy when cues are high in diagnosticity, but liberals are more accurate when cues are low in diagnosticity.

6. Ideology modulates evaluations of people who challenge efficient categorization

In this next section, I outline how a perceiver's political ideology impacts the way in which social categorization processes shape evaluations of others. I highlight that the desire for efficient categorization contributes to ideological differences in evaluations of targets based on the ease with which they can be mentally placed into a group and the degree to which they reinforce the diagnosticity of cues. I also outline how contextual activation of epistemic motivations and categorization goals play a critical role in determining when political ideology modulates evaluations derived from categorization processes.

6.1 The impact of categorization ease on liking

Targets that possess greater alignment with the stereotypes of their (social) category have been described in various ways, such as being "good targets" (Funder, 1995, 2012), possessing cue validity (Brunswik, 1955), embodying a kernel of truth to a stereotype (Kenny, 1994), and as fostering stereotype accuracy (Jussim, 2005). Independent of the specific phrase used, people whose physical appearance is stereotypical of their group membership are easier to categorize, as there is less competition among the possible judgments that could be made (Freeman et al., 2020; Freeman & Ambady, 2011). For example, there is greater competition between the categories of *male* and *female* when people categorize a gender atypical (versus typical) target person (Freeman, Ambady, Rule, & Johnson, 2008). Relatedly, people take greater amounts of time to categorize the race of multiracial than monoracial individuals, as multiracial individual often possess characteristics that are stereotypic of several racial groups (Chen & Hamilton, 2012).

The difficultly with which social information is processed corresponds to people's subsequent evaluations. Objects that are easier to encode and require the allocation of fewer cognitive resources (e.g., objects with a stronger figure-group contrast or greater symmetry) are evaluated in a more positive manner (Reber, Schwarz, & Winkielman, 2004; Winkielman & Cacioppo, 2001). A similar process occurs in the evaluation of social groups, such that targets who are easier to categorize are evaluated more favorably (Lick & Johnson, 2015, 2016). For example, greater time taken to categorize a target's sexual orientation was associated with more negative evaluations of the target (Lick & Johnson, 2013; Lick, Johnson, & Rule, 2015). Relatedly, when a social context (e.g., times of economic scarcity) impairs the fluent encoding of Black faces on a neural level, individuals allocate resources in a more racially biased manner (Krosch & Amodio, 2019).

Greater deliberation time and expense of cognitive resources reduce efficiency in the judgment input. The ECF proposes that the degree to which a person prioritizes efficient categorization modulates the connection strength between judgment difficulty and target evaluations. The ECF also contends that conservatives more strongly favor efficient categorization than do liberals. Thus, conservatives (versus liberals) are expected to more readily form negative evaluations of targets who require greater (versus less) time and cognitive effort to categorize.

Previous research has found support for this perspective in the evaluation of non-human objects. For example, greater conservatism among men is related to lower liking of polygons as they become more complex (Eisenman, Borod, & Grossman, 1972) and conservatives form more negative evaluations of abstract artwork compared to liberals (Wilson, Ausman, & Mathews, 1973). Conservatives are also more attentive than are liberals in detecting shapes that deviate from an expected pattern (Okimoto & Gromet, 2016). Some indirect evidence also suggests that similar patterns would emerge in evaluations of people. Epistemic motivations that are generally stronger among conservatives than liberals guide attitudes toward groups that exist outside of category binaries (i.e., groups harder to categorize). For example, when attitudes are assessed toward groups as a whole, a stronger motivation for cognitive closure is related to more negative attitudes toward bisexual people (Burke et al., 2017), gender nonbinary people (Morgenroth et al., 2021), and transgender people (Tebbe & Moradi, 2012).

We have also conducted several studies that examine whether expending cognitive effort during the social categorization process is more strongly associated with evaluations of human targets among conservative perceivers than liberal perceivers. In one study (Stern & Rule, 2018; Study 1) participants viewed photographs of transgender people who were in the process of undergoing hormone replacement therapy (HRT) to transition from female to male. The stimulus set included photographs of each target person over the course a year. As transgender individuals undergo HRT, their physical appearance initially becomes more androgynous (i.e., a blend of masculine and feminine characteristics) and then becomes more gender typical (e.g., a greater degree of masculine than feminine characteristics for a person identifying as male). Ratings obtained from a separate set of individuals confirmed that this was the case, in that there was variability in the degree to which target individuals were more androgynous (difficult to categorize) or gender typical (easy to categorize).

Participants in the study viewed one photograph of each target and indicated how positively they felt toward the person using a sliding scale that ranged from 0 (*not at all positively*) to 100 (*very positively*). To avoid the possibility that pre-existing feelings toward transgender people would influence evaluations, participants were not informed that targets were transgender. Among conservative perceivers, the degree to which targets possessed an androgynous physical appearance was associated with more negative evaluations. Among liberal perceivers, however, physical androgyny was not associated with evaluations of targets.

In a subsequent study (Stern & Rule, 2018; Study 2), we examined the extent to which categorization difficulty shaped conservatives' and liberals' evaluations. Participants again viewed photos of transgender individuals, but now categorized each person as male or female before indicating how positively they felt toward the person. Participants were given an unlimited amount of time to categorize each target person's gender. Greater androgyny in targets' physical appearance was, unsurprisingly, associated with longer categorization times. Importantly, however, the amount of time taken to make category judgments was differentially associated with evaluations among liberal and conservative perceivers (Fig. 5). Longer categorization times were associated with more negative evaluations of transgender targets among conservative perceivers. In contrast, response times were unrelated to evaluations among liberal perceivers. These patterns held when accounting

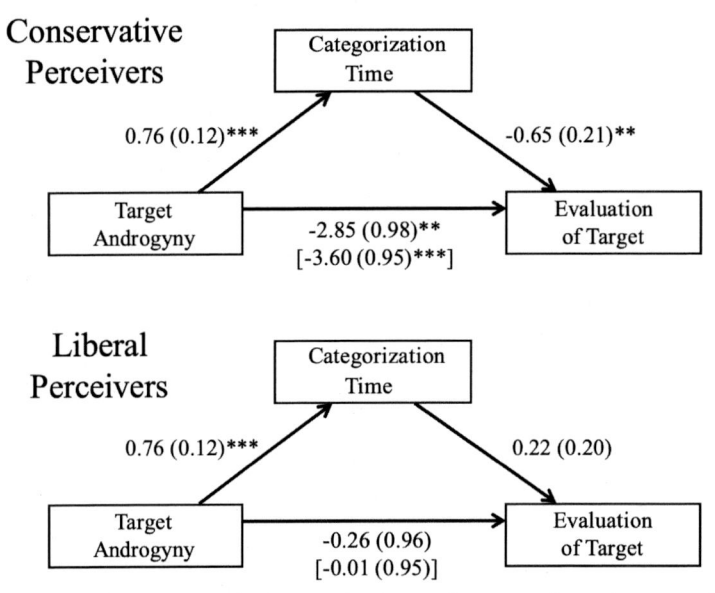

Fig. 5 Target androgyny predicting evaluations of targets through categorization response times for liberal and conservative perceivers (one standard deviation below and above the ideology mean, respectively), as reported in Study 2 of Stern and Rule (2018). Values in brackets represent direct associations; values without brackets represent associations when all variables are included in the model. **$P<.01$. ***$P<.001$.

for participants' attitudes toward transgender people in general and endorsement of traditional gender roles. These findings indicate that greater cognitive effort expended during the process of social categorization leads conservatives, more so than liberals, to form negative evaluations of targets.

Although categorization times were unrelated to target evaluations among liberal perceivers, the relationship trended in a positive direction such that longer decision times were associated with more *positive* evaluations of transgender targets. We conducted an additional analysis examining this relationship among people who reported being strongly liberal (i.e., 1.5 standard deviations more liberal than the ideology mean) and found that the relationship was significant. In other words, extreme liberals viewed a target more favorably when they expended greater cognitive effort to categorize the target's gender.

How do we make sense of this surprising relationship? Understanding this pattern of evaluation requires a nuanced consideration of exactly how liberals differ from conservatives in their motivational profiles. Some perspectives have discussed uncertainty and ambiguity as a general human dislike that people wish to minimize, with the strength of this desire varying across individuals (Buhr & Dugas, 2002; Camerer & Weber, 1992). In other words, people seek to avoid uncertainty, and some people want to do so more strongly than others. This notion is commonly reflected in discussions of epistemic motivation differences between liberals and conservatives. For example, Tetlock (2007, p. 905) noted that conservatives' greater desire for closure, certainty, order, and structure "does not mean that liberals crave uncertainty" but instead that liberals' motivation to avoid uncertainty is simply weaker. However, people sometimes find it pleasant to become immersed in effortful cognitive activity (Wilson, Westgate, Buttrick, & Gilbert, 2019) and to engage with ambiguity (Golman, Gurney, & Loewenstein, 2021), which raises the possibility that liberals' and conservatives' epistemic motivations might sometimes be the inverse of one another. For example, Carney et al. (2008, p. 817) argue that liberals display motivational patterns consistent with a desire for "openness, creativity, novelty, and rebelliousness".

Liberals might not only be more motivated than conservatives to engage in effortful cognitive processing but sometimes may actually enjoy doing so. A closer examination of epistemic motivation scales that liberals score higher on than conservatives supports this perspective. As previously noted, liberals have higher scores than conservatives on the measure of need for cognition (Jost et al., 2018). Several items on the scale reflect pleasure and interest in engaging in deliberative thought, such as *I really enjoy a task that involves coming up with new solutions to problems* and *I prefer my life to be filled with puzzles that I must solve* (Cacioppo, Petty, & Feng Kao, 1984). Greater need for cognition is also associated with higher responses on a measure that explicitly assesses enjoyment derived from thinking (Wilson et al., 2019). Thus, it is conceptually feasible that, at least to some extent, liberals approach social categorization as a complex puzzle that they hope to solve. For people who are strongly liberal, greater engagement on the task could prompt more positive feelings toward the stimulus that evoked the deliberation. Just as liberals (versus conservatives) more strongly prefer complex and abstract art that requires effortful thought to process (Wilson et al., 1973), liberals might similarly prefer social targets that require more time and mental exertion to categorize.

6.2 The impact of liking on categorization ease

Greater preferences for people who facilitate easy categorization forges a general relationship between positivity and categorization ease. As a result, liking of a target also promotes a desire for easy categorization. For example, we (Alter, Stern, Granot, & Balcetis, 2016) examined how political leaders (e.g., members of the US Congress) were represented in news articles. People associate Eurocentric (versus Afrocentric) phenotypic characteristics, such as lighter skin, with leadership abilities (Gaines, 2012; Messing, Jabon, & Plaut, 2016). We reasoned that articles describing political leaders in a more positive (versus negative) manner would display a photograph in which the person possessed lighter skin. In other words, the person would be represented in a manner that facilitated categorization as a leader. An analysis of the objective skin tone of photographs in articles supported this reasoning. When a politician was described positively (versus negatively), the skin tone of the photo that accompanied the article was objectively lighter. The relationship between positivity and skin tone did not vary across the race or gender of the politician.

A correspondence between positivity and categorization ease is more likely to emerge in contexts that prompt more conservative (versus liberal) ways of thinking. For example, in one study we (Stern, Balcetis, Cole, West, & Caruso, 2016; Study 3) had Black and White participants read information stating that an important governmental department (the Department of Education) was either highly unstable (e.g., disorganized, unpredictable future) or stable (e.g., organized, predictable future). Instability (versus stability) prompts individuals to think in more conservative (versus liberal) ways (Jost, Gaucher, & Stern, 2015; Kay & Friesen, 2011). Participants then read about a highly qualified candidate running for a position in the Department of Education. Participants were informed that the candidate either did or did not share their political views about the education system as a means of inducing favorable or unfavorable feelings toward the candidate, respectively.

Participants next indicated the extent to which three photos of the candidate were representative of him. We altered the skin tone of the photos so that participants viewed one photo in which the candidate's skin tone was lighter, one in which it was darker, and one where it was unaltered. The race of the candidate was ambiguous from the photographs. We found that when the system was presented as unstable (versus stable) and participants viewed the candidate favorably (versus unfavorably), both Black and White participants were more likely to rate the lightened photo as representative of the candidate than the unaltered and darkened photos. In other words, they formed a mental image of the candidate as possessing the stereotypical characteristics of a leader. These findings highlight that situations inducing more conservative (versus liberal) ways of thinking more strongly promote a link between positivity and ease of categorization for members of both higher and lower status groups.

6.3 Evaluations based on group stereotype alignment

The degree to which target individuals conform to or diverge from the category stereotypes of their group impacts whether perceivers continue to endorse those stereotypes. For example, exposure to counterstereotypical women (e.g., those in leadership positions) reduces gender stereotyping (Dasgupta & Asgari, 2004; Finnegan, Oakhill, & Garnham, 2015). When possible, however, people resist updating category stereotypes given their importance in structuring everyday life. People who possess an abundance of information about a counterstereotypical target form subtypes as a means of maintaining the stereotype (Kunda & Oleson, 1995). In the absence of additional information that allows for subtyping, targets who deviate from stereotypes experience backlash (Heilman & Wallen, 2010; Parks-Stamm, Heilman, & Hearns, 2008; Phelan & Rudman, 2010; Rudman & Fairchild, 2004). Perceivers defend stereotypes through derogating and stigmatizing counterstereotypical individuals. Through doing so, they construct spaces in which individuals closely conform to and reflect the stereotypes of their group (Bobbitt-Zeher, 2011; Fiske, Bersoff, Borgida, Deaux, & Heilman, 1991).

The ECF contends that once people are categorized into a group, they are still relevant to future categorization processes. Specifically, targets who challenge stereotypes involved in efficient categorization are predicted to receive backlash in the form of negative evaluations and treatment, especially from conservative (versus liberal) perceivers. Social categorization is highly efficient in contexts that are devoid of counterstereotypical people, as cues are highly diagnostic of group membership. In these situations, perceivers would need to expend few cognitive resources to make an accurate category judgment. For example, making the inference that a highly masculine person is a man and a highly feminine person is a woman when cues are diagnostic would result in correct judgments. However, people who embody attributes that diverge from the stereotypes about their social group disrupt these processes. They challenge the belief that cues are diagnostic and that cues can consistently be used to quickly achieve accurate category judgments. For example, a person with masculine physical characteristics who identifies as a woman chips away at the presumed diagnosticity of cues.

Prioritization of efficient categorization prompts conservative (versus liberal) perceivers to show greater preference toward individuals who are stereotypical and enforce the diagnosticity of cues. For example, in one study (Stern, West, & Rule, 2015; Study 6) participants viewed photographs of four White men. Each photo was accompanied with information about the person's ostensible age, sex, race, and sexual orientation. Two of the men were labeled as identifying as straight and the other two as gay. Critically, based on ratings from a separate set of individuals, one of the men within each sexual orientation group was low on gender typicality and one was high on gender typicality. In turn, two of the men were stereotypical (a masculine straight man and feminine gay man) and two were counterstereotypical (a feminine straight man and masculine gay man).

Participants decided how they would allocate $30 among the four men in whole dollars. Overall, conservatives allocated more money to the stereotypical targets than to the counterstereotypical targets, and this outcome occurred for both the gay and straight targets (Fig. 6). Interestingly, liberals showed the opposite pattern. They allocated more money to the counterstereotypical (versus stereotypical) gay targets, and their allocations to straight targets trended in the same direction. As previously noted, liberals might show a slight preference toward engaging in more complex social

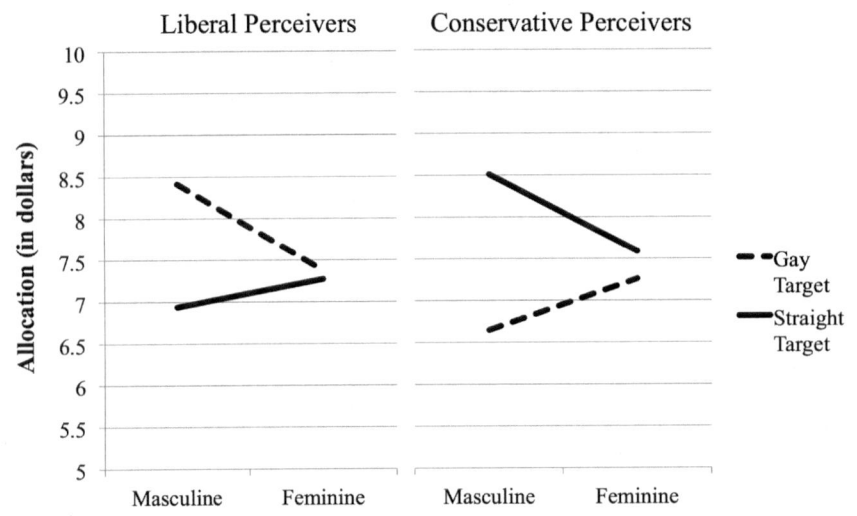

Fig. 6 Relationship between target femininity (plotted at one standard deviation below and above the mean) and allocations to gay and straight targets among liberal and conservative perceivers (one standard deviation below and above the ideology mean, respectively), as reported in Study 6 of Stern et al. (2015).

categorization processes. Showing favorability toward people who disrupt efficient categorization could function as a means of doing so.

A different way of looking at the allocation patterns in Fig. 6 highlights how the ECF makes distinct predictions from other theoretical perspectives. The ideological conflict hypothesis and social dominance theory suggest that conservatives should show greater preference for groups that are stereotyped as conservative and higher status, respectively, whereas liberals should show the opposite pattern (Brandt & Crawford, 2020; Kteily et al., 2019). Straight (versus gay) individuals are perceived as being higher status and more conservative (Brandt, Reyna, Chambers, Crawford, & Wetherell, 2014; Sirin, McCreary, & Mahalik, 2004). Consistent with social dominance and ideological conflict perspectives, we observed that conservatives allocated more money to targets labeled as straight (versus gay) whereas liberals allocated more money to targets labeled as gay (versus straight). Thus, it is theoretically and empirically compatible for conservatives (versus liberals) to display greater preference for people who bolster efficient categorization while simultaneously preferring members of higher (versus lower) status and conservative (versus liberal) groups.

Ideological differences in the treatment of (counter)stereotypical individuals extend beyond social groups that are enmeshed in existing social hierarchies. Conservatives (more so than liberals) show greater preference for people who enforce (versus challenge) stereotypes even when targets belong to experimentally created groups. In a subsequent study (Stern et al., 2015; Study 7), participants read a description that created a novel stereotype about two fictional groups: Niffites and Luupites. The description indicated that the groups differed on physical characteristics. Specifically, groups diverged in characteristics that could be used to make a category judgment from a facial photograph. One group was described as possessing more moles, and the other group possessed longer fingers. To create conditions in which the stereotype was relevant to a categorization goal, all participants were told that later in the study they would (ostensibly) view photographs of people and determine whether the person belonged to the Niffite or Luupite group. Before completing that task, however, they would choose how to allocate $30 to people who belong to each group.

Participants then viewed headshot photos of four White men in a 2×2 matrix. Two of the men clearly possessed moles and two did not. Additionally, two targets were labeled as being Niffite and the other two as Luupite, such that half of the targets possessed a physical appearance consistent with the stereotype participants had learned and half countered the stereotype. Overall, conservatives allocated more money to targets that reinforced (versus countered) the stereotype, whereas target stereotypicality did not shape liberals' allocations. These findings support the perspective that more positive treatment of stereotypical individuals among conservative (versus liberal) perceivers results from a basic desire to engage in efficient categorization.

6.4 Context modulates ideological differences in epistemic motivation

Situations shift the strength of people's goals (Kruglanski et al., 2002; Touré-Tillery & Fishbach, 2014). These changes can occur over long and sustained periods of time, such as when prolonged exposure to economic insecurity increases a chronic desire for future stability (Giuliano & Spilimbergo, 2014). Shifts also happen in a more short-term manner, such as when safety threats prompt a temporary desire to feel secure (Bonanno & Jost, 2006; Landau et al., 2004). Of greatest relevance to the present discussion, contextual factors can shape the extent to which liberals and conservatives differ in their motivations (Federico & Malka, 2018; Tetlock, 2007). In other words, ideological differences in motivation possess some degree of malleability.

Contexts activating goals are expected to affect liberals and conservatives in different ways. When a goal is situationally activated, people chronically low on the goal experience an increase in goal strength whereas those chronically high on the goal experience little or no change (Banfield, Kay, Cutright, Wu, & Fitzsimons, 2011; Cutright, Wu, Banfield, Kay, & Fitzsimons, 2011). For example, conservatives generally report a stronger motivation to connect and affiliate with like-minded others than do liberals (e.g., Graham et al., 2009). Experimental manipulations that activate feelings of social isolation increase relational motivation among liberals (but not conservatives), and information that produces feelings of social saturation decreases relational motivation among conservatives (but not liberals; Stern & West, 2016; Stern, West, Jost, & Rule, 2014). In situations where conservatives (versus liberals) are chronically higher on a goal, activating the goal should increase motivational strength among liberals more so than conservatives.

In the ECF, ideological differences in the desire for efficient categorization are proposed to emerge because liberals and conservatives diverge in epistemic motivation. When a social context reduces or eliminates these differences in epistemic motivation, the distinction between liberals and conservatives in prioritizing efficient categorization is consequentially expected to shift. Specifically, when a situation elevates liberals' epistemic motivations to be comparable to that of conservatives, liberals should be just as likely as conservatives to prioritize efficient categorization. To test this idea, participants in one study (Stern et al., 2015; Study 5) learned a fictitious stereotype that Jewish people are more likely to have moles on their faces than are non-Jewish people. Participants were then assigned to either an uncertainty salience condition in which they completed a task to activate feelings of uncertainty (e.g., they wrote down what physically happens to them when they feel uncertain) or a control condition in which they did not complete this task.

Participants next provided evaluations based on facial photographs that were either labeled as *Jewish* or *Not Jewish*. Some targets aligned with the stereotype that participants had learned (e.g., a person with moles labeled as being Jewish) and some challenged the stereotype (e.g., a person without moles labeled as being Jewish). In the control condition, conservatives evaluated stereotypical (versus counterstereotypical) targets more positively, whereas target stereotypicality did not shape liberals' evaluations. When uncertainty was made salient, however, both liberals and conservatives evaluated stereotypical (versus counterstereotypical) targets more positively. In other words, increasing epistemic motivation through activating feelings of uncertainty led liberals to favor targets who promoted efficient categorization to a similar degree as conservatives did.

6.5 Categorization goals modulate ideological differences

People are motivated to accurately categorize others because doing so is functional to pursuing additional goals (e.g., Higgins, 2019; Macrae et al., 2002). The ECF argues that the existence of a categorization goal modulates whether conservatives prioritize efficient categorization more so than liberals. When the need to accurately categorize others into groups is reduced or eliminated, conservatives (versus liberals) should show a greater reduction in prioritizing efficient categorization. As a result, the degree to which evaluations among conservative perceivers are tied to target individuals' reinforcement of cue diagnosticity should be attenuated and more comparable to that of liberal perceivers.

We (Stern et al., 2015; Study 4) directly tested this prediction. People possess a wealth of experience in categorizing others into the groups that exist in society (e.g., race, sexual orientation). Thus, we reasoned that it would be most feasible to alter categorization goals with experimentally created groups. Participants learned the novel stereotype about Niffites and Luupites that was outlined in a previously reviewed study and were informed that they would be providing evaluations of people belonging to each group. They also read that after completing the evaluation task, they would be shown a new set of faces. Some participants were told that they would categorize the group membership (i.e., Niffite or Luupite) of the people in the photos. This information ensured that participants (both liberal and conservative) assigned to this condition possessed a goal to categorize people as Niffite or Luupite. The remainder of the participants were told that they would estimate the age of the people in the photos. Given that Niffites and Liffites are fictional groups and participants had no reason to believe that they would ever encounter these groups again, we expected that participants assigned to this condition would be less likely to possess a goal to accurately categorize people as Niffite or Luupite.

We found that when participants expected to later complete a Niffite/Luupite categorization task (a categorization goal related to the stereotype), conservatives evaluated stereotypical targets more positively than counterstereotypical targets, whereas liberals did not differentially evaluate targets based on their stereotypicality. However, when participants expected to later estimate new targets' ages (a categorization goal unrelated to the stereotype), neither liberals nor conservatives differentially evaluated targets based on their stereotypicality. These findings highlight that greater prioritization of efficient categorization among conservative (versus liberal) perceivers is tailored to when a categorization goal exists. People who undermine stereotypes are innocuous when the cues are unlikely to be used in future judgments, and devaluing counterstereotypical individuals would serve little purpose in promoting categorization efficiency.

6.6 Summary

People typically evaluate others more negatively when the categorization process is disrupted. Considering the role of a perceiver's ideology adds an additional layer of nuance in understanding when and why people who are more (versus less) difficult to categorize will experience differential treatment. Conservative (versus liberal) perceivers are especially likely to evaluate targets more negatively when their group membership is ambiguous (versus unambiguous) because they require greater cognitive effort to categorize. Conservatives are also more likely than liberals to treat people in a negative manner when they challenge (versus bolster) the diagnosticity of cues that facilitate efficient categorization. These differences are sensitive to context. Situations that amplify epistemic motivations for certainty prompt negative attitudes toward counterstereotypical (versus stereotypical) individuals among liberal perceivers to a degree that their evaluations parallel those of conservative perceivers. Further, reducing a categorization goal attenuates the impact of target stereotypicality on evaluations among conservative perceivers to a degree that their evaluations are comparable to those of liberal perceivers.

7. Political attitudes and behaviors based on efficient categorization

William James, 1890/1983, p. 960) famously stated that "My thinking is first and last and always for the sake of my doing". In other words, thinking is for action (Fiske, 1992). The social categorization process constitutes an important form of thinking. For nearly seventy years, scholars have outlined how social category judgments can shape subsequent behaviors (Secord, 1958; Zebrowitz & Collins, 1997). However, most research examining the functionality of social categorization has focused on how the *outcomes* of category judgments guide behavior. For example, once an individual is categorized into a social group people systematically form judgments of competence and warmth from the category information (Fiske, Cuddy, Glick, & Xu, 2002). These evaluations in turn impact how people engage with members of different groups (Bergsieker, Shelton, & Richeson, 2010). The ECF instead focuses on the impact of the social categorization *process* for the construction of subsequent attitudes and behaviors. The ECF proposes that conservatives more readily form political attitudes and enact behaviors that are predicated on efficient social categorization than do liberals. In this section, I outline evidence supporting this argument.

7.1 Policy attitudes

Liberals and conservatives differ in their attitudes toward various social and political issues (e.g., abortion; Hodson & MacInnis, 2017). Many political issues explicitly invoke social category memberships, including immigration, affirmative action, hate crime legislation, and gender wage gaps. Explanations for ideological divides on these types of issues have typically focused on differences in prejudice (e.g., attitudes toward minorities and women; Hodson & MacInnis, 2017; van der Toorn et al., 2017) and endorsement of negative category stereotypes (e.g., thinking racial minorities are lazy and dangerous; Burns & Gimpel, 2000). Within the ECF, beliefs about efficient categorization are also proposed to play a role in guiding people's attitudes and, in turn, explaining why liberals and conservatives diverge in attitudes toward various political issues.

People work to maintain an "illusion of objectivity" about their attitudes (Kunda, 1990). They want to think that they are correct and form attitudes that they can justify (Fernbach, Rogers, Fox, & Sloman, 2013). To do so, they rely on beliefs to construct a semblance of logic in their attitudes. Indirect evidence suggests that people have sometimes used beliefs about whether group memberships can be accurately gleaned from minimal information to form attitudes toward social policies. As two salient examples, the United States previously had laws enforcing racial segregation and policies barring sexual minorities from serving in the U.S. military. Before the policies were formally ended, people tasked with enforcing segregation relied on visual information to determine whether people violated rules (e.g., if a Black person used the "wrong" water fountain or bathroom; Rothstein, 2017), and doctors giving physical exams looked for feminine bodily characteristics as cues to identify gay military personnel (Bérubé, 1990). Conservatives (versus liberals) were more supportive of these policies and believed they could be effectively enforced (Kruse, 2013; Pew Research Center, 2009), suggesting that beliefs about efficient categorization might contribute to ideological differences in policy support.

Some social policies also directly invoke the idea of efficient categorization. For example, racial profiling in law enforcement consists of using group membership to make inferences about possible criminal behavior. The act of engaging in profiling, such as pulling over a driver because of their perceived race or requiring a person to undergo more extensive screening at an airport because of their presumed religion, first requires a person to assume that they can accurately determine group membership from minimal information. Although racial profiling is illegal in many places, it still appears to be common (Pierson et al., 2020).

Conservatives are more supportive of racial profiling than are liberals. For example, we (Stern & Axt, 2021; Study 2) found that conservatives were more likely than liberals to endorse items such as *Law enforcement officers should pay particular attention to those social groups more heavily involved in crime, even if this means focusing on members of particular ethnic groups* whereas liberals were more likely to endorse items such as *Law enforcement officers should act as if members of all racial groups are equally likely to commit crimes.* A stronger motivation to deliberate among liberals (versus conservatives) in part explained this ideological divide in support for profiling. This pattern of findings remained even when accounting for the desire to uphold group-based hierarchy, cognitive ability, explicit and implicit racial attitudes, and various demographic characteristics on which liberals and conservatives sometimes differ (e.g., age, sex, race). These findings further suggest that epistemic processes, including a desire for efficient categorization, could contribute to divergent policy attitudes among liberals and conservatives.

I (Stern, 2019; Study 4) directly examined whether beliefs about cue diagnosticity uniquely contribute to understanding why conservatives and liberals hold divergent attitudes toward profiling. Participants read about a specific example of either racial or religious profiling and then indicated the extent to which they supported the practice. For example, participants assigned to the racial profiling condition read the following: *It has been reported that some police officers and security guards in the United States stop African Americans and Hispanic Americans more than White Americans while they are leaving shopping malls and stores because the officers believe that African Americans and Hispanic Americans are more likely to commit certain types of crimes.*

A stronger belief that cues are diagnostic of group membership among conservatives (versus liberals) contributed to explaining the ideological divide in support for profiling (Fig. 7). Conservatives (versus liberals)

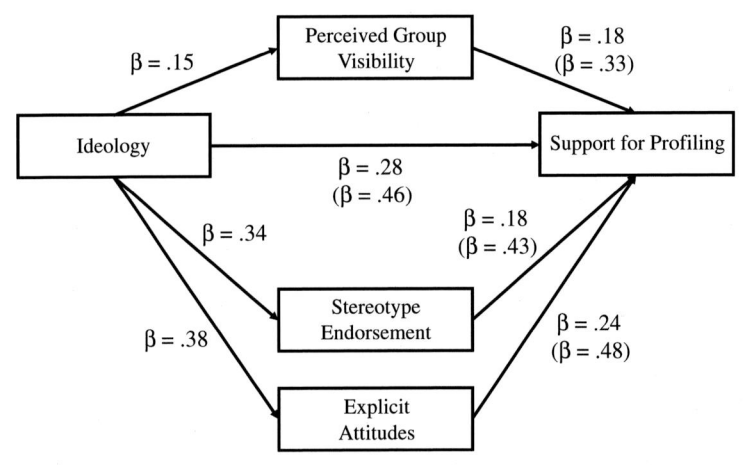

Fig. 7 Political ideology predicting support for profiling through beliefs about group visibility, endorsement of stereotypes, and explicitly negative attitudes, as reported in Study 4 of Stern (2019). Higher scores on ideology represent greater conservatism (versus liberalism). All paths $P < .001$.

also reported greater prejudice toward racial and religious minorities, and more strongly endorsed negative stereotypes about these groups (e.g., that African-Americans are untrustworthy and corrupt). Prejudice and stereotype endorsement explained additional variance in the ideological divide over support for profiling, but beliefs about cue diagnosticity continued to have a unique explanatory role even when accounting for these constructs. These findings highlight how beliefs about cue diagnosticity lead liberals and conservatives to diverge in attitudes about policies that implicate efficient categorization.

7.2 Political intentions and behaviors

Does a desire for efficient categorization also guide political intentions and behaviors? Voting behavior is generally considered one of the strongest indices of political support, as it reflects a person's interest in who should hold decision-making power. When people are unsure about what political attitudes to adopt or behaviors to enact, they often rely on their political party for guidance (Cohen, 2003; Stern & Ondish, 2018). However, a substantial percentage of people do not identify with a major political party. As of 2021 roughly 40% of people in the United States indicated that they consider themselves to be "Independent," meaning that they are not aligned with a major party (Gallup, 2021). People also vary in the degree to which they are engaged with politics (Federico, 2021), and individuals who are disengaged are unlikely to rely on political party recommendations even when they belong to a party. A substantial portion of the population relies on information other than a political party's guidance to determine political behavior, which underscores the importance of examining the role of categorization processes.

Categorization processes contribute to voting decisions. Politicians who are easier to categorize are more likely to win elections (Samochowiec, Wänke, & Fiedler, 2010). The ECF proposes that this relationship should be stronger among more conservative (versus liberal) voters. Some indirect evidence supports this possibility. For example, female Republican (i.e., conservative) representatives display greater gender typicality in their facial appearance than do Democratic (i.e., liberal) representatives (Carpinella & Johnson, 2013), possibly due to the electoral advantage that it affords among more conservative (versus liberal) voters. More direct evidence also supports the ECF's prediction. Hehman, Carpinella, Johnson, Leitner, and Freeman (2014) found that the difficultly of categorizing a female politician's gender was related to a lower likelihood of receiving votes in states with more conservative voters, but there was no relationship between categorization difficulty and voting outcomes in more liberal states. Republican candidates who look less stereotypically Republican also receive lower vote shares, but only in conservative-leaning constituencies (Olivola, Sussman, Tsetsos, Kang, & Todorov, 2012; Olivola, Tingley, & Todorov, 2018).

Contexts that prompt more conservative (versus liberal) ways of thinking also lead people to prefer candidates who promote efficient categorization. We (Stern et al., 2016; Study 3) found that the mental representations people formed about a candidate guided voting intentions. When a more conservative mindset was activated through describing the U.S. government as unstable (versus stable), both Black and White individuals who mentally represented a candidate as possessing the stereotypical characteristics of a leader (lighter skin) indicated stronger intentions to vote for the candidate.

In a subsequent study (Stern et al., 2016; Study 4a), we also found that the degree to which a candidate's actual physical characteristics allowed them to be easily categorized as a leader guided voting intentions. Black and White participants either read that the Department of Agriculture was highly unstable or stable. Participants were then presented with three racially ambiguous male candidates who were ostensibly running for a position in the Department of Agriculture and indicated how likely they would be to vote for each candidate. All three candidates were presented as being highly qualified for the position, but they differed in their skin tone. One candidate's skin tone had been altered to be lighter, one to be darker, and one was unaltered. When a more conservative mindset was (versus was not) activated through the stability manipulation, both Black and White participants favored the candidate whose characteristics allowed them to be most easily categorized as a leader. Specifically, both Black and White participants were more likely to express interest in voting for the lighter skinned candidate than the darker skinned or unaltered candidates.

To assess the motivational determinants behind these voting intentions, we also measured participants' desire to bolster society (e.g., *In general, the American political system operates as it should*; Kay & Jost, 2003). The motive to defend the status quo of society is grounded in epistemic goals for order and predictability (Hennes et al., 2012). Thus, it reflects a desire for efficiency on a system-based level. We found that when a more conservative mindset was (versus was not) activated through instability, greater motivation to bolster society (i.e., lower confidence in the current system) was associated with stronger intentions to vote for the lighter (versus darker) skinned candidate. This relationship emerged for both Black and White participants. These findings indicate that situations fostering more conservative (versus liberal) ways of thinking promote interest in leaders who are easy to categorize.

7.3 Summary

Social categorization, like other forms of thinking, contributes to action. The ECF outlines how the *process* of social categorization feeds into subsequent political attitudes and behaviors, and in particular how ideological differences in a desire for efficient categorization produce divergent outcomes. Specifically, beliefs that cues are diagnostic of group membership uniquely contribute to explaining ideological divides in the endorsement of policies that require efficient categorization. Conservatives are also more likely than liberals to vote for political candidates who are easier to categorize. Situations that activate a more conservative (versus liberal) mindset similarly lead to preferences for easily categorizable leaders. While social categorization processes are instrumental in guiding political action, they are more impactful among conservative (versus liberal) individuals and contexts.

8. Future directions and concluding remarks

The ECF and reviewed program of research integrate ideas from social cognition and political psychology to highlight how liberal-conservative ideology systematically relates to social categorization processes. The model proposes a clear mechanism—epistemic motivation—that undergirds these ideological differences. The model is also domain general, in the sense that the predictions are not tied to any particular social category. The ECF broadly contributes to social categorization research through denoting when and why a relatively stable aspect of a perceiver corresponds to beliefs about how social categories can be accurately judged, the way in which cues are processed during social categorization, and the manner in which these categorization processes subsequently guide evaluations, attitudes, and behaviors. The ECF highlights clear situational factors that are expected to attenuate ideological differences, which gives insight into when meaningful variability in social categorization is most likely to occur. The ECF additionally contributes to theorizing in political psychology through providing a novel understanding of ideological divides in social evaluation and political behaviors that are grounded in categorization processes. A focus on ideological differences in social category processing gives deeper insight into the origins of why liberals and conservatives fail to see "eye-to-eye" on various issues and policies. In this final section, I highlight several prominent directions for future work. For each of these areas, I outline predictions derived from the ECF that researchers could directly test.

8.1 Revisiting the focal goal of social categorization

The ECF assumes that the degree of cognitive effort liberals and conservatives expend in the social categorization process typically operates in pursuit of reaching a conclusion that is accurate. Proposals from some scholars deem it unlikely that the quest to render an accurate judgment would be subordinated to alternative goals (Higgins, 2019; Rossignac-Milon & Higgins, 2018; Szumowska, Czernatowicz-Kukuczka, Kossowska, Król, & Kruglanski, 2020; Trope & Thompson, 1997). However, the ECF defines the efficiency of a judgment output in relation to whether a focal goal is achieved, and so leaves open the possibility that other goals (e.g., the desire to enforce hierarchy or achieve a positive social identity) could become prioritized over accuracy goals during social categorization.

For example, in some studies examining racial categorization perceivers are exposed to target individuals who vary in their alignment with White or Black prototypes, and perceivers are then required to categorize targets as either White or Black (e.g., Krosch et al., 2013). Participants might think that researchers have provided them with a correct response option. However, it is also possible that perceivers view racially ambiguous Black-White targets as biracial or another group membership that is not provided within the binary response option (e.g., Hispanic or Middle Eastern; Nicolas, Skinner, & Dickter, 2019). Perceivers might then shift from a pursuit of accuracy (since they would view accuracy as impossible) toward the achievement of an alternative goal. If this were to occur, the amount of cognitive effort invested in a judgment would be expected to function in the service of the alternative goal. For example, cognitive resources could be dispensed in a manner that the perceiver construes as supporting extant group hierarchy even if they view the allocation of those resources as jeopardizing or yielding little impact on accuracy.

As noted at the beginning of this chapter, motivations within alternative frameworks have until now been primarily implicated in directional predictions about judgments (e.g., categorizing targets as racial outgroup members), but have remained more disconnected from questions about cognitive processing during categorization. Examining whether and when certain motives might supersede accuracy goals and subsequently shape the degree of effort expended during the social categorization process would be a generative direction for clarifying the distinctions between (and relations among) different theoretical frameworks.

8.2 Distinguishing social and economic ideology

The ECF focuses on political ideology in unidimensional and general terms (i.e., overall resistance or support for change). Some scholars have argued that ideology can also be represented in a multidimensional manner where attitudes toward social (e.g., abortion) and economic (e.g., taxation) issues are specified as distinct constructs (Lipset, 1959). Empirically, political attitudes often load onto two factors that have been classified as social and economic dimensions (Feldman & Johnston, 2014; Johnston & Ollerenshaw, 2020). However, the literature has also provided varying results concerning the strength and direction of the relationship between these dimensions (Azevedo, Jost, Rothmund, & Sterling, 2019; Benoit & Laver, 2006; Malka, Lelkes, & Soto, 2019). Further, there is a lack of conceptual clarity in whether various issues (e.g., welfare, environmental regulations) can be classified as "social" or "economic" (Gilens, 1995; Song et al., 2020). These challenges raise questions about how distinct these dimensions are from one another.

Despite these potential issues in examining ideology as multidimensional, researchers have begun to address whether psychological motivations are differentially linked to social and economic political views. Findings indicate that epistemic motivations (e.g., motives for closure and certainty) are consistently associated with more politically conservative (versus liberal) views on social issues (Costello & Lilienfeld, 2021; Feldman & Johnston, 2014; Malka et al., 2014). Given that epistemic motives undergird the predictions of the ECF, I anticipate that social ideology would contribute to patterns of categorization and evaluation that mirror those reviewed here. In contrast, there is considerable variability in whether epistemic motives are associated with economic liberalism or conservatism (Federico & Malka, 2018; Malka & Soto, 2015; Sterling, Jost, & Pennycook, 2016). Some findings suggest that political engagement contributes to explaining this variability, such that people who are more engaged often display a link between epistemic goals and economically conservative views (Czarnek & Kossowska, 2021; Johnston, Lavine, & Federico, 2017). Thus, it is possible that the ECF's predictions also apply to economic ideology, but only among people high in political engagement.

8.3 The role of political content and identity

Support for the ECF comes from studies examining social categorization processes involving gender, sexual orientation, religion, race, age, and experimentally created groups. While all of these group memberships hold implications that are political in nature, none of them inherently involve political identity. In other words, a person's political views do not define their race and gender (and vice-versa). The extent to which a social categorization is structured around politics (e.g., categorizing political party membership) or whether political identity is activated in a situation might impact ideological differences in categorization processes.

Some research suggests that epistemic motivations most readily guide liberals and conservatives when judgments are non-political, and that this occurs regardless of the broader political context. As one example, we (Ruisch & Stern, 2021) found that conservatives (versus liberals) reported greater confidence in the accuracy on their judgments on non-political tasks (e.g., estimating numbers of dots) in part because of ideological differences in the motivation to make rapid judgments. The ideological difference in confidence did not vary based on whether the current president was liberal (Obama) or conservative (Trump). Relatedly, feelings of dissimilarity in non-political domains were (marginally) more strongly associated with prejudice toward various groups among conservative (versus liberal) perceivers even during a conservative political administration (Stern & Crawford, 2021).

In contrast, being presented with overtly political judgments has the potential to activate political identity, which can shift the goals that are most accessible (Huddy, 2001). When a political identity is activated the defense of that identity is likely to take prominence over epistemic goals for deliberation. Liberals and conservatives display comparable levels of motivation to defend their political identities and beliefs (Ditto et al., 2019; Frimer, Skitka, & Motyl, 2017; Washburn & Skitka, 2018), with people on the extremes being most zealous (van Prooijen & Krouwel, 2017). Thus, for overtly political judgements, ideological extremity might be more important in guiding categorization processes than is ideological direction. For example, people who are more politically extreme (versus moderate) organize political stimuli (e.g., politicians) in a simpler manner, especially when political ideology is made salient (Lammers, Koch, Conway, & Brandt, 2017). Additionally, extremity modulates accuracy of categorizing political beliefs from photographs (Ivanov, Muller, Delmas, & Wänke, 2018).

Altogether, I anticipate that ideological differences in social categorization processes will most readily emerge when judgments are non-political in nature. In other words, the ECF as currently stated is likely to have the most value in explaining non-political category judgments and evaluation patterns. When political identity is activated, however, defending that identity might become a more focal goal than are epistemic desires. As a result, ideological extremity might take prominence in guiding judgments.

8.4 Multiple social categories

Research supporting the ECF has focused on judgments or evaluations of people within the scope of a single category. However, people occupy multiple social categories, and in recent years researchers have begun to examine how perceivers collectively manage these categories in their inferences and judgments (Kang & Bodenhausen, 2015; Petsko & Bodenhausen, 2020). In one area of work, scholars have documented how social categories can themselves function as cues for additional category inferences. For example, people rely on a target's race to make further judgments about sex (Goff, Thomas, & Jackson, 2008) and sexual orientation (Johnson & Ghavami, 2011). Researchers have also underscored how the same physical appearance cues can facilitate multiple category judgments (e.g., race, sex), resulting in more efficient judgments when category phenotypes align (Johnson, Freeman, & Pauker, 2012).

The ECF would predict that conservatives should be more reliant on social categories as cues for additional category judgments (e.g., greater likelihood of categorizing Black men as straight and Asian men as gay) than are liberals. Conservatives (versus liberals) should also display greater preference for targets when intersecting phenotypes prompt judgment efficiency (e.g., Asian women) compared to when phenotypes clash and in turn require greater deliberation for judgments (e.g., Asian men).

8.5 Applications for trait and emotion judgment processes

Studies supporting the ECF have focused on category judgments that are generally represented in a discrete manner (e.g., categorizing a person as either gay or straight). However, the ECF also holds implications for understanding social categorization processes that are more graded. For example, inferences about traits (e.g., trustworthiness, competence) and emotions (e.g., anger, disgust) are a focal and unavoidable aspect of everyday life (Barrett, Adolphs, Marsella, Martinez, & Pollak, 2019; Rule, Krendl, Ivcevic, & Ambady, 2013). People use inferences of emotions and traits to group individuals together in a manner similar to discrete category memberships (e.g., Barrett, 2006; Klapper, Dotsch, van Rooij, & Wigboldus, 2016), and these judgments appear to influence political outcomes (e.g., voting behavior; Carpinella & Johnson, 2016; Todorov, Mandisodza, Goren, & Hall, 2005).

Based on the ECF, ideological differences in epistemic motivation would be expected to lead conservatives (versus liberals) to more strongly prioritize efficiency in trait and emotion inferences. For example, conservatives (versus liberals) should display greater reliance on appearance cues when making trait and emotion judgments, and also show a stronger preference for people who facilitate efficiency in these inferences. As initial support for this possibility, people who endorse conservative (i.e., just world) beliefs more strongly believe that facial cues are diagnostic of various traits (Suzuki et al., 2019). Further exploring the impact of political ideology on trait and emotion judgment processes would be a generative extension of the ECF.

8.6 Social categorization in vivo

The vast majority of research, including work supporting the ECF, has examined social categorization processes in highly controlled settings where participants are provided with specific information about a target (e.g., a photograph). Some scholars have pointed out that there is a paucity of research exploring social categorization in more information rich environments that reflect the complexity of everyday life (Bodenhausen & Peery, 2009). For example, Todorov et al. (2015, p. 537) noted that "In real-life situations, people do not interact with disembodied faces. There is nonverbal information, bodily information, other appearance information (e.g., clothing, neatness), and rich contextual information (e.g., party setting)." At the current time, it is relatively unknown how social categorization processes play out when a person is exposed to a richer information environment.

What predictions would the ECF make concerning ideological differences in categorization processes under more "real world" conditions? Conservatives (versus liberals) should continue to be more reliant on cues that they believe are diagnostic of group membership when making category judgments. Additionally, conservatives should be more likely than liberals to form negative evaluations of targets when cues in a more information rich environment are "mixed" or "compete" in the categorization process. On the other hand, liberals' (versus conservatives') greater desire to deliberate should motivate them to engage in a broader form of information search, especially when the group membership is highly ambiguous. For example, a person interested in determining a celebrity's religion could search Wikipedia for a possible answer. Relatedly, upon meeting a new individual at a party, a person could ask questions that indirectly gauge their interaction partner's sexual orientation.

A related question concerns how ideological differences in accuracy will shift as demographics change. A growing number of people identify with groups that possess ambiguity in category membership. For example, a higher proportion of people than ever before identify as transgender and multiracial (Meerwijk & Sevelius, 2017; Parker, Horowitz, Morin, & Lopez, 2015). Physical appearance cues for these groups are typically less diagnostic than for cisgender and monoracial groups (Chen, 2019; McLemore, 2015). In situations where cues are undiagnostic of the correct answer, effortful information search and conversation foster more accurate judgments than does the usage of low effort strategies (Eyal, Steffel, & Epley, 2018). As a result, liberals might display greater accuracy than conservatives for these types of category judgments, especially for environments with abundant information.

8.7 Concluding remarks

Social categorization is a pervasive part of everyday life. Researchers have accumulated an impressive array of knowledge concerning how social category judgments shape subsequent thought and behavior. While scholars have begun to explore the factors that contribute to social categorization judgments, less is known about these processes. In this chapter, I outlined the ECF, which integrates perspectives in social cognition and political psychology to understand variability in social categorization processes. I discussed findings indicating that the political ideology of a perceiver is associated with the way in which people process information while constructing a social category judgment, as well as how this process subsequently guides evaluations, attitudes, and behaviors. I also outlined implications and potential extensions of the ECF, which will hopefully generate future discussion about the manner in which political ideology contributes to social judgment processes.

Acknowledgments

I thank Benjamin Ruisch and Christopher Petsko for helpful comments on an earlier draft of this chapter.

References

Abramowitz, A. (2010). *The disappearing center: Engaged citizens, polarization, and American democracy.* Yale University Press.

Abrams, D. E., & Hogg, M. A. (1990). *Social identity theory: Constructive and critical advances.* Springer-Verlag Publishing.

Allport, G. W. (1954). *The nature of prejudice.* New York: Addison-Wesley.

Allport, G. W., & Kramer, B. M. (1946). Some roots of prejudice. *Journal of Psychology, 22,* 9–39.

Alter, A. L., Stern, C., Granot, Y., & Balcetis, E. (2016). The "bad is black" effect: Why people believe evildoers have darker skin than do-gooders. *Personality and Social Psychology Bulletin, 42*(12), 1653–1665.

Althusser, L. (1971). *Ideology and Ideological State Apparatuses: Lenin and Philosophy and Other Essays.* London: New Left Books.

Ambady, N., & Gray, H. M. (2002). On being sad and mistaken: Mood effects on the accuracy of thin-slice judgments. *Journal of Personality and Social Psychology, 83*(4), 947–961.

Ammerman, N. T. (2003). Religious identities and religious institutions. *Handbook of the Sociology of Religion,* 207–224.

Amodio, D. M., Jost, J. T., Master, S. L., & Yee, C. M. (2007). Neurocognitive correlates of liberalism and conservatism. *Nature Neuroscience, 10*(10), 1246–1247.

Andersen, S. M., Klatzky, R. L., & Murray, J. (1990). Traits and social stereotypes: Efficiency differences in social information processing. *Journal of Personality and Social Psychology, 59*(2), 192–201.

Andrzejewski, S. A., Hall, J. A., & Salib, E. R. (2009). Anti-Semitism and identification of Jewish group membership from photographs. *Journal of Nonverbal Behavior, 33*(1), 47–58.

Axt, J., & Stern, C. (under review). A comparative investigation of predictive and construct validity among eight measures of conservatism.

Azevedo, F., Jost, J. T., Rothmund, T., & Sterling, J. (2019). Neoliberal ideology and the justification of inequality in capitalist societies: Why social and economic dimensions of ideology are intertwined. *Journal of Social Issues, 75*(1), 49–88.

Banfield, J. C., Kay, A. C., Cutright, K. M., Wu, E. C., & Fitzsimons, G. J. (2011). A person by situation account of motivated system defense. *Social Psychological and Personality Science, 2*(2), 212–219.

Banks, R. R., & Eberhardt, J. L. (1998). Social psychological processes and the legal bases of racial categorization. In J. L. Eberhardt, & S. T. Fiske (Eds.), *Confronting racism: The problem and the response* (pp. 54–75). Thousand Oaks, CA: Sage.

Barrett, L. F. (2006). Solving the emotion paradox: Categorization and the experience of emotion. *Personality and Social Psychology Review, 10*(1), 20–46.

Barrett, L. F., Adolphs, R., Marsella, S., Martinez, A. M., & Pollak, S. D. (2019). Emotional expressions reconsidered: Challenges to inferring emotion from human facial movements. *Psychological Science in the Public Interest, 20*(1), 1–68.

Bem, S. L. (1993). *The lenses of gender: Transforming the debate on sexual inequality.* Yale University Press.

Benoit, K., & Laver, M. (2006). *Party policy in modern democracies.* Routledge.

Bergsieker, H. B., Shelton, J. N., & Richeson, J. A. (2010). To be liked versus respected: Divergent goals in interracial interactions. *Journal of Personality and Social Psychology, 99*(2), 248–264.

Bérubé, A. (1990). *Coming out under fire: The history of gay men and women in World War II.* New York: Free Press.

Blair, I. V., Judd, C. M., Sadler, M. S., & Jenkins, C. (2002). The role of Afrocentric features in person perception: Judging by features and categories. *Journal of Personality and Social Psychology, 83*(1), 5–25.

Blascovich, J., Wyer, N. A., Swart, L. A., & Kibler, J. L. (1997). Racism and racial categorization. *Journal of Personality and Social Psychology, 72*(6), 1364–1372.

Bobbitt-Zeher, D. (2011). Gender discrimination at work: Connecting gender stereotypes, institutional policies, and gender composition of workplace. *Gender & Society, 25*(6), 764–786.

Bodenhausen, G. V., & Peery, D. (2009). Social categorization and stereotyping in vivo: The VUCA challenge. *Social and Personality Psychology Compass, 3*(2), 133–151.

Bonanno, G. A., & Jost, J. T. (2006). Conservative shift among high-exposure survivors of the September 11th terrorist attacks. *Basic and Applied Social Psychology, 28*(4), 311–323.

Bosson, J. K., & Vandello, J. A. (2011). Precarious manhood and its links to action and aggression. *Current Directions in Psychological Science, 20*(2), 82–86.

Brandt, M. J., & Crawford, J. T. (2020). Worldview conflict and prejudice. In B. Gawronski (Ed.), *Advances in experimental social psychology* (Vol. 61, pp. 1–66). Cambridge, MA: Academic Press.

Brandt, M. J., Reyna, C., Chambers, J. R., Crawford, J. T., & Wetherell, G. (2014). The ideological-conflict hypothesis: Intolerance among both liberals and conservatives. *Current Directions in Psychological Science, 23*(1), 27–34.

Brewer, M. B. (1988). A dual process model of impression formation. In R. S. Wyer Jr., & T. K. Srull (Eds.), *Advances in social cognition* (Vol. 1, pp. 1–36). Hillsdale, NJ: Lawrence Erlbaum.

Brunswik, E. (1955). Representative design and probabilistic theory in a functional psychology. *Psychological Review, 62*(3), 193–217.

Buck, D. M., Plant, E. A., Ratcliff, J., Zielaskowski, K., & Boerner, P. (2013). Concern over the misidentification of sexual orientation: Social contagion and the avoidance of sexual minorities. *Journal of Personality and Social Psychology, 105*(6), 941–960.

Buhr, K., & Dugas, M. J. (2002). The intolerance of uncertainty scale: Psychometric properties of the English version. *Behaviour Research and Therapy, 40*(8), 931–945.

Burke, S. E., Dovidio, J. F., LaFrance, M., Przedworski, J. M., Perry, S. P., Phelan, S. M., & van Ryn, M. (2017). Beyond generalized sexual prejudice: Need for closure predicts negative attitudes toward bisexual people relative to gay/lesbian people. *Journal of Experimental Social Psychology, 71*, 145–150.

Burns, P., & Gimpel, J. G. (2000). Economic insecurity, prejudicial stereotypes, and public opinion on immigration policy. *Political Science Quarterly, 115*(2), 201–225.

Cacioppo, J. T., & Petty, R. E. (1982). The need for cognition. *Journal of Personality and Social Psychology, 42*(1), 116–131.

Cacioppo, J. T., Petty, R. E., & Feng Kao, C. (1984). The efficient assessment of need for cognition. *Journal of Personality Assessment, 48*(3), 306–307.

Camerer, C., & Weber, M. (1992). Recent developments in modeling preferences: Uncertainty and ambiguity. *Journal of Risk and Uncertainty, 5*(4), 325–370.

Carney, D. R., Jost, J. T., Gosling, S. D., & Potter, J. (2008). The secret lives of liberals and conservatives: Personality profiles, interaction styles, and the things they leave behind. *Political Psychology, 29*(6), 807–840.

Carpinella, C. M., & Johnson, K. L. (2013). Appearance-based politics: Sex-typed facial cues communicate political party affiliation. *Journal of Experimental Social Psychology, 49*(1), 156–160.

Carpinella, C. M., & Johnson, K. L. (2016). Visual political communication: The impact of facial cues from social constituencies to personal pocketbooks. *Social and Personality Psychology Compass, 10*(5), 281–297.

Cassidy, B. S., Sprout, G. T., Freeman, J. B., & Krendl, A. C. (2017). Looking the part (to me): effects of racial prototypicality on race perception vary by prejudice. *Social Cognitive and Affective Neuroscience, 12*(4), 685–694.

Chandra, A., Copen, C. E., & Mosher, W. D. (2013). Sexual behavior, sexual attraction, and sexual identity in the United States: Data from the 2006–2010 National Survey of Family Growth. In *International handbook on the demography of sexuality* (pp. 45–66). Dordrecht: Springer.

Chen, J. M. (2019). An integrative review of impression formation processes for multiracial individuals. *Social and Personality Psychology Compass, 13*(1), e12430.

Chen, J. M., & Hamilton, D. L. (2012). Natural ambiguities: Racial categorization of multiracial individuals. *Journal of Experimental Social Psychology, 48*(1), 152–164.

Chen, J. M., Kteily, N. S., & Ho, A. K. (2019). Whose side are you on? Asian Americans' mistrust of Asian–White biracials predicts more exclusion from the in group. *Personality and Social Psychology Bulletin, 45*(6), 827–841.

Chen, J. M., Norman, J. B., & Nam, Y. (2021). Broadening the stimulus set: Introducing the American Multiracial Faces Database. *Behavior Research Methods, 53*(1), 371–389.

Choma, B. L., Hanoch, Y., Hodson, G., & Gummerum, M. (2014). Risk propensity among liberals and conservatives: The effect of risk perception, expected benefits, and risk domain. *Social Psychological and Personality Science, 5*(6), 713–721.

Cohen, G. L. (2003). Party over policy: The dominating impact of group influence on political beliefs. *Journal of Personality and Social Psychology, 85*(5), 808–822.

Cohen, J. (1988). *Statistical power analysis.* Hillsdale, NJ: Erbaum.

Converse, P. E. (1964). The nature of belief systems in mass publics. In D. E. Apter (Ed.), *Ideology and discontent* (pp. 206–261). New York: Free Press.

Conway, L. G., III, Gornick, L. J., Houck, S. C., Anderson, C., Stockert, J., Sessoms, D., & McCue, K. (2016). Are conservatives really more simple-minded than liberals? The domain specificity of complex thinking. *Political Psychology, 37*(6), 777–798.

Costello, T. H., & Lilienfeld, S. O. (2021). Social and economic political ideology consistently operate as mutual suppressors: Implications for personality, social, and political psychology. *Social Psychological and Personality Science, 12*(8), 1425–1436.

Cuddy, A. J., Fiske, S. T., Kwan, V. S., Glick, P., Demoulin, S., Leyens, J. P., & Htun, T. T. (2009). Stereotype content model across cultures: Towards universal similarities and some differences. *British Journal of Social Psychology, 48*(1), 1–33.

Cutright, K. M., Wu, E. C., Banfield, J. C., Kay, A. C., & Fitzsimons, G. J. (2011). When your world must be defended: Choosing products to justify the system. *Journal of Consumer Research, 38*(1), 62–77.

Cutting, J. E., Proffitt, D. R., & Kozlowski, L. T. (1978). A biomechanical invariant for gait perception. *Journal of Experimental Psychology: Human Perception and Performance, 4*(3), 357–372.

Czarnek, G., & Kossowska, M. (2021). The effects of needs for security and certainty on economic beliefs: The role of political engagement and the welfare state model. *Social Psychological and Personality Science, 12*(8), 1467–1475.

Czopp, A. M., Kay, A. C., & Cheryan, S. (2015). Positive stereotypes are pervasive and powerful. *Perspectives on Psychological Science, 10*(4), 451–463.

Dasgupta, N., & Asgari, S. (2004). Seeing is believing: Exposure to counterstereotypic women leaders and its effect on the malleability of automatic gender stereotyping. *Journal of Experimental Social Psychology, 40*(5), 642–658.

Devine, P. G. (1989). Stereotypes and prejudice: Their automatic and controlled components. *Journal of Personality and Social Psychology, 56*(1), 5–18.

Devine, P. G., & Elliot, A. J. (1995). Are racial stereotypes really fading? The Princeton trilogy revisited. *Personality and Social Psychology Bulletin, 21*(11), 1139–1150.

Diamond, L. M. (2003). What does sexual orientation orient? A biobehavioral model distinguishing romantic love and sexual desire. *Psychological Review, 110*(1), 173–192.

Ding, J. Y., & Rule, N. O. (2012). Gay, straight, or somewhere in between: Accuracy and bias in the perception of bisexual faces. *Journal of Nonverbal Behavior, 36*(2), 165–176.

Ditto, P. H., Liu, B. S., Clark, C. J., Wojcik, S. P., Chen, E. E., Grady, R. H., Celniker, J. B., & Zinger, J. F. (2019). At least bias is bipartisan: A meta-analytic comparison of partisan bias in liberals and conservatives. *Perspectives on Psychological Science, 14*(2), 273–291.

Eagly, A. H., Diekman, A. B., Johannesen-Schmidt, M. C., & Koenig, A. M. (2004). Gender gaps in sociopolitical attitudes: A social psychological analysis. *Journal of Personality and Social Psychology, 87*(6), 796–816.

Eagly, A. H., Nater, C., Miller, D. I., Kaufmann, M., & Sczesny, S. (2019). Gender stereotypes have changed: A cross-temporal meta-analysis of US public opinion polls from 1946 to 2018. *American Psychologist, 75*, 301–315.

Eagly, A. H., & Wood, W. (1999). The origins of sex differences in human behavior: Evolved dispositions versus social roles. *American Psychologist, 54*(6), 408–423.

Eberhardt, J. L. (2020). *Biased: Uncovering the hidden prejudice that shapes what we see, think, and do.* New York: Viking.

Eisenman, R., Borod, J., & Grossman, J. C. (1972). Sex differences in the interrelationships of authoritarianism, anxiety, creative attitudes, preference for complex polygons, and the Barron-Welsh Art Scale. *Journal of Clinical Psychology, 28*(4), 549–550.

Epley, N., Keysar, B., Van Boven, L., & Gilovich, T. (2004). Perspective taking as egocentric anchoring and adjustment. *Journal of Personality and Social Psychology, 87*(3), 327–339.

Eyal, T., Steffel, M., & Epley, N. (2018). Perspective mistaking: Accurately understanding the mind of another requires getting perspective, not taking perspective. *Journal of Personality and Social Psychology, 114*(4), 547–571.

Farmer, K., Cady, R., Bleiberg, J., & Reeves, D. (2000). A pilot study to measure cognitive efficiency during migraine. *Headache: The Journal of Head and Face Pain, 40*(8), 657–661.

Farrell, M. J. (1957). The measurement of productive efficiency. *Journal of the Royal Statistical Society: Series A (General), 120*(3), 253–281.

Fazio, R. H., & Dunton, B. C. (1997). Categorization by race: The impact of automatic and controlled components of racial prejudice. *Journal of Experimental Social Psychology, 33*(5), 451–470.

Federico, C. M. (2021). When do psychological differences predict political differences?: Engagement and the psychological bases of political polarization. In J. W. van Prooijen (Ed.), *The psychology of political polarization* (pp. 17–37). Routledge.

Federico, C. M., & Malka, A. (2018). The contingent, contextual nature of the relationship between needs for security and certainty and political preferences: Evidence and implications. *Political Psychology, 39*, 3–48.

Feldman, S., & Johnston, C. (2014). Understanding the determinants of political ideology: Implications of structural complexity. *Political Psychology, 35*(3), 337–358.

Fernbach, P. M., Rogers, T., Fox, C. R., & Sloman, S. A. (2013). Political extremism is supported by an illusion of understanding. *Psychological Science, 24*(6), 939–946.

Finnegan, E., Oakhill, J., & Garnham, A. (2015). Counter-stereotypical pictures as a strategy for overcoming spontaneous gender stereotypes. *Frontiers in Psychology, 6*, 1291.

Fiske, S. T. (1998). Stereotyping, prejudice, and discrimination. In T. Gilbert, & S. T. Fiske (Eds.), *Handbook of social psychology* (pp. 357–411). Boston, MA: McGraw-Hill.

Fiske, S. T. (1992). Thinking is for doing: portraits of social cognition from daguerreotype to laserphoto. *Journal of Personality and Social Psychology, 63*(6), 877–889.

Fiske, S. T., Bersoff, D. N., Borgida, E., Deaux, K., & Heilman, M. E. (1991). Social science research on trial: Use of sex stereotyping research in Price Waterhouse v. Hopkins. *American Psychologist, 46*(10), 1049–1060.

Fiske, S. T., Cuddy, A. J., Glick, P., & Xu, J. (2002). A model of (often mixed) stereotype content: competence and warmth respectively follow from perceived status and competition. *Journal of Personality and Social Psychology, 82*(6), 878–902.

Fiske, S. T., & Taylor, S. E. (2013). *Social cognition: From brains to culture.* Sage.

Frederick, S. (2005). Cognitive reflection and decision making. *Journal of Economic Perspectives, 19*(4), 25–42.

Freeman, J. B., & Ambady, N. (2011). A dynamic interactive theory of person construal. *Psychological Review, 118*(2), 247–279.

Freeman, J. B., Ambady, N., Rule, N. O., & Johnson, K. L. (2008). Will a category cue attract you? Motor output reveals dynamic competition across person construal. *Journal of Experimental Psychology: General, 137*(4), 673–690.

Freeman, J. B., Johnson, K. L., Ambady, N., & Rule, N. O. (2010). Sexual orientation perception involves gendered facial cues. *Personality and Social Psychology Bulletin, 36*(10), 1318–1331.

Freeman, J. B., Stolier, R. M., & Brooks, J. A. (2020). Dynamic interactive theory as a domain-general account of social perception. In *Advances in experimental social psychology* (Vol. 61, pp. 237–287). Academic Press.

Frimer, J. A., Skitka, L. J., & Motyl, M. (2017). Liberals and conservatives are similarly motivated to avoid exposure to one another's opinions. *Journal of Experimental Social Psychology, 72*, 1–12.

Funder, D. C. (2012). Accurate personality judgment. *Current Directions in Psychological Science, 21*(3), 177–182.

Funder, D. C. (1995). On the accuracy of personality judgment: A realistic approach. *Psychological Review, 102*(4), 652–670.

Gaertner, S. L., & Dovidio, J. F. (2000). *Reducing intergroup bias: The common ingroup identity model.* Philadelphia: Psychology Press.

Gaither, S. E., Chen, J. M., Pauker, K., & Sommers, S. R. (2019). At face value: Psychological outcomes differ for real vs. computer-generated multiracial faces. *The Journal of Social Psychology, 159*(5), 592–610.

Gallup. (2021). *Party affiliation.* Retrieved from https://news.gallup.com/poll/15370/party-affiliation.aspx.

Gaines, K. K. (2012). *Uplifting the race: Black leadership, politics, and culture in the twentieth century.* Chapel Hill, NC: University of North Carolina Press.

Garrison, K. E., Finley, A. J., & Schmeichel, B. J. (2019). Ego depletion reduces attention control: Evidence from two high-powered preregistered experiments. *Personality and Social Psychology Bulletin, 45*(5), 728–739.

Gieseler, C. (2019). *Gender-reveal parties as mediated events: Celebrating identity in pink and blue.* Lexington Books.

Gieseler, K., Inzlicht, M., & Friese, M. (2020). Do people avoid mental effort after facing a highly demanding task? *Journal of Experimental Social Psychology, 90*, 104008.

Gilbert, D. T., & Hixon, J. G. (1991). The trouble of thinking: Activation and application of stereotypic beliefs. *Journal of Personality and Social Psychology, 60*(4), 509–517.

Gilens, M. (1995). Racial attitudes and opposition to welfare. *The Journal of Politics, 57*(4), 994–1014.

Giuliano, P., & Spilimbergo, A. (2014). Growing up in a Recession. *Review of Economic Studies, 81*(2), 787–817.

Goff, P. A., Thomas, M. A., & Jackson, M. C. (2008). "Ain't I a woman?": Towards an intersectional approach to person perception and group-based harms. *Sex Roles, 59*(5-6), 392–403.

Golman, R., Gurney, N., & Loewenstein, G. (2021). Information gaps for risk and ambiguity. *Psychological Review, 128*, 86–103.

Graham, J., Haidt, J., & Nosek, B. A. (2009). Liberals and conservatives rely on different sets of moral foundations. *Journal of Personality and Social Psychology, 96*(5), 1029–1046.

Grant, P. R., & Holmes, J. G. (1981). The integration of implicit personality theory schemas and stereotype images. *Social Psychology Quarterly*, 107–115.

Greenberg, J., & Jonas, E. (2003). Psychological motives and political orientation- -the left, the right, and the rigid: Comment on Jost et al. (2003). *Psychological Bulletin, 129,* 376–382.

Haines, E. L., Deaux, K., & Lofaro, N. (2016). The times they are a-changing... or are they not? A comparison of gender stereotypes, 1983–2014. *Psychology of Women Quarterly, 40*(3), 353–363.

Hehman, E., Carpinella, C. M., Johnson, K. L., Leitner, J. B., & Freeman, J. B. (2014). Early processing of gendered facial cues predicts the electoral success of female politicians. *Social Psychological and Personality Science, 5*(7), 815–824.

Hehman, E., Sutherland, C. A., Flake, J. K., & Slepian, M. L. (2017). The unique contributions of perceiver and target characteristics in person perception. *Journal of Personality and Social Psychology, 113*(4), 513–529.

Heilman, M. E., & Wallen, A. S. (2010). Wimpy and undeserving of respect: Penalties for men's gender-inconsistent success. *Journal of Experimental Social Psychology, 46*(4), 664–667.

Hennes, E. P., Nam, H. H., Stern, C., & Jost, J. T. (2012). Not all ideologies are created equal: Epistemic, existential, and relational needs predict system-justifying attitudes. *Social Cognition, 30*(6), 669–688.

Hewstone, M., Hantzi, A., & Johnston, L. (1991). Social categorization and person memory: The pervasiveness of race as an organizing principle. *European Journal of Social Psychology, 21*(6), 517–528.

Hewstone, M., Islam, M. R., & Judd, C. M. (1993). Models of crossed categorization and intergroup relations. *Journal of Personality and Social Psychology, 64*(5), 779.

Higgins, E. T. (1998). The aboutness principle: A pervasive influence on human inference. *Social Cognition, 16*(1), 173–198.

Higgins, E. T. (2013). Truth motivation. In K. D. Markman, T. Proulx, & M. J. Lindberg (Eds.), *The psychology of meaning* (pp. 91–114). American Psychological Association.

Higgins, E. T. (2019). What reigns supreme: Value, control, or truth? *Motivation Science, 5*(3), 185–201.

Hill, H., Bruce, V., & Akamatsu, S. (1995). Perceiving the sex and race of faces: The role of shape and colour. *Proceedings of the Royal Society of London. Series B: Biological Sciences, 261*(1362), 367–373.

Himmelfarb, S. (1966). Studies in the perception of ethnic group members: I. Accuracy, response bias, and anti-Semitism. *Journal of Personality and Social Psychology, 4*(4), 347–355.

Ho, A. K., Kteily, N. S., & Chen, J. M. (2020). Introducing the sociopolitical motive × intergroup threat model to understand how monoracial perceivers' sociopolitical motives influence their categorization of multiracial people. *Personality and Social Psychology Review, 24*(3), 260–286.

Ho, A. K., Kteily, N. S., & Chen, J. M. (2017). "You're one of us": Black Americans' use of hypodescent and its association with egalitarianism. *Journal of Personality and Social Psychology, 113*(5), 753–768.

Ho, A. K., Sidanius, J., Cuddy, A. J., & Banaji, M. R. (2013). Status boundary enforcement and the categorization of black–white biracials. *Journal of Experimental Social Psychology, 49*(5), 940–943.

Ho, A. K., Sidanius, J., Kteily, N., Sheehy-Skeffington, J., Pratto, F., Henkel, K. E., & Stewart, A. L. (2015). The nature of social dominance orientation: Theorizing and measuring preferences for intergroup inequality using the new SDO7 scale. *Journal of Personality and Social Psychology, 109*(6), 1003.

Ho, A. K., Sidanius, J., Levin, D. T., & Banaji, M. R. (2011). Evidence for hypodescent and racial hierarchy in the categorization and perception of biracial individuals. *Journal of Personality and Social Psychology, 100*(3), 492–506.

Hodson, G., & MacInnis, C. C. (2017). Can left-right differences in abortion support be explained by sexism? *Personality and Individual Differences, 104*, 118–121.

Huddy, L. (2001). From social to political identity: A critical examination of social identity theory. *Political Psychology, 22*(1), 127–156.

Hugenberg, K., Miller, J., & Claypool, H. M. (2007). Categorization and individuation in the cross-race recognition deficit: Toward a solution to an insidious problem. *Journal of Experimental Social Psychology, 43*(2), 334–340.

Ivanov, I., Muller, D., Delmas, F., & Wänke, M. (2018). Interpersonal accuracy in a political context is moderated by the extremity of one's political attitudes. *Journal of Experimental Social Psychology, 79*, 95–106.

Iyengar, S., Lelkes, Y., Levendusky, M., Malhotra, N., & Westwood, S. J. (2019). The origins and consequences of affective polarization in the United States. *Annual Review of Political Science, 22*, 129–146.

James, W. (1890-1983). *The principles of psychology.* Cambridge, MA: Harvard University Press.

Johnson, K. L., Freeman, J. B., & Pauker, K. (2012). Race is gendered: How covarying phenotypes and stereotypes bias sex categorization. *Journal of Personality and Social Psychology, 102*(1), 116–131.

Johnson, K. L., Gill, S., Reichman, V., & Tassinary, L. G. (2007). Swagger, sway, and sexuality: Judging sexual orientation from body motion and morphology. *Journal of Personality and Social Psychology, 93*(3), 321–334.

Johnson, K. L., & Ghavami, N. (2011). At the crossroads of conspicuous and concealable: What race categories communicate about sexual orientation. *PLoS One, 6*(3), e18025.

Johnson, K. L., Lick, D. J., & Carpinella, C. M. (2015). Emergent research in social vision: An integrated approach to the determinants and consequences of social categorization. *Social and Personality Psychology Compass, 9*(1), 15–30.

Johnson, K. L., & Tassinary, L. G. (2005). Perceiving sex directly and indirectly: Meaning in motion and morphology. *Psychological Science, 16*(11), 890–897.

Johnston, C. D., Lavine, H. G., & Federico, C. M. (2017). *Open versus closed: Personality, identity, and the politics of redistribution.* Cambridge University Press.

Johnston, C. D., & Ollerenshaw, T. (2020). How different are cultural and economic ideology? *Current Opinion in Behavioral Sciences, 34*, 94–101.

Jost, J. T. (1995). Negative illusions: Conceptual clarification and psychological evidence concerning false consciousness. *Political Psychology*, 397–424.

Jost, J. T. (2006). The end of the end of ideology. *American Psychologist, 61*(7), 651–670.

Jost, J. T., & Banaji, M. R. (1994). The role of stereotyping in system-justification and the production of false consciousness. *British Journal of Social Psychology, 33*(1), 1–27.

Jost, J. T., Federico, C. M., & Napier, J. L. (2009). Political ideology: Its structure, functions, and elective affinities. *Annual Review of Psychology, 60*, 307–337.

Jost, J. T., Gaucher, D., & Stern, C. (2015). "The world isn't fair": A system justification perspective on social stratification and inequality. In J. Dovidio, & J. Simpson (Eds.), *APA handbook of personality and social psychology* (Vol. II, pp. 317–340). Washington, DC: American Psychological Association.

Jost, J. T., Glaser, J., Kruglanski, A. W., & Sulloway, F. J. (2003). Political conservatism as motivated social cognition. *Psychological Bulletin, 129*(3), 339–375.

Jost, J. T., Nosek, B. A., & Gosling, S. D. (2008). Ideology: Its resurgence in social, personality, and political psychology. *Perspectives on Psychological Science, 3*(2), 126–136.

Jost, J. T., Sterling, J., & Stern, C. (2018). Getting closure on conservatism, or the politics of epistemic and existential motivation. In C. Kopetz, & A. Fishbach (Eds.), *Volume I. The motivation-cognition interface, from the lab to the real world: A festschrift in Honor of Arie W. Kruglanski* (pp. 56–87). New York: Routledge.

Jung, K. H., White, K. R., & Powanda, S. J. (2019). Automaticity of gender categorization: A test of the efficiency feature. *Social Cognition, 37*(2), 122–144.

Jussim, L. (2005). Accuracy: Criticisms, controversies, criteria, components, and cognitive processes. *Advances in Experimental Social Psychology, 37,* 1–93.

Kahan, D. M. (2012). Ideology, motivated reasoning, and cognitive reflection: An experimental study. *Judgment and Decision making, 8,* 407–424.

Kalmoe, N. P. (2020). Uses and abuses of ideology in political psychology. *Political Psychology, 41,* 771–793.

Kang, S. K., & Bodenhausen, G. V. (2015). Multiple identities in social perception and interaction: Challenges and opportunities. *Annual Review of Psychology, 66,* 547–574.

Katz, J. N. (2007). *The invention of heterosexuality.* University of Chicago Press.

Kawakami, K., Amodio, D. M., & Hugenberg, K. (2017). Intergroup perception and cognition: An integrative framework for understanding the causes and consequences of social categorization. In *Advances in experimental social psychology* (Vol. 55, pp. 1–80). Academic Press.

Kay, A. C., Day, M. V., Zanna, M. P., & Nussbaum, A. D. (2013). The insidious (and ironic) effects of positive stereotypes. *Journal of Experimental Social Psychology, 49*(2), 287–291.

Kay, A. C., & Friesen, J. (2011). On social stability and social change: Understanding when system justification does and does not occur. *Current Directions in Psychological Science, 20*(6), 360–364.

Kay, A. C., & Jost, J. T. (2003). Complementary justice: Effects of "poor but happy" and "poor but honest" stereotype exemplars on system justification and implicit activation of the justice motive. *Journal of Personality and Social Psychology, 85*(5), 823–837.

Kenny, D. A. (1994). *Interpersonal perception: A social relations analysis.* Guilford Press.

Kinder, D. R., & Kalmoe, N. P. (2017). *Neither liberal nor conservative: Ideological innocence in the American public.* University of Chicago Press.

Klapper, A., Dotsch, R., van Rooij, I., & Wigboldus, D. H. (2016). Do we spontaneously form stable trustworthiness impressions from facial appearance? *Journal of Personality and Social Psychology, 111*(5), 655–664.

Klapper, A., Dotsch, R., van Rooij, I., & Wigboldus, D. (2017). Four meanings of "categorization": A conceptual analysis of research on person perception. *Social and Personality Psychology Compass, 11*(8), e12336.

Kleiman, T., & Hassin, R. R. (2011). Non-conscious goal conflicts. *Journal of Experimental Social Psychology, 47*(3), 521–532.

Knowles, E. D., & Peng, K. (2005). White selves: Conceptualizing and measuring a dominant-group identity. *Journal of Personality and Social Psychology, 89*(2), 223–241.

Kogan, N. (1979). A study of age categorization. *Journal of Gerontology, 34*(3), 358–367.

Krosch, A. R., & Amodio, D. M. (2014). Economic scarcity alters the perception of race. *Proceedings of the National Academy of Sciences, 111*(25), 9079–9084.

Krosch, A. R., & Amodio, D. M. (2019). Scarcity disrupts the neural encoding of Black faces: A socioperceptual pathway to discrimination. *Journal of Personality and Social Psychology, 117*(5), 859–875.

Krosch, A. R., Berntsen, L., Amodio, D. M., Jost, J. T., & Van Bavel, J. J. (2013). On the ideology of hypodescent: Political conservatism predicts categorization of racially ambiguous faces as Black. *Journal of Experimental Social Psychology, 49*(6), 1196–1203.

Kruglanski, A. W. (1989). The psychology of being "right": The problem of accuracy in social perception and cognition. *Psychological Bulletin, 106*(3), 395–409.

Kruglanski, A. W., Shah, J. Y., Fishbach, A., Friedman, R., Chun, W., & Sleeth-Keppler, D. (2002). A theory of goal systems. *Advances in Experimental Social Psychology, 34,* 311–378.

Kruse, K. M. (2013). *White flight: Atlanta and the making of modern conservatism. Vol. 89.* Princeton University Press.

Kteily, N. S., Rocklage, M. D., McClanahan, K., & Ho, A. K. (2019). Political ideology shapes the amplification of the accomplishments of disadvantaged vs. advantaged group members. *Proceedings of the National Academy of Sciences, 116*(5), 1559–1568.

Kunda, Z. (1990). The case for motivated reasoning. *Psychological Bulletin, 108*(3), 480–498.

Kunda, Z., & Oleson, K. C. (1995). Maintaining stereotypes in the face of disconfirmation: Constructing grounds for subtyping deviants. *Journal of Personality and Social Psychology, 68*(4), 565–579.

Kurzban, R., Tooby, J., & Cosmides, L. (2001). Can race be erased? Coalitional computation and social categorization. *Proceedings of the National Academy of Sciences, 98*(26), 15387–15392.

Lammers, J., Koch, A., Conway, P., & Brandt, M. J. (2017). The political domain appears simpler to the politically extreme than to political moderates. *Social Psychological and Personality Science, 8*(6), 612–622.

Landau, M. J., Solomon, S., Greenberg, J., Cohen, F., Pyszczynski, T., Arndt, J., & Cook, A. (2004). Deliver us from evil: The effects of mortality salience and reminders of 9/11 on support for President George W. Bush. *Personality and Social Psychology Bulletin, 30*(9), 1136–1150.

Lane, R. E. (1962). *Political ideology: Why the American common man believes what he does.* New York: Free Press.

Lavie, N. (2010). Attention, distraction, and cognitive control under load. *Current Directions in Psychological Science, 19*(3), 143–148.

Lick, D. J., & Johnson, K. L. (2013). Fluency of visual processing explains prejudiced evaluations following categorization of concealable identities. *Journal of Experimental Social Psychology, 49*(3), 419–425.

Lick, D. J., & Johnson, K. L. (2016). Perceptually Mediated Preferences and Prejudices. *Psychological Inquiry, 27*(4), 335–340.

Lick, D. J., & Johnson, K. L. (2015). The interpersonal consequences of processing ease: Fluency as a metacognitive foundation for prejudice. *Current Directions in Psychological Science, 24*(2), 143–148.

Lick, D. J., & Johnson, K. L. (2014). "You can't tell just by looking!" Beliefs in the diagnosticity of visual cues explain response biases in social categorization. *Personality and Social Psychology Bulletin, 40*(11), 1494–1506.

Lick, D. J., Johnson, K. L., & Rule, N. O. (2015). Disfluent processing of nonverbal cues helps to explain anti-bisexual prejudice. *Journal of Nonverbal Behavior, 39*(3), 275–288.

Lick, D. J., Johnson, K. L., Rule, N. O., & Stroessner, S. J. (2019). Perceivers infer base rates from social context to judge perceptually ambiguous social identities. *Social Cognition, 37*(6), 596–623.

Lin, H., Saunders, B., Friese, M., Evans, N. J., & Inzlicht, M. (2020). Strong effort manipulations reduce response caution: A preregistered reinvention of the ego-depletion paradigm. *Psychological Science, 31*(5), 531–547.

Lipset, S. M. (1959). Democracy and working-class authoritarianism. *American Sociological Review*, 482–501.

Lipset, S. (1960). *Political man.* Garden City, NY: Doubleday.

Livingston, R. W. (2001). What you see is what you get: Systematic variability in perceptual-based social judgment. *Personality and Social Psychology Bulletin, 27*(9), 1086–1096.

Lorber, J., & Farrell, S. A. (Eds.). (1991). *The social construction of gender* (pp. 309–321). Newbury Park, CA: Sage.

Lopez, I. F. H. (1994). The social construction of race: Some observations on illusion, fabrication, and choice. *Harvard Civil Rights-Civil Liberties Law Review, 29*, 1.

Ma, D. S., Correll, J., & Wittenbrink, B. (2015). The Chicago face database: A free stimulus set of faces and norming data. *Behavior Research Methods, 47*(4), 1122–1135.

Ma, D. S., Kantner, J., & Wittenbrink, B. (2021). Chicago face database: Multiracial expansion. *Behavior Research Methods*, *53*(3), 1289–1300.

Macrae, C. N., Alnwick, K. A., Milne, A. B., & Schloerscheidt, A. M. (2002). Person perception across the menstrual cycle: Hormonal influences on social-cognitive functioning. *Psychological Science*, *13*(6), 532–536.

Macrae, C. N., & Bodenhausen, G. V. (2000). Social cognition: Thinking categorically about others. *Annual Review of Psychology*, *51*(1), 93–120.

Maddox, K. B. (2004). Perspectives on racial phenotypicality bias. *Personality and Social Psychology Review*, *8*(4), 383–401.

Malka, A., Lelkes, Y., & Soto, C. J. (2019). Are cultural and economic conservatism positively correlated? A large-scale cross-national test. *British Journal of Political Science*, *49*(3), 1045–1069.

Malka, A., & Soto, C. J. (2015). Rigidity of the economic right? Menu-independent and menu-dependent influences of psychological dispositions on political attitudes. *Current Directions in Psychological Science*, *24*(2), 137–142.

Malka, A., Soto, C. J., Inzlicht, M., & Lelkes, Y. (2014). Do needs for security and certainty predict cultural and economic conservatism? A cross-national analysis. *Journal of Personality and Social Psychology*, *106*(6), 1031–1051.

Markus, H. R. (2008). Pride, prejudice, and ambivalence: Toward a unified theory of race and ethnicity. *American Psychologist*, *63*(8), 651–670.

McAdams, D. P., Albaugh, M., Farber, E., Daniels, J., Logan, R. L., & Olson, B. (2008). Family metaphors and moral intuitions: How conservatives and liberals narrate their lives. *Journal of Personality and Social Psychology*, *95*(4), 978–990.

McLemore, K. A. (2015). Experiences with misgendering: Identity misclassification of transgender spectrum individuals. *Self and Identity*, *14*(1), 51–74.

Meerwijk, E. L., & Sevelius, J. M. (2017). Transgender population size in the United States: a meta-regression of population-based probability samples. *American Journal of Public Health*, *107*(2), e1–e8.

Messing, S., Jabon, M., & Plaut, E. (2016). Bias in the flesh: Skin complexion and stereotype consistency in political campaigns. *Public Opinion Quarterly*, *80*(1), 44–65.

Monteith, M. J., Sherman, J. W., & Devine, P. G. (1998). Suppression as a stereotype control strategy. *Personality and Social Psychology Review*, *2*(1), 63–82.

Monteith, M. J., Spicer, C. V., & Tooman, G. D. (1998). Consequences of stereotype suppression: Stereotypes on AND not on the rebound. *Journal of Experimental Social Psychology*, *34*(4), 355–377.

Morgenroth, T., & Ryan, M. K. (2021). The effects of gender trouble: An integrative theoretical framework of the perpetuation and disruption of the gender/sex binary. *Perspectives on Psychological Science*, *16*(6), 1113–1142.

Morgenroth, T., Sendén, M. G., Lindqvist, A., Renström, E. A., Ryan, M. K., & Morton, T. A. (2021). Defending the sex/gender binary: The role of gender identification and need for closure. *Social Psychological and Personality Science*, *12*(5), 731–740.

Neuberg, S. L., & Newsom, J. T. (1993). Personal need for structure: Individual differences in the desire for simpler structure. *Journal of Personality and Social Psychology*, *65*(1), 113–131.

Neuberg, S. L., & Fiske, S. T. (1987). Motivational influences on impression formation: outcome dependency, accuracy-driven attention, and individuating processes. *Journal of Personality and Social Psychology*, *53*(3), 431–444.

Nicolas, G., de la Fuente, M., & Fiske, S. T. (2017). Mind the overlap in multiple categorization: A review of crossed categorization, intersectionality, and multiracial perception. *Group Processes & Intergroup Relations*, *20*(5), 621–631.

Nicolas, G., Skinner, A. L., & Dickter, C. L. (2019). Other than the sum: Hispanic and Middle Eastern categorizations of Black–White mixed-race faces. *Social Psychological and Personality Science*, *10*(4), 532–541.

Nosek, B. A., & Banaji, M. R. (2001). The go/no-go association task. *Social Cognition, 19*(6), 625–666.

Okimoto, T. G., & Gromet, D. M. (2016). Differences in sensitivity to deviance partly explain ideological divides in social policy support. *Journal of Personality and Social Psychology, 111*(1), 98–117.

Oldmeadow, J., & Fiske, S. T. (2007). System-justifying ideologies moderate status = competence stereotypes: Roles for belief in a just world and social dominance orientation. *European Journal of Social Psychology, 37*(6), 1135–1148.

Olivola, C. Y., Eubanks, D. L., & Lovelace, J. B. (2014). The many (distinctive) faces of leadership: Inferring leadership domain from facial appearance. *The Leadership Quarterly, 25*(5), 817–834.

Olivola, C. Y., Sussman, A. B., Tsetsos, K., Kang, O. E., & Todorov, A. (2012). Republicans prefer Republican-looking leaders: Political facial stereotypes predict candidate electoral success among right-leaning voters. *Social Psychological and Personality Science, 3*(5), 605–613.

Olivola, C. Y., Tingley, D., & Todorov, A. (2018). Republican voters prefer candidates who have conservative-looking faces: New evidence from exit polls. *Political Psychology, 39*(5), 1157–1171.

Olivola, C. Y., & Todorov, A. (2010). Fooled by first impressions? Reexamining the diagnostic value of appearance-based inferences. *Journal of Experimental Social Psychology, 46*(2), 315–324.

Osborne, D., & Sibley, C. G. (2020). Does Openness to Experience predict changes in conservatism? A nine-wave longitudinal investigation into the personality roots to ideology. *Journal of Research in Personality, 103979.*

Parker, K., Horowitz, J. M., Morin, R., & Lopez, M. H. (2015). *Multiracial in America.* Retrieved from https://www.pewsocialtrends.org/2015/06/11/multiracial-in-america/.

Parks-Stamm, E. J., Heilman, M. E., & Hearns, K. A. (2008). Motivated to penalize: Women's strategic rejection of successful women. *Personality and Social Psychology Bulletin, 34*(2), 237–247.

Pauker, K., Carpinella, C. M., Lick, D. J., Sanchez, D. T., & Johnson, K. L. (2018). Malleability in biracial categorizations: The impact of geographic context and targets' racial heritage. *Social Cognition, 36*(5), 461–480.

Payne, B. K., Vuletich, H. A., & Brown-Iannuzzi, J. L. (2019). Historical roots of implicit bias in slavery. *Proceedings of the National Academy of Sciences, 116*(24), 11693–11698.

Peery, D., & Bodenhausen, G. V. (2008). Black + White = Black: Hypodescent in reflexive categorization of racially ambiguous faces. *Psychological Science, 19*(10), 973–977.

Petsko, C. D., & Bodenhausen, G. V. (2020). Multifarious person perception: How social perceivers manage the complexity of intersectional targets. *Social and Personality Psychology Compass, 14*(2), e12518.

Petsko, C. D., & Bodenhausen, G. V. (2019). Race–Crime congruency effects revisited: Do we take defendants' sexual orientation into account? *Social Psychological and Personality Science, 10*(1), 73–81.

Pew Research Center. (2009). *Americans favor carbon cap, gays in the military and renewing U.S.-Cuba Ties.* Retrieved from https://www.pewresearch.org/politics/2009/03/25/americans-favor-carbon-cap-gays-in-the-military-and-renewing-us-cuba-ties/.

Pew Research Center. (2014). *Political ideology.* Retrieved from https://www.pewforum.org/religious-landscape-study/political-ideology/.

Phelan, J. E., & Rudman, L. A. (2010). Reactions to ethnic deviance: The role of backlash in racial stereotype maintenance. *Journal of Personality and Social Psychology, 99*(2), 265–281.

Pierson, E., Simoiu, C., Overgoor, J., Corbett-Davies, S., Jenson, D., Shoemaker, A., & Goel, S. (2020). A large-scale analysis of racial disparities in police stops across the United States. *Nature Human Behaviour, 4,* 736–745.

Pierson, P., & Schickler, E. (2020). Madison's Constitution under stress: A developmental analysis of political polarization. *Annual Review of Political Science, 23*, 37–58.

Pietraszewski, D., Cosmides, L., & Tooby, J. (2014). The content of our cooperation, not the color of our skin: An alliance detection system regulates categorization by coalition and race, but not sex. *PLoS One, 9*(2), e88534.

Pinsof, D., & Haselton, M. (2016). The political divide over same-sex marriage: Mating strategies in conflict? *Psychological Science, 27*(4), 435–442.

Pratto, F., Sidanius, J., Stallworth, L. M., & Malle, B. F. (1994). Social dominance orientation: A personality variable predicting social and political attitudes. *Journal of Personality and Social Psychology, 67*(4), 741–763.

Proulx, T., & Brandt, M. J. (2017). Beyond threat and uncertainty: The underpinnings of conservatism. *Social Cognition, 35*(4), 313–323.

Prusaczyk, E., & Hodson, G. (2019). The roles of political conservatism and binary gender beliefs in predicting prejudices toward gay men and people who are transgender. *Sex Roles*, 1–9.

Reber, R., Schwarz, N., & Winkielman, P. (2004). Processing fluency and aesthetic pleasure: Is beauty in the perceiver's processing experience? *Personality and Social Psychology Review, 8*(4), 364–382.

Richeson, J. A., & Shelton, J. N. (2007). Negotiating interracial interactions: Costs, consequences, and possibilities. *Current Directions in Psychological Science, 16*(6), 316–320.

Rieger, G., Linsenmeier, J. A., Gygax, L., Garcia, S., & Bailey, J. M. (2010). Dissecting "gaydar": Accuracy and the role of masculinity–femininity. *Archives of Sexual Behavior, 39*(1), 124–140.

Roberts, B. W., & DelVecchio, W. F. (2000). The rank-order consistency of personality traits from childhood to old age: A quantitative review of longitudinal studies. *Psychological Bulletin, 126*(1), 3–25.

Rodeheffer, C. D., Hill, S. E., & Lord, C. G. (2012). Does this recession make me look black? The effect of resource scarcity on the categorization of biracial faces. *Psychological Science, 23*(12), 1476–1478.

Rokeach, M. (1968). *Beliefs, attitudes, and values*. San Francisco: Jossey-Bass.

Rossignac-Milon, M., & Higgins, E. T. (2018). Epistemic companions: Shared reality development in close relationships. *Current Opinion in Psychology, 23*, 66–71.

Rothstein, R. (2017). *The color of law: A forgotten history of how our government segregated America*. Liveright Publishing.

Rudman, L. A., & Fairchild, K. (2004). Reactions to counterstereotypic behavior: the role of backlash in cultural stereotype maintenance. *Journal of Personality and Social Psychology, 87*(2), 157–176.

Ruisch, B. C., Shook, N. J., & Fazio, R. H. (2021). Of unbiased beans and slanted stocks: Neutral stimuli reveal the fundamental relation between political ideology and exploratory behaviour. *British Journal of Psychology, 112*, 358–361.

Ruisch, B., & Stern, C. (2021). The confident conservative: Ideological differences in judgment and decision-making confidence. *Journal of Experimental Psychology: General, 150*, 527–544.

Rule, N. O., & Ambady, N. (2008). Brief exposures: Male sexual orientation is accurately perceived at 50 ms. *Journal of Experimental Social Psychology, 44*, 1100–1105.

Rule, N. O., & Ambady, N. (2010). Democrats and Republicans can be differentiated from their faces. *PLoS One, 5*(1), e8733.

Rule, N. O., Ambady, N., Adams, R. B., Jr., & Macrae, C. N. (2008). Accuracy and awareness in the perception and categorization of male sexual orientation. *Journal of Personality and Social Psychology, 95*(5), 1019–1028.

Rule, N. O., Garrett, J. V., & Ambady, N. (2010). On the perception of religious group membership from faces. *PLoS One, 5*(12), e14241.

Rule, N. O., Krendl, A. C., Ivcevic, Z., & Ambady, N. (2013). Accuracy and consensus in judgments of trustworthiness from faces: Behavioral and neural correlates. *Journal of Personality and Social Psychology*, *104*(3), 409–426.

Rule, N. O., Rosen, K. S., Slepian, M. L., & Ambady, N. (2011). Mating interest improves women's accuracy in judging male sexual orientation. *Psychological Science*, *22*(7), 881–886.

Rypma, B., Berger, J. S., Prabhakaran, V., Bly, B. M., Kimberg, D. Y., Biswal, B. B., & D'Esposito, M. (2006). Neural correlates of cognitive efficiency. *NeuroImage*, *33*(3), 969–979.

Saad, L. (2019). *U.S. still leans conservative, but liberals keep recent gains.* In Gallup. https://news.gallup.com/poll/245813/leans-conservative-liberals-keep-recent-gains.aspx.

Secord, P. F. (1958). Facial features and inference processes in interpersonal perception. In R. Tagiuri, & L. Petrullo (Eds.), *Person perception and interpersonal behavior.* Stanford, CA: Stanford University Press.

Samochowiec, J., Wänke, M., & Fiedler, K. (2010). Political ideology at face value. *Social Psychological and Personality Science*, *1*(3), 206–213.

Shook, N. J., & Fazio, R. H. (2009). Political ideology, exploration of novel stimuli, and attitude formation. *Journal of Experimental Social Psychology*, *45*(4), 995–998.

Sibley, C. G., Osborne, D., & Duckitt, J. (2012). Personality and political orientation: Meta-analysis and test of a Threat-Constraint Model. *Journal of Research in Personality*, *46*(6), 664–677.

Sickles, R. C., & Zelenyuk, V. (2019). *Measurement of productivity and efficiency.* Cambridge University Press.

Sidanius, J., & Pratto, F. (2001). *Social dominance: An intergroup theory of social hierarchy and oppression.* Cambridge University Press.

Sirin, S. R., McCreary, D. R., & Mahalik, J. R. (2004). Differential reactions to men and women's gender role transgressions: Perceptions of social status, sexual orientation, and value dissimilarity. *The Journal of Men's Studies*, *12*(2), 119–132.

Skitka, L. J., Mullen, E., Griffin, T., Hutchinson, S., & Chamberlin, B. (2002). Dispositions, scripts, or motivated correction? Understanding ideological differences in explanations for social problems. *Journal of Personality and Social Psychology*, *83*(2), 470–487.

Song, H., Lewis, N. A., Jr., Ballew, M. T., Bravo, M., Davydova, J., Gao, H. O., & Romero-Canyas, R. (2020). What counts as an "environmental" issue? Differences in issue conceptualization by race, ethnicity, and socioeconomic status. *Journal of Environmental Psychology*, 101404.

Spielmann, J., & Stern, C. (2021). Gender transition shapes perceived sexual orientation. *Self and Identity*, *20*, 463–477.

Sterling, J., Jost, J. T., & Pennycook, G. (2016). Are neoliberals more susceptible to bullshit? *Judgment and Decision making*, *11*(4).

Stern, C. (2019). Political ideology predicts beliefs about the visibility of social category memberships. *Social Cognition*, *37*, 18–40.

Stern, C., Ruisch, B., & Rule, N. O. (under review). Conservatives express greater confidence in social category judgments than do liberals.

Stern, C., & Axt, J. (2021). Ideological differences in race and gender stereotyping. *Social Cognition*, *39*, 259–294.

Stern, C., & Axt, J. (2020). Investigating whether group status modulates the relationship between individual differences in epistemic motivation and political conservatism. *Journal of Research in Personality*, *86*, 103940.

Stern, C., Balcetis, E., Cole, S., West, T. V., & Caruso, E. (2016). Government instability shifts skin tone representations of and intentions to vote for political candidates. *Journal of Personality and Social Psychology*, *110*, 76–95.

Stern, C., & Crawford, J. T. (2021). Ideological conflict and prejudice: An adversarial collaboration examining correlates and ideological (a) symmetries. *Social Psychological and Personality Science, 12*, 42–53.

Stern, C., & Ondish, P. (2018). Political aspects of shared reality. *Current Opinion in Psychology, 23*, 11–14.

Stern, C., & Ondish, P. (2019). Political attitudes. In D. Albarracín, & B. Johnson (Eds.), *The handbook of attitudes* (2nd Ed., Vol. II. pp. 498–534). New York, NY: Psychology Press.

Stern, C., & Rule, N. O. (2018). Physical androgyny and categorization difficulty shape political conservatives' attitudes toward transgender people. *Social Psychological and Personality Science, 9*, 24–31.

Stern, C., & West, T. V. (2016). Ideological differences in anchoring and adjustment during social inferences. *Personality and Social Psychology Bulletin, 42*, 1466–1479.

Stern, C., West, T. V., Jost, J. T., & Rule, N. O. (2014). "Ditto Heads": Do conservatives perceive greater consensus within their ranks than liberals? *Personality and Social Psychology Bulletin, 40*, 1162–1177.

Stern, C., West, T. V., Jost, J. T., & Rule, N. O. (2013). The politics of gaydar: Ideological differences in the use of gendered cues in categorizing sexual orientation. *Journal of Personality and Social Psychology, 104*, 520–541.

Stern, C., West, T. V., & Rule, N. O. (2015). Conservatives negatively evaluate counter-stereotypical people to maintain a sense of certainty. *Proceedings of the National Academy of Sciences, 112*, 15337–15342.

Stern, C., West, T. V., & Schoenthaler, A. (2013). The dynamic relationship between accuracy and bias in social perception research. *Social and Personality Psychology Compass, 7*(5), 303–314.

Suzuki, A., Tsukamoto, S., & Takahashi, Y. (2019). Faces tell everything in a just and biologically determined world: Lay theories behind face reading. *Social Psychological and Personality Science, 10*(1), 62–72.

Szumowska, E., Czernatowicz-Kukuczka, A., Kossowska, M., Król, S., & Kruglanski, A. W. (2020). Truth and significance: A 3N model (needs, narratives, networks) perspective on religion. In *The science of religion, spirituality, and existentialism* (pp. 225–242). Academic Press.

Tajfel, H. (1981). *Human groups and social categories: Studies in social psychology.* Cambridge, England: Cambridge University Press.

Tajfel, H., & Turner, J. C. (1979). An integrative theory of intergroup conflict. In W. G. Austin, & S. Worchel (Eds.), *The social psychology of intergroup relations* (pp. 33–47). Monterey, CA: Brooks/Cole.

Tamir, D. I., & Mitchell, J. P. (2013). Anchoring and adjustment during social inferences. *Journal of Experimental Psychology: General, 142*(1), 151–162.

Taylor, S. E., Fiske, S. T., Etcoff, N. L., & Ruderman, A. J. (1978). Categorical and contextual bases of person memory and stereotyping. *Journal of Personality and Social Psychology, 36*(7), 778–793.

Tebbe, E. N., & Moradi, B. (2012). Anti-transgender prejudice: A structural equation model of associated constructs. *Journal of Counseling Psychology, 59*(2), 251–261.

Tetlock, P. E. (2007). Psychology and politics: The challenges of integrating levels of analysis in social science. In A. W. Kruglanski, & E. T. Higgings (Eds.), *Social psychology: Handbook of basic principles* (2nd ed., pp. 888–912). New York: Guilford Press.

Todorov, A., Mandisodza, A. N., Goren, A., & Hall, C. C. (2005). Inferences of competence from faces predict election outcomes. *Science, 308*(5728), 1623–1626.

Todorov, A., Olivola, C. Y., Dotsch, R., & Mende-Siedlecki, P. (2015). Social attributions from faces: Determinants, consequences, accuracy, and functional significance. *Annual Review of Psychology, 66*, 519–545.

Touré-Tillery, M., & Fishbach, A. (2014). How to measure motivation: A guide for the experimental social psychologist. *Social and Personality Psychology Compass*, *8*(7), 328–341.

Trope, Y., & Thompson, E. P. (1997). Looking for truth in all the wrong places? Asymmetric search of individuating information about stereotyped group members. *Journal of Personality and Social Psychology*, *73*(2), 229–241.

Tskhay, K. O., & Rule, N. O. (2013). Accuracy in categorizing perceptually ambiguous groups: A review and meta-analysis. *Personality and Social Psychology Review*, *17*(1), 72–86.

van der Toorn, J., Jost, J. T., Packer, D. J., Noorbaloochi, S., & Van Bavel, J. J. (2017). In defense of tradition: Religiosity, conservatism, and opposition to same-sex marriage in North America. *Personality and Social Psychology Bulletin*, *43*(10), 1455–1468.

Van Hiel, A., Onraet, E., & De Pauw, S. (2010). The relationship between social-cultural attitudes and behavioral measures of cognitive style: A meta-analytic integration of studies. *Journal of Personality*, *78*(6), 1765–1800.

van Prooijen, J. W., & Krouwel, A. P. (2017). Extreme political beliefs predict dogmatic intolerance. *Social Psychological and Personality Science*, *8*(3), 292–300.

Washburn, A. N., & Skitka, L. J. (2018). Science denial across the political divide: Liberals and conservatives are similarly motivated to deny attitude-inconsistent science. *Social Psychological and Personality Science*, *9*(8), 972–980.

West, T. V., & Kenny, D. A. (2011). The truth and bias model of judgment. *Psychological Review*, *118*(2), 357–378.

White, K. R., Kinney, D., Danek, R. H., Smith, B., & Harben, C. (2020). The resistance to change-beliefs scale: Validation of a new measure of conservative ideology. *Personality and Social Psychology Bulletin*, *46*(1), 20–35.

Wilder, D. A. (1986). Social categorization: Implications for creation and reduction of intergroup bias. In *19. Advances in experimental social psychology* (pp. 291–355). Academic Press.

Wilson, G. D., Ausman, J., & Mathews, T. R. (1973). Conservatism and art preferences. *Journal of Personality and Social Psychology*, *25*(2), 286–288.

Wilson, T. D., Westgate, E. C., Buttrick, N. R., & Gilbert, D. T. (2019). The mind is its own place: The difficulties and benefits of thinking for pleasure. In *Advances in experimental social psychology* (Vol. 60, pp. 175–221). Academic Press.

Winkielman, P., & Cacioppo, J. T. (2001). Mind at ease puts a smile on the face: Psychophysiological evidence that processing facilitation elicits positive affect. *Journal of Personality and Social Psychology*, *81*(6), 989–1000.

Xie, S. Y., Flake, J. K., & Hehman, E. (2019). Perceiver and target characteristics contribute to impression formation differently across race and gender. *Journal of Personality and Social Psychology*, *117*(2), 364–385.

Yzerbyt, V., Castano, E., Leyens, J. P., & Paladino, M. P. (2000). The primacy of the ingroup: The interplay of entitativity and identification. *European Review of Social Psychology*, *11*(1), 257–295.

Zebrowitz, L. A., & Collins, M. A. (1997). Accurate social perception at zero acquaintance: The affordances of a Gibsonian approach. *Personality and Social Psychology Review*, *1*(3), 204–223.

Zell, E., & Bernstein, M. J. (2014). You may think you're right… Young adults are more liberal than they realize. *Social Psychological and Personality Science*, *5*(3), 326–333.

CHAPTER FIVE

Testosterone tradeoffs in close relationships

Robin S. Edelstein*

University of Michigan, Ann Arbor, MI, United States
*Corresponding author: e-mail address: redelste@umich.edu

Contents

Abstract

Research on testosterone has long been dominated by a focus on "high testosterone" behaviors, such as aggression, competition, and dominance. The vast majority of this work, including in humans, has also been conducted in exclusively male samples, based in part on presumed links between testosterone and masculinity. Yet testosterone is implicated in many psychological and interpersonal processes for *both* men and women, and "low testosterone" behaviors may be particularly critical for ongoing close relationships. This fairly narrow focus on high testosterone, in men, leaves major gaps in our understanding of the social neuroendocrinology of close relationships, particularly as related to positive processes like caregiving, support-seeking, and intimacy. The goal of this review is to integrate the literature on testosterone in close relationships, in both men and women, with an eye toward closeness, intimacy, and other positive processes that likely contribute to and are supported by individual differences in testosterone and changes in testosterone over time. I focus on testosterone in the context of romantic and parent-child relationships, and highlight directions for future research that can help to fill important gaps in this literature. Further, I argue that, because close relationships are inherently dynamic and dyadic, longitudinal research that includes both men and women, and ideally both couple members, is critical for a complete understanding of the role of testosterone in close relationship processes.

1. Overview

In the media and popular culture, testosterone is often depicted as critical for seemingly "masculine" behaviors, such as competition, sexual prowess, and physical strength (Jordan-Young & Karkazis, 2019). "Low testosterone" is often considered problematic, particularly (and in some cases exclusively) for men, and opportunities abound for men to increase their testosterone. Based on these kinds of characterizations, one might reasonably assume that high levels of testosterone are essential for men, and potentially problematic for women, with few limits on the benefits of increasing (men's) testosterone. In reality, but perhaps not surprisingly, empirical research reveals a much more nuanced picture: Although there are certainly many benefits of high(er) testosterone, particularly for attracting and obtaining sexual partners and defending offspring, *lower* testosterone may in fact be more beneficial for maintaining close relationships—both with romantic partners and children—once those relationships have been established (Edelstein & Chin, 2018). This "tradeoff", between attracting sexual partners and defending offspring on the one hand, versus maintaining romantic relationships and nurturing offspring on the other hand, is thought to be evolutionarily adaptive in that it allows for flexibility in the allocation of resources to the most pressing tasks facing an individual at a given point in time (van Anders, Goldey, & Kuo, 2011; Wingfield, Hegner, Dufty, & Ball, 1990).

Despite consensus on such tradeoffs, most research on the psychological correlates and implications of testosterone in humans and other animals, even in the context of close relationships, tends to center around processes associated with *higher* testosterone, such as aggression, competition, dominance, and sexual attraction or desire (e.g., Eisenegger, Haushofer, & Fehr, 2011; Geniole & Carré, 2018; see van Anders et al., 2011). Perhaps as a consequence, these studies also typically focus exclusively on men; very few studies include both men and women, let alone couples or dyads, making it difficult to assess within-couple associations or gender differences in links between testosterone and relationship processes (Edelstein & Chin, 2018). Although men typically have higher baseline or endogenous levels compared to women, testosterone plays an important role in many psychological and interpersonal processes in *both* men and women (Goldey & van Anders, 2015). Thus, this narrow focus on men and "high testosterone" processes leaves major gaps in our understanding of more nurturant aspects of close relationships, such as those related to support-seeking, caregiving, emotional and physical intimacy, and other positive relationship processes. This gap is particularly striking in that it diverges from the close relationships literature more generally, which has long focused on nurturant constructs such as perceived partner responsiveness, closeness, and social support (Reis & Gable, 2003; Warren & Donaldson, 2017).

The goal of this review is to integrate the literature on testosterone in close relationships, in humans, with an eye toward closeness, intimacy, and other positive relationship processes that are likely supported by and feed into individual differences in testosterone and changes in testosterone over time. I will highlight major gaps in our understanding of the role of testosterone in romantic and parent-child relationships, and consider directions for future research that can help to fill these gaps. I argue that adopting a dyadic, longitudinal approach is critical for a complete understanding of links between testosterone and relationship dynamics. Relationships with partners and children are inherently dyadic, in that they include more than one person. Thus, research with couples should be considered the gold standard for understanding dyadic processes, such as how one partner's provision of support might influence his or her partner's hormone levels. Moreover, questions about hormonal synchrony or coordination between partners can *only* be answered with dyadic data. Relationships with partners and children also change over time, and many fundamental questions about close relationships involve major life transitions, such as relationship initiation, divorce, and becoming a parent. Thus, longitudinal data are particularly important for understanding how relationship processes unfold over time and for teasing apart causality between hormones and relationship outcomes.

In the following sections, I review the implications of differences and changes in testosterone for romantic and parent-child relationships, with a particular focus on processes that are thought to be evolutionarily adaptive. I consider assessments of individual differences in testosterone (e.g., links between baseline testosterone and relationship outcomes) as well as changes in testosterone over time (e.g., in the short-term as a function of experimental manipulations or longer-term as a function of developmental changes). Given that several recent reviews focus on the implications of partnering and parenting exclusively for men's testosterone (e.g., Gettler, 2020;

Grebe, Sarafin, Strenth, & Zilioli, 2019; Meijer, van IJzendoorn, & Bakermans-Kranenburg, 2019; Zilioli & Bird, 2017), I highlight research conducted with women whenever possible, and particularly research that includes couples or dyads.

2. The costs and benefits of testosterone in close relationship contexts

Testosterone is a steroid hormone that is found in virtually all vertebrates, including birds, reptiles, and mammals (Hirschenhauser & Oliveira, 2006). It is an end-product of the hypothalamic-pituitary-gonadal (HPG) axis, produced primarily in the testes in men and in the ovaries and adrenal glands in women. Although commonly thought of as a "male" hormone, and despite fairly large sex differences in baseline or endogenous levels, testosterone plays an important role in physical development, sexual differentiation, and behavioral regulation in both male and female animals, including humans (e.g., Goldey & van Anders, 2015). In fact, in some studies, small changes or differences in testosterone appear to be more strongly associated with outcomes for women than for men (e.g., Dhillon et al., 2020; Edelstein, van Anders, Chopik, Goldey, & Wardecker, 2014; Raisanen, Chadwick, Michalak, & van Anders, 2018), perhaps in part *because* women have relatively lower baseline levels compared to men (Sherwin, 1988).

From an evolutionary perspective, testosterone "tradeoffs" have typically been framed as a tension between attracting sexual partners and producing offspring (i.e., mating) on the one hand versus caring for those offspring (i.e., parenting) on the other hand (e.g., Gettler, 2020). One of the most widely adopted frameworks for understanding such tradeoffs—the "Challenge Hypothesis"—was initially developed to understand sources of variability among monogamously mating male birds and, ultimately, male animals (including humans) more broadly (Wingfield et al., 1990; Wingfield, Ramenofsky, Hegner, & Ball, 2020). In its original form, the challenge hypothesis built on observations that (1) in many male animals, testosterone is typically higher during mating compared to non-mating seasons and (2) both within and between species, males who devote more resources to mating than parenting typically have higher testosterone than those who devote more resources to parenting than mating. Increases in male animals' testosterone have also been linked to territorial aggression and intra-sex competition for access to receptive females. Critically, from this perspective, higher testosterone is adaptive for attracting sexual partners and defending offspring; however, because the production of testosterone is metabolically costly (e.g., potentially impairing immune functioning; Foo, Nakagawa, Rhodes, & Simmons, 2017), and because aggression directed towards offspring may decrease reproductive success, high levels of testosterone are thought to be incompatible with parental care. Thus, particularly for species in which paternal care is more common, flexibility in males' testosterone responses across contexts may be especially adaptive.

van Anders et al. (2011) expanded upon the Challenge Hypothesis, proposing the "Steroid/Peptide Theory of Social Bonds." This theoretical perspective accounts for distinctions among different kinds of parental and sexual behavior and attempts to explain apparent inconsistencies in prior studies linking seemingly similar behaviors with both low and high testosterone. In this framework, parental behavior that is nurturant and focused on the provision of care is hypothesized to be linked with relatively low testosterone and/or decreases in testosterone; parental behavior in the service of infant protection and defense is hypothesized to be linked with relatively high testosterone and/or increases in testosterone (e.g., van Anders, Tolman, & Volling, 2012). Similarly, sexual behavior that is centered around nurturance and emotional intimacy is thought to be more closely tied to low testosterone; sexual behavior that is more explicitly erotic and less nurturant should be more closely tied to high testosterone (Goldey, Avery, & van Anders, 2014; Goldey & van Anders, 2011; van Anders, Hamilton, Schmidt, & Watson, 2007). van Anders and colleagues also extended their theorizing more explicitly to women, arguing that the Challenge Hypothesis' nearly exclusive focus on men limits our understanding about how testosterone is implicated in women's parenting and sexual behavior (and more nurturant aspects of behavior more generally).

Research conducted in the decades since the Challenge Hypothesis was originally formulated generally supports the distinction between contexts and benefits associated with high versus low testosterone (Gray, Straftis, Bird, McHale, & Zilioli, 2020; Wingfield et al., 2020): Outcomes associated with competition, dominance, aggression, and attracting sexual partners tend to be linked with relatively high levels of testosterone, and/or increases in testosterone (e.g., Book, Starzyk, & Quinsey, 2001; Slatcher, Mehta, & Josephs, 2011). Outcomes associated with caregiving, nurturance, and pair-bonding tend to be linked with relatively low levels of testosterone, and/or decreases in testosterone, (e.g., Edelstein et al., 2017, 2014; Kuo et al., 2016). As women are increasingly included in this research, more recent findings also suggest many similarities in associations across sex or gender. The following sections review this research, with a focus primarily on findings with relevance for romantic and parent–child relationships.

3. Implications of testosterone for dominance, competition, aggression, and sexuality

3.1 Social dominance, competition, and aggression

Despite diurnal declines, assessments of testosterone (and other hormones) show fairly high rank–order stability over repeated assessments, particularly when those assessments occur at the same time of day (e.g., Liening, Stanton, Saini, & Schultheiss, 2010). Baseline or endogenous testosterone measures are therefore considered somewhat "trait-like" (Sellers, Mehl, & Josephs, 2007), making it possible to assess correlations between testosterone and other stable constructs, such as personality traits. In general, baseline testosterone has not been consistently associated with individual differences in broad personality traits, such as the "Big Five" (i.e., neuroticism, extraversion, openness to experience, agreeableness, and conscientiousness): A recent meta-analysis of nearly 4,000 participants from 25 samples revealed fairly weak and mostly nonsignificant associations between baseline salivary testosterone levels and the Big Five personality traits, although there was some evidence for small negative associations with conscientiousness (Sundin et al., 2021).

Instead, higher baseline testosterone has been most consistently been linked with somewhat narrower traits that are implicated in competition and dominance, including higher self-reported competitiveness, need for power, social dominance, and sensation- or novelty-seeking (e.g., Arnocky, Albert, Carré, & Ortiz, 2018; Campbell et al., 2010; Määttänen et al., 2013; Perini, Ditzen, Hengartner, & Ehlert, 2012; Sellers et al., 2007; Stanton & Schultheiss, 2009; Turan, Guo, Boggiano, & Bedgood, 2014). Participants with higher baseline testosterone levels, and those whose testosterone has been temporarily increased via pharmacological administration or experimental manipulation, also show more risk-taking and competitive behavior (e.g., Apicella, Dreber, & Mollerstrom, 2014; Goudriaan et al., 2010; Kordsmeyer & Penke, 2019; Stanton, Liening, & Schultheiss, 2011; Zilioli & Watson, 2014). Importantly, although women are much less likely than men to be included in these studies, associations are often similar for men and women when both are included in the same study (e.g., Sellers et al., 2007; Stanton et al., 2011; Sundin et al., 2021).

Engaging in competitive activities, such as sports or videogames, can also increase testosterone in both men and women (Casto & Edwards, 2016; Edwards & Casto, 2013). For instance, in a study of male and female cross-country runners, both men and women showed pre- to post-race increases in testosterone, and these increases were unrelated to the runners' finish times (Casto, Elliott, & Edwards, 2014). In attempt to isolate the effects of competition specifically from those involved in physical exertion more generally, the "competition effect" has also been assessed in more tightly controlled laboratory scenarios (e.g., using video games or competitive puzzles). Findings from such studies suggest that competition that does not involve physical exertion may nevertheless increase testosterone in both men and women, regardless of the competition outcome (see Casto & Edwards, 2016, for a review). Competition effects from laboratory studies appear to be less consistent than those conducted in the field, however, and point to considerable variability in testosterone responses.

At least one source of variability in testosterone responses is the competition outcome: In many cases there is evidence for a "winner-loser effect," such that testosterone increases are often larger among winners compared to losers, who in some cases show testosterone decreases (e.g., Casto & Edwards, 2016; Geniole, Bird, Ruddick, & Carré, 2017; Jiménez, Aguilar, & Alvero-Cruz, 2012). In one study, for instance, men who won a (rigged) videogame competition against another male participant showed increases in testosterone following the competition compared to men who lost the competition. Moreover, men who showed larger testosterone increases, regardless of whether they won or lost the competition, performed better in a subsequent competitive activity (Zilioli & Watson, 2014), suggesting that increases in testosterone may feed forward to influence competitive behavior.

Perceptions of ability and performance have also been associated with testosterone levels and changes in testosterone: Female flag football players showed a pre-to post-game increase in testosterone, regardless of whether they won or lost; however, both winners and losers who felt more positively about their performance showed higher testosterone across time points and larger pre- to post-game increases in testosterone (Casto, Rivell, & Edwards, 2017). Interestingly, findings from a recent meta-analysis suggest that winner-loser effects also appear to be stronger for studies conducted in the field (e.g., sporting events) versus the lab (e.g., playing videogames; Geniole et al., 2017). Differences between lab and field studies suggest not only that it may be more difficult to elicit winner-loser effects in the lab, but also that there are likely contextual factors influencing testosterone reactivity that are not yet fully understood. Winner-loser effects also appear to be more consistently observed among male versus female participants; however, women are much less likely to be included in studies of competition than men (Carré & Olmstead, 2015).

Higher testosterone has also been linked with dominance and aggression in romantic relationships specifically: In a sample of partnered men, those with higher baseline testosterone reported more verbal and physical aggression directed toward their female partners (Soler, Vinayak, & Quadagno, 2000). Similarly, in a study of dating couples—one of the few to include both men and women—Kaiser and Powers (2006) found that men with higher baseline testosterone were more likely to report using physically and psychologically aggressive strategies with their female partners during conflict, but only when their partners also had relatively high testosterone compared to other women in the sample. When higher testosterone men were paired with lower testosterone women, they were *less* likely to engage in physically aggressive behaviors. The authors argued that lower testosterone women may have been more effective in diffusing tension and conflict in the relationship, perhaps contributing to higher testosterone men's lower aggression in this particular pairing. Effects were largely nonsignificant for women's behavior, although there was a trend suggesting similar patterns for women's physical aggression. Together, these findings suggest that conflict strategies may be at least somewhat dependent on the relative hormone concentrations of each partner, and that women's aggression may be less closely tied than men's to their or their partner's testosterone levels. More generally, these findings highlight the importance of considering the hormone levels of *both* relationship partners when assessing interpersonal outcomes.

3.2 Sexual attraction and behavior

3.2.1 Number of sexual partners
Sexual behavior, including the ability to attract sexual partners and the extent of one's sexual experience, has been associated with relatively high levels of testosterone and increases in testosterone (Goldey & van Anders, 2015). For example, among heterosexually oriented young adults, a higher number of (self-reported) lifetime sexual partners has been linked with higher testosterone (e.g., Edelstein, Chopik, & Kean, 2011; Peters, Simmons, & Rhodes, 2008; Puts et al., 2015); these associations have also been observed among older men and women, who typically have

significantly lower average levels of circulating testosterone than their younger counterparts (Pollet, van der Meij, Cobey, & Buunk, 2011). Although my lab's initial research on this topic revealed stronger links between uncommitted sexual behavior among partnered young women compared to men (Edelstein et al., 2011), associations between testosterone and number of sexual partners are often stronger among men versus women (e.g., Pollet et al., 2011). Both men and women in polyamorous relationships (i.e., who have more than one sexual and/or romantic partner) also tend to have higher levels of testosterone compared to those who are monogamously partnered (van Anders, Hamilton, & Watson, 2007), suggesting that opportunities for sexual experience may be facilitated by and/or lead to testosterone increases.

What might account for links between higher testosterone and number of sexual partners? In a study of male undergraduates, those with higher baseline testosterone reported having had more "mating success," which was defined by a composite variable that included lifetime number of short- and long-term sexual partners (Peters et al., 2008). Yet men's testosterone was unrelated to observer ratings of masculinity or attractiveness, suggesting that factors other than physical appearance may have contributed to higher testosterone men's success in the dating market. Although such factors were not investigated in this particular study, other work suggests that both men and women with higher testosterone display more interpersonal confidence (Dabbs, Bernieri, Strong, Campo, & Milun, 2001), which could be attractive to potential partners. Further, in a laboratory study, men with higher baseline testosterone displayed more socially dominant behaviors (e.g., assertiveness, taking control of an interaction with another male participant), and female confederates reported "clicking" more with higher than lower testosterone men (Slatcher et al., 2011). Interestingly, however, neither men's testosterone nor women's reports of "clicking" with them were related to independent ratings of men's masculinity from facial photographs, again suggesting that something other than men's physical appearance likely drove these associations.

Other studies have linked *changes* in testosterone with behaviors that may increase men's attractiveness to potential dating partners: Roney, Lukaszewski, and Simmons (2007) found that men showed testosterone increases following relatively brief laboratory interactions with a female confederate. The confederates also rated men's behavior during the interaction, and men who showed larger testosterone increases were rated as more extraverted and as engaging in more self-disclosure during the interaction.

Men who showed larger testosterone increases following a competitive task against other men were similarly rated by female observers as smiling more, making more eye contact, and showing more interest with a female confederate in a subsequent interaction (van der Meij, Almela, Buunk, Fawcett, & Salvador, 2011); any of these factors could have made men more attractive to potential partners. Together, these findings also provide some evidence for bidirectional links between testosterone and behavior: Interactions with women raised men's testosterone, and men who showed larger testosterone increases behaved in ways that were more attractive to female confederates.[1] Comparable studies have not yet been conducted to identify mechanisms that might contribute to links between testosterone and women's attractiveness to sexual partners, and further work is clearly needed to disentangle causal mechanisms, but extant findings suggest that less tangible (but nevertheless perceivable) affiliative behaviors may contribute to links between high testosterone and the ability to attract sexual partners (at least among men).

3.2.2 Changes in testosterone in sexual contexts

Women's testosterone responses to potential sexual partners, and sexual stimuli more generally, have been much less extensively studied, but there is some evidence to suggest that women also experience testosterone changes in sexual contexts. For instance, single heterosexual women's testosterone increased following a speed-dating session in which they had brief interactions with male participants, but decreased in a control condition involving interactions with female participants; male participants did not show any significant changes in testosterone in either condition (van der Meij et al., 2019). Given that men's testosterone would be expected to decline over the course of the session without any sort of intervention (due to diurnal changes), van der Meij et al. suggested that the men in their study may have perceived other male participants as competitors, and female participants as potential sexual partners; either of these possibilities could have contributed to similar testosterone responses in both conditions (i.e., no discernable changes from baseline). Testosterone changes were not significantly associated with either men's or women's attractiveness to other speed dating participants in this study. In another study, women's testosterone increased after watching clips from a movie ("The Notebook") in

---

[1] Associations between men's baseline testosterone and ratings of their behavior were not reported by Roney et al. and were not statistically significant in the van der Meij study.

which an attractive man attempts to "court" a young woman, but not in response to other videoclips depicting an unattractive man or an attractive women with no men present (Lopez, Hay, & Conklin, 2009). Together, these findings suggest that women's testosterone may be particularly sensitive to context, that women's testosterone increases might not necessarily make them more attractive to potential partners, and that the circumstances that elicit changes in women's testosterone may differ from those that elicit changes in men's testosterone.

Indeed, in a series of studies, Goldey and van Anders (2011) found that simply fantasizing about a pleasant sexual experience led to an increase in women's testosterone compared to thinking about other kinds of non-sexual experiences (e.g., celebrating a work accomplishment with a friend, a job interview, a routine interaction at the post office). Thinking about sexual experiences did not change men's testosterone levels compared to the other conditions (Goldey & van Anders, 2012). However, consistent with the idea that nurturance is associated with lower testosterone, follow-up analyses revealed that men whose sexual fantasies included less nurturant content showed larger increases in testosterone in the sexual condition (Goldey et al., 2014); fantasy content was unrelated to hormone changes among women. Together, these findings again point to potential differences in contextual factors that may elicit testosterone changes in men versus women, but also to the difficulty of comparing men's and women's responses when they are not included in the same study or exposed to the same experimental manipulations.

It is also important to note that the effects reported by Goldey and van Anders (2011) and Lopez et al. (2009) were obtained *only* among naturally cycling women; women using hormonal contraceptives, which typically decrease women's testosterone and often dampen testosterone responses (Liening et al., 2010; van Anders, Goldey, & Bell, 2014), did not show testosterone changes as a function of the experimental manipulation in either study. Given that a sizable percentage of partnered women use hormonal methods of contraception at some point in their lives (Jones, Mosher, & Daniels, 2012), limiting research participation to naturally cycling women, particularly when conducting studies with couples in committed relationships, is likely to result in a particularly unrepresentative sample. Yet including women on hormonal contraceptives may make it difficult to interpret associations (or lack thereof) between testosterone and other outcomes.

The issue of hormonal contraception is particularly thorny and ubiquitous in the social neuroendocrinology literature, but it deserves further empirical attention with more highly powered samples. Sample sizes in these kinds of studies tend to be fairly small to begin with, particularly when women using hormonal contraceptives are excluded (e.g., approximately 60 naturally cycling women across conditions in Goldey & van Anders, 2011 and Lopez et al., 2009), and comparing naturally cycling women to women taking hormonal contraceptives necessarily requires larger samples and more financial resources. Combined with the somewhat flawed assumption that women's testosterone shows large fluctuations across the menstrual cycle, and that menstrual cycles are too complicated to account for statistically, concerns about hormonal contraception have in many cases contributed to the exclusion of women from hormone research altogether (van Anders et al., 2014). Future research would benefit from more explicit and deliberate comparisons between naturally cycling women and those taking hormonal contraceptives.

3.2.3 Changes in testosterone following interactions with romantic partners

Relatively few studies have examined the effects of interactions between couple members on testosterone changes and the extent to which different kinds of interactions may elicit different patterns of change. In one of the few exceptions, Makhanova, McNulty, Eckel, Nikonova, and Maner (2018) assessed testosterone in 50 newlywed couples before and after they participated in a conflict discussion. Given links between aggression, conflict, and testosterone, this kind of interaction might be expected to lead to testosterone increases; however, on average, both men and women showed *declines* in testosterone following the discussion, which the authors attributed to diurnal changes. Men who perceived their partners to be more oppositional during the conversation showed smaller declines, consistent with the idea that interpersonal conflict may increase testosterone. However, without any sort of comparison or control condition, it is difficult to determine how the conflict per se may have affected participants' hormone levels. Similar declines in both men's and women's testosterone were observed among 90 couples after discussing an emotional video (Peters, Hammond, Reis, & Jamieson, 2016), but again without a comparison condition, the effects of the emotional discussion per se are difficult to parse from those associated with the passage of time. A critical next step for this area of research is to compare the effects of different kinds of couple interactions (e.g., nurturant versus competitive) on testosterone responses in both couple members.

A recent study from my lab was designed to better understand whether and how emotionally intimate discussions may lead to hormones change in couples, and particularly whether such changes differ from those that might be expected in less intimate contexts (Chin, Reese, Ascigil, Sim, & Edelstein, 2021). Over 100 couples (the majority of whom were not married) participated in one of two 30-min semi-structured discussions, based on the "Fast Friends Task" developed by Aron, Melinat, Aron, and Vallone (1997). In the high-closeness (i.e., "fast friends") condition, couples took turns asking and answering a series of questions designed to encourage increasingly higher levels of self-disclosure and emotional intimacy (e.g., "When did you last cry in front of another person?"). The low-closeness (i.e., "small talk") condition was similar in structure and format, but the questions were designed to elicit minimal self-disclosure or emotional intimacy (e.g., "When did you last walk for an hour?"). In general, people tend to report increases in closeness, passionate love, and relationship satisfaction after engaging in the high- versus low-closeness discussion with their partner (e.g., Stanton, Campbell, & Pink, 2017; Welker et al., 2014).

In contrast to the few existing studies of testosterone reactivity in couples, we found that testosterone *increased* among both men and women in the high- versus low-closeness condition; there were no significant changes in testosterone in the low-closeness condition (see Fig. 1). Further, participants reported disclosing (marginally) more to their partners in the high- versus

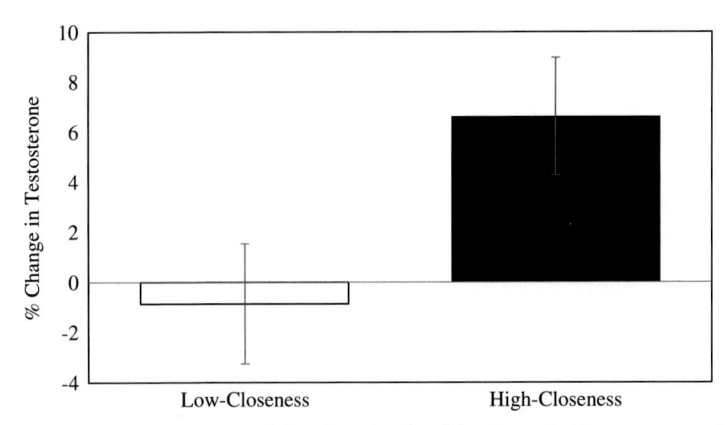

Fig. 1 Changes in testosterone following the fast-friends task. Testosterone changes were significantly larger in the high- versus low closeness condition, b = 4.39, $P < 0.001$, and significantly different from zero only in the high-closeness condition, t(104) = 2.83, $P < 0.01$. Error bars represent standard errors of the mean. N = 105 couples (Chin et al., 2021).

low-closeness condition, and differences in disclosure mediated the effect of condition on testosterone reactivity. Participants did not perceive the high-closeness discussion to be more enjoyable or more positive, however, and participants in both conditions were equally likely to say that they would like to do the task again. Thus, something about disclosure per se in the high-closeness condition appears to have contributed to testosterone reactivity, over and above participants' enjoyment of the task. Testosterone may be elevated in the early stages of a romantic relationship (Farrelly, Owens, Elliott, Walden, & Wetherell, 2015; Goldey, Conley, & van Anders, 2018; Marazziti & Canale, 2004), which could be due to heightened passion, sexual attraction, or excitement. Perhaps our manipulation of closeness also increased these kinds of feelings, or reminded participants of what initially attracted them to their partner, any of which could have contributed to short-term increases in testosterone. As noted earlier, men who showed testosterone increases following brief interactions with female confederates were also rated as engaging in more self-disclosure with those confederates (Roney et al., 2007). Moreover, Ketay, Welker, and Slatcher (2017) found a pattern of testosterone reactivity suggesting testosterone increases following the fast-friends task among unacquainted same-sex dyads; however, their comparison condition was different in structure and content than the small-talk task used in our study, making direct comparisons somewhat difficult. It is also not yet clear how unacquainted dyads might experience these tasks differently from people in established relationships, and how those differences might play out at the neuroendocrine level. In future studies, we hope to further disentangle the mechanisms that contribute to testosterone changes in couples by assessing potential mediating constructs like passion, sexual attraction, and excitement more directly. More generally, studies that explicitly manipulate nurturance versus sexual attraction, competition, and/or dominance will be critical for teasing apart whether and how these theoretically relevant contexts may affect testosterone responses in both men and women.

3.2.4 Sexual desire

Testosterone is often assumed to be positively, and directly, related to sexual desire in both men and women (e.g., Jordan-Young & Karkazis, 2019). This assumption is based largely on (1) observations that men typically have higher circulating testosterone and report higher sexual desire compared to women and (2) studies of men and women with clinically low testosterone—or clinical conditions that affect testosterone and/or sexual desire—that suggest supplementation with exogenous testosterone can increase sexual desire (e.g., Achilli et al., 2017; reviewed in Baumeister, Catanese, & Vohs, 2001; Corona et al., 2014). Research with nonclinical samples of healthy men and women reveals a much less consistent picture (e.g., van Anders, 2012), however, and suggests that there may be value in distinguishing between dyadic and solitary sexual desire. van Anders (2013) argues that *solitary* sexual experiences, such as masturbation, are more erotic than nurturant, and thus such experiences should be more closely tied to high versus low testosterone; *dyadic* or partnered sexual experiences, in contrast, typically involve more nurturance and intimacy, and thus should be more closely tied to low versus high testosterone in this framework.

Consistent with these hypotheses, in nonclinical samples, desire for solitary sexual experiences has (in some cases) been linked with higher baseline testosterone, whereas desire for dyadic sexual experiences has been more consistently linked with lower baseline testosterone (Raisanen et al., 2018; Sim, Chopik, Wardecker, & Edelstein, 2020; van Anders, 2012). Rarely are men and women (let alone couples) included in the same study; however, across studies, links between testosterone and sexual desire are often stronger among women than men (e.g., Sim et al., 2020; see van Anders, 2012). In many cases, men's baseline testosterone is unrelated to either solitary or dyadic sexual desire (Raisanen et al., 2018; van Anders, 2012), although in one study we found that desire for *uncommitted* sex was positively associated with baseline testosterone among undergraduate men but not women (Edelstein et al., 2011).

Taken together, these findings suggest that, despite prevailing assumptions, differences in women's sexual desire may be more closely tied than men's to differences in testosterone. Sex or gender differences in any domain are likely driven as much (if not more) by context, experience, and culture as biology; however, gender differences in sexual behavior may be especially prone to social influences insofar as in most cultures women's sexuality is more heavily policed than men's (Petersen & Hyde, 2010). As just one example, women who engage in sexual activity outside of a committed relationship tend to be judged more harshly than men who engage in the same behavior (e.g., Conley, Ziegler, & Moors, 2013). These judgements likely contribute to the fairly large gender differences in self-reported desire for uncommitted sexual experiences (e.g., Edelstein et al., 2011), and potentially links between such desire and testosterone. Moreover, as with other research in this area, it is difficult to discern gender differences and similarities in findings when the vast majority of studies focus exclusively on men *or* women.

It also is particularly surprising that studies of sexual desire and behavior overwhelmingly focus on individuals as opposed to couples, despite the inherently dyadic nature of most sexual experiences and the centrality of such experiences to romantic relationships. In one of the few dyadic studies to date on this topic, we recently assessed changes in testosterone and sexual desire in a sample of 29 first-time expectant couples (Sim et al., 2020). As described in more detail in the following sections, expectant parents (both mothers and fathers) typically show changes in testosterone throughout the perinatal period (e.g., Berg & Wynne-Edwards, 2002; Edelstein et al., 2015; Storey, Walsh, Quinton, & Wynne-Edwards, 2000). Many expectant and new parents also experience declines in sexual desire, and particularly dyadic desire, during this time (e.g., Von Sydow, Ullmeyer, & Happ, 2001), making it an especially interesting period in which to assess links between testosterone and sexual desire. We found that, consistent with previous research, both men and women reported declines in dyadic but not solitary desire throughout the prenatal period. Further, among expectant mothers, prenatal testosterone was negatively correlated with dyadic sexual desire, consistent with the idea that higher testosterone may impede more nurturant sexual experiences. Among expectant fathers, however, testosterone was *positively* correlated with dyadic desire, such that men who showed larger declines in testosterone throughout the prenatal period reported lower dyadic sexual desire. One interpretation of these findings is that declines in expectant fathers' testosterone may help both to prepare men for fatherhood and to orient them towards their partners. Indeed, Gettler, McDade, Agustin, Feranil, and Kuzawa (2013) found that men who showed smaller declines in testosterone after becoming fathers reported engaging in more frequent sexual intercourse with their female partners compared to men who showed larger declines.

Neither men's nor women's solitary desire was related to average levels of testosterone or changes in testosterone in our study, and we did not find any evidence for links between one partner's testosterone and his or her partners' sexual desire; however, these kinds of "partner effects" tend to be smaller in magnitude than "actor effects" (i.e., associations between one's own hormones and behavior), and it is likely that our sample was not sufficiently powered to detect them. Nonetheless, our findings are consistent with the idea that dyadic sexual desire may be more closely tied to differences and changes in testosterone than solitary desire, and that men and women may show different associations among these constructs.

More generally, these and other findings complicate what has long been assumed to be a straightforward association between testosterone and sexual desire.

It is also worth noting the difficulty of discerning the direction of causality for most hormone-behavior links, even with longitudinal designs; constructs that are especially sensitive to social and cultural context, like sexual desire, may be particularly challenging in this respect. Changes in testosterone likely influence changes in desire (e.g., Sim et al., 2020), but it is equally probable that changes in desire feed back to influence changes in testosterone, and in reality most links are likely bidirectional. For instance, sexual activity can increase testosterone in both men and women (van Anders, Hamilton, Schmidt, & Watson, 2007), at least in the short term, which could influence desire for subsequent sexual activity. Future research would benefit from more comprehensive designs that include highly powered samples of both men and women, and ideally couples, who are studied over time to better understand how short- and long-term fluctuations in testosterone influence and are influenced by fluctuations in sexual desire.

4. Implications of testosterone for nurturance and caregiving

As described above, behavior and outcomes in competitive, aggressive, and sexual contexts have generally been linked with high(er) levels of testosterone and increases in testosterone. Often missing from this picture, however, is the role that testosterone plays in caregiving and nurturant relationships. In particular, because research on testosterone has been dominated by a focus on "high testosterone" behaviors and outcomes, we know considerably less about how close relationships may both promote and benefit from *lower* levels of testosterone and/or declines in testosterones over time. Moreover, and arguably relatedly, work in this area has disproportionately centered on men's experiences and perspectives (van Anders et al., 2014, 2011); similar trends have long been evident in research with non-human animals (Beery & Zucker, 2011). Even neuroendocrine research on parenting tends to emphasize fatherhood, in contrast to most psychological research on parenting, which tends to be much more "mother-focused" (Cabrera, Volling, & Barr, 2018). In fact, although women are increasingly included in research on testosterone, several recent reviews and meta-analysis of key outcomes and mechanisms (e.g., the Challenge Hypothesis) focus exclusively on effects observed among men (e.g., Grebe et al., 2019; Meijer et al., 2019).

This disproportionate emphasis on correlates of "high testosterone," primarily among men, also contributes to a critical disconnect between the social neuroendocrinology and close relationship literatures. Close relationships researchers have long focused not only on negative processes such as conflict, loneliness, and separation, but also on positive processes, such as caregiving, social support, and communication (Finkel, Simpson, & Eastwick, 2017). Indeed, these positive processes are often what make close relationships particularly meaningful, beneficial, and rewarding (Reis & Gable, 2003). Reflecting a trend in psychology more generally to understand not only what causes psychological distress but also what allows people to flourish, many close relationships researchers have increasingly encouraged greater focus on positive relationship processes (e.g., Reis & Gable, 2003; Warren & Donaldson, 2017). With some notable exceptions—such as work on oxytocin (e.g., Algoe, Kurtz, & Grewen, 2017; Crockford, Deschner, Ziegler, & Wittig, 2014), often coined the "love" or "cuddle" hormone, and that on the potentially buffering effects of partner support on physiological stress responses (see Pietromonaco & Collins, 2017; Slatcher & Selcuk, 2017)—positive relationship processes have been largely neglected in neuroendocrine research on close relationship processes.

The following sections focus on what we do know about the role of testosterone in more nurturant aspects of close relationships, and the ways in which ongoing relationships may both benefit from and contribute to lower levels of testosterone.

4.1 Prosocial personality traits and behavior

Prosocial behavior, and personality traits that promote such behavior, have been most consistently linked with lower baseline or endogenous testosterone. Men with lower baseline testosterone, for instance, report lower attachment avoidance (i.e., greater comfort with closeness), disconnection from others, and loneliness, but higher empathy (Harris, Rushton, Hampson, & Jackson, 1996; Turan et al., 2014). Fewer relevant studies include women, but in women, higher empathy and pro-social tendencies such as nurturance and positive feelings toward children, have similarly been linked with lower testosterone (Deady, Smith, Sharp, & Al-Dujaili, 2006; Harris et al., 1996). Both men and women with lower testosterone may also be higher in perspective-taking and "empathic accuracy," or the ability to read others' emotions (Ronay & Carney, 2013), which could contribute to better interpersonal outcomes. In a similar vein, testosterone administration has been shown to decrease trust, empathy, and generosity in both men and women (e.g., Bos, Panksepp, Bluthe, & van Honk, 2012; Ou et al., 2021).

Experimental research further suggests that experiences that foster or encourage nurturance tend to elicit declines in testosterone; however, these kinds of experiences have been much less extensively studied than those likely to elicit *increases* in testosterone (Zilioli & Bird, 2017). For instance, in a sample of new and expectant parents, men showed decreases in testosterone after listening to recorded infant cries; declines in testosterone were strongest among men who reported more couvade or "pregnancy symptoms" (e.g., weight gain, nausea) and those who reported a stronger desire to comfort the infant (Storey et al., 2000). Women's testosterone was not measured in this study, but insofar as couvade symptoms reflect identification with pregnant partners and/or investment in parenting (e.g., Brennan, Ayers, Ahmed & Marshall-Lucette, 2007), these findings suggest that men's nurturant tendencies may have contributed to changes in testosterone as a function of exposure to infant cries. van Anders et al. (2012) further demonstrated that men's testosterone responses to a crying infant doll depended on the quality of their interactions with the doll: Men who were given the opportunity to provide comfort to the doll tended to show decreases in testosterone following the interaction, whereas those who did not have this opportunity tended to show *increases* in testosterone, perhaps due to protective or defensive responses.

Much less is known about women's testosterone reactivity in caregiving situations and the implications of such reactivity for subsequent behavior; however, in one study, women similarly showed declines in testosterone after providing care to a crying (but unsoothable) infant doll (Voorthuis, Bakermans-Kranenburg, & van IJzendoorn, 2017). More recently, in one of the few studies to include both men and women, my colleagues and I examined testosterone changes following a mildly stressful parent-infant interaction, the Strange Situation (commonly used to assess parent-infant attachment dynamics). In a sample of 300 parents, both mothers and fathers showed pre- to post-interaction testosterone declines (Edelstein et al., 2019), consistent with the idea that nurturant or caregiving behavior elicits short-term changes in testosterone. Further, fathers who reported lower attachment avoidance showed larger testosterone declines, again suggesting that this interaction pulled for nurturant behavior (see Fig. 2). Mothers'

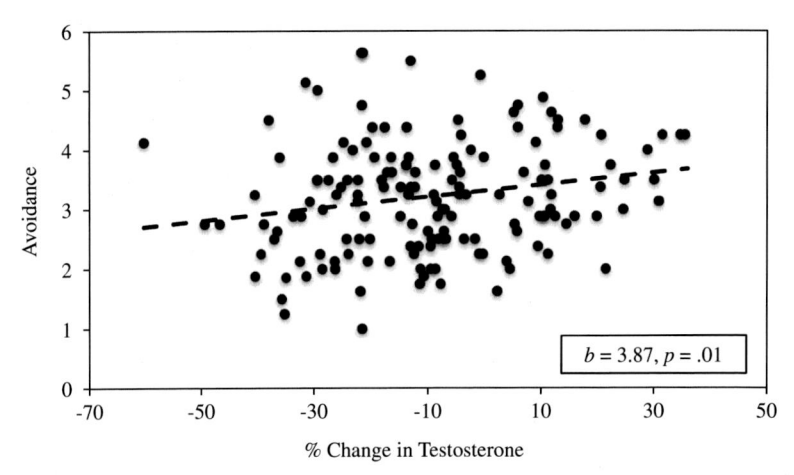

Fig. 2 Associations Between Fathers' Avoidance and Changes in Testosterone Following the Strange Situation Procedure. N = 150 (Edelstein et al., 2019).

testosterone reactivity did not vary as a function of attachment avoidance, despite overall declines following the interaction; given that mothers typically spend more time engaging in infant care than fathers, including in this sample, the laboratory interaction may have been less novel or stressful for avoidant mothers versus fathers, which could have attenuated links between avoidance and testosterone reactivity.

Of note, neither mothers nor fathers in this sample showed significant changes in testosterone following a subsequent teaching task (Kuo et al., 2016; Volling, unpublished data), suggesting that the changes we observed cannot be attributed simply to the passage of time. Other studies similarly demonstrate that playing or sitting with children in a non-stressful setting does not elicit changes in parents' (exclusively fathers in these studies) testosterone (e.g., Gettler, McDade, Agustin, & Kuzawa, 2011; Kuo et al., 2018; Storey, Noseworthy, Delahunty, Halfyard, & McKay, 2011). Thus, situations that pull more strongly for parental caregiving behavior, such as the Strange Situation, might be necessary to elicit short-term changes in testosterone. Further research is clearly needed to better understand the contexts that elicit testosterone declines and the predictors of variability in these responses, particularly among women. Given that nurturant versus protective responses to infant distress appear to differentiate decreases versus increases in testosterone, respectively, future research would also likely benefit from more explicit assessments of these constructs and their links with both baseline testosterone and testosterone reactivity.

4.2 Partnering and parenting

Among the most consistent findings in the literature on testosterone in close relationships is that people in committed romantic relationships, and those who are parents, tend to have lower levels of testosterone than their counterparts who are single and/or do not have children (e.g., Gettler & Oka, 2016; van Anders & Goldey, 2010; see Edelstein & Chin, 2018; Grebe et al., 2019; Meijer et al., 2019, for reviews). Differences in testosterone as a function of partnering and parenting are reliably observed among both men and women (e.g., Barrett et al., 2013; Edelstein et al., 2011; Gettler & Oka, 2016; van Anders & Goldey, 2010); however, fewer studies include women, and rarely are *both* men and women included in the same study, making direct comparisons difficult. As noted earlier, men and women in polyamorous relationships—simultaneous emotional and/or sexual relationships with multiple partners—typically have *higher* testosterone than those who are involved with only one partner (e.g., Alvergne, Faurie, & Raymond, 2009; van Anders, Hamilton, & Watson, 2007), suggesting that commitment to a single partner, rather than partnering or sexual activity per se, may be a key determinant of differences in testosterone.

The age of children in the home may also be important: In one study, accounting for differences in marital status, women with children ages three and younger had the lowest testosterone compared to women with older children and those without children; testosterone levels did not differ between the latter two groups of women (Barrett et al., 2013). Kuzawa, Gettler, Huang, and McDade (2010) similarly found that differences in testosterone between Filipino mothers and non-mothers were most evident when comparing women with children younger than two years old to those without children. And in a sample of fathers in the Philippines, those with younger children showed larger diurnal declines in testosterone (reflecting lower overall testosterone output) compared to men with younger children (Rosenbaum, Gettler, McDade, Bechayda, & Kuzawa, 2018), again suggesting lower testosterone in the presence of younger versus older children. Together, these findings suggest that involvement in direct care of dependent children may be a critical mechanism underlying parenting-testosterone associations. Indeed, as discussed in more detail below, men who are more involved in parental care are more likely to show declines in testosterone associated with fatherhood (Gettler, McDade, Feranil, & Kuzawa, 2011).

Partnering and parenting "effects" have been found among people in many different cultures and geographic locations, such as women in Norway (Barrett et al., 2013) and the Philippines (Kuzawa et al., 2010) and men from a polygynous (i.e., having multiple wives) agricultural community in rural Senegal (Alvergne et al., 2009). Although there is certainly some variability in these links across cultures, one takeaway from cross-cultural research appears to be that testosterone varies as a function of investment in one's role as a partner and/or parent more so than as a function of the cultural or societal labels applied to a particular relationship (see Gettler, 2020, for a recent review). For instance, in cultures that emphasize and value paternal involvement in childrearing, fathers are more likely to have lower testosterone compared to men without children; these differences tend to be less prominent (and may even be reversed) in cultures in which men are less directly involved in parental care (e.g., Gettler, Lew-Levy, Sarma, Miegakanda, & Boyette, 2020; Muller, Marlowe, Bugumba, & Ellison, 2009). Partnering and parenting effects also appear to be fairly independent of potential confounds, such as age, body mass index (BMI), and socioeconomic status (e.g., Alvergne et al., 2009; Barrett et al., 2013); thus involvement in these relationships, as opposed to changes that may co-occur with them, may be a key predictor of differences in testosterone. More generally, these findings suggest a commonality, or even potential universality, of differences or changes in testosterone as a function of partnering and parenting.

4.2.1 Longitudinal changes in testosterone and relationship status

Links between testosterone and partnering/parenting are generally assumed to be causal, in that changes in one's relationships are thought to *lead* to changes in testosterone (and other hormones) over time. Yet the vast majority of research on this topic is cross-sectional, making it difficult to draw firm conclusions about causality. It is certainly possible that changes in testosterone precede changes in relationship status, and many links are likely bidirectional in that neuroendocrine and interpersonal processes feed back to mutually influence one another (e.g., Mazur & Booth, 1998). However, the few existing longitudinal studies on this topic generally support the idea that changes in partnering and parenting in fact precede changes in hormones (e.g., Das & Sawin, 2016; Edelstein et al., 2015; Gettler, McDade, Feranil, & Kuzawa, 2011; but see Goldey et al., 2018; van Anders & Watson, 2006). For example, in a large study of over 4,000

United States Army veterans, men who were married had significantly lower serum testosterone levels than those who had never been married, and both married and never married men had lower testosterone that men who were currently divorced (Mazur, 2014). Longitudinal analyses in this sample further revealed that, controlling for age, men who divorced showed increases in testosterone in the years surrounding divorce; men who became or remained married showed decreases in testosterone during this time (Mazur & Michalek, 1998).

Another ten-year longitudinal study of over 1,000 Danish men (ages 30–60 at the initial assessment) similarly demonstrated that, on average, men's serum testosterone declined with age, a common phenomenon among both men and women (e.g., Fabbri et al., 2016; Liu et al., 2007); however, men who became partnered during the study showed a larger decline compared to those who became unpartnered (Holmboe et al., 2017). Moreover, there was relatively little support for the reverse causal pathway, in that men's testosterone levels at the beginning of the study did *not* predict changes in their partnered status over the next 10 years. These findings held after controlling for BMI, smoking, and physical activity, suggesting that changes in relationship status may moderate normative age-related declines in testosterone over and above other relevant demographic variables. Taken together, these studies provide compelling evidence for causal links between changes in relationship status and changes in testosterone, at least among men.

Comparably large-scale studies of changes in *women's* testosterone and relationship status have not yet been conducted; however, two smaller studies that included women ($Ns = 78$ and 28, respectively) found some evidence for bidirectional pathways from testosterone to relationship status: College-aged and young adult women with lower testosterone were more likely to become partnered over the course of these studies, approximately 8 months after the initial assessment (Goldey et al., 2018; van Anders & Watson, 2006). In one sample, women who transitioned from single to partnered showed small increases in testosterone during the initial phases of their relationship; those who remained single also showed higher testosterone compared to those who remained committed (Goldey et al., 2018). Cross-sectional studies provide some converging evidence that men's and women's testosterone may be higher during the initial compared to later stages of a relationship (Farrelly et al., 2015; Marazziti & Canale, 2004). Together, these findings provide intriguing evidence for bidirectional links between testosterone and relationship status, at least in women;

however, it is important to note that, in both samples, there was relatively little change in relationship status over the course of the (relatively short-term) study, making it difficult to fully assess the extent to which changes in partnering were associated with changes in testosterone. Further research with highly powered samples and over longer time periods would be helpful to better understand whether and how changes in relationship status are linked with changes in testosterone, particularly among women.

4.2.2 Longitudinal changes in testosterone and parental status

The limited longitudinal research on the neuroendocrinology of parenthood similarly suggests that hormones, including testosterone, change in response to (rather than precede) the process of becoming a parent. For instance, in one longitudinal study, a representative sample of over 600 men in Cebu City, Philippines was followed over a four-year period as men experienced transitions in partnering and parenthood (Gettler, McDade, Feranil, & Kuzawa, 2011). Men who became partnered fathers during this time showed larger declines in testosterone compared to single men who did not have children; however, the relatively small percentage of men who became partnered but did *not* have children had testosterone levels similar to men who remained unpartnered. These findings suggest that parenting per se may be a particularly critical mechanism driving testosterone changes over time. Moreover, testosterone declines were most pronounced among fathers who were more directly involved in infant care, again suggesting that caregiving specifically may contribute to testosterone changes, above and beyond partnering more generally or hormone changes associated with aging.

In a more recent but smaller longitudinal study of first-time parents in the United States ($N = 58$), we found evidence that changes in fathers' testosterone may begin even before babies are born: Couples were followed from the first through the third trimester of pregnancy, and expectant fathers showed small but reliable declines in salivary testosterone from the beginning through the end of the prenatal period (Edelstein et al., 2015). That these changes were detectable this early among expectant fathers suggests that they may be driven by something other than the physical presence of an infant—perhaps the experience of preparing for a baby or increased commitment to their partner or parental role. Surprisingly little attention has been paid to predictors of change in fathers' testosterone, particularly during the prenatal period, but it would be reasonable to hypothesize that changes in psychological variables, such as one's identity as a (soon-to-be-) parent or investment in the family, would predict declines in men's testosterone throughout the transition to parenthood.

Of note, expectant mothers in this and other longitudinal studies show fairly large *increases* in salivary testosterone throughout the prenatal period (e.g., Edelstein et al., 2015; Fleming, Ruble, Krieger, & Wong, 1997). These changes appear to be independent of the sex of the fetus (at least when testosterone is assessed via saliva; Voegtline, Costigan, Kivlighan, Henderson, & DiPietro, 2013). Prenatal increases in maternal testosterone are thought to support fetal development, maintain the pregnancy, and generally prepare women to become mothers (e.g., by increasing focus on infant defense and protection; Fleming et al., 1997; Makieva, Saunders, & Norman, 2014). Prenatal testosterone levels that are *too* high have been linked with adverse birth outcomes such as shorter gestational periods and low birthweight (e.g., Carlsen, Jacobsen, & Romundstad, 2006; Schonblum et al., 2018; Voegtline et al., 2013), however, suggesting that there may be an optimal level of testosterone during this period. Further, after delivery, new mothers' testosterone levels decline fairly quickly back to pre-pregnancy levels (Fleming et al., 1997), and the cross-sectional comparisons described above indicate that mothers have *lower* baseline testosterone compared to women without children. Thus, the shorter-term testosterone increases observed during pregnancy may not extend into the postpartum, and may in fact reverse as a function of motherhood.

4.3 Implications of individual differences in testosterone for established relationships

4.3.1 Romantic relationships

As described above, differences in testosterone as a function of partnering and parenting have been fairly well documented; these differences have been found among both men and women and in a variety of cultural contexts. Although limited, some evidence suggests that changes in relationships precede changes in testosterone (e.g., Holmboe et al., 2017; Mazur & Michalek, 1998), but also that changes in testosterone may feed back to influence close relationships (e.g., Goldey et al., 2018). These findings cannot speak directly to the *adaptive benefit* of any changes in testosterone, however, or to the mechanisms that may support testosterone-relationship links. From an evolutionary perspective, testosterone production is metabolically costly, and "high testosterone" behaviors such as aggression, competition, and extradyadic sexual activity can interfere with engagement in more nurturant behaviors, such as caring for offspring and maintaining ongoing intimate relationships (van Anders et al., 2011; Wingfield et al., 2020). Thus, insofar as differences or changes in testosterone associated with partnering and parenting are evolutionarily adaptive, they should be associated with measurable benefits in close relationship contexts (Roney & Gettler, 2015; Wardecker, Smith, Edelstein, & Loving, 2015).

Indeed, correlational research demonstrates not only that people who are partnered and/or parents have lower testosterone than those who are not partnered or do not have children, but also that, among those who are partnered and/or parents, lower testosterone is associated with better relationship functioning (e.g., Denes, Afifi, & Granger, 2017; Edelstein et al., 2014; see Meijer et al., 2019, for review). For instance, among partnered men and women, lower testosterone is associated with higher self-reported relationship quality, including greater investment in and commitment to romantic partners (e.g., Edelstein et al., 2014; Gettler et al., 2020; Gray et al., 2017). Partnered men with lower testosterone also report less interest in extradyadic sexual activity (Edelstein et al., 2011; Farrelly et al., 2015; McIntyre et al., 2006); partnered women with lower testosterone report lower levels of (prior) uncommitted sexual activity, and sensation-seeking (Costa, Correia, & Oliveira, 2015; Edelstein et al., 2011), individual differences that could promote interest in alternative romantic or sexual partners (Penke & Asendorpf, 2008). Finally, as described earlier, partnered men with lower testosterone report directing less aggression and violence toward their female partners (e.g., Kaiser & Powers, 2006; Soler et al., 2000).

Lower testosterone individuals may also perceive their partners' behavior more positively: In a laboratory study of 50 couples, women with lower testosterone reported that their partners were more accommodating during a conflict discussion, and they were more satisfied with how that conversation went. Perceived accommodation mediated the association between women's testosterone and satisfaction with the conversation (Dhillon et al., 2020), suggesting that women with lower testosterone may have been more charitable in their interpretations of their partner's behavior or that their partners may have engaged in more effective conflict management strategies. There were no significant associations between men's testosterone and their perceptions of the conversation or satisfaction with it in this study.

Of course, partners of lower testosterone women in the Dhillon et al. (2020) study may have actually *been* more accommodating; men's behavior

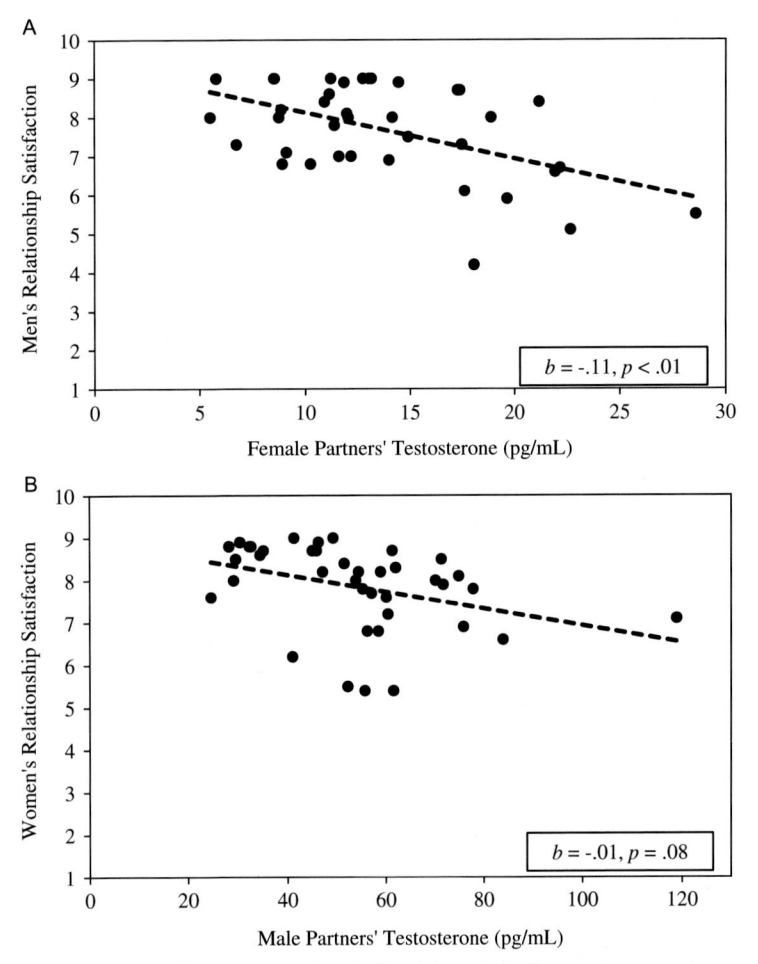

Fig. 3 (A) Associations between men's relationship satisfaction and women's testosterone. N = 39 (Edelstein et al., 2014). (B) Associations between women's relationship satisfaction and men's testosterone. N = 39 (Edelstein et al., 2014).

was not assessed but could also have contributed to women's satisfaction with the conflict discussion. Indeed, the few studies that include both couple members reveal that the benefits of low(er) testosterone may also extend to partners: In an initial study, we found that men and women reported higher relationship satisfaction and commitment not only when they themselves had lower testosterone, but also when their *partners* had lower testosterone (Edelstein et al., 2014; see Fig. 3A and B). As discussed in more detail later, testosterone levels also tend to be correlated within couples (e.g., Rodriguez, Granger, & Leerkes, 2021; Saxbe, Edelstein, et al., 2017), which could reflect assortative mating (i.e., people are attracted to those with similar testosterone levels) or correlated changes in testosterone over time. Thus, insofar as individuals with relatively low testosterone also tend to have partners with relatively low testosterone, the benefits to relationship functioning may be additive.

Along these lines, in a sample of first-time parents, women whose partners had lower testosterone (assessed at 6–9 months postpartum) reported higher relationship satisfaction, less intimate aggression, and fewer depressive symptoms at subsequent follow-up assessments (Saxbe, Schetter, Simon, Adam, & Shalowitz, 2017). Moreover, the association between men's testosterone and women's depressive symptoms was mediated by women's relationship satisfaction, suggesting that testosterone may have had more proximal influences on women's perceptions of their relationships, which then contributed to their overall well-being and mental health. Because testosterone was only assessed at one point in time, and only among men, these data cannot speak to the direction of causality in these associations or to the role of women's testosterone. Yet they provide converging evidence that an individual's testosterone has implications not only for their own relationship outcomes, but also those of their partner.

As with research on partnering and parenting status per se, most studies of links between hormones and relationship outcomes are cross-sectional, making it difficult to infer causality. In one notable exception, relationship quality and testosterone were assessed longitudinally in a representative sample of over 1,200 older Americans (average age of 67 at the first assessment; Das & Sawin, 2016). Among men, higher testosterone at the first assessment predicted lower relationship quality at the second assessment five years later, but relationship quality at the first assessment was not significantly associated with testosterone at the second assessment, suggesting that changes in testosterone may have led to changes in men's relationship quality. In contrast, women's testosterone at the first assessment was not significantly associated with relationship quality at the second assessment, but there was a trend suggesting that relationship quality at the first assessment predicted testosterone at the second assessment. These findings provide some evidence that changes in testosterone precede changes in relationship outcomes, at least in men, and for potentially different causal pathways for men versus women. However, data from men and women were analyzed separately, so it is not entirely clear whether the pattern of findings in fact differs significantly by gender. It is also unclear whether these results might generalize to younger populations, particularly given that both men's and women's testosterone levels generally decline with age (e.g., Fabbri et al., 2016; Liu et al., 2007). Further research that includes repeated assessments of both testosterone and relationship quality over time, and direct comparisons between findings for men and women, would go a long way towards addressing questions about causality in this literature.

4.3.2 Parent-child relationships

Lower testosterone has also been consistently linked with better parenting outcomes among both mothers and fathers, including greater involvement in childcare and more responsive behavior toward children, particularly in stressful contexts (e.g., Edelstein et al., 2017; Kuo et al., 2018). For instance, in a sample of first-time parents, assessed when their children were 18 months old, mothers and fathers with lower baseline testosterone self-reported better ability to tolerate frustration (Rodriguez et al., 2021). Fathers with lower testosterone also scored lower on measures associated with risk for abusive parenting and were rated by trained observers as engaging in more positive and less negative parenting behaviors during a structured laboratory interaction; there were no significant associations between mothers' testosterone at 18 months and their observed parenting behavior. Kuo et al. (2018) similarly found that new fathers who had lower testosterone on the day after their babies were born reported more involvement with childcare several months later.

Our study of expectant couples provides additional evidence for prospective links between prenatal hormones and postpartum outcomes, as well as for the dyadic implications of these links: At three months postpartum, fathers who had shown larger prenatal declines in testosterone reported that they provided more infant care and that they were more satisfied with, committed to, and invested in their romantic relationships (Edelstein et al., 2017; Saxbe, Edelstein, et al., 2017; see Fig. 4, Panel A). Their female partners corroborated these reports, indicating that they received more postpartum support and assistance with household tasks from fathers who showed larger prenatal declines in testosterone. In a similar vein, despite normative prenatal increases in testosterone, expectant mothers who showed smaller testosterone increases were rated by their male partners as providing more postpartum parenting support (Edelstein et al., 2017).

We observed many similar associations in one of the rare studies to include sexual minority participants (Chin et al., 2020): In a longitudinal sample of 25 lesbian couples expecting their first child, pregnant women showed fairly large increases in testosterone, as expected, throughout the

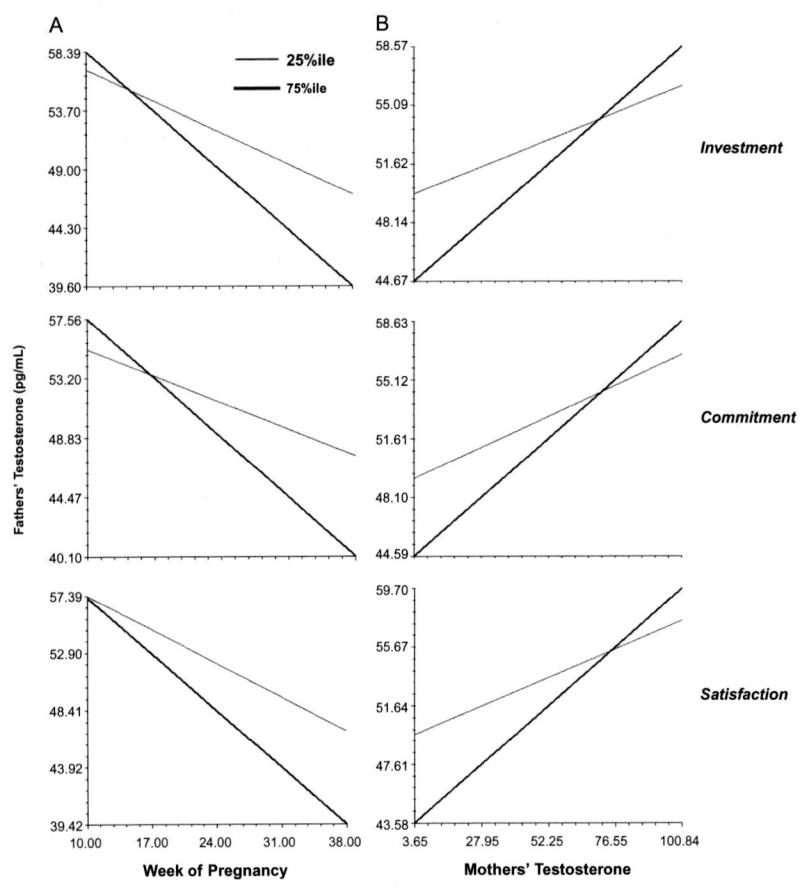

Fig. 4 Associations between Fathers' Testosterone and Postpartum Relationship Quality: Change Over Pregnancy (Panel A) and Associations With Mothers' Testosterone (Panel B). Slopes are Plotted at the 25th and 75th Percentile for Each Relationship Quality Subscale. N = 27 couples (Saxbe, Edelstein, et al., 2017).

prenatal period. There were no significant changes in their female partners' testosterone levels during this time; however, for both partners, lower testosterone was generally associated with more positive relationship and parenting outcomes at 3 months postpartum. Birth mothers with lower testosterone throughout the prenatal period reported doing more infant care, feeling more parenting self-efficacy, and engaging in less hostile parenting behavior; non-birth mothers with lower testosterone reported providing more postpartum support to their partner. For both partners, lower testosterone prenatally was associated with greater postpartum relationship commitment; for non-birth mothers, lower testosterone was also associated with greater postpartum investment and satisfaction. Birth mothers whose *partners* had lower testosterone also reported greater commitment.

Taken together, these findings provide support for the idea that lower testosterone may be functional in helping people prepare for parenthood by reducing aggression toward infants, facilitating parent-infant attachment, and maintaining the bond between parents (Zilioli & Bird, 2017). Our findings also suggest potentially important dyadic effects, such that testosterone matters not only for one's own parenting but also for that of one's partner. Moreover, the findings of Chin et al. (2020) provide much-needed data on hormones and hormone changes in sexual minority populations, suggesting many similarities in links between testosterone and relationship outcomes for lesbian and heterosexual couples. One potentially important difference between our two samples (and compared to samples of heterosexual couples more generally) is that nonbirth mothers in our study did not show significant changes in testosterone during the prenatal period. The relatively small and homogenous nature of our sample could have made it more difficult for us to detect prenatal testosterone changes among non-birth mothers, particularly given that (nonexpectant) women have relatively low levels of testosterone to begin with. Moreover, because we did not assess new parents' hormones postpartum, we do not yet know whether nonbirth mothers may have shown postpartum declines in testosterone, as is typically found among both new fathers and birth mothers. It is also possible that our initial prenatal assessment, which typically occurred during the first trimester, failed to detect testosterone changes that could have occurred during the very early stages of pregnancy in nonbirth mothers. Given the dearth of data on sexual minority couples, and the fact that there are no a priori reasons to expect that non-birth mothers would show different patterns of hormone changes compared to new and expectant fathers, further research on this topic, with larger and more diverse samples of sexual minority participants, is critically needed.

Longitudinal data also suggest, however, that testosterone levels may "rebound" as children get older, at least among fathers: In a study of over 200 new fathers, postpartum testosterone declined from pre- to postpartum, but then appeared to return to prenatal levels by about 10 months postpartum (Corpuz & Bugental, 2020). Moreover, new fathers whose testosterone levels rebounded more slowly reported spending (marginally) more time with their infants (Corpuz, D'Alessandro, & Collom, 2021), again consistent with the idea that lower testosterone and declines in testosterone facilitate infant care. Mothers' testosterone was not assessed in this study, and similar models have not yet been applied to changes in new mothers' hormones; however, as described earlier, cross-sectional data suggest that women with older children have higher testosterone than those with younger children, suggesting that their testosterone may similarly rebound as children get older.

It is also noteworthy that fathers whose testosterone rebounded more slowly in the Corpuz et al. (2021) study were rated by observers as providing *lower* quality care during a laboratory interaction. These findings may be surprisingly in light of fairly consistent negative associations between testosterone and parental responsiveness; however, the interaction task used in this study was designed to elicit fear in the infants (by presenting visitors wearing a series of potentially aversive masks). The authors argue that the rebound in testosterone may impede more *direct* forms of care, as indexed by self-reported time spent with the infant, but facilitate more *indirect* forms of care, such as those indexed by the laboratory task. Insofar as testosterone increases as a function of infant protection (Wynne-Edwards & Reburn, 2000) and unsuccessful attempts to soothe a distressed infant (van Anders et al., 2012), it is also possible that fathers' responses to this particular (aversive) laboratory task were more closely tied to protection as opposed to caregiving. This explanation is consistent with van Anders et al. (2011) proposal that not all parenting behavior should be linked with lower testosterone, only that which involves nurturant caregiving.

4.4 Synchrony in hormone levels and responses

Studies that include both partners can shed light not only on dyadic or partner effects, but also on hormonal coordination or synchrony *between* partners, which may have implications for relationship outcomes (Timmons, Margolin, & Saxbe, 2015). For instance, couples often show reliable between-partner correlations in cortisol, one of the body's major stress hormones, and couples whose cortisol levels are more strongly correlated tend to report poorer relationship quality and less optimal relationship functioning (e.g., Braren, Brandes-Aitken, Ribner, Perry, & Blair, 2020; Schneiderman, Kanat-Maymon, Zagoory-Sharon, & Feldman, 2014). These findings suggest that cortisol covariation might be an indicator of greater relationship stress; people whose cortisol levels are more closely tied to their partner's might also be more impacted by their partner's experiences of stress and/or have more difficulty coping with stressful experiences (e.g., Khaled et al., 2021).

Much less is known about synchrony in other hormones, but as described above, there is some evidence for within-couple correlations in testosterone (e.g., Booth, Johnson, & Granger, 2005; Rodriguez et al., 2021). In our longitudinal sample of expectant parents, for instance, we found that average levels of testosterone were positively correlated within couples throughout the prenatal period (Saxbe, Edelstein, et al., 2017). These correlations were evident by the second prenatal assessment (approximately week 20 of gestation), but increased in magnitude throughout the pregnancy and were statistically significant only at the last assessment (approximately week 36 of gestation; Edelstein et al., 2015). These findings, although preliminary and based on a relatively small sample of couples, suggest that the strength of coordination in testosterone may have increased over time[2]. Because there are currently no other published data on within-couple synchrony in testosterone, it is not yet clear whether couples simply show increased coordination over time or whether these findings are specific to a major life event like the transition to parenthood.

Moreover, in our study, the magnitude of within-couple correlations in testosterone predicted fathers' postpartum relationship outcomes: Men who showed stronger prenatal correlations in testosterone with their female partners reported higher relationship satisfaction, commitment, and investment at three months postpartum (Saxbe, Edelstein, et al., 2017; see Fig. 4, Panel B). These findings were specific to testosterone; in our sample, within-couple synchrony in other hormones (i.e., cortisol, estradiol, and progesterone) did not predict fathers' postpartum relationship quality. Further, *prenatal* relationship quality did not predict within-couple correlations in testosterone, suggesting that coordination in testosterone may precede rather than stem from individual differences in relationship quality. Of course, any null effects should be interpreted cautiously given our relatively small and homogenous sample; however, taken together, our findings suggest that within-dyad covariation in testosterone (unlike cortisol) may reflect or predict positive relationship processes, perhaps due to links between testosterone and nurturance or caregiving (van Anders et al., 2011). Given the dearth of work on this topic, further research is warranted to better understand the extent of within-dyad coordination of testosterone across relationship types and contexts, and the implications of such coordination for parenting and romantic relationship outcomes.

---

[2] In our sample of lesbian couples, within-couple correlations in testosterone were positive, and largest in magnitude at the last prenatal assessment, but were not significantly significant (Chin et al., 2020).

5. Open questions and future directions

The research reviewed here is generally consistent with the idea of testosterone trade-offs, in that contexts that require or pull for competition,
dominance, and/or the acquisition of sexual partners tend to be associated
with relatively high levels of testosterone and increases in testosterone; contexts that require or pull for nurturance and/or caregiving are generally associated with relatively low levels of testosterone and decreases in testosterone.
For instance, both men and women with higher testosterone report having
had more lifetime sexual partners; they are also more likely to show affiliative
behaviors (e.g., smiling, eye contact, self-confidence) during interactions
with potential partners, which could contribute to their ability to attract
those partners. Interactions with potential partners, or in some cases thinking
about such interactions, can also lead to testosterone increases. The effects
of interactions with *current* romantic partners have been less extensively
studied, but there is evidence for both testosterone increases and decreases
following such interactions.

Benefits in the context of ongoing nurturant relationships, in contrast,
have been more consistently linked with lower testosterone and decreases
in testosterone: Both men and women who are partnered and/or parents
generally have lower testosterone than their single counterparts and compared to people without children. Among those in already established relationships, lower testosterone has been associated with better outcomes in
both romantic and parent-child domains. These positive associations also
appear to extend to partners, such that both men and women whose *partners*
have lower testosterone also report higher relationship quality and better
parenting outcomes. And preliminary evidence suggests that coordination
or synchrony in testosterone may be associated with higher relationship
quality, at least among men. Extant longitudinal data generally point to
changes in relationships preceding changes in testosterone, with some evidence for bidirectional links between testosterone and relationship outcomes (particularly among women).

To move this area of inquiry forward, additional longitudinal and experimental research is critically needed to better understand causal links
between testosterone and relationship outcomes. For better or worse,
many of the questions most central to close relationship processes—what
drives relationship transitions, why some relationships persist while
others do not, to name just a few—are not particularly amenable to

random assignment or experimental manipulation, particularly in humans. However, research on testosterone and social behavior more generally has benefitted from experimental approaches that temporarily increase testosterone via pharmacological administration, and many effects obtained with this approach are consistent with those observed in correlational studies (e.g., Bos et al., 2012). For instance, administration of testosterone has been shown to reduce markers of empathy in women (Hermans, Putman, & van Honk, 2006) and perceptions of dominance in men (Welling, Moreau, Bird, Hansen, & Carré, 2016). Further, in a sample of young women without children, Bos et al. (2021) recently found that testosterone administration increased emotional reactivity to photographs depicting distressed infants; this effect was particularly strong among women who reported more protective tendencies. Although preliminary, these findings are consistent with the Steroid/Peptide Theory of Social Bonds (van Anders et al., 2011) in suggesting that contexts that elicit infant protection (as opposed to nurturance) may be facilitated by experimentally induced increases in testosterone.

As noted by Carré and Robinson (2020), however, very few pharmacological administration studies include both men and women, making it difficult to assess sex or gender differences in the effects of exogenous testosterone on behavior. Perhaps more importantly, it remains unclear whether effects obtained in pharmacological administrations studies are generalizable to those observed in correlational studies of naturally occurring differences in testosterone. Research on aggression, for instance, suggests that associations may be stronger when testosterone is measured endogenously as opposed to experimentally manipulated (Geniole et al., 2020). In other studies, effects of pharmacological administration appear to be in the *opposite* direction of those obtained for endogenous testosterone (e.g., Brannon, Carr, Jin, Josephs, & Gawronski, 2019). Moreover, several highly powered studies have failed to find evidence for the effects of exogenous testosterone on theoretically relevant outcomes, such as empathy (Nadler et al., 2019) and economic risk-taking (Stanton, Welker, Bonin, Goldfarb, & Carré, 2021). Additional work with highly powered pre-registered studies is clearly necessary to assess the reliability of any effects of experimentally induced testosterone as well as links between naturally occurring testosterone and relationship outcomes.

Future studies would also benefit from the collection of larger samples that are sufficiently powered to detect both sex or gender differences and partner effects. The findings reviewed here point to some potentially important gender differences in links between testosterone and relationship outcomes. For instance, women's testosterone may be more closely tied to sexual desire than men's, and men's testosterone may be more closely tied to interpersonal aggression than women's. Many studies also document partner effects in associations between testosterone and relationship outcomes. Yet very few studies include both men and women, and those that do often analyze data separately by sex or gender, making it nearly impossible to empirically assess sex or gender differences and/or partner effects. Given the necessarily interdependent nature of close relationships, this information is critical for a complete understanding of the social neuroendocrinology of close relationship processes.

The inclusion of women taking hormonal contraceptives is another potentially important concern for future research. Hormonal contraceptives typically lower women's testosterone, and in many cases blunt women's testosterone responses; yet a sizable number of women (particularly those in committed relationships) have used some form of hormonal contraceptives at some point in their lives. There are currently no systematic assessments of the effects of women's hormonal contraceptive use on links between women's testosterone and relationship outcomes, however, and excluding women taking hormonal contraceptives altogether may have unintended negative consequences for generalizability. Future research would benefit from a more explicit and comprehensive examination of whether and how women's contraceptive use is associated with their own and their partners' relationship outcomes, including short- and longer-term changes in testosterone.

In addition, despite growing recognition of the importance of diversity in many areas of psychology, research on testosterone, and social neuroendocrinology more generally, has long been dominated by a focus on Western, cisgender, heterosexually oriented participants (DuBois, Gibb, Juster, & Powers, 2021; van Anders et al., 2014). Greater attention to diversity in gender, sexual, and racial/ethnic identity would go a long way toward increasing representation and inclusivity in social neuroendocrinology research. Capitalizing on these and other kinds of diversity (e.g., in socioeconomic status) would also allow for novel tests of critical components of major theories and allow researchers to more fully assess the generalizability of their theories and findings.

Finally, in the vast majority of work reviewed here, testosterone levels were assessed via immunoassays of salivary measures. Salivary measures have long been used in research with humans, in part because they are generally less invasive and less expensive to collect compared to other bodily substances, such as blood or urine (Mazur, 2018; Schultheiss, Dlugash, & Mehta, 2018); however, salivary immunoassays may be more prone to measurement error than other techniques, particularly at lower concentrations. This is of particular concern for assessments of testosterone in women, who tend to have low levels of baseline testosterone compared to men (e.g., Miller, Plessow, Rauh, Gröschl, & Kirschbaum, 2013; Welker et al., 2016). Other techniques, such as mass spectrometry, are thus likely to become preferred assessment tool over immunoassays in the near future (Schultheiss et al., 2018).

6. Conclusions

Close relationships are an important source of support, pleasure, and companionship across the lifespan. Psychological research on close relationships has long focused on positive relationship processes, such as caregiving and social support, in an effort to understand what makes these relationships especially meaningful and rewarding. In contrast, neuroendocrine research, particularly that involving testosterone, has tended to focus on more negative aspects of close relationships, such as conflict and aggression. This work has also tended to be centered around the experiences of men and fathers, as opposed to women and mothers, and too infrequently includes dyads or couples.

Moving forward, research on the social neuroendocrinology of close relationships would benefit from greater focus on more positive and nurturant aspects of close relationships, including contexts that, from a theoretical perspective, should elicit testosterone *decreases* as well as increases. Work with couples and dyads is also critical to better understand how testosterone contributes to and is influenced by ongoing relationships. And more explicit measures of theoretically relevant constructs, like sexual attraction and nurturance, will likely help to disentangle the mechanisms that contribute to different patterns of testosterone reactivity in both individuals and couples. Finally, although hormones such as testosterone show fairly high rank-order stability, they nevertheless can and do change over time (e.g., following relationship transitions) and across situations (e.g., following discussions with romantic partners). Additional longitudinal and experimental data will be crucial for beginning to disentangle causal links between testosterone (and other hormones) and close relationship processes.

Acknowledgments

I am grateful to Amie Gordon and Kristi Chin for their feedback on an earlier version of this manuscript, and to my many collaborators on the studies reviewed here, including Esra Ascigil, Bill Chopik, Kristi Chin, Patty Kuo, Onawa LaBelle, Amy Moors, Zachary Reese, Darby Saxbe, Oliver Schultheiss, Lester Sim, Sari van Anders, Brenda Volling, and Britney Wardecker.

References

Achilli, C., Pundir, J., Ramanathan, P., Sabatini, L., Hamoda, H., & Panay, N. (2017). Efficacy and safety of transdermal testosterone in postmenopausal women with hypoactive sexual desire disorder: A systematic review and meta-analysis. *Fertility and Sterility, 107*, 475–482.

Algoe, S. B., Kurtz, L. E., & Grewen, K. (2017). Oxytocin and social bonds: The role of oxytocin in perceptions of romantic partners' bonding behavior. *Psychological Science, 28*, 1763–1772.

Alvergne, A., Faurie, C., & Raymond, M. (2009). Variation in testosterone levels and male reproductive effort: Insight from a polygynous human population. *Hormones and Behavior, 56*, 491–497.

Apicella, C. L., Dreber, A., & Mollerstrom, J. (2014). Salivary testosterone change following monetary wins and losses predicts future financial risk-taking. *Psychoneuroendocrinology, 39*, 58–64.

Arnocky, S., Albert, G., Carré, J. M., & Ortiz, T. L. (2018). Intrasexual competition mediates the relationship between men's testosterone and mate retention behavior. *Physiology & Behavior, 186*, 73–78.

Aron, A., Melinat, E., Aron, E. N., & Vallone, R. D. (1997). The experimental generation of interpersonal closeness: A procedure and some preliminary findings. *Personality and Social Psychology Bulletin, 23*, 363–377.

Barrett, E. S., Tran, V., Thurston, S., Jasienska, G., Furberg, A. S., Ellison, P. T., & Thune, I. (2013). Marriage and motherhood are associated with lower testosterone concentrations in women. *Hormones and Behavior, 63*, 72–79.

Baumeister, R. F., Catanese, K. R., & Vohs, K. D. (2001). Is there a gender difference in strength of sex drive? Theoretical views, conceptual distinctions, and a review of relevant evidence. *Personality and Social Psychology Review, 5*, 242–273.

Beery, A. K., & Zucker, I. (2011). Sex bias in neuroscience and biomedical research. *Neuroscience & Biobehavioral Reviews, 35*, 565–572.

Berg, S. J., & Wynne-Edwards, K. E. (2002). Salivary hormone concentrations in mothers and fathers becoming parents are not correlated. *Hormones and Behavior, 42*, 424–436.

Book, A. S., Starzyk, K. B., & Quinsey, V. L. (2001). The relationship between testosterone and aggression: A meta-analysis. *Aggression and Violent Behavior, 6*, 579–599.

Booth, A., Johnson, D. R., & Granger, D. A. (2005). Testosterone, marital quality, and role overload. *Journal of Marriage and Family, 67*, 483–498.

Bos, P. A., Lesemann, F. H. P., Spencer, H., Stein, D. J., van Honk, J., & Montoya, E. R. (2021). Preliminary data on increased reactivity towards children in distress after testosterone administration in women: A matter of protection? *Biological Psychology, 165*, 108176.

Bos, P. A., Panksepp, J., Bluthe, R. M., & van Honk, J. (2012). Acute effects of steroid hormones and neuropeptides on human social-emotional behavior: A review of single administration studies. *Frontiers in Neuroendocrinology, 33*, 17–35.

Brannon, S. M., Carr, S., Jin, E. S., Josephs, R. A., & Gawronski, B. (2019). Exogenous testosterone increases sensitivity to moral norms in moral dilemma judgements. *Nature Human Behaviour*, *3*, 856–866.

Braren, S. H., Brandes-Aitken, A., Ribner, A., Perry, R. E., & Blair, C. (2020). Maternal psychological stress moderates diurnal cortisol linkage in expectant fathers and mothers during late pregnancy. *Psychoneuroendocrinology*, *111*, 104474.

Brennan, A., Ayers, S., Ahmed, H., & Marshall-Lucette, S. (2007). A critical review of the Couvade syndrome: The pregnant male. *Journal of Reproductive and Infant Psychology*, *25*, 173–189.

Cabrera, N. J., Volling, B. L., & Barr, R. (2018). Fathers are parents, too! Widening the lens on parenting for children's development. *Child Development Perspectives*, *12*, 152–157.

Campbell, B. C., Dreber, A., Apicella, C. L., Eisenberg, D. T., Gray, P. B., Little, A. C., … Lum, J.K. (2010). Testosterone exposure, dopaminergic reward, and sensation-seeking in young men. *Physiology & Behavior*, *99*, 451–456.

Carlsen, S. M., Jacobsen, G., & Romundstad, P. (2006). Maternal testosterone levels during pregnancy are associated with offspring size at birth. *European Journal of Endocrinology*, *155*, 365–370.

Carré, J. M., & Olmstead, N. A. (2015). Social neuroendocrinology of human aggression: Examining the role of competition-induced testosterone dynamics. *Neuroscience*, *286*, 171–186.

Carré, J. M., & Robinson, B. A. (2020). Testosterone administration in human social neuroendocrinology: Past, present, and future. *Hormones and Behavior*, *122*, 104754.

Casto, K. V., & Edwards, D. A. (2016). Testosterone, cortisol, and human competition. *Hormones and Behavior*, *82*, 21–37.

Casto, K. V., Elliott, C., & Edwards, D. A. (2014). Intercollegiate cross country competition: Effects of warm-up and racing on salivary levels of cortisol and testosterone. *International Journal of Exercise Science*, *7*, 318–328.

Casto, K. V., Rivell, A., & Edwards, D. A. (2017). Competition-related testosterone, cortisol, and perceived personal success in recreational women athletes. *Hormones and Behavior*, *92*, 29–36.

Chin, K., Chopik, W. J., Wardecker, B. M., LaBelle, O. P., Moors, A. C., & Edelstein, R. S. (2020). Longitudinal associations between prenatal testosterone and postpartum outcomes in a sample of first-time expectant lesbian couples. *Hormones and Behavior*, *125*, 104810.

Chin, K., Reese, Z., Ascigil, E., Sim, L., & Edelstein, R. S. (2021). Closeness-inducing discussions with a romantic partner increase cortisol and testosterone. *Psychoneuroendocrinology*, *132*, 105357.

Conley, T. D., Ziegler, A., & Moors, A. C. (2013). Backlash from the bedroom: Stigma mediates gender differences in acceptance of casual sex offers. *Psychology of Women Quarterly*, *37*, 392–407.

Corona, G., Isidori, A. M., Buvat, J., Aversa, A., Rastrelli, G., Hackett, G., … Maggi, M. (2014). Testosterone supplementation and sexual function: A meta-analysis study. *The Journal of Sexual Medicine*, *11*, 1577–1592.

Corpuz, R., & Bugental, D. (2020). Life history and individual differences in male testosterone: Mixed evidence for early environmental calibration of testosterone response to first-time fatherhood. *Hormones and Behavior*, *120*, 104684.

Corpuz, R., D'Alessandro, S., & Collom, G. K. (2021). The postnatal testosterone rebound in first-time fathers and the quality and quantity of paternal care. *Developmental Psychobiology*, *63*, 1415–1427.

Costa, R. M., Correia, M., & Oliveira, R. F. (2015). Does personality moderate the link between women's testosterone and relationship status? The role of extraversion and sensation seeking. *Personality and Individual Differences*, *76*, 141–146.

Crockford, C., Deschner, T., Ziegler, T. E., & Wittig, R. M. (2014). Endogenous peripheral oxytocin measures can give insight into the dynamics of social relationships: A review. *Frontiers in Behavioral Neuroscience*, *8*, 68.

Dabbs, J. M., Jr., Bernieri, F. J., Strong, R. K., Campo, R., & Milun, R. (2001). Going on stage: Testosterone in greetings and meetings. *Journal of Research in Personality*, *35*, 27–40.

Das, A., & Sawin, N. (2016). Social modulation or hormonal causation? Linkages of testosterone with sexual activity and relationship quality in a nationally representative longitudinal sample of older adults. *Archives of Sexual Behavior*, *45*, 2101–2115.

Deady, D. K., Smith, M. J., Sharp, M. A., & Al-Dujaili, E. A. S. (2006). Maternal personality and reproductive ambition in women is associated with salivary testosterone levels. *Biological Psychology*, *71*, 29–32.

Denes, A., Afifi, T. D., & Granger, D. A. (2017). Physiology and pillow talk: Relations between testosterone and communication post sex. *Journal of Social and Personal Relationships*, *34*, 281–308.

Dhillon, A., Denes, A., Crowley, J. P., Ponivas, A., Winkler, K. L., & Bennett, M. (2020). Does testosterone influence young adult romantic partners' accommodation during conversations about stressors? *Human Communication Research*, *46*, 444–469.

DuBois, L. Z., Gibb, J. K., Juster, R.-P., & Powers, S. I. (2021). Biocultural approaches to transgender and gender diverse experience and health: Integrating biomarkers and advancing gender/sex research. *American Journal of Human Biology*, *33*, e23555.

Edelstein, R. S., & Chin, K. (2018). Hormones and close relationship processes: Neuroendocrine bases of partnering and parenting. In O. C. Schultheiss, & P. H. Mehta (Eds.), *Routledge international handbook of social neuroendocrinology* (pp. 281–297). Routledge.

Edelstein, R. S., Chin, K., Saini, E. K., Kuo, P. X., Schultheiss, O. C., & Volling, B. L. (2019). Adult attachment and testosterone reactivity: Fathers' avoidance predicts changes in testosterone during the strange situation procedure. *Hormones and Behavior*, *112*, 10–19.

Edelstein, R. S., Chopik, W. J., & Kean, E. L. (2011). Sociosexuality moderates the association between testosterone and relationship status in men and women. *Hormones and Behavior*, *60*, 248–255.

Edelstein, R. S., Chopik, W. J., Saxbe, D. E., Wardecker, B. M., Moors, A. C., & LaBelle, O. P. (2017). Prospective and dyadic associations between expectant parents' prenatal hormone changes and postpartum parenting outcomes. *Developmental Psychobiology*, *59*, 77–90.

Edelstein, R. S., van Anders, S. M., Chopik, W. J., Goldey, K. L., & Wardecker, B. M. (2014). Dyadic associations between testosterone and relationship quality in couples. *Hormones and Behavior*, *65*, 401–407.

Edelstein, R. S., Wardecker, B. M., Chopik, W. J., Moors, A. C., Shipman, E. L., & Lin, N. J. (2015). Prenatal hormones in first-time expectant parents: Longitudinal changes and within-couple correlations. *American Journal of Human Biology*, *27*, 317–325.

Edwards, D. A., & Casto, K. V. (2013). Women's intercollegiate athletic competition: Cortisol, testosterone, and the dual-hormone hypothesis as it relates to status among teammates. *Hormones and Behavior*, *64*, 153–160.

Eisenegger, C., Haushofer, J., & Fehr, E. (2011). The role of testosterone in social interaction. *Trends in Cognitive Sciences*, *15*, 263–271.

Fabbri, E., An, Y., Gonzalez-Freire, M., Zoli, M., Maggio, M., Studenski, S. A., ... Ferrucci, L. (2016). Bioavailable testosterone linearly declines over a wide age spectrum in men and women from the Baltimore Longitudinal Study of Aging. *Journals of Gerontology Series A: Biomedical Sciences and Medical Sciences*, *71*, 1202–1209.

Farrelly, D., Owens, R., Elliott, H. R., Walden, H. R., & Wetherell, M. A. (2015). The effects of being in a "new relationship" on levels of testosterone in men. *Evolutionary Psychology*, *13*. 147470491501300130.

Finkel, E. J., Simpson, J. A., & Eastwick, P. W. (2017). The psychology of close relationships: Fourteen core principles. *Annual Review of Psychology*, *68*, 383–411.

Fleming, A. S., Ruble, D., Krieger, H., & Wong, P. Y. (1997). Hormonal and experiential correlates of maternal responsiveness during pregnancy and the puerperium in human mothers. *Hormones and Behavior*, *31*, 145–158.

Foo, Y. Z., Nakagawa, S., Rhodes, G., & Simmons, L. W. (2017). The effects of sex hormones on immune function: A meta-analysis. *Biological Reviews*, *92*, 551–571.

Geniole, S. N., Bird, B. M., McVittie, J. S., Purcell, R. B., Archer, J., & Carré, J. M. (2020). Is testosterone linked to human aggression? A meta-analytic examination of the relationship between baseline, dynamic, and manipulated testosterone on human aggression. *Hormones and Behavior*, *123*, 104644.

Geniole, S. N., Bird, B. M., Ruddick, E. L., & Carré, J. M. (2017). Effects of competition outcome on testosterone concentrations in humans: An updated meta-analysis. *Hormones and Behavior*, *92*, 37–50.

Geniole, S. N., & Carré, J. M. (2018). Human social neuroendocrinology: Review of the rapid effects of testosterone. *Hormones and Behavior*, *104*, 192–205.

Gettler, L. T. (2020). Exploring evolutionary perspectives on human fatherhood and paternal biology: Testosterone as an exemplar. In H. E. Fitzgerald, K von Klitzing, N. J. Cabrera, J Scarano de Mendonça, & T Skjøthaug (Eds.), *Handbook of Fathers and Child Development* (pp. 137–152). Springer.

Gettler, L. T., Lew-Levy, S., Sarma, M. S., Miegakanda, V., & Boyette, A. H. (2020). Sharing and caring: Testosterone, fathering, and generosity among BaYaka foragers of the congo Basin. *Scientific Reports*, *10*, 1–14.

Gettler, L. T., McDade, T. W., Agustin, S. S., Feranil, A. B., & Kuzawa, C. W. (2013). Do testosterone declines during the transition to marriage and fatherhood relate to men's sexual behavior? Evidence from the Philippines. *Hormones and Behavior*, *64*, 755–763.

Gettler, L. T., McDade, T. W., Agustin, S. S., & Kuzawa, C. W. (2011). Short-term changes in fathers' hormones during father–child play: Impacts of paternal attitudes and experience. *Hormones and Behavior*, *60*, 599–606.

Gettler, L. T., McDade, T. W., Feranil, A. B., & Kuzawa, C. W. (2011). Longitudinal evidence that fatherhood decreases testosterone in human males. *Proceedings of the National Academy of Sciences of the United States of America*, *108*, 16194–16199.

Gettler, L. T., & Oka, R. C. (2016). Are testosterone levels and depression risk linked based on partnering and parenting? Evidence from a large population-representative study of US men and women. *Social Science and Medicine*, *163*, 157–167.

Goldey, K. L., Avery, L. R., & van Anders, S. M. (2014). Sexual fantasies and gender/sex: A multimethod approach with quantitative content analysis and hormonal responses. *The Journal of Sex Research*, *51*, 917–931.

Goldey, K. L., Conley, T. D., & van Anders, S. M. (2018). Dynamic associations between testosterone, partnering, and sexuality during the college transition in women. *Adaptive Human Behavior and Physiology*, *4*, 42–68.

Goldey, K. L., & van Anders, S. M. (2011). Sexy thoughts: Effects of sexual cognitions on testosterone, cortisol, and arousal in women. *Hormones and Behavior*, *59*, 754–764.

Goldey, K. L., & van Anders, S. M. (2012). Sexual thoughts: Links to testosterone and cortisol in men. *Archives of Sexual Behavior*, *41*, 1461–1470.

Goldey, K. L., & van Anders, S. M. (2015). Sexual modulation of testosterone: Insights for humans from across species. *Adaptive Human Behavior and Physiology*, *1*, 93–123.

Goudriaan, A. E., Lapauw, B., Ruige, J., Feyen, E., Kaufman, J.-M., Brand, M., & Vingerhoets, G. (2010). The influence of high-normal testosterone levels on risk-taking in healthy males in a 1-week letrozole administration study. *Psychoneuroendocrinology*, *35*, 1416–1421.

Gray, P. B., Reece, J., Coore-Desai, C., Dinall, T., Pellington, S., & Samms-Vaughan, M. (2017). Testosterone and Jamaican fathers: Exploring links to relationship dynamics and paternal care. *Human Nature*, 1–18.

Gray, P. B., Straftis, A. A., Bird, B. M., McHale, T. S., & Zilioli, S. (2020). Human reproductive behavior, life history, and the challenge hypothesis: A 30-year review, retrospective and future directions. *Hormones and Behavior*, *123*, 104530.

Grebe, N. M., Sarafin, R. E., Strenth, C. R., & Zilioli, S. (2019). Pair-bonding, fatherhood, and the role of testosterone: A meta-analytic review. *Neuroscience and Biobehavioral Reviews*, *98*, 221–233.

Harris, J. A., Rushton, J. P., Hampson, E., & Jackson, D. N. (1996). Salivary testosterone and self-report aggressive and pro-social personality characteristics in men and women. *Aggressive Behavior*, *22*, 321–331.

Hermans, E. J., Putman, P., & van Honk, J. (2006). Testosterone administration reduces empathetic behavior: A facial mimicry study. *Psychoneuroendocrinology*, *31*, 859–866.

Hirschenhauser, K., & Oliveira, R. F. (2006). Social modulation of androgens in male vertebrates: Meta-analyses of the challenge hypothesis. *Animal Behaviour*, *71*, 265–277.

Holmboe, S. A., Priskorn, L., Jørgensen, N., Skakkebaek, N. E., Linneberg, A., Juul, A., & Andersson, A.-M. (2017). Influence of marital status on testosterone levels—A ten year follow-up of 1113 men. *Psychoneuroendocrinology*, *80*, 155–161.

Jiménez, M., Aguilar, R., & Alvero-Cruz, J. R. (2012). Effects of victory and defeat on testosterone and cortisol response to competition: Evidence for same response patterns in men and women. *Psychoneuroendocrinology*, *37*, 1577–1581.

Jones, J., Mosher, W. D., & Daniels, K. (2012). Current contraceptive use in the United States, 2006–2010, and changes in patterns of use since 1995. *National Health Statistics Reports*, *60*.

Jordan-Young, R. M., & Karkazis, K. (2019). *Testosterone: An unauthorized biography*. Harvard University Press.

Kaiser, H., & Powers, S. (2006). Testosterone and conflict tactics within late-adolescent couples: A dyadic predictive model. *Journal of Social and Personal Relationships*, *23*, 231–248.

Ketay, S., Welker, K. M., & Slatcher, R. B. (2017). The roles of testosterone and cortisol in friendship formation. *Psychoneuroendocrinology*, *76*, 88–96.

Khaled, M., Corner, G. W., Morris, A., Havaldar, S., Luo, E., & Saxbe, D. E. (2021). Physiological linkage in pregnancy: Couples' cortisol, negative conflict behavior, and postpartum depression. *Biological Psychology*, *108075*.

Kordsmeyer, T. L., & Penke, L. (2019). Effects of male testosterone and its interaction with cortisol on self-and observer-rated personality states in a competitive mating context. *Journal of Research in Personality*, *78*, 76–92.

Kuo, P. X., Braungart-Rieker, J. M., Burke Lefever, J. E., Sarma, M. S., O'Neill, M., & Gettler, L. T. (2018). Fathers' cortisol and testosterone in the days around infants' births predict later paternal involvement. *Hormones and Behavior*, *106*, 28–34.

Kuo, P. X., Saini, E. K., Thomason, E., Schultheiss, O. C., Gonzalez, R., & Volling, B. L. (2016). Individual variation in fathers' testosterone reactivity to infant distress predicts parenting behaviors with their 1-year-old infants. *Developmental Psychobiology*, *58*, 303–314.

Kuzawa, C. W., Gettler, L. T., Huang, Y., & McDade, T. W. (2010). Mothers have lower testosterone than non-mothers: Evidence from the Philippines. *Hormones and Behavior*, *57*, 441–447.

Liening, S. H., Stanton, S. J., Saini, E. K., & Schultheiss, O. C. (2010). Salivary testosterone, cortisol, and progesterone: Two-week stability, interhormone correlations, and effects of time of day, menstrual cycle, and oral contraceptives use on steroid hormone levels. *Physiology and Behavior*, *99*, 8–16.

Liu, P. Y., Beilin, J., Meier, C., Nguyen, T. V., Center, J. R., Leedman, P. J., ... Handelsman, D.J. (2007). Age-related changes in serum testosterone and sex hormone binding globulin in Australian men: Longitudinal analyses of two geographically separate regional cohorts. *The Journal of Clinical Endocrinology & Metabolism, 92,* 3599–3603.

Lopez, H. H., Hay, A. C., & Conklin, P. H. (2009). Attractive men induce testosterone and cortisol release in women. *Hormones and Behavior, 56,* 84–92.

Määttänen, I., Jokela, M., Hintsa, T., Firtser, S., Kähönen, M., Jula, A., ... Keltikangas-Järvinen, L. (2013). Testosterone and temperament traits in men: Longitudinal analysis. *Psychoneuroendocrinology, 38,* 2243–2248.

Makhanova, A., McNulty, J. K., Eckel, L. A., Nikonova, L., & Maner, J. K. (2018). Sex differences in testosterone reactivity during marital conflict. *Hormones and Behavior, 105,* 22–27.

Makieva, S., Saunders, P. T., & Norman, J. E. (2014). Androgens in pregnancy: Roles in parturition. *Human Reproduction Update, 20,* 542–559.

Marazziti, D., & Canale, D. (2004). Hormonal changes when falling in love. *Psychoneuroendocrinology, 29,* 931–936.

Mazur, A. (2014). Testosterone of young husbands rises with children in the home. *Andrology, 2,* 125–129.

Mazur, A. (2018). History of social neuroendocrinology in humans. In *Routledge International Handbook of Social Neuroendocrinology* (pp. 7–25). Routledge.

Mazur, A., & Booth, A. (1998). Testosterone and dominance in men. *Behavioral and Brain Sciences, 21,* 353–363.

Mazur, A., & Michalek, J. (1998). Marriage, divorce, and male testosterone. *Social Forces, 77,* 315–330.

McIntyre, M. H., Gangestad, S. W., Gray, P. B., Chapman, J. F., Burnham, T. C., O'Rourke, M. T., & Thornhill, R. (2006). Romantic involvement often reduces men's testosterone levels—But not always: The moderating role of extrapair sexual interest. *Journal of Personality and Social Psychology, 91,* 642–651.

Meijer, W. M., van IJzendoorn, M. H., & Bakermans-Kranenburg, M. J. (2019). Challenging the challenge hypothesis on testosterone in fathers: Limited meta-analytic support. *Psychoneuroendocrinology, 110,* 104435.

Miller, R., Plessow, F., Rauh, M., Gröschl, M., & Kirschbaum, C. (2013). Comparison of salivary cortisol as measured by different immunoassays and tandem mass spectrometry. *Psychoneuroendocrinology, 38,* 50–57.

Muller, M. N., Marlowe, F. W., Bugumba, R., & Ellison, P. T. (2009). Testosterone and paternal care in East African foragers and pastoralists. *Proceedings of the Royal Society B: Biological Sciences, 276,* 347–354.

Nadler, A., Camerer, C. F., Zava, D. T., Ortiz, T. L., Watson, N. V., Carré, J. M., & Nave, G. (2019). Does testosterone impair men's cognitive empathy? Evidence from two large-scale randomized controlled trials. *Proceedings of the Royal Society B: Biological Sciences, 286,* 20191062.

Ou, J., Wu, Y., Hu, Y., Gao, X., Li, H., & Tobler, P. N. (2021). Testosterone reduces generosity through cortical and subcortical mechanisms. *Proceedings of the National Academy of Sciences of the United States of America, 118,* e2021745118.

Penke, L., & Asendorpf, J. B. (2008). Beyond global sociosexual orientations: A more differentiated look at sociosexuality and its effects on courtship and romantic relationships. *Journal of Personality and Social Psychology, 95,* 1113–1135.

Perini, T., Ditzen, B., Hengartner, M., & Ehlert, U. (2012). Sensation seeking in fathers: The impact on testosterone and paternal investment. *Hormones and Behavior, 61,* 191–195.

Peters, B. J., Hammond, M. D., Reis, H. T., & Jamieson, J. P. (2016). The consequences of having a dominant romantic partner on testosterone responses during a social interaction. *Psychoneuroendocrinology, 74,* 308–315.

Peters, M., Simmons, L. W., & Rhodes, G. (2008). Testosterone is associated with mating success but not attractiveness or masculinity in human males. *Animal Behaviour, 76*, 297–303.

Petersen, J. L., & Hyde, J. S. (2010). A meta-analytic review of research on gender differences in sexuality, 1993–2007. *Psychological Bulletin, 136*, 21–38.

Pietromonaco, P. R., & Collins, N. L. (2017). Interpersonal mechanisms linking close relationships to health. *American Psychologist, 72*, 531–542.

Pollet, T. V., van der Meij, L., Cobey, K. D., & Buunk, A. P. (2011). Testosterone levels and their associations with lifetime number of opposite sex partners and remarriage in a large sample of American elderly men and women. *Hormones and Behavior, 60*, 72–77.

Puts, D. A., Pope, L. E., Hill, A. K., Cárdenas, R. A., Welling, L. L., Wheatley, J. R., & Breedlove, S. M. (2015). Fulfilling desire: Evidence for negative feedback between men's testosterone, sociosexual psychology, and sexual partner number. *Hormones and Behavior, 70*, 14–21.

Raisanen, J. C., Chadwick, S. B., Michalak, N., & van Anders, S. M. (2018). Average associations between sexual desire, testosterone, and stress in women and men over time. *Archives of Sexual Behavior, 47*, 1613–1631.

Reis, H. T., & Gable, S. L. (2003). *Toward a positive psychology of relationships*. American Psychological Association.

Rodriguez, C. M., Granger, D. A., & Leerkes, E. M. (2021). Testosterone associations with parents' child abuse risk and at-risk parenting: A multimethod longitudinal examination. *Child Maltreatment, 26*, 50–62.

Ronay, R., & Carney, D. R. (2013). Testosterone's negative relationship with empathic accuracy and perceived leadership ability. *Social Psychological and Personality Science, 4*, 92–99.

Roney, J. R., & Gettler, L. T. (2015). The role of testosterone in human romantic relationships. *Current Opinion in Psychology, 1*, 81–86.

Roney, J. R., Lukaszewski, A. W., & Simmons, Z. L. (2007). Rapid endocrine responses of young men to social interactions with young women. *Hormones and Behavior, 52*, 326–333.

Rosenbaum, S., Gettler, L. T., McDade, T. W., Bechayda, S. S., & Kuzawa, C. W. (2018). Does a man's testosterone "rebound" as dependent children grow up, or when pairbonds end? A test in Cebu, Philippines. *American Journal of Human Biology, 30*, e23180.

Saxbe, D. E., Edelstein, R. S., Lyden, H. M., Wardecker, B. M., Chopik, W. J., & Moors, A. C. (2017). Fathers' decline in testosterone and synchrony with partner testosterone during pregnancy predicts greater postpartum relationship investment. *Hormones and Behavior, 90*, 39–47.

Saxbe, D. E., Schetter, C. D., Simon, C. D., Adam, E. K., & Shalowitz, M. U. (2017). High paternal testosterone may protect against postpartum depressive symptoms in fathers, but confer risk to mothers and children. *Hormones and Behavior, 95*, 103–112.

Schneiderman, I., Kanat-Maymon, Y., Zagoory-Sharon, O., & Feldman, R. (2014). Mutual influences between partners' hormones shape conflict dialog and relationship duration at the initiation of romantic love. *Social Neuroscience, 9*, 337–351.

Schonblum, A., Arnon, L., Ravid, E., Salzer, L., Hadar, E., Meizner, I., ... Koren, L. (2018). Can hair steroids predict pregnancy longevity? *Reproductive Biology, 18*, 410–415.

Schultheiss, O. C., Dlugash, G., & Mehta, P. H. (2018). Hormone measurement in social neuroendocrinology: A comparison of immunoassay and mass spectrometry methods. In O. C. Schultheiss, & P. H. Mehta (Eds.), *Routledge international handbook of social neuroendocrinology* (pp. 26–40). Routledge.

Sellers, J. G., Mehl, M. R., & Josephs, R. A. (2007). Hormones and personality: Testosterone as a marker of individual differences. *Journal of Research in Personality, 41*, 126–138.

Sherwin, B. B. (1988). A comparative analysis of the role of androgen in human male and female sexual behavior: Behavioral specificity, critical thresholds, and sensitivity. *Psychobiology, 16*, 416–425.

Sim, L., Chopik, W. J., Wardecker, B. M., & Edelstein, R. S. (2020). Changes in prenatal testosterone and sexual desire in expectant couples. *Hormones and Behavior, 125*, 104823.

Slatcher, R. B., Mehta, P. H., & Josephs, R. A. (2011). Testosterone and self-reported dominance interact to influence human mating behavior. *Social Psychological and Personality Science, 2*, 531–539.

Slatcher, R. B., & Selcuk, E. (2017). A social psychological perspective on the links between close relationships and health. *Current Directions in Psychological Science, 26*, 16–21.

Soler, H., Vinayak, P., & Quadagno, D. (2000). Biosocial aspects of domestic violence. *Psychoneuroendocrinology, 25*, 721–739.

Stanton, S. C., Campbell, L., & Pink, J. C. (2017). Benefits of positive relationship experiences for avoidantly attached individuals. *Journal of Personality and Social Psychology, 113*, 568–588.

Stanton, S. J., Liening, S. H., & Schultheiss, O. C. (2011). Testosterone is positively associated with risk taking in the Iowa Gambling Task. *Hormones and Behavior, 59*, 252–256.

Stanton, S. J., & Schultheiss, O. C. (2009). The hormonal correlates of implicit power motivation. *Journal of Research in Personality, 43*, 942–949.

Stanton, S. J., Welker, K. M., Bonin, P. L., Goldfarb, B., & Carré, J. M. (2021). The effect of testosterone on economic risk-taking: A multi-study, multi-method investigation. *Hormones and Behavior, 134*, 105014.

Storey, A. E., Noseworthy, D. E., Delahunty, K. M., Halfyard, S. J., & McKay, D. W. (2011). The effects of social context on the hormonal and behavioral responsiveness of human fathers. *Hormones and Behavior, 60*, 353–361.

Storey, A. E., Walsh, C. J., Quinton, R. L., & Wynne-Edwards, K. E. (2000). Hormonal correlates of paternal responsiveness in new and expectant fathers. *Evolution and Human Behavior, 21*, 79–95.

Sundin, Z. W., Chopik, W. J., Welker, K. M., Ascigil, E., Brandes, C. M., Chin, K., ... McLarney-Vesotski, A.R. (2021). Estimating the associations between Big Five personality traits, testosterone, and cortisol. *Adaptive Human Behavior and Physiology, 7*, 307–340.

Timmons, A. C., Margolin, G., & Saxbe, D. E. (2015). Physiological linkage in couples and its implications for individual and interpersonal functioning: A literature review. *Journal of Family Psychology, 29*, 720–731.

Turan, B., Guo, J., Boggiano, M. M., & Bedgood, D. (2014). Dominant, cold, avoidant, and lonely: Basal testosterone as a biological marker for an interpersonal style. *Journal of Research in Personality, 50*, 84–89.

van Anders, S. M. (2012). Testosterone and sexual desire in healthy women and men. *Archives of Sexual Behavior, 41*, 1471–1484.

van Anders, S. M. (2013). Beyond masculinity: Testosterone, gender/sex, and human social behavior in a comparative context. *Frontiers in Neuroendocrinology, 34*, 198–210.

van Anders, S. M., & Goldey, K. L. (2010). Testosterone and partnering are linked via relationship status for women and "relationship orientation" for men. *Hormones and Behavior, 58*, 820–826.

van Anders, S. M., Goldey, K. L., & Bell, S. N. (2014). Measurement of testosterone in human sexuality research: Methodological considerations. *Archives of Sexual Behavior, 43*, 231–250.

van Anders, S. M., Goldey, K. L., & Kuo, P. X. (2011). The steroid/peptide theory of social bonds: Integrating testosterone and peptide responses for classifying social behavioral contexts. *Psychoneuroendocrinology, 36*, 1265–1275.

van Anders, S. M., Hamilton, L. D., Schmidt, N., & Watson, N. V. (2007). Associations between testosterone secretion and sexual activity in women. *Hormones and Behavior, 51*, 477–482.

van Anders, S. M., Hamilton, L. D., & Watson, N. V. (2007). Multiple partners are associated with higher testosterone in North American men and women. *Hormones and Behavior, 51*, 454–459.

van Anders, S. M., Tolman, R. M., & Volling, B. L. (2012). Baby cries and nurturance affect testosterone in men. *Hormones and Behavior, 61*, 31–36.

van Anders, S. M., & Watson, N. V. (2006). Relationship status and testosterone in North American heterosexual and non-heterosexual men and women: Cross-sectional and longitudinal data. *Psychoneuroendocrinology, 31*, 715–723.

van der Meij, L., Almela, M., Buunk, A. P., Fawcett, T. W., & Salvador, A. (2011). Men with elevated testosterone levels show more affiliative behaviours during interactions with women. *Proceedings of the Royal Society B: Biological Sciences, 1726*, 202–208.

van der Meij, L., Demetriou, A., Tulin, M., Méndez, I., Dekker, P., & Pronk, T. (2019). Hormones in speed-dating: The role of testosterone and cortisol in attraction. *Hormones and Behavior, 116*, 104555.

Voegtline, K. M., Costigan, K. A., Kivlighan, K. T., Henderson, J. L., & DiPietro, J. A. (2013). Sex-specific associations of maternal prenatal testosterone levels with birth weight and weight gain in infancy. *Journal of Developmental Origins of Health and Disease, 4*, 280–284.

Von Sydow, K., Ullmeyer, M., & Happ, N. (2001). Sexual activity during pregnancy and after childbirth: Results from the sexual preferences questionnaire. *Journal of Psychosomatic Obstetrics & Gynecology, 22*, 29–40.

Voorthuis, A., Bakermans-Kranenburg, M. J., & van IJzendoorn, M. H. (2017). Testosterone reactivity to infant crying and caregiving in women: The role of oral contraceptives and basal cortisol. *Infant Behavior and Development, 56*, 101191.

Wardecker, B. M., Smith, L. K., Edelstein, R. S., & Loving, T. J. (2015). Intimate relationships then and now: How old hormonal processes are influenced by our modern psychology. *Adaptive Human Behavior and Physiology, 1*, 150–176.

Warren, M. A., & Donaldson, S. I. (2017). *Toward a positive psychology of relationships: New directions in theory and research*. ABC-CLIO.

Welker, K. M., Baker, L., Padilla, A., Holmes, H., Aron, A., & Slatcher, R. B. (2014). Effects of self-disclosure and responsiveness between couples on passionate love within couples. *Personal Relationships, 21*, 692–708.

Welker, K. M., Lassetter, B., Brandes, C. M., Prasad, S., Koop, D. R., & Mehta, P. H. (2016). A comparison of salivary testosterone measurement using immunoassays and tandem mass spectrometry. *Psychoneuroendocrinology, 71*, 180–188.

Welling, L. L. M., Moreau, B. J. P., Bird, B. M., Hansen, S., & Carré, J. M. (2016). Exogenous testosterone increases men's perceptions of their own physical dominance. *Psychoneuroendocrinology, 64*, 136–142.

Wingfield, J. C., Hegner, R. E., Dufty, A. M., & Ball, G. F. (1990). The "challenge hypothesis": Theoretical implications for patterns of testosterone secretion, mating systems, and breeding strategies. *The American Naturalist, 136*, 829–846.

Wingfield, J. C., Ramenofsky, M., Hegner, R. E., & Ball, G. F. (2020). Whither the challenge hypothesis? *Hormones and Behavior, 123*, 104588.

Wynne-Edwards, K. E., & Reburn, C. J. (2000). Behavioral endocrinology of mammalian fatherhood. *Trends in Ecology and Evolution, 15*, 464–468.

Zilioli, S., & Bird, B. M. (2017). Functional significance of men's testosterone reactivity to social stimuli. *Frontiers in Neuroendocrinology, 47*, 1–18.

Zilioli, S., & Watson, N. V. (2014). Testosterone across successive competitions: Evidence for a 'winner effect' in humans? *Psychoneuroendocrinology, 47*, 1–9.